NO WAY TO
RUN A RAILROAD

NO WAY TO
RUN A RAILROAD
The Untold Story of the
Penn Central Crisis

Stephen Salsbury

McGraw-Hill Book Company

New York   St. Louis   San Francisco   Auckland
Bogotá   Singapore   Johannesburg   London
Madrid   Mexico   Montreal   New Delhi
Panama   São Paulo   Hamburg
Sydney   Tokyo   Paris
Toronto

Library of Congress Cataloging in Publication Data

Salsbury, Stephen.
 No way to run a railroad.

 Includes index.
 1. Penn Central Railroad. I. Title.
HE2791.P4326S24   385'.065'74   80–15712
ISBN 0–07–054483–2

1234567890   DODO   8987654321

ISBN 0-07-054483-2

The editors for this book were Kiril Sokoloff and Christine M.
Ulwick, the designer was Mark E. Safran, and the production
supervisor was Paul A. Malchow. It was set in Garamond by
ComCom.

Printed and bound by R. R. Donnelley & Sons Company.

For Glenn S. Dumke, Oscar Handlin,
and Alfred D. Chandler, Jr.

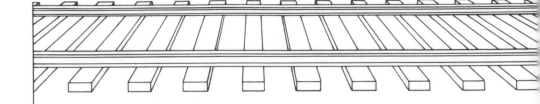

CONTENTS

Foreword   ix
Preface   xiii

PART 1   The Bankruptcy

1. The Significance of the Penn Central   3
2. A Giant Enterprise in Distress   29
3. Moves to Modernize Management   37
4. Financial Improvements, 1951–1963   45
5. Diversifying into Earnings and Growth   57
6. The Dream of Solution Through Merger   75
7. Turmoil at the Top   89
8. Collision Course   99
9. Merging into Chaos   117
10. Toward Disaster: Operating Failure   135
11. Toward Disaster: Mounting Chaos at the Top   147
12. Disaster   171
13. A Task Unfinished   187

PART 2   False Allegations Concerning Causes of the Penn Central Bankruptcy

14. Scapegoat   203
15. Penphil   215

16.   Executive Jet Aviation: The First Phase   237
17.   The Failure of Executive Jet   259
18.   The Mystery of the Missing $4 Million   291
19.   The Trial and Acquittal   309

APP. A   The Pension Fund   325

APP. B   Pennsylvania Railroad–New York Central Capital
Expenditures: A Comparison   337

APP. C   Penphil Group Stockholding in Kanab   343

Index   347

FOREWORD

People such as the original Cassandra have never been wanted, let alone popular or highly valued. The myth is that because she would not make love with Apollo, he used his god-given powers to prevent her prophecies from ever being believed, but always to be proved true. In the 1960s, David Bevan filled the classic but unenviable role of Cassandra on the Pennsylvania and Penn Central Railroads. Most of his warnings of trouble turned out to be true. Unfortunately, his prophecies were disregarded by top management. The two chief officers of the merged railroads, Stuart Saunders and Alfred Perlman, did not fully appreciate the calamitous results from the inadequately planned merger and huge capital expenditures involved. It seems, in retrospect, as if they may have been under the spell of an Apollonian curse.

After 13 years of missionary efforts, David Bevan had, by 1964, convinced the chief Pennsylvania Railroad executives that they were running a marginal operation where costs had to be carefully scrutinized, planned for, and trimmed wherever possible. The new regime was headed by Saunders, a lawyer whose only railroad experience had been with the Norfolk & Western, a railroad whose high profits came from controlled traffic in coal. He disregarded many of the checks and safeguards developed by Bevan and based his strategy principally on the assumed but largely unexplored economies that would result from a merger with the New York Central.

In retrospect, the two roads, literally thrown together in 1968, had no chance for survival with the existing operating problems and management structure. Because, like Cassandra, Bevan refused to share top-level euphoria, he was virtually eliminated as an influence during most of the first 2 years of the merger by being relieved of the major part of his duties. The merger was followed by a breakdown in railroad services, accompanied by questionable expenditures for new equipment and capital improvements. The borrowed money that had to be poured into the merged roads during the ensuing years appears in retrospect to have been sufficient in the course of time to bankrupt a corporation with such small normal earning power even if a bad winter in 1970, government interference, and mounting nonrail competition had not made financial liquidity impossible.

But what of the board of directors? Could they not have moderated the steadily rising expenditures for operations and maintenance, and recognized Saunders' lack of administrative expertise? Unfortunately, the board had only a couple of nonofficer members who understood the marketing of railroad service. The remaining outsiders were traditional representatives of financial and other institutions who assumed the mighty Pennsylvania Railroad and its successor, the Penn Central, were financially invulnerable. Unhappily, Richard K. Mellon, the senior director in both service and knowledge of the road, was taken ill in the critical year of 1968 and never attended a board meeting after the merger took place. Such a board—one that in the absence of personal knowledge is almost forced to believe whatever management tells it—is unfortunately not unusual in big companies. The failure to assess the position of the company, even from its annual reports, was a strong, contributing factor in the passage of resolutions authorizing the enormous capital borrowing necessitated by the approval of operating budget deficits and of new investment in the railroad from 1968 to 1970.

Had the two roads been merely put under a common board of directors and top management in 1968 and allowed to operate as separate entities until carefully tested plans for combining services had been worked out, survival might have been possible; at least, Bevan thought so at the time. But the two systems were placed under common operation, when such vital elements as safety controls necessary for the operation of trains and rules for the allotment and movement of freight cars of the two roads were based on incompatible systems. The result, as could readily have been anticipated, was a breakdown in rail service that lost customers to trucks which, incidentally were being indirectly subsidized by the interstate highway program. It was questionable whether these customers could ever be recovered, and their loss, as well as the general confusion, contributed to staggering operating deficits.

These, then, are the facts that underlay the truth of Cassandralike forecasts of disaster. Bevan's real miscalculation was to remain as the financial officer at the urgent request of Richard Mellon. By the time Bevan had been restored to workable financial authority in 1969, the damage to both operations and the financial structure had been done. It had always been Bevan's hope that the income from the diversified investments of the Pennsylvania Company might support a railroad that was nearly breaking even, but such returns were insignificant in comparison with the $400-million operating loss of the early months of 1970.

This greatest bankruptcy in world history, one that led to government entrance into what had previously been a privately owned industry, illustrates ills to which very large corporations are sometimes prone: ineffective top managers, unchecked by knowledgeable representatives of stockholders on the board of directors; lack of proper information through accounting of what was going on in the operations; government interference with corporate efforts to find new avenues to profit; and overoptimism regarding future expenses in relation to sales.

Stephen Salsbury's history is the first study of the Penn Central prepared and documented from a very large collection of records, many of them generated by Bevan and including government reports, transcripts of depositions and trial testimony in numerous suits, and of testimony before government agencies, all of which stretch over many years following the bankruptcy. These materials are supplemented by personal interviews and letters. The pertinent parts of the collection will be deposited in the Eleutherian Mills Historical Library and made available to the public.

In the first part of the book, the author reveals amazing naivete on the part of some of the major actors. The narrative, while involved, possesses the excitement that comes from a sense of impending disaster, and it should hold the attention of anyone interested in business.

In the second part of the book, Professor Salsbury analyzes in more detail the difficulties for which government investigators blamed David Bevan. Chapter 14, "Scapegoat," emphasizes the threat to the rights of private individuals from uncoordinated and competitive investigations by government agents, each seeking political advantage from sensational news releases. Salsbury closes with a plea for a single, special investigating body, similar to royal commissions in Britain, for cases having wide public ramifications. Chapter 15, on Penphil, is a provocative discussion of the doctrine of conflict of interest as it applies to officers making decisions to have their companies buy stock in smaller enterprises in which they are directors or have other access to "inside" knowledge. Focused on real people and situations, the chapter holds much more interest than abstract discussions in management texts. The chapters on Executive Jet and its European connections tell a fascinating and disturbing business history. This outside venture, trivial compared to the Penn Central Railroad, was seized upon by government investigators of the bankruptcy and written up in releases that appeared under lurid newspaper headlines. As business history, the chapters are particularly interesting in illustrating the problems of dealing with an agency such as the Civil Aeronautics Board (CAB). In the beginning, the chief officers and directors of Penn Central were enthusiastic about investing a few million dollars in an air-taxi service, but the ambitions of the managers of Executive Jet Aviation and the slowness and unpredictability of the CAB, which would not allow the railroad to control airline policies, ended in ruinous overexpansion of equipment which could neither be operated nor sold. While the success of this small enterprise might have substantially benefited Penn Central, its failure resulted in a loss that, although small in relation to the railroad's operating deficits, diverted official attention from Penn Central affairs.

Salsbury's unusual book, written by an experienced scholar from extensive public and private records, should be read by all teachers and students of management of railway history, and of recent government regulation. By tracing these widely applicable lessons from history, the discussion illustrates what may happen increasingly often in the future.

THOMAS C. COCHRAN
Benjamin Franklin Professor of History, Emeritus
University of Pennsylvania

PREFACE

This is a story of both a man, David Bevan, and a bankruptcy—it is a business biography. The book traces the role of the chief financial officer of what was America's largest transportation enterprise, the Penn Central, and his relationship to America's largest and most celebrated business failure.

The Penn Central resulted from the merger in February 1968 of America's two largest railroad corporations, the Pennsylvania and the New York Central. Both these enterprises traced their ancestry back into the first half of the nineteenth century. Each railroad had been one of four great trunk lines, which in the 1850s had first linked the Atlantic seaboard with the tributaries to the Mississippi River system. The Pennsylvania, in particular, under the presidency of J. Edgar Thomson in the 1850s, pioneered new forms of business organization that set the stage for a revolution in business management in the United States. Throughout the nineteenth century, the Pennsylvania grew so strong that it called itself, with much justification, "the Standard Railroad of the World." For decades, it and its greatest rival, the New York Central, dominated transportation in a large part of the United States lying between the mid-Atlantic states and Chicago. The two railroads reached their greatest power during the first two decades of the twentieth century. After 1920 they began a slow decline, which was at first gradual and barely noticeable. After the end of World War II, the decline accelerated and the once highly profitable corporations remained solvent largely through the earnings of their substantial nonrailroad holdings. By the middle of the 1950s, it became clear that business could not continue as usual for any of the railroads in the eastern part of the United States. Nevertheless, the Pennsylvania and the New York Central were crucial to large segments of the American economy.

The major problem that faced eastern railroad managements in the

1950s was how to restore the enterprises to financial health. Some observers, largely from the outside, noted that the massive railroad corporations, which had been leaders in business innovation in the nineteenth century, had become backward and inefficient. These critics saw the answer in internal managerial reform that would enable railroads to adopt modern practices. They hoped that a new organizational structure, new philosophies in accounting, and radically improved data processing would enable executives to identify scientifically areas where railroads could handle traffic competitively with other forms of transportation. They also hoped the new methods would reduce staff, increase efficiency, and aid in clearing away those parts of the railroads' system that were no longer competitive. Simultaneously, other leaders, largely traditional railroad managers, saw the solution in quite different terms. They focused upon the excess trackage that had been built up in the eastern part of the United States in the days when railroads had an effective monopoly of internal commerce. These men, many of whom lacked solid knowledge of modern methods of business administration, saw merger as the primary solution for the ills of eastern railways. However, they did not associate merger with managerial reform. For them, a unified system would provide the mechanism to clear away duplicate trackage and to make some saving through the elimination of parallel managements. The chief proponent of this view was the Pennsylvania Railroad's James Symes, and the Penn Central resulted from his efforts.

Although this is a business biography which focuses on a man, Part I of this book attempts to analyze the causes of the Penn Central's failure. To do this I have developed five major propositions. First, while the Pennsylvania Railroad had a high measure of operating success in the post-World War II period, its managerial structure and practices were backward when compared with other large American enterprises. Second, there was no planning prior to the Pennsylvania–New York Central merger at the crucial operating or managerial levels. Third, the Penn Central failed operationally. Fourth, the railroad's top management, specifically Board Chairman and Chief Executive Officer Stuart Saunders and President and Chief Operating Officer Alfred Perlman, rejected advance planning and modern concepts of business management, particularly those in budget-making and forward financial planning, and these factors together with operational failure caused the bankruptcy. Fifth, diversification did not cause the bankruptcy.

David C. Bevan's career provides a unique insight into the problems that engulfed the Penn Central. Bevan started his railroad life with the old Pennsylvania in 1951 when he became its financial vice-president. In the Penn Central, he was the chief financial officer and thus one of the corporation's three top men, along with Stuart Saunders, the board chairman and chief executive officer, and Alfred Perlman, the president and chief operating officer. Of the three, Bevan's career with the railroad spanned the longest period of time. He was also the most centrally involved in the events that followed the bankruptcy.

David Bevan was not the traditional railroad executive. After taking a master of business administration degree at the Harvard Business School, he went into banking and then life insurance. In his earlier positions, he became familiar with the most advanced concepts of business organization, accounting, and financial analysis. In the Pennsylvania and its arch-rival, the New York Central, he encountered the most venerable, but also two of the most backward, large business organizations in the United States. This book analyzes Bevan's attempt to modernize the Pennsylvania's and then the Penn Central's finances and accounting. The story of initial success and ultimate defeat sheds brilliant light on the problems that eastern railroads in general faced as they attempted to reorganize themselves to meet the challenges of the latter half of the twentieth century.

Because the government investigations that followed the Penn Central's bankruptcy so distorted the picture of what happened, this book must also devote considerable attention to them. Every effort has been made to place the investigations in proper perspective. The emphasis has been placed on separating fact from myth, a task which in itself has been substantial. There has been only a passing attempt to analyze the forces that caused the various government officials and investigators to act as they did; that is a large topic and more properly the subject for another full-length book.

This study is based both on the voluminous public record and on private sources. I have used many government documents, including those emerging from the investigations made by the Interstate Commerce Commission, the Securities and Exchange Commission, the House of Representatives Committee on Banking and Currency, and the Senate Commerce Committee. I have gone beyond the printed reports of these organizations to examine the testimony and documents upon which the investigators based their conclusions. In addition, I have read much of the testimony in a large number of court actions concerning the Penn Central. I have also used a full range of railroad corporation reports and have followed the reporting of the Penn Central affair in the news media, especially the Philadelphia press. Although these sources have proved enlightening, this study could not have been written without the full cooperation of David Bevan. After the railroad's collapse, he collected a vast quantity of primary source material on the Pennsylvania and New York Central Railroads as well as on the Penn Central. Because he was involved in numerous court actions and government investigations, his lawyers were given the opportunity to copy a large quantity of railroad records, including much of the correspondence in and out of his office when he was chief financial officer. This correspondence included copies of many official documents of the parent railroad, its subsidiaries, and affiliated companies. Although this material contains many letters and memoranda produced by Bevan in the course of his railroad career, most of the documents were originated by other people. David Bevan has given me complete access to his files, and I prevailed upon him to deposit this material (it took a large truck to move all of the documents) in the Eleutherian Mills Historical Library in Greenville, Delaware. For want of a better name, I have referred to these files as the "Bevan Papers" and documents cited as such may be consulted at Eleutherian Mills by persons interested in further research on the Penn Central.

In addition to making all his records available, Mr. Bevan subjected himself to lengthy, detailed, and searching interviews. Although I had never met him previously, I was impressed from the first by the full and frank manner in which he answered my many questions. These interviews provided the source for the numerous unfootnoted quotations in this book. Mr. Bevan graciously read the full text of this book prior to publication. He was extremely helpful in clearing up many complex problems of fact. We did not, however, always agree on interpretations of the facts. In every case, my viewpoint has prevailed. I wish to emphasize that the final selection of the material in this work and its interpretations has always been mine, and that I must be held wholly accountable for any errors of fact or interpretation.

While this book is basically about the largest bankruptcy of all time and the underlying causes, I, as the author, found myself on the horns of a dilemma. Various government agencies, politicians, and others, through reports and statements to the news media, created in the minds of the public a belief that the downfall of the Penn Central was precipitated by Executive Jet Aviation and Penphil. Actually, neither one was a factor, but so much publicity was devoted to them that I have felt impelled to deal with them in considerable detail in order to dispel the prevailing misconception. In order to keep things in the right perspective, it seems best to deal first with the bankruptcy, and then, in a separate and distinct part of the book, to review both Executive Jet and Penphil as factors in the Penn Central debacle.

This work has been more than five years in the writing and many people have contributed. Thomas C. Cochran, Benjamin Franklin Professor of History, Emeritus, at the University of Pennsylvania, called my attention to the unique opportunity of studying America's largest business failure from the inside. I owe Professor Cochran an enormous debt. He has read several drafts of the manuscript, and he has always been ready with sharp insight and good advice. The late Charles R. Whittlesey, who for many years was professor of finance and economics in the Wharton School at the University of Pennsylvania, also served as a tireless and stimulating critic. He made numerous suggestions about organization, analysis, and style, which I have greatly appreciated. Ralph Goodwin, professor of history at East Texas State University, read a number of the earlier chapters and made valuable suggestions about style and organization. Richard Overton, Professor of History Emeritus of the University of Western Ontario, took time from his busy publishing schedule to read and thoroughly criticize my book. I benefitted greatly from his sharp, but always helpful, analysis. I also owe a very large debt to Kiril Sokoloff, Senior Editor at McGraw-Hill, whose careful, insightful comments helped me to better express my ideas.

A large number of people connected with the Penn Central and its aftermath have generously given of their time in order to answer my many questions. I particularly want to thank Edwin P. Rome, partner in the Philadelphia law firm of Blank, Rome, Klaus & Comisky, who was special counsel for the trustees of the Penn Central and Stewart Dalzell and Raymond Denworth, both partners in the firm of Drinker, Biddle and Reath. This firm represented 21 of the outside Penn Central directors and a former Penn Central president, Paul Gorman, in the legal actions that were a result of the railroad's failure. The law firm was also liaison counsel for all defendants in the Multi-District Litigation that the bankruptcy caused. Finally, I want to thank Edward German, who represented David Bevan in many of the legal actions taken against him after the Penn Central's collapse. These busy Philadelphia lawyers all tolerated my questioning with helpful good humor, and they placed at my disposal many important documents. Others who took time from their busy schedules for interviews were Carl G. Sempier, former assistant vice-president for data systems of the Penn Central, and Henry A. Quinn, a partner in the Philadelphia office of Peat, Marwick, Mitchell & Co.

All these people may take credit for good things in this volume. While many helped, the final work is mine, and for all errors of interpretation and of fact I take full responsibility.

I owe two very important institutional debts. I started this study while I was a professor of history at the University of Delaware. That institution granted me both time and funds to support my work. In 1977 I took the Chair of Economic History at the University of Sydney in Australia. I am deeply grateful to that university for granting secretarial assistance and a travel allowance so that I might return to Philadelphia to finish the final stages of this work.

STEPHEN SALSBURY

Part 1
THE
BANKRUPTCY

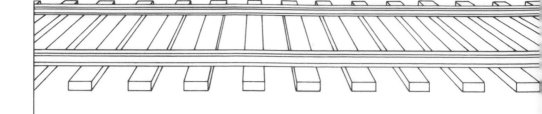

Chapter 1
THE SIGNIFICANCE
OF THE PENN CENTRAL

Although this book focuses on a large railroad, it is not about trains. It deals with business institutions in a particular industry in the two decades following 1950. Because railroads are America's oldest large-scale business organizations, observing what has happened to them has great value in understanding fundamental issues facing American businesses in the 1980s.

Recently, Alfred D. Chandler, Jr., analyzed the forces shaping the managerial revolution in American business in his Pulitzer-prize-winning book, *The Visible Hand* [1]. Chandler began his study by discussing the creation of what he called "the first modern business enterprises," which were the railroads, and he continued by analyzing the emergence of new managerial techniques throughout the American economy until the end of World War II. Chandler's emphasis on innovation in large enterprises is relevant to transportation companies, such as railroads and airlines; industrial concerns, such as meat-packers, steelmakers, and chemical manufacturers; and mass distributors, such as supermarket chains and department stores. All these businesses have at one time or another been at the center of the transformation of America from a small colonial agricultural venture to one of the most complex and powerful economies on earth.

Railroads have played a decisive role in creating the modern American economic system. They are the oldest large businesses, and for a long period of time—over 60 years—they were the nation's dominant corporations. Railroads pioneered in many ways. They brought into being new methods of finance; they were innovators in the use of the corporation as a legal entity; they created new forms of administration; they developed new types of accounting, particularly cost accounting; they undertook new methods of competition; and they caused new patterns of labor-management relations. Most of the creativity in managerial techniques took place between the 1840s and 1900. After that the railroad managerial structures ossified, and innovation in business administration shifted to such rising industrial corporations as the electrical manufacturers, the explosives makers, and (later on) the automakers, and also to mass distribution firms, such as mail-order and chain retailers. Chandler made this point forcefully. Slightly more than one-sixth of his volume was spent on analyzing the managerial revolution in the railroads. Almost all of this was concerned with the decades prior to 1900. In the twentieth century, railroads had little place in America's business revolution. The major issue which arises is this: Why did railroads cease to be innovative in a managerial sense? Is there something in the nature of railroads that caused this? Or were there more basic forces at work that might be applicable to all large enterprises?

Alfred Chandler's analysis dwelt on the cutting edge of institutional development. In so doing, it passed over some fundamental forces that are at work in the American economy and need attention if we are to understand what is happening to American business in the 1980s. The Penn Central debacle illustrates this point clearly.

RAILROADS AND THE RISE OF MODERN AMERICAN BUSINESS INSTITUTIONS

Before we go any further, it is necessary to examine Chandler's findings in some detail. Chandler focused on institutional innovation. He started with the sedentary merchants on the eastern seaboard of the United States in the early nineteenth century and explained how they moved into manufacturing. He analyzed how new transportation enterprises arose, especially railroads, and how they faced challenges never before experienced by American businesses. These new problems were partly in response to a revolution in technology: in transportation there was the development of the steam engine, and in communication there was the emergence of the telegraph and the transoceanic cable. Problems began with the rise, beginning as early as the 1830s, of new railroad corporations which were far larger than any previous business enterprises and which also extended over vast distances. For example, even a small predecessor of the New York Central, the 160-mile Western Railroad of Massachusetts, had by 1842 more than $7 million of capital invested in it. In comparison, the 360-mile Erie Canal, which was finished in 1825 and was the nation's biggest enterprise at the time, cost only $7 million. In 1873 the Pennsylvania Railroad, which had completed extending its control over lines that reached from Philadelphia to Chicago, represented an investment of more than $400 million. Early railroads loomed especially large when compared with contemporary industrial enterprises. As Chandler pointed out, in the mid-nineteenth century only exceptional mills [2] ". . .cost as much as $500,000. In fact, in 1850, only 41 American plants had a capitalization $250,000." It was not just financial size, however, that was crucial. By 1870 the two predecessors to the Penn Central, the Pennsylvania and the New York Central, controlled lines extending over distances exceeding 1000 miles between the Atlantic Ocean and Chicago. Old administrative methods were not sufficient to manage organizations of the size and complexity of these railroads.

Prerailroad American business institutions had been formed by the sedentary merchants, especially those residing in the major eastern seaboard cities. Although the merchants' interests were worldwide, their assets were small. Because transportation and communication were slow and unreliable, merchants who were engaged in global trading were forced to delegate authority to agents picked on the basis of reputation. Since merchants knew most about their friends and relatives, the bonds of friendship and kinship (rather than bureaucratic organization) cemented their empires [3].

The sedentary merchants founded most of the manufacturing enterprises before the American Civil War. They particularly dominated cotton textiles, but, as has been previously noted, these were minuscule compared with the new railroads. More importantly, the industrial enterprises were located in one place and were easily supervised without a bureaucratic administrative structure. Thus the traditional methods sufficed.

Almost from the first, railroads presented extraordinary challenges. Because their capital requirements were large, they could not be financed, as the textile industry had been, by single individuals or small groups. Railroads needed investment bankers, stock exchanges, and even a financial press. They fostered all these things [4].

Although railroads were not the first business in the United States to use the corporate form (that honor belongs to banks), they did pioneer here as well. Railways were the first big corporations with vast numbers of stockholders whose shares were regularly traded on exchanges. With very few exceptions, railroad charters were issued by states, not by the federal government. Since railways routinely operated across state boundaries, they developed what amounted to holding companies, enabling lines chartered in one state to control those chartered in another. The Pennsylvania, chartered in the state of Pennsylvania, used such a device in 1870. Its president, Thomas Scott, had the Pennsylvania legislature charter the Pennsylvania Company—as opposed to the parent Pennsylvania Railroad—to hold the shares and leases of the lines that it came to control between Pittsburgh, Chicago, and St. Louis [5].

Almost from the beginning, circumstances forced railroads to discard the administrative devices used by merchants. The experience of America's first heavily trafficked trunk line, Massachusetts' Western Railroad, proved the need for a new administrative structure. This line, which in 1900 came under the control of The New York Central, ran for 160 miles between Worcester and Albany. Construction of the line was finished in December 1841, and almost immediately safety became a major issue. The connecting Boston & Worcester, a short 44-mile road which had been completed in 1836, had solved the problem of preventing wrecks in a manner that avoided institutional innovation. The Boston & Worcester originally started with one passing track located halfway between the terminal cities and had trains start simultaneously from each end of the line and meet in the center. A train, once reaching the midpoint, could not proceed until the other train arrived. This made it unnecessary for the Boston & Worcester to develop a complex system of organization and employee discipline [6]. The Western could not operate in this way. Its long line required the morning passenger from Worcester to Albany to start at 9:30 A.M.: the train did not reach the Albany terminal until 6:35 P.M. In the beginning the Western scheduled three daily trains each way between Worcester and Albany. This meant that twelve times each day, trains going in opposite directions passed one another. The necessity for extra movements and work trains posed a difficult scheduling problem, particularly on a single track line that ran through mountains and lacked even elementary signaling. Even before the Western was completed, the system had a series of fatal wrecks, ending with a head-on collision of two passenger trains in October 1841. This accident killed two people and injured seventeen.

Safety problems on the Western resulted in major innovations. A radically new plan of administration was adopted; it attempted to develop definite lines of authority and responsibility for every phase of the railway's business. The Western's new bureaucratic administrative structure had little in common with the methods of the sedentary merchants who had previously dominated America's economic life. At the top of the railway's new administration was the corporation's head office, located in Springfield, Massachusetts, where the president of the company sat with a main administrative aide, the chief engineer, whose duties were soon assumed by a new office: that of general superintendent. Also at the central office was the master of transportation, whose job was to oversee freight and passenger transportation and maintenance of engines and rolling stock. The Springfield headquarters also had the firm's major repair shops supervised by a master mechanic. Thus, in a tentative way, the Western began to establish a functionally departmentalized administrative system separating such functions as transportation, maintenance, and so on, and placing them in different departments all located at a general headquarters (Springfield). The new structure broke the railway into three independent divisions about 50 miles in length. Each division was supervised by a roadmaster so that control could be extended to every part of the system. Later, these divisions were supervised by a deputy superintendent. Each division was in itself almost a mini-railroad company. The division or deputy superintendents had line authority to supervise the various functions, that is, movement of trains, repairs to rolling stock at divisional maintenance facilities, and track upkeep. Thus, in the words of Alfred Chandler [7]: "The need to assure a safety of passengers and employees on the new, high-speed mode of transportation made the Western Railroad the first American business enterprise to be operated through a formal administrative structure manned by full-time salaried managers. This embryonic modern business enterprise included two middle managers—the master of transportation and the master mechanic—and two managers—the superintendent and president." It also included several lower-level managers at the divisional level.

Written reports were a key factor in the Western's new administrative structure. They were made at divisional levels by all personnel (railway operators, divisional repair mechanics, divisional superintendents, and so on). The reports were made on a regular basis—some daily, some weekly, and some monthly. Most were forwarded to the railroad's headquarters, where they were analyzed by top management. The railway's speed made it possible for reports filed at Albany to arrive in company headquarters on the same day. Thus the controlling executives came to rely less on delegated authority. They could quickly evaluate performance on the basis of hard data and issue new directives as necessary. The bonds of friendship and kinship which had been crucial for the success of mercantile enterprises became less important on the railroads [8].

Railroads also had to pioneer in cost accounting. While it is true that textile mills also did this, the problems facing railroads were much more complex. Early railroads were, from the start, common carriers, which meant that they were forced to transport every kind of traffic, from passengers to high-value freight and bulk commodities. Each of these kinds of traffic required different types of facilities. For example, high-value freight could often be handled on baggage or express cars attached to passenger trains. Bulk freight such as grain or coal posed different problems. Grain was seasonal, and hauling it required the construction of large terminal facilities and the purchase of cars which would be used only part of the year. Coal was different: It could be mined the year round, and thus facilities erected to transport it had to be amortized differently than those erected for seasonal agricultural commodities. In short, in order to construct sensible tariff structures, the railroads had to segregate the specific costs associated with moving each kind of traffic. The Western Railroad faced this problem in the 1840s when it was deciding whether or not to compete against the water route between Albany and Boston for carrying bulk quantities of wheat and flour between upstate New York and industrial New England. Complex calculations on the part of the Western Railroad soon convinced its management that there was little profit in handling this type of bulk commodity [9].

Railroads also utilized new methods of competition. By the 1850s, four great trunk lines crossed the divide to link the Atlantic's waters with those of the West, either the Ohio-Mississippi Rivers system or the Great Lakes. The Baltimore & Ohio linked the Chesapeake Bay with Wheeling. The Pennsylvania connected Philadelphia with Pittsburgh. The Erie ran between Hoboken (across the Hudson River from New York City) and Dunkirk on Lake Erie, while the New York Central linked Albany with Buffalo. After the Civil War the Central came under the control of the steamboat king Cornelius Vanderbilt, who gave the Central two rail connections from Albany to New York City by purchasing the Hudson River Railroad and the Harlem Railroad.

It soon became clear that the four major trunk lines would compete for much of the through traffic that was beginning to flow between the Midwest and the eastern American seaboard. What form this competition would take was unknown. People like Vanderbilt worried that it might take the ruinous cutthroat form he experienced when he operated steamboats on the Hudson River and Long Island Sound. Railroad managers, as early as 1854, tried to forestall this through two methods. They created associations (cartels) to set noncompetitive uniform tariff agreements. Secondly, they secured traffic through alliances with connecting roads. Almost at the same time that the four great eastern trunk lines reached their western terminals, construction began on lines extending further westward toward Chicago and St. Louis. To capture through traffic, all four great eastern trunk lines made alliances with their western counterparts. For example, the Pennsylvania tried to link itself with the Pittsburgh, Fort Wayne & Chicago, the Steubenville & Indiana, and the Marietta & Cincinnati railroad companies. The Baltimore & Ohio and the New York Central also attempted to form alliances with other connecting lines. The Erie Railroad, financially the weakest of the four and therefore in most need of attracting traffic, behaved differently. Under the leadership of Jay Gould, it attempted to create alliances and also, by secret agreement, tried to undermine the alliances which its rivals had made. The Erie also undercut the cartel agreement sponsored by the associations, which, being contrary to public policy, could not be enforced in court.

The railroad managers of the eastern trunk lines quickly realized that because traffic originated at points far from their lines, it was essential to move closer to the source of the business. The failure of both associations and alliances forced railroad executives to turn to a policy of "system building." Railroads such as the Pennsylvania and the New York Central extended their control over western lines through leases or direct ownership of the connecting routes. In this way, each system obtained control over trunks running from the western terminals in the Northeast (Pittsburgh and Buffalo) to all-important midwestern cities, such as Cincinnati, Indianapolis, St. Louis, Cleveland, Detroit, Toledo, and Chicago. By the 1880s both the Pennsylvania and the New York Central systems had emerged into giant systems controlling trackage between New York City and the Midwest.

Railroads also saw the emergence of some of America's first effective trade unions. Originally these began during the 1860s as fraternal organizations, or brotherhoods; their primary object was providing insurance for their members. Outside organizations had to assume this role because railway work was dangerous and companies often retreated into their legal rights in order to avoid paying compensation to workers killed or injured on the job. It did not take the railroad brotherhoods long to become craft unions and to use the strike weapon to secure their demands. Because, as will be seen later, railroads were so important, the government quickly became involved.

THE UNIQUE CONDITIONS ALLOWING MANAGERIAL INNOVATION ON THE RAILROADS

Railroads in the nineteenth century were fortunate. They arrived at a time when management had almost total freedom to innovate. There were few precedents for any of their activities. The corporate form was new. Legal institutions were unprepared to deal with them. No better illustration of this can be seen than the case made famous by the Adams brothers in their book, *Chapters of Erie.* Charles Francis Adams, Jr., and Henry Adams, writing in the *North American Review* of July 1869, told a story which has become infamous in the annals of American railway history. C. F. Adams, Jr., chronicled how Cornelius Vanderbilt attempted to stifle competition of the New York Central by trying to purchase the rival Erie Railroad. Had Vanderbilt been successful, he would have monopolized all the important rail routes between New York City and Lake Erie. Vanderbilt failed because he ran afoul of some of the most clever Wall Street manipulators, namely, Daniel Drew, Jay Gould, and Jim Fisk, who controlled the Erie. The details of this struggle need not concern us here; note, however, that New York State's court system proved itself hopelessly inadequate in ironing out conflict between contending Vanderbilt–Erie groups. The reasons are clear. First, even within New York, it was possible for a corporation extending from one end of the state to the other to come under the jurisdictions of many state courts; the courts could and did issue orders countermanding one another. Second, the Erie posed still more difficult problems. Its eastern terminal, Hoboken, was in another state (New Jersey), and when Erie management did not like a decision made by a New York court, it picked up its records and crossed the state boundary, thus placing itself out of reach of New York's judicial system. The Erie case, which occurred in 1868, highlighted a problem which took years to solve. In the meantime, railroad entrepreneurs had enormous latitude for action.

It was not only the legal system that gave railroad management a free hand. Railroads emerged when governments, at both state and federal levels, were relatively weak. In the beginning there were few (if any) well-organized business or labor movements. Also, the lack of a tradition of managerial organization which the railroads could adopt ensured innovation.

FORCES RETARDING RAILROAD MANAGERIAL INNOVATION

After Alfred Chandler described the rise of new managerial traditions on the railroads, he turned to developments in other businesses where innovation continued. By focusing on innovation, Chandler missed some very important elements in American managerial history. The 100 years between 1840 and 1940 were unusual in human history, particularly so in the history of business institutions. Basically, human beings are conservative. I do not mean this in the political sense but in the institutional sense. People prefer stable arrangements because they safeguard status, property, and hard-won rights. Once institutional agreements are made, it generally takes some major change to alter them, such as drastic economic, technological, or political upheavals. The 100 years between 1840 and 1940 were unique because of the rapid change of business institutions. Previously, business institutions had been stable for centuries. Sedentary merchants of Boston in 1800 could have readily understood the business frameworks of their Italian counterparts in Medici-dominated Florence in the fifteenth century. Actually, Boston in the days of John Hancock had more in common with fifteenth-century Venice than with twentieth-century New York. The same generalization could also be made about technology. In the third decade of the nineteenth century, the rate of technological change in transportation and communication suddenly soared. After the innovations in water transport (canals and steamboats), technological innovation focused on railroads and then spread to other areas, such as manufacturing and distribution. This created a need for a new business framework, and for a time all seemed carried before the new tide. However, once an institutional structure came into being within an industry, conservative forces took over and acted to retard innovation.

The railroads illustrate this perfectly. Between 1840 and 1870, vast new bureaucratic structures arose to administer them. Once these enterprises became large and profitable, say between 1870 and 1890, the private bureaucracies became amazingly stable and resistant to change. One reason may have been the railroads' very great success. Throughout the nineteenth century they dominated inland transportation. Well-constructed systems linking key cities, particularly in the industrial Northeast, were remarkably profitable. This was especially true for the Penn Central's predecessors, the New York Central and the Pennsylvania. Once the initial problems of administration had been satisfactorily solved, there was little incentive for further innovation. Actually, new forces sprang up to stop further change. After the Civil War, governments, at first weak, passed legislation to regulate railroads. This was in direct response to abuses by railroad entrepreneurs. Stock market upheavals, such as those associated with the Erie, frightened investors. But even stronger voices for state regulation came from the users of rail transportation, particularly farmers. The Granger movement during the 1870s brought into being state regulatory commissions in several midwestern states. The target of many of the complaints was rate discrimination, particularly different charges for the same commodity applied to large shippers as against small shippers [10]. In the end, state regulation proved unsatisfactory. Much traffic moved across state lines, and under the U.S. Constitution it could not be controlled by the individual states. Thus the federal government became the major regulator of railroads.

Labor was also a conservative factor. Railroad managements fiercely opposed railway labor unions in the nineteenth century. The Pennsylvania used armed force to break a massive strike in 1877. At first, only weak railroad managements succumbed to union demands. Strong railroads, like the Chicago, Burlington & Quincy, preferred to shut down or hire strikebreakers rather than yield [11]. But as the nineteenth century wore on and the twentieth century began, railway unions grew stronger and began to achieve substantial victories.

INSTITUTIONAL INNOVATION AND STAGNATION IN THE PENN CENTRAL'S PREDECESSORS

Railroads are particularly significant, not because they are railroads but because as business organizations they achieved a new institutional arrangement so early. Railroad managerial structures were essentially complete by 1890, just about the time that the industrial sector was beginning to go through its own administrative reform. By 1900, railroads had brought into being forces that served to freeze their positions. Analysts have suggested that because railroads were so far ahead of any other industry, their problems came from technological obsolence, and the analysts have failed to see in railroad history a broader significance for American business.

The story of the Penn Central and its two predecessor railroads, the Pennsylvania and the New York Central, vividly illustrates the problem of institutional development and change. Although both systems served essentially the same region and were approximately the same size (the New York Central was always slightly smaller than the Pennsylvania), they often did things in a very different manner. For example, the two adopted very different administrative structures. The Pennsylvania under the direction of J. Edgar Thomson built a managerial structure that drew on the experience of the Western Railroad and the Erie Railroad. By 1857, Thomson had divided his railway into geographical divisions, each controlled by a superintendent who reported to a general superintendent, who in turn had operational responsibility for the entire system. As Alfred Chandler noted [12], the Pennsylvania's main achievement

> was a clarification in the relationship between the central office and the geographic subdivisions. Both the central headquarters and the several divisions carried on at least three functional activities—transportation, maintenance of way, and maintenance of locomotives, rolling stock, and other machinery. Thomson explicitly delegated the full powers to control the road to the officers in charge of transportation—to the general superintendent in the central headquarters and to the division superintendents in the geographic subunits. The other functional officers at the headquarters set standards and procedures but could not order their subordinates in the divisions when to work and what to work on. On the Pennsylvania, therefore, the division superintendent directed the daily work of all the men in his division. This meant, for example, that all workers in the division's shops were under his control; while the master of machinery set the rules and standards for "the discipline and economy of conducting the business of their [the division superintendents'] shops." In short, this was the beginning in industry of the line and staff system where the executives on the line of authority handled people and the other officers, the staff executives, handled things.

The Pennsylvania's way was not the only method of organization. The New York Central did things differently. In fact, the New York Central's early history was the opposite of the Pennsylvania. While the Pennsy had been built as a major trunk line initially linking Harrisburg with Pittsburgh, the New York Central was a consolidation of ten separate short lines. Chandler noted that the system's first senior executives, men like Erastus Corning, Dean Richmond, and E. D. Worcester, were rich New York politicians rather than professional railroad administrators. Initially, the New York Central's problems were financial and political rather than operational, and its early leaders paid little attention to administrative innovations. The administrative structure which emerged on the Central at the same time Thomson built his structure on the Pennsy emphasized a high degree of centralization. The Pennsylvania adopted what became known as a "decentralized divisional" structure. In contrast, the New York Central adopted a "departmental" structure. It was not a line and staff administration. On the Central the president and his functional department managers did not delegate their authority. Although the New York Central was divided into divisions, these divisions were for operational purposes only. However [13]: "The functional managers on the geographical divisions—transportation, motive power, maintenance of way, passenger, freight, and accounting, reported directly to their functional superiors at the central office." As will be demonstrated in later chapters of this book, the institutional administrative forms adopted on these railroads in the 1850s lasted almost intact until the day in 1968 when they merged to form the Penn Central. It would be difficult to cite a better example of institutional rigidity than this. One of the mistakes made by the Penn Central's top management, which escalated operational confusion, was the failure to decide whether to operate the consolidated railroad on a centralized or decentralized basis.

Although the Pennsylvania and the New York Central developed very different administrative structures, there were also similarities. Both railroads adopted what in the nineteenth century was a sophisticated accounting system. They each used cost accounting, which was essential for rate making. Also, in a vast organization such as the Pennsy or the Central, an accurate accounting procedure was necessary to ensure that top management could keep control over assets and to ensure the honesty of employees who were hundreds of miles away from company headquarters. Significantly, top management of the Penn Central's two predecessor railroads did not, until after World War II, use accounting data for forecasting or planning purposes. This innovation only began to appear in selected industrial firms after 1900. As early as 1907, the du Pont company of Wilmington, Delaware, an explosives firm, began to use statistics produced in the accounting department for the planning of capital expenditures as well as for production and inventory control. It was not until after 1920 that this knowledge was passed on to other firms in which the du Ponts were interested, particularly General Motors. For reasons which will be analyzed in later chapters, railroads clung to accounting systems which developed in the nineteenth century and did not share the advances in industrial and distribution firms [14].

The Pennsylvania and the New York Central were also alike in building comprehensive systems which linked the eastern seaboard with the Midwest. In many places tracks of the two railroads ran almost side by side, connecting such cities as Indianapolis and St. Louis. Both systems refrained from gaining direct control over lines west of Chicago and St. Louis. And neither system expanded its routes substantially after 1900. In fact, a hasty glance at maps of the New York Central- and the Pennsylvania-controlled lines, one drawn at the beginning of the twentieth century and another on the eve of the merger, would disclose very small differences in the extent of the two giant systems. This was despite the continuous shift of the center of economic gravity in the United States away from the eastern seaboard toward the West and South. This should have encouraged both railroads to gain control of western lines, creating a truly transcontinental system comparable to the Canadian Pacific in Canada.

The ossification of the Central and the Pennsy can only be understood against the background of railroad history in the latter part of the nineteenth century. Between 1870 and 1893 America went through a major railroad boom. This was the time when most of the great transcontinental lines were built: the Northern Pacific and the Great Northern on the northern route, and the Santa Fe and the Southern Pacific in the South. Other major lines were built in the West, such as the Oregon Short Line, which united the Union Pacific at Ogden with Portland. The South also witnessed a large-scale reconstruction of its railway lines after the Civil War and the addition of many new ones. There was also considerable railroad building in the older areas, particularly the Midwest. Much of this construction in older areas duplicated existing lines and added to railroad competition. By the 1890s America had far more railroad mileage than it needed.

A depression in 1893, together with the overbuilt state of railways, brought on a severe financial crisis for many companies, and during this period almost one-third of America's railroad mileage was in bankruptcy. This provided great opportunities to reshape the U.S. railroad networks, and some of the most important investment bankers stepped into the breach, particularly the House of Morgan and Kuhn Loeb & Company. It is significant that the eastern lines, particularly the Pennsylvania and the New York Central, remained profitable throughout this period. It was the West that saw much of the turmoil. At the center of the action were the two great railroad magnates: Edward H. Harriman and James J. Hill. Harriman had risen to prominence by gaining control of the financially ailing, but potentially strong, Union Pacific. Using this as a base after 1900, he came into control of the late Collis P. Huntington's railroads, particularly the giant Southern Pacific, which linked New Orleans, Louisiana with Portland, Oregon, and also formed the connection between Ogden (the Union Pacific's western terminal) and San Francisco. James J. Hill had begun by seizing control of local railroads in Minnesota and then extending them across the United States to Seattle to form the Great Northern Railway. At the same time Hill managed to control a parallel line, the Northern Pacific, which was the original northern transcontinental which linked Duluth and St. Paul in Minnesota with Portland and Seattle on the Pacific Coast. As of 1900 neither Hill's lines nor Harriman's reached Chicago. Hill's interests terminated at

the Twin Cities in Minnesota, and Harriman's at Omaha, Nebraska. Both
Hill and Harriman desired a Chicago connection, and they seized simultaneously on the very profitable and well-constructed Chicago, Burlington &
Quincy, which linked both the Twin Cities and Omaha with Chicago. Details
of this story are complex, but the fight to delineate imperial railroad boundaries in the West was fierce, with J. P. Morgan backing Hill and Jacob Schiff
of Kuhn-Loeb supporting Harriman. The struggle for domination culminated in the famous Northern Pacific Corner in 1901, which created a
sharp but short Wall Street panic.

Morgan and Schiff recognized that a settlement was necessary, and out of
this came a giant transportation monopoly in the Pacific Northwest known
as the Northern Securities Company, which was to control the following
railroads: the Northern Pacific; the Great Northern; the Spokane, Portland
& Seattle; and the Chicago, Burlington & Quincy. The decision to create the
Northern Securities Company was a private one reached solely by the participants in the struggle, particularly the investment bankers. Unfortunately for
them, it occurred almost simultaneously with Theodore Roosevelt's acciden-
tal succession to the presidency. Roosevelt, a Progressive, heeded the cries
against a new railroad monopoly by opponents of the Hill-Harriman settlement and used the power of the federal government to attack the Northern
Securities Company in the courts. Roosevelt used as a weapon the previously
dormant Sherman Antitrust Act. The case reached the courts in 1902, and
in 1904 the Supreme Court of the United States, in a five-to-four-decision,
made history by declaring, for the first time, a major corporate merger a
violation of the Sherman Act and requiring the dissolution of the Northern
Securities Company. Many historians belittle the effect of this decision on
railroad history. They point out that while the Supreme Court dissolved the
Northern Securities Company, it did nothing to alter the actual ownership
of the stock in the various component railroads, thus effectively leaving
Morgan and Hill in their controlling positions. Furthermore, in 1904 the
various components in the Northern Securities combination had not been
administratively integrated, so that as far as the general public was concerned, the individual railroads seemed to operate much as before. Nevertheless, the successful application of the Sherman Antitrust Act to thwart
railroad combination and monopoly made it very clear to investment bankers
and railroad presidents that they were no longer free to reshape the railroad
map of the United States at their pleasure. It is no accident that after the
Northern Securities decision few major railroad mergers took place until
well after World War II. This was certainly one of the factors preventing
America from following the Canadian example, which by the 1920s saw the
emergence of two nationwide railroad systems, the Canadian Pacific and the
Canadian National. It was not until railroads ran into dire financial straits in
the 1960s that mergers were again seen as a method of solving railroad ills

the way they had been in the 1890s. The sixties spawned several important mergers, among them being those between the Norfolk & Western, the Virginian, the Nickel Plate, and the Wabash; the union of the Chesapeake & Ohio and Baltimore & Ohio; and the almost exact reincarnation of the Northern Securities Company with the formation of the Burlington Northern. The Penn Central merger fits nicely into this pattern.

Another force retarding change in the railroad industry was the emergence of federal regulation. This began in 1887 with the creation of the first federal regulatory agency, the Interstate Commerce Commission. One of the purposes behind the ICC was to ensure that railroad rates would be [15] "just and reasonable." For a number of years the ICC did little to achieve railroad rate regulation, but gradually pressure from shippers and geographic interests built up. Then, as the Progressives came to power in Washington during the presidency of Roosevelt, Congress passed a number of acts giving the ICC expanded authority. These included the Elkins Act of 1903, which gave the ICC the authority to actually prohibit rebating, which had continued until then despite its supposed prohibition in the original Interstate Commerce Act. In 1906 the Hepburn Act [16] "gave the Commission power to fix maximum rates," and more importantly "shifted the burden of proof in rate proceedings from the Commission to the railroads, and made ICC decisions effective as soon as they were reached." The Mann-Elkins Act of 1910 further broadened the ICC's rate-making authority. Finally, the Transportation Act of 1920 gave the ICC power to set minimum as well as maximum rates, and it introduced the Commission to the area of investment banking by giving it the power to oversee the issuance of new railroad securities.

Today it is dogma to criticize the ICC. The Commission's historians, Ari and Olive Hoogenboom, wrote in the foreword to their book on the history of the ICC [17]: "Nearly everyone agrees that the Interstate Commerce Commission has failed." I agree with this judgment but would emphasize that the ICC has had an enormous impact upon railroads. Much of the nature of this impact has not been recognized even now. Because the ICC was concerned with rate making, it began to set standards for bookkeeping and statistical reporting. From the first, the ICC drew many of its staff and advisers from the ranks of the railroad industry. It was only natural that the ICC, in setting the format for reporting, drew heavily on the administrative and bureaucratic experience of the great railroads prior to 1900. In short, as will be seen later in this book, the cost accounting concepts current in the railroad industry in the nineteenth century were frozen in ICC regulations and practice, and these concepts continued to dominate railway thinking through the Penn Central merger. In the beginning there was probably very little difference between railroad, industrial, and ICC accounting procedures. The important point here is that the Commission adopted these methods before industrial enterprises went through a further accounting revolution which involved using accounting information as a tool in managerial decision making. When the ICC, using the powers granted to it by the Hepburn Act and the Mann-Elkins Act, started in 1910 to regulate actual railroad rates, the railway management was forced to think in ICC terms. This obsession with justifying rates before the ICC continued to grow throughout the twentieth century. As will be demonstrated, the result was that railroads were cut off from crucial innovations in business management which were occurring elsewhere. This kept railroad managers from adopting analytical techniques that had been a key to success in such corporations as du Pont, General Motors, and Sears.

The ICC regulations did further harm. As Albro Martin has shown in his important book, *Enterprise Denied,* the ICC started to regulate railroad rates at a time when they were already relatively low. This coincided with the beginning of a long-term inflation that characterized the American economy from 1900 through 1929, with some short exceptions. After 1910 the railroads found themselves in a position of having their rates regulated when almost nothing else was. These rates remained low while their labor and supply costs soared. As Martin pointed out, this drove capital out of railroads and into more attractive fields, of which there were many [18].

Another problem was that the ICC started its regulation at the height of railroad power and prosperity. Much of the regulation was based on the idea that railroads had a natural monopoly of land transportation and that other forms had to be nurtured or protected against them. There also persisted the idea that the main form of transportation competition was one railroad against another, not railroads against other forms of transportation, such as roads or waterways. Indeed, the Transportation Act of 1920 specifically authorized the Commission to set minimum rates. This power was used to protect other forms of transportation, particularly barges on internal waterways and trucks. Finally, the ICC's authority to regulate the issuance of railroad securities occurred before other industries were similarly controlled.

The regulation of railroads when few other enterprises were regulated dampened the enthusiasm of major investment bankers. It hastened a trend which emphasized that railroad managers would be engineers and operators, not financiers. As the twentieth century wore on, these operators became further separated from the world of finance. In contrast, many, although not all, of the great railroad entrepreneurs of the nineteenth century combined a solid operational knowledge with an appreciation of finance. This was especially true of magnates like the Great Northern's James J. Hill, the Union Pacific's Edward Harriman, the Southern Pacific's Collis P. Huntington, the Pennsylvania's Thomas Scott, and the Chicago, Burlington & Quincy's Charles E. Perkins. Because throughout the 1920s rail firms continued to remain relatively profitable, no one at the time recognized clearly the long-term damage which ICC regulation inflicted on the railroad system.

Other forces also acted to restrict management options. Not the least of these was the continued rise of organized railroad labor. By the beginning of World War I, four major brotherhoods (conductors, engineers, trainmen, and firemen) had organized and dominated the running of trains. These unions exerted a strong influence on the federal government long before most industries found it necessary to bargain with organized labor. In 1916 Congress intervened directly in railroad labor relations by passing the Adamson Act, which legislated the 8-hour day for railway employees. This reduced working time from the normal 10-hour day with no loss in pay. World War I brought further government interference in railway labor-management relations. In the middle of the war, America's railroad system broke down and the government took over the operation of all the lines under the United States Railroad Administration. This organization further strengthened unions by encouraging collective bargaining. As a result, unionization spread from the operating employees to other functions, such as shops and maintenance of way [19].

After World War I, the Transportation Act of 1920 established a Railroad Labor Board which attempted to settle industrial disputes on the systems. Thus, if collective bargaining failed, the Board had the power to resort to compulsory arbitration. This had mixed results since neither side was bound to accept the results of arbitration. Nevertheless, by 1920 railroad labor was clearly far stronger than labor in any other major industry (except, possibly, parts of the coal-mining industry). The strength of organized labor, particularly in the operating departments, had the tendency to freeze work rules on the rails at a time when substantial technological innovation was possible.

RAILROAD MANAGEMENT IN A
PERIOD OF STAGNATION

Since the end of World War II, it has been fashionable in many circles to label railroad management as stodgy, conservative, unimaginative, and backward. Although there may be truth in some or all of these characterizations, they have to be considered against the reality facing twentieth-century railroad managers. Railroad leaders lacked many of the options routinely open to other businessmen. For example, they found it difficult, if not impossible, to merge with other railroads and thus create a more efficient network in tune with shifting national demographic and industrial trends. It also proved nearly impossible to develop a full line of transportation services. While railroads dominated inland transportation up to 1900, this situation rapidly changed with the rise of motor transportation, the introduction of the airplane, and the reemergence of inland waterways. Yet attempts to coordinate railroad services with these modes of transportation suffered because the federal government would not allow railroads to own these competing transportation enterprises. Both the Pennsylvania and the New York Central moved early to ally themselves with airlines. The Pennsy was instrumental in 1928 in founding Transcontinental Air Transport, the predecessor of Trans World Airlines (TWA). And immediately after World War II, the New York Central purchased a substantial interest in Flying Tiger Airlines, which was primarily a freight carrier. Ownership of air transportation by railroads, which was routine in Canada, became illegal under the rules of the federal Civil Aeronautics Board. Later in this book another Pennsylvania experiment with airline services will be described in detail, illustrating the enormous problems faced by railroad management when it attempted to move toward an integrated rail–air service. Similarly, significant ownership of motor carriers and water transportation lines by railroads has been hindered, although there has been slightly more success in these areas than with airlines.

In other critical areas, railroad managements found their hands tied. With the exception of the public utilities (electricity, telephone, gas, and water), almost all American businesses have had the freedom in peacetime to set prices for their goods and services, and to determine the level and nature of their business activities. In constrast, the ICC regulated almost every aspect of the railroads. The Commission set minimum and maximum railroad rates. It often forced railroads to set joint rates with other carriers, such as barge lines, making the railroads share lucrative business with these competing forms of transportation. This was done at the same time that the U.S. Army Corps of Engineers spent massive sums of public money to improve waterways and charged the users no tolls. The ICC also regulated the level of railway service. Branch lines could not be abandoned without permission, and regulators often forced the continuation of money-losing passenger trains. The ICC not only specified an accounting system for railroads but also had control over the issuance of railroad securities. This happened long before other firms came under the regulation of the Securities and Exchange Commission. Ironically, as will be seen later in this book, when the SEC did come into existence, it resented the fact that railroads were under ICC, rather than SEC, control. However, the line between the two regulatory agencies was not clear-cut; if a railroad engaged in any other business (for example, if it operated a real estate company), that business *did* fall under the SEC.

Finally, the railroads faced problems with their bureaucratic structure and their personnel. Because the railroad bureaucracies were old, well entrenched, and, for many years, successful, these structures built up a momentum of their own which proved hard to change. Workers and even executives resisted change as long as things could be done in a traditional manner. In the area of labor relations, things were even more complex because of the early strength of railroad unions. These organizations froze work rules in the operating area by the 1920s, and this made it difficult for management to take full advantage of technological improvements. Railroad unions set the number of the crew on trains and postulated work rules that gave employees a full day's pay based upon the mileage run rather than the hours worked. This was done early, when speeds were slow, and railroads were denied much of the benefit of increased productivity. Rapid inflation exacerbated the squeeze since railroad rate increases lagged behind wage hikes. The experience of the Pennsylvania when it shifted to long-distance electric trains in the eastern corridor in the early 1930s demonstrated union power. When electrification first started railroad, firemen recognized that they would have no duties on electric locomotives. One wrote in 1911 that [20]: "It will be a great change for [the firemen] to sit in a nice clean cab equal to a pullman coach, with little more to do than keep his eyes open, ring the bell for crossings, and look wise." The unions were so powerful that the Pennsylvania did not even consider abolishing firemen on electric locomotives. As Michael Bezilla observed, this did not even become an issue until the 1950s, by which time the Pennsylvania and other major railroads were in desperate financial straits.

For many years the plight of the railroads has been considered unique. Nevertheless, all American industry has become subject to the same types of pressures affecting the railroads, that began slowly in the New Deal and then accelerated rapidly in the 1960s and 1970s. Most large corporations, especially the older ones which for many years were successful, have built up large private bureaucracies which have been more difficult to change. More important, government regulation has spread from railroads to almost every phase of economic activity. Industrial firms which once had the freedom to locate their activities at any point now face stringent environmental restrictions enforced by the government. Even rebuilding a plant at the same location is strictly regulated. Hiring and firing have become government-controlled. Another government agency sets strict standards for occupational health and safety conditions. Most major industrial concerns have become unionized, and as in the case of railroads, government has passed laws encouraging unionization. The SEC supervises the issuance of stocks and securities for most corporations. The Federal Antitrust Division examines most mergers. And since World War II, major industries have increasingly had to be concerned with government price control. This has long been true in the steel industry, but price regulation has spread to such key areas as natural gas and oil. Even the right of management to close down an operation has been undermined. More and more pressure has been exerted to keep firms from shifting production out of old established regions, such as the Northeast. Finally, the government has acted to prevent the collapse of certain major industrial concerns (for example, Lockheed and Chrysler). Much of the institutional rigidity which was associated with railroads after the turn of the twentieth century exists in other businesses as well. This fact may be a key to the depressing lack of productivity increase which has come to characterize the American economy since 1970.

RAILROAD MANAGERIAL RESPONSE TO INSTITUTIONAL RIGIDITY

How did railroad management after 1900 cope with the problems of institutional rigidity? If top executives could not freely set prices, control conditions of employment, or establish a full line of services, what options were open? First, the character of management changed. The executive positions, especially on the larger and more prosperous systems, gravitated almost entirely to men who came up through the operating divisions. Often these men were engineers. Since traditional entrepreneurial maneuvers were impossible, they attempted to solve problems through technology. In fact, they had extraordinary success, since the period 1900–1960 saw a technological revolution. For example, managers decreased the use of work force by increasing the length and weight of trains. To do this, railroads laid down heavier rails. This made possible the use of heavier cars with larger capacities. Fewer cars cut down maintenance and also saved dead weight by reducing couplings, wheels, and car superstructure. To move longer, heavier trains, railroads built larger and more powerful locomotives. This was but the beginning. Railway engineers sought new types of motive power which were free of the restrictions of steam. The Pennsylvania, in the mid-1920s, embarked on a large-scale program of electrification, and by the end of the 1930s trackage running from New York to Washington and west from Philadelphia to Harrisburg was under wires. Electric locomotives were far more efficient than steam. The Pennsy's investigation of savings conducted in 1938 indicated that electrics, when compared with the most modern steam engines, were cheaper to repair and spent less time undergoing inspections at terminals. Furthermore, while multiple units of electric locomotives could be operated with one crew, steam trains that were double- or triple-headed needed a crew for each engine [21].

The Pennsylvania's large pre-World War II electrification program was unique. Other railroad managers beginning in the mid-thirties seized on the diesel-electric engine to solve their motive power problems. After the war, diesel locomotives swept all before them. They had many advantages of conventional electric locomotives, and in addition they did not require the enormous capital cost associated with the erection of wires and electric substations.

The motive power revolution was only part of the story of railroad technological change. New concepts in signaling and train dispatching, such as centralized train control, reduced the need for a large work force in signaling and made possible far more effective use of trackage. Engineers estimated that centralized train control allowed two main line tracks to do the work of three, making it possible for systems like the New York Central and the Pennsylvania to reduce some of their key lines from four tracks to three and sometimes to two. This allowed savings in real estate taxes and track maintenance. The technological innovations brought to the railroads by their engineer-managers should not be underestimated. The innovations enabled the firms to meet drastically altered competitive conditions which came with the rise of road, water, and air transportation. Despite both a serious erosion of its passenger business and the challenges by motor traffic to its high-value short-haul freight, the Pennsylvania remained profitable even through the Great Depression. The New York Central was less successful, although it remained solvent.

A major problem of the new technology was money. The Pennsylvania's electrification scheme in the 1930s cost in excess of $200 million. This sum loomed large against the railway's depressed earnings; the Pennsy's net income fell as low as $19.5 million in 1931 and remained relatively low throughout the Depression. The railway had to resort to government-supported loans, first from the Reconstruction Finance Corporation and then, at the suggestion of President Roosevelt's Secretary of the Interior, Harold L. Ickes, from the Public Works Administration. Fortunately for the Pennsylvania and many other railroads which continued to be technologically innovative during the 1930s, World War II caused business profits to rise, allowing some debt retirement. After the war, however, for many railroads, particularly those in the northeastern part of the United States, financial conditions worsened. Both the Pennsylvania's and the Central's capital needs always greatly exceeded supply of money. This led railroad leaders to think about the reorganization of the whole northeastern network. This idea came from the railroad management, especially from operators such as the Pennsylvania's James M. Symes.

MANAGERS AND INSTITUTIONS

This book concentrates on business institutions, but it also is about managers. The Penn Central had three major leaders: Stuart Saunders, the chief executive officer and chairman of the board; Alfred Perlman, president and chief operating officer; and David Bevan, chairman of the finance committee and the chief financial officer. These three men attempted to reverse the deteriorating fortunes of railroading in the Northeast. At the time the Penn Central came into existence in 1968, business analysts and outsiders felt that the corporation had an effective management. There were solid reasons for this belief. All three men had in common a good education. Saunders and Bevan both graduated from prestigious small liberal arts colleges. Both did graduate work at Harvard. Saunders received a law degree and Bevan received a masters in business administration. Perlman was an engineer, a graduate of the Massachussets Institute of Technology. He also had some graduate training at the Harvard Business School.

Although the three men had excellent educations, they each brought to the Penn Central very different but complementary talents. Saunders was a lawyer. It is often said that contrary to the popular image of lawyers defending clients in spectacular court battles, most lawyers work strenuously to keep cases out of court. This is particularly true in business, where they specialize in bringing antagonistic groups together for the benefit of both parties. Saunders was this kind of lawyer. He was a skilled politician and a good mediator, and he was sensitive to the desires of conflicting groups. Before he reached the Penn Central, he demonstrated an extraordinary ability to facilitate railroad mergers which previously had been thwarted for the same reasons that Theodore Roosevelt had opposed the formation of the Northern Securities Company.

Unlike traditional presidents on the Pennsylvania, Saunders was not an operating man, although he was chosen by James Symes, who *was* an operator. Nevertheless, Saunders's qualities as a lawyer and as a successful achiever of mergers seemed to make him the ideal person to bring the New York Central and the Pennsylvania together in a successful new transportation enterprise.

Alfred Perlman was a very different kind of person. He had much in common with traditional railroad leaders. Although an engineer, Perlman had worked primarily in operations since his graduation from MIT. Perlman followed in the best tradition of twentieth-century railroad executives. He had been brought to the New York Central by that Wall Street rebel Robert R. Young, a financier who hoped to infuse American railroad management with innovative ideas. Young was an optimist who had great faith in trains; he caught the public imagination with his battle for improved passenger service and his successful fight in 1954 to capture the New York Central. Young picked Perlman to manage the Central, and the big attraction was Perlman's competence as an innovative operations man. Perlman had been an early advocate of the diesel locomotive. He alertly used technology to cut labor costs. On the Central, Perlman acted quickly to encourage innovation. He fostered the adoption of centralized train control on the system's most heavily trafficked lines. Perlman also built modern classification yards designed to speed the makeup of freight trains at key junctions and to minimize the use of expensive labor and locomotives. Ever alert for new methods, Perlman strongly advocated using computers for the solution of railroad problems. At the time of the Penn Central's merger, Perlman's reputation as an astute technician stood extraordinarily high.

David Bevan, the chief financial officer, was different still. Although he came from a railroad family, his early career had nothing to do with trains. He was a professionally educated financial analyst with long experience in banks and insurance companies. Like Saunders, Bevan had been picked by an operating man. In this case the goal was to bring outside talent to focus on the problems associated with the Pennsylvania's post-World War II debt of over $1 billion. Bevan viewed the railroad neither as an operating man nor as a lawyer but primarily as an outsider well-versed in the administrative and financial techniques which had revolutionized American business since 1900. As chief financial officer he was well placed to begin a program of modernization in the railroad's managerial structure [22].

In theory, the Penn Central's management should have worked well. In Stuart Saunders the company had a first-rate lawyer and politician who could explain the railroad's problems to the outside world and thus help break the institutional straitjacket which was preventing the reconstruction of the Northeast's transportation network. In Alfred Perlman the firm had a brilliant operations expert with a solid record of applying new technology on two railroads: the Denver & Rio Grande Western and the New York Central. In David Bevan the Penn Central had a financial officer with wide experience who understood the latest concepts in the administration of large-scale enterprises. Yet the Penn Central failed, and as this book will demonstrate, its top management must accept a considerable portion of the blame. One of the reasons was that Saunders, Perlman, and Bevan could not, or would not, work together as a team. Why should this have been so?

Part of the problem undoubtedly lies in the personalities of each of the individuals involved. Certainly none of these top administrators could effectively communicate with one another. But there is another explanation as well. A standard issue that historians have almost always faced is the problem of the relationship of humans to their environment. This is the question of free will versus predetermination. How much freedom do humans have to shape their own destiny? How much is an individual a prisoner of his or her environment?

The case of the Penn Central poses these questions starkly. Saunders, Perlman, and Bevan did not operate in a vacuum. In the Pennsylvania and the New York Central they inherited very rigid private bureaucracies—more than a century old—which had shown a strong resistance to change. As will become clear, Perlman, an operating man from the beginning, was heavily influenced by the administrative structures and traditions which had shaped the New York Central from the middle of the nineteenth century. In addition, the very problems faced by the Penn Central tended to separate the operators from the newcomers like Bevan and Saunders, who did not share in the old ways. Perlman, true to his calling, saw the technological innovation as the railroad's salvation. This conflicted with Bevan's priority.

The chief financial officer, looking from an outside perspective, placed a primary emphasis on solving the railroad's financial problems, and this meant restricting capital expenditures to the company's ability to finance them. He also saw a pressing need for administrative reform. This set the stage for a direct conflict. Perlman could achieve his goals only through massive capital projects, and this meant more debt. Bevan and his ideas stood in the way. To make matters worse, as will become clear, neither understood the institutional background of the other. The Penn Central tragedy is, therefore, a classic struggle between two concepts rooted in vastly different traditions. Ironically, both Bevan and Perlman were struggling toward the same goal through drastically different methods. Stuart Saunders, who came to the railroad from still a different background, proved unable to bridge the gap.

In other circumstances, the divisions within the Penn Central might not have led to disaster. But by the time of the Penn Central's creation in 1968, the margin for error was so slight that it could not afford mistakes. Although the three men understood the seriousness of the railroad's position, none fully recognized the thinness of the margin for error. After all, the Pennsylvania had a continuous record of dividends since before the American Civil War. It had survived the Depression, and during that dark period it had undertaken an enormous electrification project partly at the urging of the highest executives in the federal government. Furthermore, Perlman and Saunders thought the railroad was so important that it would not be allowed to fail even if it got into temporary financial difficulties. The Penn Central has much of the elements of a classic Greek tragedy. Its human actors were caught in an institutional web that in the end controlled them. This is not to say that they had no responsibility for what happened; rather, the large weight of tradition overwhelmed much of the small latitude for action which existed.

A word needs to be said about the rest of this book. This study is not a history of the Penn Central. It is the story of one man, David Bevan, and his part in this greatest of American business failures. It is an important story because Bevan met head-on the challenges of dealing with an old, established, ailing, but still vital American industry. His story shows in bold relief the major issues in the failure and, by inference, problems that will be central to many large business ventures in the last two decades of the twentieth century.

Bevan's career has another significance. He was the one who faced the brunt of the investigations that occurred after the railroad's collapse. These probes, mainly launched by government, shaped the public view of the Penn Central disaster. There is a great deal of irony in all this. From the brief institutional sketch which this chapter has provided, it should be clear that government agencies and policies had much to do with the predicament in which railroads found themselves after World War II. No one can deny that government itself was a major factor in the tragedy. Yet who investigated the railroad's collapse? Government officials, both elected and appointed, who were directly involved in the events, carried out the investigation. Thus, Wright Patman, chairman of the Banking and Currency Committee of the House of Representatives, who torpedoed the railroad's last-minute plea for government aid to avoid bankruptcy, launched a major probe. So did the Senate Committee on Commerce. The ICC undertook a separate investigation, as did the SEC.

This book will demonstrate that the current governmental institutional framework scatters the responsibility for investigation and prosecution in a disaster of the Penn Central type. In fact, it does more than that. It ensures that investigations will be carried out by a large number of separate governmental agencies, most of which have axes to grind. For example, the ICC and the SEC had overlapping jurisdictions and were at war with one another. The Penn Central's collapse gave the SEC an opportunity to attack the ICC for an alleged failure to protect investors in railroad securities. It enabled the SEC to argue that it should be given jurisdiction over these matters currently with the ICC. There is still another issue here. The Penn Central's failure and the strain which it caused to the northeastern transportation system and the nation's banking and security systems seriously embarrassed both the ICC and the SEC. These regulatory agencies were supposed to monitor the activities of large ventures such as the Penn Central, and they should not have been caught unaware by its failure. The public might have asked—indeed Wright Patman did ask—whether the regulatory agencies were performing their function properly. It is evident that there is a strong potential for conflict in a governmental investigation of a corporate disaster when the government was supposed to be regulating that industry. As will be seen, David Bevan's experiences illustrate this point forcefully.

References

1.   Alfred D. Chandler, Jr., *The Visible Hand: The Managerial Revolution in American Business,* Harvard University Press, Cambridge, 1977.

2.   Alfred D. Chandler, Jr., and Stephen Salsbury, "The Railroads: Innovators in Modern Business Administration," in Bruce Mazlish (ed.), *The Railroad and the Space Program,* M.I.T. Press, Cambridge, 1965.

3.   For a general discussion of prerailroad business institutions, see Stephen Salsbury, "American Business Institutions Before the Railroad," in Glenn Porter (ed.), *Encyclopedia of American Economic History,* vol. II, Charles Scribner's Sons, New York, 1980, pp. 601–618.

4.   See Alfred D. Chandler, Jr., *Henry Varnum Poor: Business Editor, Analyst and Reformer,* Harvard University Press, Cambridge, 1956.

5. Chandler and Salsbury, op. cit., p. 152.

6. It is interesting to note that canals—which were much longer—needed no such planning since the canal authorities did not operate the canal boats. Canals operated like turnpikes, allowing individuals to own the methods of transportation.

7. Chandler, *The Visible Hand,* pp. 97–98.

8. For a full discussion of the managerial revolution on the Western Railroad, see Stephen Salsbury, *The State Investor and the Railroad: The Boston & Albany, 1825–1867,* Harvard University Press, Cambridge, 1967. See especially Chapter 9.

9. Ibid., Chapter 10.

10. For a discussion relating to the Midwest, see Henrietta M. Larson, *The Wheat Market and the Farmer in Minnesota, 1858–1900* Columbia University, New York, 1926. For a slightly different view, see Lee Benson Merchants, *Farmers and Railroads: Railroad Regulation and New York Politics, 1850–1887,* Harvard University Press, Cambridge, 1955.

11. See Robert U. Bruce, *1899: Year of Violence,* Bobbs & Merrill, Indianapolis, 1959, and Donald L. McMurry, *The Great Burlington Strike of 1888: A Case History in Labor Relations,* Harvard University Press, Cambridge, 1957, and also Richard C. Overton, *Burlington Route,* New York, 1965, pp. 158–160 and 206–214.

12. Chandler and Salsbury, op. cit., pp. 140–141.

13. Chandler, *The Visible Hand,* p. 107.

14. See Alfred D. Chandler, Jr., and Stephen Salsbury, *Pierre Du Pont and the Making of the Modern Corporation,* Harper & Row, New York, 1971. See especially Chapter 8.

15. Data for the ICC come from Thomas K. McGraw, "Regulatory Agencies," in Porter, op. cit., p. 797.

16. Ibid.

17. Ari Hoogenboom and Olive Hoogenboom, *A History of the ICC from Panacea to Palliative,* W. W. Norton and Co., New York, 1976, p. ix.

18. Albro Martin, *Enterprise Denied: Origins of the Decline of American Railroads, 1897–1917,* Columbia University Press, New York, 1971.

19. George Soule, *Prosperity Decade: From War to Prosperity, 1917–1929,* M. E. Sharpe, White Plains, New York, 1975 (reprint), p. 191.

20. This quotation, from the *Brotherhood of Locomotive Firemen* of February 1911, was quoted in Michael Bezilla, *Electric Traction on the Pennsylvania Railroad, 1895–1968,* The Pennsylvania State University Press, University Park, 1980, p. 135.

21. Bezilla, op. cit., pp. 161–162.

22. I would like to thank Professor Richard Overton for calling the similarities and contrasts in the careers of Saunders, Perlman, and Bevan to my attention.

Chapter 2
A GIANT ENTERPRISE IN DISTRESS

At midcentury the Pennsylvania Railroad was America's largest transportation enterprise. With assets of almost $3 billion, its more than 10,100 miles of tracks stretched westward from New York City to Chicago and St. Louis. Even as late as 1956, the Pennsylvania ranked as one of the United States' largest business ventures. In that year, *Fortune* magazine noted that the road's assets totaled slightly more than $3,037,000,000, substantially greater than the second largest transportation company, the New York Central, with assets of over $2,638,-000,000. Only three of *Fortune's* 500 largest industrial corporations, General Motors, Standard Oil of New Jersey, and United States Steel, had more assets than the Pennsylvania. And among the utilities, only the giant American Telephone and Telegraph surpassed the Pennsy, as it was familiarly, almost affectionately, known.

THE HISTORICAL LEGACY

Unfortunately, the Pennsylvania was vulnerable as well as venerable. It had been chartered in 1846 by the Commonwealth of Pennsylvania to build a railway between Harrisburg and Pittsburgh. The Pennsylvania was, along with the Baltimore & Ohio, the New York & Erie, and the New York Central, one of the four great trunk railway lines that in the 1850s linked the Atlantic seaboard with the Ohio-Mississippi valley.

As the nineteenth century wore into the twentieth, the Pennsylvania Railroad moved from strength to strength. It paid its stockholders their first dividend in 1848, an amount equal to a 6 percent return on paid-in capital. This was but the first of an unbroken string of annual dividend payments, which lasted throughout the entire life of the Pennsylvania Railroad until its absorption into the Penn Central in 1968.

The railroad reached the peak of its strength during the presidency of Alexander Johnston Cassatt (1899–1906). Under the Cassatt regime, there was enormous physical expansion. Little of this growth involved the addition of new route miles; rather, Cassatt emphasized the upgrading of the railroad's ability to haul people and goods. He finished the quadrupling of the trackage between New York City and Altoona, Pennsylvania. Cassatt's biggest accomplishment, however, was building the railway directly into Manhattan. Traditionally, passengers bound for New York on the Pennsylvania ended their rail journey at Jersey City, where they transferred to ferries for the trip across the Hudson River to New York City. Cassatt changed this. In 1900, the Pennsylvania purchased control of the Long Island Railroad. Then, in conjunction with the Long Island, the Pennsylvania started to construct an underground railway which ran from New Jersey under the Hudson River to a terminal in New York City and thence eastward under the East River to Long Island. Construction began on this expensive and complex project in 1904, and the first trains arrived in New York's Pennsylvania Station in 1910.

THE DECLINING PENNSYLVANIA

Despite temporary reprieves, the decline of the Pennsy, though gradual, was inexorable. By midcentury its days of glory were past and the system was living on borrowed time. This condition was evident to anyone who cared to make a detailed examination of the railroad's annual reports.

Although the railroad industry as a whole declined after World War II, the Pennsy's problems were far more serious than those experienced by many lines. Financial analysts have traditionally used a railroad's operating ratio as a measure of its success. This ratio is the percentage of operating revenues necessary to meet operating expenses. It should be noted that operating expenses do not include such important items as interest on bonded indebtedness, rental payments for leased lines (such as the Pennsylvania's long-term obligations with such corporations as the Pittsburgh, Fort Wayne, and Chicago), or the equipment trust payments, which finance the purchase of new rolling stock. The higher the operating ratio, the worse the performance of the railroad. Thus the Pennsylvania's subsidiary, the Long Island, in 1951 required 95.17 percent of its operating revenues to pay its operating expenses [1]. This was one of the most unfavorable ratios of any major railroad in 1951.

The Pennsylvania's operating ratio of 85.5 percent was relatively high. The railroad's ratio had been bad since the end of World War II, fluctuating from a low of 83.29 percent in 1948 to a high of 90.71 percent in 1946 [2]. The Pennsylvania's management well knew the significance of these data and commented in its 1951 annual report: "This ratio does not produce a margin sufficient to meet interest, rents, taxes, and other requirements to afford a satisfactory return to the stockholders and provide sufficient funds for reinvestment to continue financial stability. The management," the report continued, "is well aware of this situation and is persistently striving to improve it" [3].

It seems ironic that the Pennsylvania, so strong in the 1890s that it withstood a depression that brought low such railroads as the Southern, the Union Pacific, and the Santa Fe could be so weak in the 1950s. But there were solid reasons for this turn of events. In fact, the very forces that worked in favor of the Pennsylvania in the 1890s undermined it in the 1950s. Transportation experts have long observed that railroads achieve their greatest efficiency in moving large quantities of bulky, low-value commodities over great distances. Such traffic moves in long trains and achieves substantial economies in labor and fuel. Railroads are at their worst in the movement of light-weight, high-value commodities, such as clothing, electronic equipment, typewriters, and light machinery. Such traffic does not require long trains but often fits readily into a small part of a freight car. When railroads move small, high-value shipments in short trains, they incur high labor and fuel costs.

Traditionally, railroads have set freight rates according to the value of the commodity carried. A bulky, low-value commodity, such as wheat or coal, is charged a low rate. Railroads were forced to adopt this policy because transportation costs of a low-value commodity represent an important part of that commodity's delivered price. Coal, for example, might sell at the mine head at $7.50 a ton. A freight rate of $3 a ton would have an important impact on its delivered price. The freight rate would in this case often determine whether or not the commodity could be sold at its destination. If a railroad sets the rates for bulky, low-value commodities too high, it risks driving them from their markets, thereby destroying the traffic altogether. The railroad traffic officers try to set a tariff that produces a profit for the railroad and ensures a market for low-value, bulky commodities, thus encouraging traffic. In the case of high-value commodities, freight rates are not so critical. For example, wool might sell at 30 to 50 cents per pound, or from $600 to $1000 a ton. A freight rate of $4 or $5, or even $10, a ton would represent an insignificant part of the wool's delivered price. Railroads, therefore, were free to charge this type of traffic more and did so almost from their beginning as freight carriers.

From the 1860s until the outbreak of World War I in 1914, railroads had a near-monopoly of land transportation. This favored systems like the Pennsylvania, which moved a wide variety of agricultural and industrial products, including a substantial amount of high-value manufactured items. Starting in the 1920s, highways began to challenge the railroads' monopoly of inland transportation. In competition with trucks, they face several serious disadvantages. Railroads have high terminal costs. They are forced to maintain large marshaling and freight yards in all major cities. Terminal costs remain the same no matter how far a commodity is shipped. These factors work against short-distance rail shipments.

Trucks avoid many of the problems involved in railroading. In the movement of high-value commodities, their small capacity is a virtue, not a hindrance. Roads reach to every part of a city or town. Trucks pick up freight directly at its origin and move it quickly over a short distance to its destination. High-value commodities can easily afford to pay a higher rate for this service. Starting in the 1920s, trucks began to capture from the railroads traffic in high-value commodities that were to be moved short distances. This diversion of traffic speeded up in the 1930s and was temporarily reversed by the gasoline and rubber shortages of World War II, but continued at an ever-accelerating rate after 1945.

Statistics give some idea of the vulnerability of the Pennsylvania Railroad to the shift of traffic from rail to rubber. In 1951, for example, 33 percent of the Pennsy's freight traffic consisted of manufactured and miscellaneous commodities. Less than 1 percent was wheat, and 32 percent was bituminous coal [4]. The comparison with the Norfolk & Western, which had an operating ratio of 66.92 percent, is striking. The Norfolk & Western had been built as a railroad designed to haul bituminous coal. In the 1890s, nearly 80 percent of its traffic was coal. Lacking the opportunity to carry large quantities of high-value merchandise, Norfolk & Western did not do as well in the 1890s as the Pennsylvania. The situation reversed itself in the 1950s. Because of Norfolk & Western's inherent efficiencies, trucks did not drain traffic from it as they did from the Pennsy. In 1951, 73.5 percent of the N&W's traffic was bituminous coal [5]. Statistics revealed other weaknesses in the Pennsylvania's freight traffic. In 1951 its average freight haul was only 243.9 miles, a sharp contrast to 517 miles on the Santa Fe and 600 miles on the Union Pacific [6].

Passenger traffic was also a serious problem for the Pennsylvania. The Pennsy, its wholly owned subsidiary, the Long Island, the New York Central, and the New York, New Haven & Hartford were the most important passenger-carrying railroads in the United States. In 1951, about 20 percent of all the Pennsylvania's rail revenues came from passenger trains. This compared with an average of 12.84 percent for all railroads and about 2 percent for the Norfolk & Western. Unfortunately, suburban and commuter traffic in the New York and Philadelphia metropolitan regions accounted for a substantial portion of the Pennsylvania Railroad's passengers.

Few aspects of railway operations were more seriously affected by the highway revolution than suburban traffic. As cars became common in the 1920s, midday, evening, and weekend travelers deserted the rails and did their shopping, theater going, and recreational travel by automobile. In the West where cities were smaller and not so densely populated, it proved relatively easy for railroads to get out of the suburban business. Thus, in 1929 the Southern Pacific ended its Portland suburban operations. In the early 1940s, it shifted its Oakland commuter traffic to another system. In Los Angeles, where the Southern Pacific ran its commuter service through a subsidiary, the management easily demonstrated overwhelming losses and therefore gradually abandoned the passenger traffic between 1940 and the mid-1950s. The Pennsylvania found it difficult to abandon suburban service. While business dwindled, a strong demand for rush-hour service into the central cities continued. This produced the worst possible situation because it forced the Pennsylvania to maintain large pools of equipment and a substantial labor force to operate a service that handled most of its passengers between 6:00 and 9:30 A.M. and 4:30 and 7:00 P.M. For the rest of the time, the Pennsylvania's equipment and labor sat idle. The results were ever-increasing passenger deficits that the railroad could not avoid.

MANAGEMENT PROBLEMS

On May 16, 1951, David Bevan arrived at his new office in the Pennsylvania Railroad's executive suite in the suburban station building directly across the street from Philadelphia's City Hall. The new vice-president in charge of finance came about 9:00 A.M., thinking that he was probably far too early and "would probably not have an opportunity to see anyone for some time." To his surprise and embarrassment, he "found that Walter Franklin, then president and chief executive of the Pennsylvania Railroad, had telephoned from Washington at 8:30 to apologize for not being present personally" to welcome him to the railroad. This incident typified "the thoughtfulness and kindness" that permeated the relationship with Franklin until his death in 1972. Bevan admired him from the outset, and this feeling increased through the years.

The warm, friendly reception masked a tense and uncertain atmosphere in the Pennsylvania Railroad's executive suite. Bevan found a venerable, but troubled, railroad. Great portions of its once-lucrative high-value freight traffic had been diverted to motor carriers. Much of the system's trackage, built to handle this business, had become obsolete. More ominously, the extensive roadbuilding that took place after World War II posed a further threat to much of the Pennsylvania's remaining high-value freight. Terminal congestion and short hauls made the Pennsy especially vulnerable and its outlook particularly dismal when compared with western railroads, such as the Union Pacific, Southern Pacific, and the Santa Fe. Similarly, the railroad's comparatively high stake in passenger traffic boded ill for the future.

The Pennsy's decline had been continuous ever since the beginning of the Depression in 1929. It had been reflected in the system's low rate of return on its investments and its decreased dividends. The railroad's management was clearly aware of the line's problems. A continuation of this decline could soon push the railroad into deficit operations and would imperil its existence as a private enterprise. Bevan recognized the problems, but he believed that vigorous, new operational and financial policies could infuse new life into the old system. For the next 19 years, he devoted his life to meeting the railroad's financial needs. In the early years, he achieved apparent success. But in the long run, the cause proved hopeless.

OPERATING SUCCESS, MANAGEMENT FAILURE

Looming in the background was the dominant personality of Martin W. Clement, then in his final 7 months as chairman of the board. Clement served the Pennsylvania for 51 years. He had come to the system from Trinity College, Hartford, in 1901 and worked his way through the ranks until he became vice-president for operations on September 16, 1926, then a member of the railroad's board of directors in 1929. In 1933 he was named executive vice-president. In April 1935, Clement became the Pennsylvania's eleventh president, a position which he held until he became chairman of the board in 1949.

Bevan had a warm feeling for Clement that resulted from the memory of his father's funeral in 1938. He had been very close to his father and was deeply upset by his death. After the funeral, Martin Clement came up to Bevan, said nothing, but put his arm around his shoulders. Bevan remembered this silent gesture of friendship 13 years later when he joined the railroad and began to notice the tension in the system's top management. During Clement's presidency, he ran the railroad as a czar. Bevan recalled him "as a large man with a booming voice . . . who dominated all conversations and when necessary raised the level of his voice to drown out any contenders for attention." Most Pennsylvania employees seldom had the opportunity to see the sympathetic side of Clement's personality. Nevertheless, he was respected by all and feared by many.

Martin Clement rose through the railroad's operational side. Accounts of his exploits were legend. Years later, Bevan was walking across the Boston Common with James M. Symes, then the Pennsy's president, when Clement's name came into the conversation. Bevan asked Symes for his frank evaluation of the man. Bevan recalls that Symes looked at "me very seriously and with the greatest sincerity said, 'Dave, in my opinion, in all probability he is the greatest operating man that ever walked the earth'." Most people who worked with Clement "shared this opinion whether or not they liked him."

Although a superlative operating man, Clement rejected modern concepts of business administration. He considered himself an expert in all fields of the railroad's endeavor, and he delegated very little authority. This constraint particularly affected the financial department, which during his administration was little more than an adjunct to the president's office. Clement expressed disdain for "statisticians," and he had little interest in developing the statistical tools that had become the hallmark of advanced management in such corporations as du Pont and General Motors. He himself made the most important financial decisions. He shared a close friendship with Thomas Parkinson, president of New York's Equitable Life Assurance Society, and on many occasions the two worked out the railroad's financing. Clement's intervention in almost all major railroad decisions hindered the development of a strong, sophisticated managerial structure. This administrative history made it difficult for the Pennsylvania to adjust to the serious challenges in the period between Clement's retirement and the creation of the Penn Central.

Despite a compelling need to strengthen the management structure in order to face the problems that lay ahead, there was no real recognition of this fact internally. With the retirement of George Pabst as financial vice-president, a vacancy existed in the top hierarchy for which a successor had to be found. As noted later, Bevan was engaged because of his national reputation and not because of any recognition of the need for an overall strengthening of management. There was no premeditated plan for a thorough reorganization of management. Business was expected to go on as usual.

References

1. Interstate Commerce Commission, *Sixty-fifth Annual Report on the Statistics of Railways in the United States for the Year Ending December 31, 1951*, Government Printing Office, Washington, D.C., 1953, p. 369.

2. Pennsylvania Railroad, *Annual Report for 1946*, p. 3, and *Annual Report for 1951*, table facing p. 1.

3. Pennsylvania Railroad, *Annual Report for 1951*, p. 4.

4.   Ibid., Statistical Section, p. 26.

5.   Joseph T. Lambie, *From Mine to Market, The History of Coal Transportation on the Norfolk and Western Railway*, New York University Press, New York, 1954, p. x.

6.   Interstate Commerce Commission, *Statistics of Railways for 1951*, pp. 471, 475, 375.

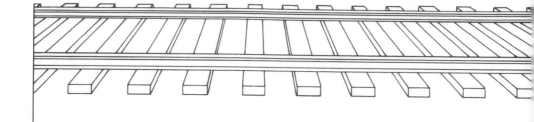

Chapter 3
MOVES TO MODERNIZE MANAGEMENT

The Pennsylvania, like most American railroads, was dominated by operating men. Its presidents traditionally rose through the ranks of the operating department or, in unusual cases, through the traffic department. Most of them were engineers and lacked formal training in business management. Some, like Martin Clement, scoffed at the collection and interpretation of statistical data, which had become the heart of modern managerial techniques. Fortunately for David Bevan, the new financial officer, Walter Franklin and his successor James Symes were sympathetic to new administrative practices, especially those involving finance. Consequently, in the years between 1951 and Symes's retirement in 1963, Bevan had solid support for his efforts to develop a modern financial structure for the railroad.

TOP MANAGEMENT: WALTER FRANKLIN AND JAMES SYMES

With Clement's retirement on December 31, 1951, all power passed to the president, Walter S. Franklin. Like Clement, Franklin had spent most of his life with the Pennsy, having joined the system in 1912. He was an expert traffic man whose duties largely involved the development and encouragement of the freight business. He served as vice-president in charge of traffic until 1947, when Clement picked him to become executive vice-president and made him second in command

and heir apparent. In 1949, Franklin became the Pennsylvania's president. In many respects, he was the opposite of Clement. He was quiet, soft-spoken, and seldom used forceful or rough language. He neither smoked nor drank. But, like Clement, Franklin had the confidence and trust of the entire system.

Franklin's age assured him a relatively short term as president and made his administration one of transition. He had already picked his successor, James M. Symes, who in 1952 was elected executive vice-president. As chief executive of the Pennsylvania from 1954 through 1963, Symes had a critical role in shaping its future. He was a self-made man, having started as a clerk with the railroad at the age of 19. Company legend had it that he owed his initial appointment more to his ability to play baseball on the railroad's team than to any innate executive talent. He had a photographic mind and a capacity for hard work. Gradually, he began to move up the ladder on the operational side. In 1942, he became vice-president of the Pennsylvania's western region and in 1947 was made vice-president in charge of operations for the entire system. Upon Clement's retirement, Franklin made Symes executive vice-president and heir apparent.

Symes was a complex man. Although he "had a warm and outgoing personality," he had "no close friends," apparently because of his "inherent shyness or reserve which kept him from going the last step toward long and lasting friendships." At first meeting, Symes appeared to have a deep insight into human nature, but Bevan soon realized that his greatest weakness was "his inability to select capable personnel." Part of Symes's problems may have stemmed from his experience working under Martin Clement, who did not encourage an effective administrative bureaucracy managed by strong department heads working as a team. Perhaps it was because Symes received most of his business education on the Pennsylvania that he lacked a real understanding of corporate bureaucracy. Clement had run the railroad successfully without resorting to modern administrative techniques, and Symes tended to appoint men who operated in a similar manner. Unfortunately, few had Franklin's or Clement's ability, and the challenges to the Pennsylvania became ever greater as the years passed.

While Symes chose many top officers, probably the two most significant were James P. Newell, who, through Symes's influence, became vice-president in charge of operations in 1952, and Stuart Saunders, who became the Pennsylvania's top executive on Symes's retirement in 1963. Newell was a particularly inauspicious choice. The vice-presidency in charge of operations was the traditional road to power on the Pennsylvania. But, where Symes had served in that position with modesty, never acting as though he would be anything but a vice-president, Newell was highly ambitious. He quickly came to resent Fred Carpi, vice-president for traffic. This vice-presidency was also a familiar route to the presidency of the Pennsylvania, and Newell soon considered Carpi his major threat to that position. Consequently, he initiated a campaign to destroy Carpi in Symes's eyes. Part of this struggle revolved around the introduction of piggy-back freight trains, that is, the carrying of truck trailers on flat cars. Symes believed that this concept had an important future because it combined the flexibility of highway transportation and the speed and economy of long-distance rail haulage. Piggy-back, Symes felt, gave the railroad a chance to win back traffic that had been diverted to the highways. In July 1954, the Pennsylvania initiated piggy-back under the name "Tructrain." This was a service operated entirely by the Pennsylvania, using its own trucks and trailers to pick up merchandise at the customer's door and to deliver it to the railroad, where it was loaded on specially designed, Pennsylvania-owned flat cars. Both Newell from the operations side and Carpi from sales took a major part in the initiation of piggy-back. At high-level meetings, Carpi, "analytical and conservative, tried to point out both the pros and the cons involved, and the problems that had to be solved, and the advantages as he saw them." Newell, on the other hand, tried "to give Symes the impression that Carpi was undermining Symes's efforts" to establish piggy-back. Newell continued his attacks until he convinced himself that he had destroyed Carpi as a presidential candidate when Symes retired.

In the long run, Newell's efforts failed, and in 1963 he was forced to take early retirement. Nevertheless, his behavior had weakened the Pennsylvania's top management and had led Symes to go outside to select a chief executive officer to succeed him. It was one of the factors that opened the way for the accession of Stuart Saunders to the presidency in 1963.

When Bevan came to the Pennsylvania, he found the corporation dominated by the retiring board chairman, Martin Clement. The new president, Walter Franklin, took hesitant steps to substitute modern techniques of business administration in lieu of Clement's personal governance. Franklin was not president long enough to place his stamp indelibly upon the railroad. Symes's accession brought to the company's top administration a remarkably talented operating man. But he lacked the knowledge of how to build an effective administrative organization and made some serious mistakes in appointments to top-level positions. A few areas of the railroad's administration did improve, but in the crucial operations sector, the old order remained. The operating men resisted new administrative techniques at the highest level. All these factors were to have dire consequences in the years ahead.

DAVID BEVAN: THE MAKING OF A FINANCIAL REFORMER

In the beginning, Bevan's position as vice-president in charge of finance had limited responsibilities. It did not include budgeting, accounting, taxes, and many other functions, nor did it involve the housekeeping area. Bevan's principal duties were corporate finance and included the supervision of the company's treasury and banking operations, investments, and debt management. Gradually, his powers expanded; but in the early years, his narrower responsibilities provided ample challenges.

David Crumley Bevan was 44 years old when in 1951 he became the Pennsylvania Railroad's vice-president in charge of finance, chief financial officer, and a director. Although he had never thought of working for the Pennsylvania, much in his past prepared him for his position there. The railroad's new financial executive came from an old Pennsylvania family. He was born on August 5, 1906, in Wayne, Pennsylvania, a town 15 miles west of Philadelphia on the route of the Paoli local, which traverses the famed Pennsylvania Main Line. He could trace his American lineage back to a Quaker ancestor, John Bevan, who migrated to Pennsylvania in 1682 and received a grant of land from William Penn in what is today the Main Line community of Wynnewood. John Bevan was a member of Pennsylvania's First Assembly and he also founded the first Quaker Meeting in Delaware County at a site about 10 miles outside Philadelphia. David's father, Howard Sloan Bevan, was a railroad man. He worked for the Pennsy more than 47 years; his death in 1938 deprived him of achieving his cherished goal of a 50-year railroad pin. Howard was a part of middle management and held the title of special agent in charge of demurrage.

The new vice-president had spent his entire youth on the Pennsylvania Main Line. For most of the time, the family lived in Ardmore, a 20-minute commute from the city. Every day his father rode the Paoli local to the Pennsylvania Railroad's office building in center city. Young David attended public schools, graduating from Lower Merion High School. Greatly interested in athletics, he played on the football team and captained the basketball and tennis teams. When it came time for college, he chose Haverford, a Quaker institution located just one stop beyond Ardmore on the Paoli local. The family had long ceased to be Quakers, and he was raised in the Episcopal church of his mother. Nonetheless, he fell under the influence of well-known Quaker teachers, especially the philosopher Rufus Jones, at Haverford College. But his main college interest was economics, although he found history fascinating. At Haverford he continued his interest in sports, playing on the varsity football and basketball teams. He received his bachelor of arts degree in 1929 and took a summer job in Philadelphia's Provident Trust Company, now the Provident National Bank.

Young Bevan realized that his training at Haverford was not adequate for a business career, and in the fall of 1929, he entered the Harvard Graduate School of Business Administration. He made a good impression at the Provident Trust, and he had a reasonable expectation of a position there when he finished his graduate work. Accordingly, he concentrated on accounting and finance. Receiving his M.B.A. degree in 1931, he joined the Provident on a permanent basis. While there, he held various titles, including those of assistant trust officer and assistant vice-president.

Bevan could not have picked a more exciting time to join the Provident. The stock market crash in 1929 had marked the beginning of the nation's most serious economic depression, which did not hit the bottom until the beginning of Franklin Roosevelt's first administration in the spring of 1933. The Provident's Investment Department, headed by S. Francis Nicholson, a brilliant Harvard Business School graduate, faced serious Depression-related problems. The division managed estates for wealthy Philadelphia families and had responsibility for the investment portfolios of many of southeast Pennsylvania's most important eleemosynary institutions. The widespread business collapses that accompanied the Depression left the department with a large and varied number of securities of corporations whose bonds were in default and whose stock appeared valueless. Bevan recalled that his early duties centered on watching over the troubled stocks and bonds, "making exchanges for securities that seemed to have a better outlook, liquidating some, and analyzing proposed reorganization plans." Philadelphia's six largest trust companies created an informal committee comprising one representative from each bank. This group met weekly to review the securities under their control. The six companies pooled information and developed a common front to work out reorganization plans for companies in which they held substantial interests. Bevan represented the Provident Trust on the committee and soon became familiar with refinancing and reshaping ailing business firms.

As the Depression lengthened into the middle thirties, the Provident often found itself in charge of estates in which a single family had working control of a large, troubled business firm. In these cases, the Trust Company assumed a long-term responsibility for nursing the corporation back to health. In 1936, Bevan moved from the Investment Department and worked directly with Carl W. Fenninger, senior vice-president in charge of the Trust Department, who had responsibility for the business firms which the Provident Trust effectively controlled. Often Fenninger sat on the boards of these companies, and his assistant became responsible to him for "the analyses of their operations, results, personnel, financial structure, and everything else" that might come up at board meetings for decisions. Success in this assignment brought Bevan into contact with many of Philadelphia's leading businessmen and bankers. It also gave him experience in business management far beyond that usually encountered by an employee of an institution such as the Provident.

World War II interrupted Bevan's banking career. In 1942, he resigned to join the War Production Board in Washington. There he worked with the Board's scrap division, which had the job of salvaging for the war effort all available scrap iron in the United States. He stayed only a few months, and then transferred to Lend-Lease, a government program that provided vital supplies to allied governments. Early in 1943, he flew to Australia as a member of a three-man Lend-Lease mission. Based in Sydney, he oversaw the distribution of a sizable amount of American equipment, which bolstered not only the Australian armed forces but also the nation's civilian economy, which was producing for war. In his work Bevan came to know and respect "honest" John Curtin, Australia's Labor Prime Minister. He stayed down under until the end of 1944, and during the last year in Sydney, he was acting head of the mission.

Bevan spent Christmas of 1944 at home with his wife, the former Mary Gilbert Heist, whom he had married in Philadelphia on June 10, 1936. At the beginning of 1945 he went to London as deputy head of the Mission of Economic Affairs at the United States Embassy. In England, he coordinated the many American business missions that were helping to reconstruct war-torn Europe. Bevan was endowed with an intensely competitive spirit. He accepted and indeed defended the capitalist order of society. Furthermore, he did not have political ambitions. Rather, his competitive spirit found an outlet in working within established structures. His rise had been based on hard, meticulous work. Moreover, he had a flair for statistical detail and organizational structure. When he joined a firm, he drove himself to learn more than anyone else about the various functions of the company and their significance.

Bevan soon came to have a reputation with subordinates for being efficient, cold, hard-driving, and distant. As an employee, he worked hard to fulfill the expectations of his employers; as a boss, he expected similar loyalty from his staff. But, beneath Bevan's formidable exterior was a deep sympathy and respect for his coworkers. He believed in leading not by exhortation or threats but by example. Bevan had a fierce pride in his abilities and his accomplishments, and he assumed that others took a similar pride in their achievements. Bevan always exercised strict self-discipline, believing that a public display of anger was self-demeaning. Even when he was angry or dissatisfied with a subordinate's performance, he never publicly embarrassed or criticized his employees.

Bevan worked best in a large organization where roles were sharply defined and formal expectations clear. He was at his worst in the give-and-take of a political situation. This was true even though his experiences in Australia and England had introduced him to some of the most capable politicians of the twentieth century.

Bevan had no desire for a government career. Germany's surrender on the seventh of May, followed by Japan's collapse in September, opened the way for his return to peacetime activity. At the end of 1945, he resigned from government service and returned to the Provident Trust Company, where at his request he was given a position in the firm's commercial banking operations. He did not stay long with the Provident. During the 1930s, when he was working for the Provident to resuscitate ailing corporations, he met a Philadelphia lawyer, John F. Sinclair, then a partner in one of the law firms representing the bank. Later, Sinclair became president of the Federal Reserve Bank of Philadelphia and, after that, the executive vice-president of the New York Life Insurance Company. In the fall of 1946, Sinclair brought Bevan into New York Life with the title of assistant treasurer.

The new position expanded Bevan's horizons. It gave him the opportunity to meet many of the nation's top financial leaders, since his duties required him to work closely with the heads of major corporations that sought direct placement loans. He moved quickly up the ladder at New York Life. In 1947, he became an assistant vice-president, and in 1949, treasurer. The treasurership made him the direct supervisor of New York Life's banking operations and its investment division. He also became a member of the company's Mortgage Loan Committee. In 1950, his final full year at New York Life, he participated directly in investing over a billion dollars of the insurance company's funds.

At New York Life, Bevan accomplished a number of important tasks that won him widespread recognition in New York City's financial community. Within the organization itself, he surprised many by trimming functions away from the treasury department that he thought could be better handled by other company departments. He turned over to the accounting department a large amount of accounting work that had traditionally been in the treasury. He worked closely with the First National City Bank to streamline New York Life's banking operations and managed to reduce "the float," that is, checks in transit, by $20 million. He also instituted a detailed system for follow-up reviews of direct placement loans. This was an innovation in the life insurance industry and provided better security for the company's assets. It became apparent that he had a keen eye for managerial talent. New York Life's subsequent president, Marshall Bissell, was a Bevan protégé whom he discovered within the company. He also recommended employing Manning Brown, who later became chairman of New York Life, and also Donald Meads, subsequently the chairman of Certain-Teed Products. He eventually left New York Life with the feeling that he had created the best financial department in the industry.

Opportunities to move on were not limited to the Pennsylvania's invitation to join the railroad. While at New York Life, he had developed a close working relationship with Frank Denton, chief executive officer of the Mellon National Bank and Trust Company in Pittsburgh. The Mellon Bank and New York Life often jointly participated in the financing of corporate ventures. Furthermore, Bevan had structured the very complex financial arrangements needed for the construction of Pittsburgh's new Mellon–United

States Steel Building. Richard King Mellon, whose family controlled the Mellon Bank, was so pleased with Bevan's work that he made a special visit to the chairman of the board of New York Life to compliment him. At the same time that the Pennsylvania Railroad was preparing for changes in its top management, the Mellon Bank was looking for a replacement for Frank Denton, who was nearing retirement age. Denton asked Bevan if he would accept the position.

Thus in early 1951 Bevan considered two attractive opportunities. He chose the railroad. As he explained to Mellon and Denton, the bank was "running like a Swiss watch." He believed that all he could hope to do was "to maintain its excellent operations." In contrast, the Pennsylvania Railroad offered an enormous challenge. Its financial structure was archaic and it presented opportunities to use the experience that he had accumulated in reorganizing and refinancing companies during his days at the Provident Trust. The Pennsylvania also offered him a chance to return home to the Main Line, where his family owned a substantial acreage of rolling countryside in Gladwyne, not too far from the Bryn Mawr station of the Paoli local.

Bevan joined the Pennsylvania Railroad as vice-president in charge of finance in May 1951. In line with Franklin's promise to upgrade the position, he also became a company director. At his first directors' meeting, he again met Richard K. Mellon, then chairman of the board of the Mellon National Bank and a director of the Pennsylvania Railroad since 1934. Bevan had told no one except his friend Charles Dickey, a J. P. Morgan partner, of the opportunity at the Mellon Bank. Much to his embarrassment, Mellon stood up and revealed the facts. He said, "I am very happy to welcome Dave Bevan here today, whom I have known for some time, and I think Mr. Franklin and the railroad are to be congratulated on obtaining his services. In all honesty, however, I must say that it is the first time that I have ever questioned his good judgment." Mellon paused, then went on, "For your information, we recently tried to get Dave to come to the Mellon Bank, but he turned us down in favor of the railroad. Since we could not get him, I am extremely glad, as a director, that the Pennsylvania was successful." In looking back on what later happened at the Penn Central, Bevan often reflected on this incident. Rejecting the Mellon Bank in favor of the railroad was clearly one of the biggest mistakes he ever made.

Chapter 4
FINANCIAL IMPROVEMENTS, 1951–1963

The financial vice-presidency provided a unique insight into the problems that later caused the Penn Central's failure. The Pennsylvania, when Bevan joined it, had large capital requirements. However, it faced the dual impediments of a large debt and poor earnings. Management's overriding problem was to keep capital expenditures to the point where they could be carried by income. This was an issue to which Bevan had to address himself on his first day in the railroad's headquarters.

Bevan's attempts to keep the railroad solvent disclosed an even greater potential deficiency: an obsolete managerial system. Although the railroad was one of America's largest businesses, it lacked most of the elementary administrative systems common to large corporations. The company had long been run by operating men who did not understand, and often opposed, new managerial techniques. Therefore, the railroad lacked such basic financial tools as income budgets, cash-flow projections, responsibility accounting, and cost and profit data geared to help top management in arriving at intelligent decisions about the allocation of its scarce resources.

One of the most fascinating and significant aspects of the Penn Central's failure is the story of the sharp conflict within the railroad over the introduction of new managerial concepts. It was the railroad's failure to adopt these methods that eventually ensured its downfall. Bevan's significance lies in his vain attempt to provide a reformed administrative structure first for the Pennsylvania and then for the Penn Central.

As the Pennsylvania's financial vice-president, Bevan's most immediate concern in 1951 was the railroad's meager return on its rail investments and its narrow profit margin. Despite consolidated revenues of more than $1,082,000,000, the Pennsylvania, after it paid its operating costs, taxes, and fixed charges, had a 1951 profit of only about $36,800,000. Ominously, $12 million, or about one-third of the $36 million, came, not from the Pennsylvania Railroad's operations, but from dividends paid to the Pennsy on the stocks of three railroads in which it had a controlling interest: the Wabash; the Detroit, Toledo & Ironton; and, most important, the Norfolk & Western. It is significant that in 1951 the income from these three stocks just about equaled the $13,100,000 that the Pennsylvania appropriated for dividends on its own shares [1]. The Pennsylvania's retained income amounted to only a little more than $11,656,000, an extremely small sum when compared with the earnings retained by industrial corporations of similar magnitude. For example, in 1951 the Shell Oil Company in America had sales of about $1,072,000,000, an amount fairly close to the Pennsy's income. But, whereas the railways' net income was $29,750,000, Shell's was $97,000,-000. Furthermore, the approximately $1 billion invested in Shell represented only one-quarter of the capital locked up in the Pennsylvania [2].

PROVIDING WORKING CAPITAL

As Bevan looked at the Pennsylvania Railroad's financial situation, he saw a number of problems. He noted that the railroad lacked adequate working capital. To illustrate the Pennsy's working capital shortage for the benefit of the board of directors' Finance Committee, Bevan compared the railroad with a series of typical industrial corporations. In each case, he measured total working capital against gross operating revenues. On the Pennsylvania in 1953, the working capital equaled about 10.4 percent of its gross operating revenues (volume of business). Even steel, which also faced serious financial problems, was better off than the railroad. It had working capital equal to 16 percent of its business volume. Oil's ratio of working capital to gross operating revenues was 22.9 percent. The chemical industry's ratio was nearly 32 percent [3].

Large cash reserves were needed because revenues often experienced sharp temporary downturns. Unlike industrial corporations, the railway found it difficult to curtail expenses in tune with business fluctuations. Passenger trains had to run whether empty or full. Fixed charges continued irrespective of the business done by the system. Consequently, expenses continued near normal during periods of economic depression. Industrial corporations, with their larger working capital and their greater flexibility in adjusting expenditures to business conditions, found it easier to ride out business downturns. Bevan knew from his experience during the Great Depression of the 1930s that working capital shortages forced a number of important railroads, including the Missouri Pacific and the Milwaukee Road, into receivership and reorganization. He felt it vital that the Pennsylvania increase its liquidity. In order to accomplish this, in 1954 he negotiated with a group of banks, headed by First National City Bank of New York, a standby revolving credit of $50 million. This was the first such arrangement ever made in the railroad industry. It assured the railroad of an absolute call on its banks for $50 million in the event of an unforeseen emergency. Bevan advised his board that this privilege should be used only if the "house were on fire"—not every time things became a little tight.

THE RESTRUCTURING AND REDUCTION OF DEBT

As Bevan surveyed the Pennsy's financial organization in 1951, he saw a number of opportunities for constructive reform. He also realized that the entire railroad industry, because of meager earnings, had no real access to the stock market, and also that for capital improvements, including equipment, the only outside source was through borrowing. The railroad's capital needs were vast. In 1952, the Pennsy either completed or had underway engineering projects with an aggregate authorized expenditure of about $121 million. In the same year, new projects were authorized which would cost over $63 million. Against these requirements, retained earnings were minuscule. In 1951, they amounted to little more than $11,600,000, and in 1952, they slightly exceeded $24,300,000 [4]. Although retained earnings provided for some of the Pennsy's capital needs, the option to sell stock had long since vanished. This meant that either the sale of bonds or the issuance of equipment trusts was the only way to raise large amounts of capital.

But even the option to raise money through debt had severe limitations. The decline in revenues, which began soon after the 1929 stock market crash, reduced retained earnings and made the sale of common shares unattractive as early as 1930. Therefore, the 1930s saw a substantial rise in the Pennsylvania's debt. By 1939, its total publicly held debt amounted to $1,052,000,000 and required yearly interest payments of slightly over $44,600,000. The highly profitable war years enabled the corporation to reduce this debt to a low of $891,897,000 in 1946. However, the postwar era brought massive capital requirements for the modernization of the railroad's war-worn physical plant and for new equipment. Starting in 1947, the debt began to creep up. By 1951, it amounted to $1,080,000,000, larger than its 1939 prewar peak. To make matters worse, the debt's postwar composition was markedly different. Before World War II, $990 million of the Pennsy's debt was in the form of bonds issued to finance permanent improvements to the railway's physical plant. Only about $62 million represented equipment trust obligations. In contrast with the bonded debt, equipment trusts were relatively short-term loans, usually maturing in equal semiannual installments over a 15-year period, under which the new rolling stock was pledged as security. Starting in 1940, the Pennsylvania's bonded debt began a slow but steady decrease, so that by 1951 it had fallen from $990 million to slightly more than $765 million. At the same time, equipment obligations had risen from $62,300,000 to $288,114,000. These data explain why the Pennsylvania's total debt was actually larger in 1951 than it had been in 1939, despite a substantial decrease in the long-term bonded debt [5]. Furthermore, the debt's composition was much more unsatisfactory.

Among the most urgent problems was unevenness in the maturity dates of the Pennsylvania's bonded debt. For example, slightly less than $10 million of bonds came due in 1953, whereas, in 1960, about $65 million of bonds matured. In 1965, total bonded debt maturities approached $125 million. Bevan realized that this pattern held substantial dangers because, in most cases, the railroad would be unable to repay the debt at maturity and would find it necessary to "roll over" the obligations. Rolling over debt meant the Pennsy would merely sell new long-term securities to replace the old. Large maturities falling due in a single year posed a hazard in the event of a weak bond market, high interest rates, or unsatisfactory earnings. In addition to the bonded debt, about $30 million of equipment trust obligations, maturing annually, had to be paid in cash, not refinanced. The shift from bonded debt to equipment obligations threatened to make long-range financial planning increasingly problematic for the railroad [6].

The first important task was the restructuring of the Pennsylvania's debt. This was made difficult by the vast and complicated corporate structure of the Pennsylvania and its subsidiaries. When Bevan became financial vice-president, the Pennsylvania's system comprised 181 different incorporated entities. Past financial reporting had presented the data for many of these firms separately from the parent company or not at all. This format clouded the true financial picture. Beginning with the 1952 annual report, he ensured that such reporting would provide much more detailed information. Thereafter, the reports contained the consolidated figures for the entire Pennsylvania system and its subsidiaries. However, the chief financial officer was always careful to maintain a section of the report that presented the operations of the parent railroad itself, a practice that later enabled outsiders to compare readily the performance of the railroad and the diversified enterprises. To further aid the railroad's top management in understanding the debt problem, the financial department embarked on a simplification program whereby the number of subsidiary corporations affiliated with the Pennsylvania was reduced from 181 to a low of 89 in 1963. Thereafter, because of diversification, the number of companies gradually increased somewhat until the merger with the New York Central in 1968.

Bevan had to work hard to promote his ideas. When he began, Martin Clement still served as the railroad's board chairman. Bevan later recalled discussing debt reduction with Clement. He pointed out that the railway had huge, noncallable maturities that would be difficult to refinance in the event they had to be rolled over during a depression or in a weak bond market. Clement's reaction revealed a great deal about his business philosophy and his concept of the railroad's importance. Bevan remembered that Clement looked at him with "a benevolent smile and said, 'It's all right with me [the debt reduction program], but I do not think it's necessary. On the other hand, I know you well enough to realize that you will go ahead and do whatever you think is right irrespective of my thoughts'." Clement went on discussing the railroad's status in the United States. He recalled that during the Depression of the 1930s, Harold Ickes, head of the Public Works Administration (PWA) asked him to arrange for the railroad to borrow $100 million from the PWA and to use it to provide jobs for the unemployed. Clement did so, receiving enough money to underwrite electrification of the Pennsylvania's long-distance line between New York City and Washington. He said that the railroad was "too dominant a factor in the economy of the country for the government ever to allow it to go into bankruptcy." Bevan did not share Clement's optimism about the government and felt it necessary to do everything possible to avoid the railroad's dependence upon federal aid.

In his campaign for change, he instructed the financial department to develop a series of charts depicting the Pennsylvania's debt problem and the need for reform. These were presented to the railroad's top management and the Finance Committee of the board of directors. Bevan won the support of Walter Franklin and James Symes, as well as of the influential Richard K. Mellon, the senior member of the railroad's board. Bevan's long-range goal was to reduce the railroad's bonded debt and, at the same time, to restructure the remaining debt so that it matured more evenly. His efforts quickly began to bear fruit. In 1954, he reported that the Pennsylvania's debt had been reduced by slightly more than $52,390,000. In 1953, the reduction had been $30,600,000. He obtained funds from two major sources. First, he used depreciation cash for the purchase of new equipment, thus reducing the need for equipment trust certificates. Second, the railroad had opportunely received cash from deals on real estate, such as on the land made surplus by the abandonment of Philadelphia's Broad Street Station and on the sale of air rights over trackage in cities such as Chicago and New York. Land-sale proceeds were used to reduce bonded debt, purchasing obligations due in years when there were large maturities. When he started, the railroad faced the prospect of rolling over $125 million of bonded debt of a single issue in 1965. By 1960, this issue had been reduced to $77 million [7].

Toward the end of 1963 when James Symes retired from the railroad, impressive results could be claimed. The bonded debt, which had amounted to $765 million in 1952, had been reduced to $548 million, a drop of slightly over 28 percent. Equipment obligations had fallen from $350 million to $233 million, a decrease of 34 percent. The total debt had decreased from $1,116,000,000 to $781,200,000, a fall of about 30 percent. The decrease in the debt had an important impact upon fixed charges. Annual interest payments fell from $39 million in 1952 to $32 million in 1964, a decrease of $7 million, approximately 18 percent [8]. The debt reduction program was even more significant than these figures indicate, since the years between 1952 and 1963 saw a slow but steady rise in interest rates, a trend that would have greatly increased the railroad's fixed costs even if borrowing had remained constant.

MODERNIZATION OF MANAGERIAL PRACTICES

As Bevan reduced the railroad's debt, he found serious shortcomings in the Pennsylvania's managerial structure. He knew that intelligent decisions by top management required accurate and detailed information flowing upward from the various operating divisions. Yet, in 1951, the firm's managerial practices were at least 40 years behind the times. This backwardness was an irony. In the nineteenth century, the railroad had pioneered modern concepts of business administration. Prior to the 1840s, the merchant dominated American business. The emergence of railroads in the following decade was revolutionary. By standards of that day, they were extremely large and complex enterprises. The Pennsylvania Railroad, when it completed its expansion program in 1873, had cost more than $400 million. As the business historian Alfred D. Chandler, Jr., observed, "Size was only one dimension of the unique challenges facing the managers of the new large railroads in the 1850s." He noted that day-to-day decisions on the railways were far more complicated and numerous than those involving a mill or canal [9].

On the eve of World War II, complex statistical control became the rule rather than the exception in large businesses. Railroads, and particularly the Pennsylvania, failed to share in these managerial advances [10]. Instead, their practices had became frozen at the beginning of the twentieth century. Nothing better illustrates this fact than the situation Bevan found when he began to investigate the way funds were handled and accounted for on the Pennsy. The vice-president in charge of finance did not have control over real estate or taxes, nor did he supervise the comptroller or accounting. Furthermore, the railroad had no capital and income budgets or cash-flow estimates. The rudimentary budgets that did exist were "made up by the staff of the operating vice-president for his use, and were changed from time to time as he saw fit. They were not generally available to top management." Consequently, there was no forward planning as to how to meet maturing obligations or to forecast the need for capital improvements in future years. When Bevan studied the accounting department, he was astounded. After careful examination, he concluded that he could not determine how many people were working in accounting, but he did find the function overstaffed. Historically, he noted, "the heads of the operating department in times past had been much stronger than the accounting chiefs, had greater authority, and had gradually taken over many important accounting functions and absorbed them into the operating departments. No one actually knew how many people were really involved in accounting, and, as far as we could ascertain, there was not a single person in the accounting department who was a qualified certified public accountant, not even the comptroller!" Bevan did discover that there were nearly 2700 people in the accounting department alone and "nobody knew how many more in the operating departments doing accounting work."

More significant than the confusion and overstaffing was the firm's concept of accounting. The department merely followed Interstate Commerce Commission (ICC) regulations. This meant that the ICC policy determined the various accounts and dictated which figures should be placed in what account. Bevan recollected that it did not take him "long to learn that ICC accounting was not only obsolete, but actually impossible to utilize effectively in controlling costs."

As he saw the ICC accounting system in use on the Pennsylvania, it had many defects. The main difficulty was that it could not be used as an effective management tool. The accounting system was passive, that is, it merely recorded facts. It had no built-in requirements for forward planning; therefore, the very concepts of capital budgets, income budgets, and cash-flow statements were foreign to the ICC system. The ICC accountants looked backward at what had happened, rather than forward to what should happen. And the ICC formula had another grave defect as a management tool. The public accounting firm of Peat, Marwick, Mitchell & Company, in a special analysis undertaken at Bevan's request, pinpointed the problem. The ICC format allocated costs against a division or a function regardless of whether the supervisor of that function was responsible for the costs. The accounting firm observed, for example, that "the regional superintendent of transportation normally received charges from other departments which may approximate 35 percent of his total budget. While it is true that such charges are for services rendered on behalf of the transportation activity, the amount of the charges or effectiveness of the work performed is not within the control of the Superintendent of Transportation" [11]. Under the ICC system, it was impossible to analyze the real effectiveness of a manager, since he reported statistical data over which he exercised no control. Thus, top management could not separate out the cost over which a regional superintendent of transportation had control and, therefore, could not effectively compare his performance against that of others or against past data.

In Bevan's attempt to restructure the Pennsylvania Railroad's debt, he faced the railroad's antiquated managerial structure. He soon determined to modernize the system. His experience with the Provident Trust before World War II and New York Life after the war enabled him to develop a constructive program for change. He discussed his ideas with his superiors, Presidents Walter Franklin and (later) James Symes. Both encouraged him to proceed, and gradually a number of new functions were placed under his jurisdiction. Responsibility for taxes had been split among four departments. These were consolidated under Bevan in 1957. Symes also placed insurance and the accounting department under his supervision.

All this readjustment prepared the way for building a new system for recording and reporting statistical data that was to serve as the basis for developing new managerial tools for the railroad's top administrators. Bevan recognized that the firm lacked employees with experience in creating such a system. Therefore, with the full support of President James Symes, he selected an outside consultant. Because Symes was already thinking of a merger between the New York Central and the Pennsylvania Railroads, Bevan decided to retain the world's largest accounting and auditing firm, Peat, Marwick, Mitchell & Company. It was already auditing the New York Central Railroad's accounts, and Bevan realized that if merger occurred, having a common outside accountant would serve the interest of both firms. Prior to the selection of Peat, Marwick, no independent firm of certified public accountants had ever routinely audited the Pennsylvania Railroad's books. In May 1959, Peat, Marwick began to advise the railroad in the adoption of two separate systems. The first was a management control devices program, and the second was a centralized data processing installation.

CONTROL DEVICES AND
RESPONSIBILITY REPORTING

As it started its assignment, Peat, Marwick recognized that it was breaking new ground. In a progress report to the Pennsy's top executives, it commented that "of all members of the American business community, railroads constitute perhaps the only industry which does not use a conventional industrial management control structure, consisting of budgetary control, work measurement, and responsibility accounting and reporting." The accounting firm added that while many railroads employed "certain aspects of these tools . . ., only the roads owned by the United States Steel Corporation employ all of them on an integrated basis" [12]. Because of the novelty of the new managerial control system, it was necessary to experiment and phase the program in over a period of several years. Having started its investigation in May 1959, Peat, Marwick introduced the first aspects of the new system in mid-1961. It was not, however, until the end of the following year that the program took effect over the entire railroad, and the full impact of the innovations did not become apparent until 1963.

The new control devices program utilized the regional structure that the Pennsylvania Railroad had adopted in November 1955. Under it, the railroad had been divided into nine regions, each of which was headed by a regional manager who controlled what amounted to a separate railroad. Peat, Marwick added a comptroller to the staff of each region. The system had three major aspects. The first was responsibility reporting. This concept abandoned the ICC practice of allocating expenses according to a set formula that did not take into account the person who directly supervised the work done. Instead, responsibility reporting held each function accountable only for what it actually expended and disbursed. Thus, a manager was relieved of responsibility for the effectiveness of work performed but not under his control. Responsibility reporting attributed expenses to "the supervisor who actually controlled the money spent for labor, materials, and so forth" [13]. Overhead, such as taxes and insurance, was not allocated to an operating department that did not control them.

Work measurement constituted the second aspect of the control devices program. The idea behind work measurement was to compare the dollars spent with the work actually produced. As the accounting firm put it, "It is not sufficient for management to assure itself that a supervisor does not exceed his dollar budget. Management must be certain that the money spent within the budget produces a reasonable amount of work" [14]. Work measurement set time standards for each operation or group of operations on the railroad. These standards were fixed by determining the "time a normal man (or men), working at a normal rate of speed, needs to complete a unit of work." Along with labor standards went material standards. Peat, Marwick conferred with industrial engineers to develop these standards, which became the basis for measuring the effectiveness of the management on any single division of the Pennsylvania Railroad. As the standards were installed, management was able to compare the work actually performed with the standard (the work that should have been performed in the same time interval). These data were reported together with payroll documents. Armed with information on the dollars spent, the work output, and the material consumed, and the responsibility reports, Pennsylvania's top management was able for the first time to have detailed and accurate information on performance in each division.

Budgetary control formed the third aspect of the control devices program. Under budgetary control, supervisors built the budgets for their own divisions. Again, included in each budget were only the expenses over which the supervisor had direct control. These budgets were forwarded to the Pennsy's general office in Philadelphia, where they could be analyzed and funds allocated for the most important projects. This was an essential step in the development of a rational and effective capital budget, as well as an integrated income budget, a step which was largely impossible prior to the institution of the control devices program. Thus, in four years, through Bevan's efforts, the Pennsylvania Railroad moved from a backward managerial system based on outmoded Interstate Commerce Commission accounting concepts to one of the most sophisticated cost and control systems in American industry.

Simultaneously with the control devices program, Peat, Marwick began work on a second major undertaking: the development and installation of an integrated data processing program. Its purpose was to install a centralized computer facility at the railroad's Philadelphia headquarters that would comprehend "the reporting and clerical aspects of the transportation function, operating statistics, sales analysis, car utilization and distribution, and car accounting" [15]. Although each of these categories utilized the same basic information, they were handled separately on the Pennsylvania in 1959. As Peat, Marwick pointed out, working up each category separately resulted in costly duplication of clerical effort. However, the worst fault was the difficulty for top management to utilize the information gathered in such a cumbersome manner. Although many of the nation's largest railroads had recognized the importance and desirability of centralizing the computer capability and integrating the information on the various functions, as late as 1961 no railroad had succeeded in installing a complete program. Typically, reported Peat, Marwick [16],

A railroad will start by developing a data processing system to deal with . . . car tracing. The company would plan to concentrate on this new procedure until it became routinized. Then it would plan to expand the system to include, let us say, sales statistics. Thereafter, each of the various functions would be absorbed sequentially until the entire program was complete. While several railroads [concluded Peat, Marwick] have started on such a program and have even completed the first phase of it, no appreciable progress has been made in developing and installing a comprehensive system.

In 1960, Peat, Marwick developed specifications for the Pennsylvania's new centralized computer system. The effort was so striking that *The Wall*

Street Journal reported that the Pennsylvania's data processing program was one of the two largest such proposals then under consideration. Experimentation with various computer prototype equipment began in 1961. Under Peat, Marwick's supervision, the railroad began to install the final system in 1962, and by 1963 it began to make an important impact on the railroad. The new centralized computer worked surprisingly well. It provided the Pennsylvania with a "comprehensive, well-disciplined data origination system [that collected] both waybill and movement information with error rates below four-tenths of 1 percent for movement and below seven-tenths of 1 percent for waybills" [17]. Not only did the new system provide more reliable and accessible information to top management, but it also saved money. Between 1963 and 1967, it enabled the railroad as a whole to save over "$14 million in clerical expenses."

David Bevan's first 12 years with the Pennsylvania produced important results. His accomplishments included initiation of a systematic debt management program as well as a strong start in the direction of reducing the railroad's massive debt. The same 12 years saw a number of important functions, such as taxes, insurance, and accounting, come under his supervision. This was essential in his campaign to modernize the Pennsylvania's obsolete administrative procedures. Acting with the enthusiastic support of President James Symes, he achieved in a short period the establishment of a new accounting system that, together with an administrative structure, gave management new and more effective tools in its struggle to make the railroad an economically successful venture. At the same time, his leadership resulted in a centralized computer center which integrated the data flowing from various important railway activities. This reinforced the railroad's new control devices program. While he was working to provide the Pennsylvania with a new managerial structure, other events were afoot that would radically alter the railroad network in the eastern United States. In these affairs, David Bevan was not a mover but a deeply interested observer.

References

1.   All the above statistical data taken from Pennsylvania Railroad, *Annual Report for 1952,* pp. 25, 29, 65.

2.   Kendall Beaton, *Enterprise in Oil, A History of Shell in the United States,* Appleton-Century-Crofts, New York, 1957, pp. 782, 783.

3.   Bevan Papers, charts presented by David C. Bevan to the Finance Committee on October 27, 1954, revised January 1955.

4.   Pennsylvania Railroad, *Annual Report for 1952,* pp. 16, 25.

5.   Ibid., p. 65.

6.   Ibid., pp. 8–9.

7.   Bevan Papers, Charts presented by David C. Bevan to the board of directors on April 27, 1960; also Pennsylvania Railroad, *Annual Report for 1954,* pp. 10–11.

8.   Pennsylvania Railroad, *Annual Report for 1963,* pp. 6–7.

9.   Alfred D. Chandler, Jr., *The Railroads, The Nation's First Big Business,* Harcourt, Brace and World, New York, 1965, pp. 97, 98.

10.   For a more detailed analysis of the changes in railroad administration, see Stephen Salsbury, "Twentieth Century Railroad Management Practices: The Case of the Pennsylvania Railroad," in Robert Gallman (ed.), *Recent Developments in the Study of Economic and Business History: Essays in Memory of Herman E. Krooss,* JAI Press, Greenwich, Conn., 1977, pp. 43–54.

11.   Bevan Papers, Progress Report to the Pennsylvania Railroad Company by Peat, Marwick, Mitchell & Co., dated Spring 1961, p. 3.

12.   Ibid., p. 1.

13.   Ibid., p. 3.

14.   Ibid., p. 4.

15.   Ibid., p. 6.

16.   Ibid., p. 7.

17.   Bevan Papers, C. G. Sempier's memorandum to W. S. Cook, "New York Central Data Processing Appraisal," December 5, 1967.

Chapter 5
DIVERSIFYING INTO EARNINGS AND GROWTH

The second major goal of the new financial leadership was to guide the Pennsylvania in its entirety into more promising channels, both immediately and in the future. Notable successes, as well as some failures, were achieved under a succession of presidents, Franklin, Symes, and Saunders. The major achievements of the Bevan years, however, were to be realized, and his judgments most amply vindicated, only after the dismal collapse of the Penn Central and the long torture of bankruptcy and reorganization that followed.

It was soon apparent to David Bevan that the railroad's operations-oriented executives had little understanding or appreciation of the importance of the company's vast real estate holdings. But to him the Pennsylvania's legacy in land and salable assets, such as the Long Island Railroad properties, focused attention on nonrailroad opportunities. Similar opportunities involved the Madison Square Garden, Chicago's Gateway Center, Philadelphia's Penn Center, and the ill-fated Pittsburgh program. All these pursuits were compatible with, and even complementary to, continuing railroad operations. In most of these developments, Bevan played a leading role in their realization. They helped to convince management that new ventures could be more profitable than the operation of the railroad itself. Much of this thinking lay behind Bevan's diversification program.

CENTER-CITY REAL ESTATE

A start was made when Bevan examined plans for developing approximately 17 acres in downtown Philadelphia that had been made available by the demolition of the old Broad Street Station. For decades, Pennsylvania trains entered Philadelphia on elevated tracks that diverged from the railroad's main New York–Washington line in West Philadelphia. This elevated line crossed the Schuylkill River near 30th and Market Streets and proceeded parallel to Market as far as 15th Street on a structure Philadelphians nick-named the Chinese Wall. In 1925, the Pennsylvania initiated plans to replace Broad Street Station. They called for the construction of a major, new long-distance passenger station at 30th and Market, together with an underground station exclusively for commuter trains adjacent to the old Broad Street Terminal. Work commenced in the mid-1920s; the Suburban Station opened in 1930, and the 30th Street Station in 1933. At that time, the Pennsylvania hoped to remove both the old Broad Street Station and the Chinese Wall. The Depression and World War II stopped this undertaking and it was not until 1952 that the railroad finally tore down Broad Street Station, thus freeing 17 acres for development.

The possibilities opened by Broad Street Station's demolition excited Bevan, who wanted the railroad to supervise and profit directly from the opportunity. James Symes, burdened with operating problems, did not wish to assume such great responsibilities. He preferred to sell the entire property outright to a developer, Albert M. Greenfield, for around $10 million. Only after Greenfield withdrew did Symes relent and agree to a plan controlled by the railroad with necessary cash, however, being provided by outside interests. The result was Penn Center, a striking group of office buildings, hotels, and transportation terminals that began the rejuvenation of one of center-city Philadelphia's most depressed areas. By the time Saunders succeeded Symes in 1963, Penn Center had become a financial success. At that time, the railroad had realized almost $25 million in land sales and was receiving, in addition, $550,000 a year in rentals [1].

The railroad's success in Philadelphia land redevelopment called attention to similar opportunities elsewhere. In 1962, Bevan helped work out a scheme to utilize the air rights above New York's Pennsylvania Station. This project involved tearing down the old station, building a new terminal, and above it constructing a $100-million sports, entertainment, and office building complex. The railroad entered the Pennsylvania Station project in part-nership with the old Madison Square Garden Corporation, which transferred its activities to the new center. While this meant the destruction of historic Penn Station, it made financial sense. Large crowds attracted by Madison Square Garden events would add to off-peak riding on the Pennsylvania's suburban trains as well as those on the Long Island, which also used Penn

Station. Work started on the project in 1963; the rebuilding of the railway facilities, the new Madison Square Garden Center, and the 29-story Penn Plaza office building was completed in February 1968. In that year, a major financial reorganization took place. Prior to the reorganization, the railroad, which by this time had become the Penn Central, had a 25 percent direct ownership in the sports center and it also had a 55 percent interest in the office building above it. Under the new management, the Penn Central exchanged its holdings for a 23 percent interest in a reorganized parent Madison Square Garden Corporation, which became a holding company for the various underlying projects. The new stock had a market value of approximately $25.7 million. This arrangement gave the railroad securities that had a ready market value. It was an asset that could be quickly sold or pledged as collateral for a loan. In addition, the railroad kept certain rights to long-term rentals under the main air-right lease [2].

The Pennsylvania also participated in another real estate venture, Chicago's $100-million Gateway Center. This undertaking involved the construction of three 20-story office buildings that utilized the air space over the tracks of the city's Union Station, of which the Pennsylvania had a 50 percent ownership [3].

SOLVING THE LONG ISLAND RAILROAD PROBLEM

Among the most frustrating and important of the Pennsylvania's unproductive properties was the Long Island Railroad. This company, a wholly owned subsidiary of the Pennsylvania, had not been a strong money earner since 1900, when President A. J. Cassatt acquired it in his drive to extend the Pennsylvania under the Hudson River and into midtown Manhattan. In 1930, the Long Island ceased to be profitable altogether and thereafter never paid a dividend on its capital stock. Nevertheless, it remained an important passenger carrier. In 1950, the Long Island hauled over 83 million passengers, but its finances were in disarray. In March 1949, it could not pay the interest on almost $40 million of its bonds, which the Pennsylvania had guaranteed. The Pennsylvania, therefore, attempted to reorganize its subsidiary under Section 77 of the Federal Bankruptcy Act.

Long Island's bankruptcy failed to solve the problem. The railroad continued to lose money, yet it was too important to abandon. Worse yet, the Long Island remained a financial burden to the Pennsylvania, since it needed a massive infusion of new capital to improve its electric power system and to acquire new rolling stock. The Pennsylvania Railroad had no surplus to provide the Long Island with fresh capital. The Long Island's problems provided the parent Pennsylvania with constant streams of bad publicity, which undermined the Pennsy's image with many of its major shippers with headquarters in New York City.

In 1954, the Pennsylvania Railroad attempted to end the Long Island's troubles by reorganizing the firm under a New York law as a railroad redevelopment corporation. This status could continue up to 12 years and exempted the railroad from all state and local taxes (except real estate taxes) for 9 years. The Long Island Transit Authority sponsored the new program, which included a $60-million fund for new rolling stock and improvement of the line's electrical facilities and shops. Under this plan, the Pennsylvania Railroad agreed to lend Long Island a further $5.5 million [4].

The Pennsylvania had a very important stake in the Long Island's success. It owned 100 percent of the company's common stock, which it carried on its books at a value in excess of $47,600,000. In addition, the Long Island owed the Pennsylvania $39,930,000 for general mortgage bonds which, during the 12-year redevelopment period, paid no interest [5]. Railroad officials hoped that the combination of reduced taxes, new capital, and for-giveness of interest on debts might revive the Long Island. Experience soon proved such hopes vain. For the Pennsylvania, therefore, the problem be-came that of how to rescue something from its large investment. The rail-road's top management decided to try selling its interest to the state of New York.

Starting about 1960, Bevan began exploratory talks with William Ronan, secretary to New York's Governor Nelson Rockefeller and soon to become the chairman of New York State's metropolitan commuter transportation authority. Both sides had something to gain. If the state took over the railroad, it could proceed to rehabilitate it with more confidence than if the system remained under the cloudy title of the quasi-governmental Redevel-opment Corporation. The Pennsylvania stood to recoup some of its lost investment. Governor Rockefeller's administration wanted to win the sup-port of hundreds of thousands of his constituents who desired improved commuter rail transportation. Nevertheless, there was the danger that poli-tics could ruin the negotiations. Fortunately for the Pennsylvania, Governor Rockefeller was one of the first politicians of stature to recognize that the preservation of rail commuter service required the substantial infusion of public funds. The Pennsylvania's chief financial officer handled the negotia-tions from beginning to end. He quickly developed a strategy. His aim was to keep the actual cash price as low as possible because he knew that the state legislature would have to approve any agreement and appropriate the funds.

Bevan started negotiations to sell the Long Island several years before Stuart Saunders became the Pennsylvania's chief executive. After the negotiations were well under way, Saunders asked Bevan how much the railroad could expect to receive. The chief financial officer prepared a de-tailed memorandum. After scanning it, Saunders told Bevan, "You are going to have to get a lot more realistic than this if you expect to sell the Long Island." Bevan replied that while he anticipated sharp bargaining, the railroad should get a price close to the original figure. To his surprise, Saunders stated that he wanted to join the negotiations. This disturbed Bevan. Saunders was still too new at the Pennsylvania to have had time to develop the knowledge needed to discuss intelligently the complex Long Island situation. However, Bevan had no choice in the matter and Saunders started to attend the sessions with Ronan.

It quickly became apparent to Bevan that Saunders thought Governor Rockefeller would take an active part in the bargaining. Saunders liked to deal with politicians and he looked forward to working closely with New York's governor. When Rockefeller did not attend any sessions, Saunders lost interest and left Bevan and Ronan to hammer out an agreement without him. Bevan felt that Saunders undermined his position by telling Ronan that the railroad's chief financial officer was only Saunders's representative. After that, Ronan consistently threatened to appeal to Saunders over Bevan's head, and on some occasions he did so. This maneuver prolonged the difficult negotiations.

In December 1965, Bevan and Ronan reached an agreement. It was far better than anything Saunders or the directors of the Pennsylvania had anticipated. Under the arrangements, the railroad received a payment of $65 million in cash. In addition, the state turned over profits from the Long Island concourse concessions to the Pennsylvania Railroad, the Bay Ridge branch, and a number of important air rights that had potential for real estate development. Other parts of the package included substantial tax relief. Altogether, the value of the agreement to the Pennsylvania Railroad amounted to about $120 million.

Saunders was delighted with the Long Island settlement, but he seemed reluctant to give Bevan any credit. His attitude became clear when Ronan sent an informal memorandum outlining the agreement for both Saunders and Bevan to sign. Bevan remembered that when the agreement came, Saunders grew angry, asserting that the request for Bevan's signature undermined his own authority. Bevan answered that as far as he was concerned, "It did not matter in the slightest," but since he had done practically all the negotiating, it was apparent that Ronan thought he should sign the agreement. Bevan later recalled that Saunders insisted that "I ask Ronan for a new memorandum without any reference to myself in it."

Bevan stated that under no circumstances would he tell the state of New York how to run its affairs by asking Ronan to withdraw his request for his signature. After sober second thoughts, Saunders decided not to make a further issue of this matter, and both men signed the document.

Next, Saunders asked Bevan to draft a report for the board of directors so that they could approve the sale. Saunders said that he would present the details to the board personally. Bevan sat through the board meeting as a detached observer while Saunders expounded on the brilliance of the negotiations that had led to Long Island's agreement with the state of New York. At one point, almost as an aside, he casually commented that Bevan had been of some help to him in the negotiations. The chief financial officer made no attempt to present a different version.

THE PITTSBURGH FIASCO

Richard King Mellon, chairman of the board of the Mellon National Bank and Trust Company, was the Pennsylvania Railroad's senior director, having served on the board continuously since 1934. He had also been a driving force behind the city of Pittsburgh's post-World War II renaissance. In the 1960s, the revitalized Golden Triangle, with its gleaming new office buildings and hotels, contrasted starkly with the Pennsylvania Railroad's adjacent property, which included a dilapidated station, ugly yards, and dingy warehouses. On numerous occasions when Bevan dropped in to see his friend Dick Mellon, the Pittsburgh industrialist walked over to his window, which looked down on the Pennsylvania property. He would point at the area and argue that the land was an eyesore, bad for Pittsburgh, and bad for the railroad's public relations. Bevan would always agree, but then add that he had nothing to do with his company's real estate or passenger operations. These answers never satisfied Mellon.

Things came to a climax in 1965. One day, after the railroad's board of directors met in Philadelphia, Stuart Saunders called Bevan into his office. Saunders said that Richard Mellon had just left and that he was very upset because a Pittsburgh firm had worked out a redevelopment plan for the railroad's Pittsburgh property. When the developers approached the railroad, they had been rebuffed. The railroad's real estate department argued that the proposition did not benefit the Pennsylvania and would actually cost the company money. Mellon, very much disturbed, went directly to Saunders and asked him to take the project away from the Pennsylvania's real estate department and give it to someone who could do something constructive for Pittsburgh and the railroad. Saunders told Bevan about the discussion with Mellon and then put the matter in Bevan's hands. It was obviously a very hot potato and Saunders had no desire to handle it personally.

The first step was to have the financial staff analyze the proposal that had been submitted to the railroad. They concluded that the real estate department had been correct. The development would cost the railroad a substantial sum of money; however, if it was successful, another company would reap the benefits. Bevan called Mellon and told him that the proposed plan would not serve the Pennsylvania, but he then promised to find another approach.

Mellon said that he was disappointed but he recognized that the project had been suddenly assigned to the financial vice-president. He ended the telephone conversation by stating that he "wanted and expected action."

Next, Bevan went to Pittsburgh, taking with him his assistant, William Gerstnecker. For 2 days, they walked the Pittsburgh streets to get "a true feel of the situation." It finally became evident that, including the station and freight yard, the railroad had the last flat land available in downtown Pittsburgh. It was clear, however, that for a proper development, the Pennsylvania would have to accumulate several isolated parcels in order to have a solid tract. On his return to Philadelphia, Bevan discussed certain problems with the operating department, and then went on to New York to see Robert Dowling, who had been the railroad's consultant on the Philadelphia Penn Center complex. Bevan asked Dowling to make an independent survey to determine whether or not commercial development of the land was feasible.

Dowling went to Pittsburgh and confirmed Bevan's conclusions. Then he, in association with Vincent C. Kling, the renowned Philadelphia architect, prepared preliminary sketches for what promised to be one of the most imaginative developments of its kind on the eastern seaboard. After consultation with Saunders, Dowling, and Kling, Bevan made a presentation to Richard Mellon, who immediately endorsed the scheme. Saunders and Bevan then obtained authority from the Pennsylvania's board of directors to formalize the development plans and quietly to acquire land not already under the Pennsylvania's control. At this stage, everything depended on confidentiality. Once plans were disclosed, the price of the nonrailroad land would rise. It was also important that the public not know that the railroad was definitely committed to the project until definitive agreements with the city were reached. A premature disclosure would destroy bargaining power with the city.

While the final plans were being drawn, Bevan left Philadelphia on a 2-week business trip. When he returned, he was "astounded to learn from Saunders that he had arranged and set a date with Dick Mellon for a so-called kick-off dinner when the whole plan would be unveiled to the public." Bevan opposed this announcement, explaining that much of the isolated property had still to be acquired and that no negotiations had yet been undertaken with the city. Saunders remained unconvinced, stating that "plans had gone too far to turn back." Thus, in May 1966, Saunders organized a Pittsburgh dinner to be attended by the city's leading citizens, industrialists, bankers, and politicians. He presided at this meeting and Dowling presented the preliminary sketches. Bevan was amused. Saunders took total credit for the project and his chief financial officer was not even on the dais.

Although the Pittsburgh redevelopment plan was well received, it did not bear fruit. The railroad's Real Estate Department estimated that the premature announcement had increased the cost of the unacquired land by at least

$5 million. Worse yet, the railroad became locked in protracted negotiations with the city that had not been completed when the Penn Central collapsed in 1970.

MAJOR ISSUES

Beginning in 1963, David Bevan led the Pennsylvania Railroad into a major diversification program that included four large purchases and three minor ventures. The large acquisitions were the Buckeye Pipeline, the Great Southwest Corporation, the Macco Corporation, and the Arvida Corporation. Relatively small-scale investments included Executive Jet Aviation and Madison Square Garden. In addition, the New York Central controlled the Strick Holding Company. The total invested in these nonrailroad properties amounted to slightly more than $209 million in cash plus $70 million in stock issued by the Pennsylvania Railroad's fully owned subsidiary, Pennsylvania Company [6]. The entire diversification program was planned and carried out between 1963 and 1968, and all but $15.2 million was expended prior to the 1968 merger of the New York Central and the Pennsylvania [7].

After the Penn Central's collapse in 1970, Bevan's efforts came under sharp attack. The Interstate Commerce Commission's investigation of the bankruptcy concluded that the program drained a total of $209 million of cash from the railroad between 1963 and 1970, thus weakening an already shaky financial structure [8]. The Staff Report of the House of Representatives Committee on Banking and Currency on the Penn Central failure was even more harsh. It called diversification "the road to ruin" [9]. The House Committee's argument was similar to that of the ICC. It asserted that diversification robbed the railroad of cash and had materially contributed to the bankruptcy. Actually, both the ICC and the House of Representatives Committee reports gave distorted pictures of the impact of diversification on the railroad's fortune.

Although Bevan emerged as the champion of diversification, the program might never have happened had it not been for the Penn Central merger. At the 1961 White Sulphur Springs summit meeting between Symes of the Pennsylvania and Tuohy of the Chesapeake & Ohio, one of the conditions of the proposed New York Central–Pennsylvania merger was the latter's voluntary liquidation of its interest in the Norfolk & Western. This divestiture posed serious problems. In 1963, the Pennsy held approximately 2.3 million shares of Norfolk & Western common; it would receive 700,000 additional shares within 6 years in exchange for the railroad's Wabash common stock holdings, which the Norfolk & Western purchased as part of the N&W–Wabash merger. In 1963, Norfolk & Western common sold at prices ranging between $126 and $135 a share; the market value of the shares amounted to more than $360 million. The questions for the Pennsy were how to dispose of this vast asset and what to do with the proceeds. The complex problem generated considerable debate in the railroad's high councils.

Early in 1963, Bevan, in his role as the Pennsylvania's chief financial officer, analyzed the possible solutions to the Norfolk & Western problem. He noted that the Pennsylvania Railroad did not own Norfolk & Western shares directly. It controlled them through its wholly owned subsidiary, the Pennsylvania Company. Over the decades, the Pennsy's top management had used the Pennsylvania Company to hold new acquisitions, such as the Norfolk & Western and the Wabash. Bevan regarded the Pennsylvania Company as the railroad's crown jewel. Every year the company received dividends from its major holdings, largely the Wabash and the Norfolk & Western, and in turn passed them on to the parent firm. In 1960, for example, the Pennsylvania Company received $14.8 million of such dividends. This allowed the parent Pennsylvania Railroad's consolidated return to show a narrow profit of $1,143,000, while the railroad itself lost $7,819,000 [10]. Between 1961 and 1963, the combined dividends from the Pennsylvania's holdings of Wabash and Norfolk & Western stock averaged around $20 million each year.

For Bevan, the Pennsylvania Company's role was clear. Its earnings had often in the past made the difference between profitability and deficit for the parent Pennsylvania system. Had it not been for the Pennsylvania Company, the Pennsylvania Railroad could not have maintained its unbroken record of consecutive annual dividends paid since 1848. But to Bevan, the Pennsylvania Company had another value; its financial strength backed the parent system's credit worthiness. The solid value underlying the company enabled Bevan to borrow money at the lowest rates even in time of crisis.

Not all the Pennsylvania directors shared Bevan's views on what to do with the assets to be realized from the sale of the Norfolk & Western shares. Moreover, their ideas were often in conflict. Some saw an opportunity to reduce the Pennsylvania's large debt. Others wanted to maximize the flow of cash into the hands of the railroad's stockholders. Still others suggested that a portion of the money be used for capital improvements, including improved passenger service. William L. Day, a member of the Board's Finance Committee and chairman of the First Pennsylvania Banking and Trust Company of Philadelphia, made a large-scale submission. He saw three major benefits from the sale of the Norfolk & Western. He thought some of the proceeds should be used to retire a portion of the railroad's large indebtedness. Day also recommended that Norfolk & Western stock ought to be distributed to Pennsylvania Railroad shareholders on a favorable basis. Finally, he advised that additional Norfolk & Western assets could be converted for new railway equipment and improvements in the system's physical plant [11]. Another director, Howard Butcher III, proposed that most of the Norfolk & Western stock should be sold within 18 months. He felt that this step would allow the railroad to avoid the sale of $50 million of new bonds. In addition, Butcher suggested that $20 million of the proceeds be put into the Madison Square Garden project, another $20 million into new passenger equipment, and an unspecified amount into improving the Pennsylvania's physical plant. He also hoped some cash from the sale of Norfolk & Western stock could be used to increase the railroad's dividend [12].

Bevan spoke against all these ideas. He argued that the Pennsylvania Company's assets should be gradually transferred from the Norfolk & Western's securities to other types of investment. In this way, he hoped to preserve the Pennsylvania Company's income, which had proved so vital to the consolidated corporation's profitability. He also wanted to retain solid assets in the Pennsylvania Company so that they could be used as collateral for borrowing. He opposed the use of Norfolk & Western assets to retire the Pennsylvania's debt. Of course, Bevan supported debt reduction. From 1951 through 1963, he had reduced the total debt of the consolidated Pennsylvania Railroad system from $1,116,000,000 to $781 million. However, he insisted that "the purchase of our own debt will neither preserve our liquidity nor will it maintain the current income realized from capital N&W stock." He observed that funds used in this manner would "be gone irrevocably and, therefore, would not be available for" emergencies. In his words [13]:

> Despite the reduction in debt, this loss of liquidity in my judgment would seriously affect our overall credit. The sale of marketable assets to retire debts is a form of liquidation and indicates a lack of ability to meet obligations in the normal manner. This, in turn, may well weaken the confidence of the various institutions on which we are dependent for current financing.

Further, Bevan observed that debt retirement was the equivalent of investing funds at the rate of 3 or 4 percent after taxes. In contrast, by acquiring 80 percent of the voting stock of other companies, it would be possible to utilize the 300 million to 400 million dollars of the Pennsylvania Railroad's carry-forward tax loss to take the acquired companies out of taxes. This held strong promise of profit for the railroad.

Bevan also warned against putting the proceeds of the Norfolk & Western stock sales into the fixed assets of the Pennsylvania Railroad. In the past, he had supported large capital improvements for the railroad. In fact, in 1959, he helped Symes finance the largest equipment program in American railroad history. This consisted of the acquisition of nearly 24,000 new freight cars, 116 new locomotives, and 7 diesel tugboats with an overall expenditure of $260 million. All this equipment had gone into service by the middle of 1960.

Bevan had two objections to using Norfolk & Western funds for the railroad's capital improvements. First, he saw no evidence that the massive expenditure of funds on the railroad, such as Symes's 1959 equipment program, resulted in positive and dependable earnings. To the contrary, despite Symes's program, 1960, 1961, and 1962 were, financially, three of the railroad's worst years since World War II. Finally, Bevan argued that if Norfolk & Western funds were "invested in fixed assets with the Pennsylvania Railroad, we will have destroyed our liquidity and also seriously injured our credit position."

Bevan desired the transfer of the railroad's investment in the Norfolk & Western to other investments that could be used as collateral for loans and that would at the same time provide income to replace the Norfolk & Western dividends. There was still another factor that shaped his thoughts. The Pennsylvania Company carried the Norfolk & Western's shares on its books at a value of $26 a share. Because the 1963–1964 market value of these securities exceeded $125 a share, the railroad faced a capital gain if it sold the stock outright. Bevan estimated that the gain would be about $300 million and would incur a capital gains tax of nearly $75 million. "It might be argued," Bevan observed, that since the railroad "had a substantial tax carried forward loss, this had no significance, but on the other hand, it would have meant using up, on a capital gains basis (taxed at 25 percent), a loss which would otherwise be available to offset ordinary income taxable at 52 percent" [14]. Bevan decided that it would be unsound to sell any substantial amount of Norfolk & Western stock, since the capital gain would use up too much of the railroad's tax credits that would better be saved to match against ordinary income.

Finally, Board Director Day's idea of distributing Norfolk & Western stock to Pennsylvania Railroad stockholders was unacceptable. The distribution would not be equitable to the holders of the Pennsylvania Company's debt, who might sue for dissipation of assets. So, too, distribution would deprive the parent railroad of assets upon which it depended.

Bevan's arguments converted even the most skeptical directors. William Day later testified before the Securities and Exchange Commission that "on the basis of what I had learned in the operations of the railroad and the difficulty of keeping it solvent," putting money in the railroad "would have been imprudent" [15].

PRINCIPAL ACCOMPLISHMENTS

Out of lengthy discussions concerning the problems surrounding the liquidation of the Pennsylvania's Norfolk & Western stock came the diversification program. The idea, a simple one, was to replace the dependable earnings which the Pennsylvania had received from the Norfolk & Western with equally dependable earnings from other investments. It is important to note here that this solution, although strongly advocated by Bevan, had the strong support of Stuart Saunders and the railroad's other directors. All agreed that the railroad should continue to use the Pennsylvania Company as a vehicle to hold the investments of the parent Pennsylvania system. To avoid dumping large quantities of Norfolk & Western shares on the market and the loss of all Norfolk & Western dividends, Bevan advocated that about one-third of the railroad's holdings of N&W common be exchanged into convertible subordinate debentures of that company. These convertible debentures would carry no vote and would fulfill the Pennsylvania's agreement to divest itself of control in the Norfolk & Western. The Pennsy's management approved and, as part of this program, in 1966 the Pennsylvania Company arranged for the exchange of 800,000 shares of "N&W common stock for 4.58% N&W convertible subordinated debentures with a par value of $104 million" [16]. This assured the Pennsylvania Company a reliable income in excess of $4.6 million a year.

The plan to dispose of the railroad's remaining interest in Norfolk & Western shares was complex. After considerable research, the railroad's tax counsel advised Bevan about the capital gains tax consequences of the disposal of new shares if the Pennsylvania Company "issued preferred stock convertible into Norfolk & Western stock, and used this in an acquisition program." Under this plan, "the initial exchange would be tax-free, provided the preferred stock was nonconvertible for a period of at least 3 years. Further, when it was converted, although taxable to the individual holder at that time, there would be no capital gains tax involved as far as the railroad was concerned." Even more attractive, if the Pennsylvania Company used its new preferred shares to acquire at least 80 percent of another firm, it could place that firm under the railroad's tax shelter, thus removing its income from taxes and thereby taking advantage of the Pennsylvania's tax-loss carry-forward in the most advantageous way [17].

The first candidate for purchase was the Buckeye Pipeline Company. This firm operated a 7900-mile pipeline that transported crude oil and petroleum products in the northeastern states served by the Pennsylvania Railroad. The Pennsylvania's board of directors approved and, in 1963, the Pennsylvania Company made a cash investment of approximately $30 million and acquired a one-third ownership of Buckeye. In 1964 the Pennsylvania Company issued $70 million of preferred shares convertible into Norfolk & Western stock at $137 a share and "escrowed 516,308 shares against this conversion." The Pennsylvania Company then used its new preferred shares to purchase the remaining Buckeye stock. The Buckeye Pipeline had a long and proven earning record. In 1965, it earned slightly more than $11.2 million; in 1966, $12.4 million; and in 1967, $13.6 million. In each of these years, Buckeye paid substantial dividends in amounts ranging from a low of $5.8 million in 1966 to $6.62 million in 1967 [18]. As expected, Buckeye remained a dependable source of income. In the early 1970s, Buckeye common stock dividends, all of which went to the Pennsylvania Company, averaged around $6 million. However, beginning in 1975, they rose sharply, with $19 million in such dividends declared [19].

While the goal was to protect the Pennsylvania Railroad with conservative, dividend-producing securities, all the directors also desired to provide an opportunity for substantial capital growth. This meant buying corporations that reinvested most of their earnings and paid small or no dividends. Because the Pennsylvania, in such ventures as Philadelphia's Penn Center, had become involved in real estate, Bevan favored further expansion in this area. Under his leadership, the Pennsylvania Company invested in three major real estate firms. The Pennsylvania's interest in the first of these, the Great Southwest Corporation, began in 1964. This company had over 6000 acres of industrial land midway between Dallas and Fort Worth. Ultimately the Pennsylvania Company put almost $52 million into Great Southwest and acquired 90 percent of its securities [20]. Starting in July 1966, the company invested in the Arvida Corporation, which was developing more than 100,000 acres of Florida land for resorts and residential, commercial, farm, and industrial purposes. The Pennsylvania committed approximately $22 million to Arvida and acquired 58 percent of the common stock. Between October 1965 and July 1966, the Pennsylvania, on the recommendation of Angus Wynne, head of Great Southwest, purchased the Macco Realty Company, which had large land holdings in Southern California, particularly in the San Fernando Valley, in Orange County near San Juan Capistrano, and at Rancho California in Riverside County. The investment in Macco represented total control and amounted to slightly more than $39.4 million. In 1969 Great Southwest and Macco merged, creating a real estate firm with major holdings in Georgia, Texas, and California.

CRITICS OF THE DIVERSIFICATION PROGRAM

A Pennsy subsidiary, the Pennsylvania Company became the vehicle for the railroad's purchase of Buckeye and the three real estate firms. In addition, another Pennsylvania Railroad subsidiary, the American Contract Company, made an investment in a small company, Executive Jet Aviation. The Pennsylvania's first support of Executive Jet began in 1964; ultimately, the railroad committed about $21 million to Executive Jet. Although relatively small, this investment became a matter of major controversy. Congressional investigators and others later claimed that Executive Jet and Penphil, a small investment club in which various railroad executives participated, were major causes in the Penn Central's bankruptcy. As will become evident, Executive Jet and Penphil were largely irrelevant factors in the complex events leading to the railroad's collapse. It is sufficient for the present to observe that Executive Jet was only a tiny part of the railroad's overall diversification scheme. The $21 million invested in the airline represented only about one-thirteenth of the $279 million that the Pennsylvania committed to diversification. Furthermore, when compared with the Penn Central's operating losses of over $460 million, investment in Executive Jet takes on even less significance.

After the Penn Central's failure in 1970, the strongest criticism of diversification came from the staff of the House of Representatives Committee on Banking and Currency. As noted earlier, the main thrust was that diversification drained cash from the railroad and significantly contributed to the bankruptcy. This argument was unrealistic because it overlooked some significant factors. Most important, the program did not invest earnings generated by the railway operation in nonrailway operations. The Financial Department's strategy was merely to transfer outside investments that the Pennsylvania Railroad had made in earlier years into new areas. The total cash invested in the diversification program amounted to approximately $163.5 million. Of this, about $98 million resulted from opportunities made possible by the forced divestiture of the Norfolk & Western shares. The remaining $65 million, used largely to buy into Great Southwest and Macco, came from the sale of the Long Island Railroad, the dubious asset that had paid no dividends since 1930 and that, since World War II, had been a drain on the Pennsylvania Railroad [21].

The Banking and Currency Committee Staff Report argued that had the cash not been invested in diversification, it could have been applied to reduce the Pennsylvania Railroad's debt. By not reducing this debt, the report contended, the railroad was forced to continue to borrow in excess of $163 million from banks. The report calculated that between 1963 and 1970, this cost the railroad about $51 million [22]. Bevan saw the situation differently. He felt it was wrong to use the Pennsylvania Railroad's outside investments to retire the debts incurred by the railway in the normal course of operations. He argued that the railroad would ultimately have to find a way to stand on its own and, if it did not, using its crown jewels to retire debt was merely a form of liquidation. It is difficult to credit the House Committee's assertion that the cash drain from diversification contributed substantially to the Penn Central's bankruptcy. The Penn Central's operating losses alone, which amounted to more than $460 million in the company's brief lifetime, were accelerating at the time of the corporation's bankruptcy. The railroad's failure was so massive and its problems so deep-seated that even the total commitments of the proceeds of divestiture of the

Norfolk & Western stock would have postponed the disaster for a few months at the most.

The House Committee's other arguments seemed largely quibbles. For example, it criticized Bevan's strategy for issuing Pennsylvania Company preferred stock in exchange for Buckeye Pipeline common. Said the Committee, this "eliminated potential methods of raising cash for use by the railroad." The Committee asserted that if the Pennsylvania Company had not issued preferred stock to acquire Buckeye, the company could possibly have sold preferred shares to the public to raise cash for the railroad. In addition, the existence of the preferred stock as a result of the Buckeye acquisition adversely affected a proposed public offering of a Pennsylvania Company common stock to raise funds. In either case, said the Committee, money raised through the sale of Pennsylvania Company stock—whether preferred or common—could have been made directly available to the railroad [23]. This argument clearly misunderstands the problem. The Pennsylvania had to divest itself of control of Norfolk & Western shares. If these securities were sold on the open market, the railroad faced unfavorable tax consequences. The issuance of the Pennsylvania Company's preferred shares, which were then exchanged for Buckeye common, allowed the railroad to avoid paying capital gains taxes. Furthermore, the Pennsylvania Company had securities outstanding with the public. An immediate transfer of company assets to the parent company risked opening the way for a suit by outside security holders who could charge dissipation of assets.

The real question was whether the railroad should liquidate its outside investments and pump the proceeds into the faltering railway business. Bevan, in common with Stuart Saunders, felt this step would be unwise. While they regarded the railway as unprofitable, they did not foresee its rapid collapse. Based on the Pennsylvania's experience since World War II, the objective was to try to get the railroad on a basis where it broke even or lost only a small amount of money. If this were achieved, then the diversification into more profitable enterprises, together with the utilization of the railroad's tax-loss carry-forward on a consolidated basis, would enable the parent company to achieve substantial profits for its stockholders. The Buckeye diversification merely transferred the railroad's highly profitable investment in the Norfolk & Western to an equally profitable investment in pipelines. In no case was cash lost to the railroad. In a serious crisis, Buckeye common had a solid value and could be sold for the railroad's benefit. If the cash crisis were merely temporary, Buckeye common could be used as the basis for a bank loan or for issuance of preferred or common stock in the Pennsylvania Company with the proceeds going to the railroad. In short, given the assumptions Bevan made, the purchase of Buckeye through an issuance of Pennsylvania Company preferred stock was both logical and sound.

The Banking and Currency Committee Staff Report also asserted that the diversification program dried up "bank lines of credit potentially available to the railroad" [24]. The staff argued that the Pennsylvania Company's real estate subsidiaries embarked on major expansion programs and, in so doing, borrowed cash from the same sources of credit as the railroad. The Committee found that these subsidiaries borrowed a total of $20 million from seven eastern banks, which also loaned money to the railroad itself. Three of these banks were in New York City: the First National City Bank, the Chase Manhattan Bank, and the Chemical Bank of New York, and they were among the largest financial institutions in the United States. The loans the Pennsylvania Company real estate subsidiaries received were small when measured against the total loan activity of any one of the giant New York banks. Furthermore, as will be seen, the credit requirements of the Penn Central Railroad during its final days amounted to more than 20 times loans made by the eastern banks to the real estate corporations. Further, the loans in question were made on the subsidiaries' own credit, and there is no reason to believe that the same loans would have been made directly to the Pennsy. It is difficult to maintain that the ultimate fate of the Penn Central's credit lines would have been any different had the diversification program not existed.

As the brief for the Bureau of Enforcement of the Interstate Commerce Commission noted, "All but $15.2 million [of the money that went into the diversification program] was invested prior to the 1968 merger" [25]. In the premerger period, when nearly all the diversification took place, the Pennsylvania Railroad itself showed no signs of financial collapse. It was, however, a time when money invested in the railroad did not produce profits, and the financial picture appeared to grow dimmer year by year. In those years when the railroad actually ran deficits, these losses were easily counterbalanced by earnings from the Pennsylvania system's outside investments, such as the Norfolk & Western, the Wabash, and real estate ventures. The Pennsylvania Railroad itself was suffering a long-term decline, a trend that had been in effect, with the exception of the World War II period, since the onset of the Depression in the 1930s. There was nothing in the past history of the Pennsylvania or, for that matter, in that of the New York Central indicating that a rapid, precipitous decline in the railroad's financial situation would begin with the merger of the two corporations. The decisions about diversification must be viewed in the light of the financial picture as it could be seen at the time they were made. In fact, after the railroad's fortune drastically changed in 1968, the system ceased to plow large amounts of capital into diversification. From its own point of view, this did not mean an end to the program, but merely a prudent step in which the Penn Central stopped investments in nonrailroad activities until the financial affairs of the transportation enterprise could be brought under control. In the meantime, Bevan used the considerable assets tied up in diversification as collateral for loans that were used to aid the financially ailing rail enterprise.

References

1. Pennsylvania Railroad, *Annual Report for 1964,* p. 19.

2. Penn Central, *Annual Report for 1967,* p. 9; *The Financial Collapse of the Penn Central Company,* a Staff Report of the Securities and Exchange Commission to the [House of Representatives] Special Sub-Committee on Investigations, Hon. Harley O. Staggers, Chairman, Government Printing Office, Washington, D.C., August 1972, pp. 58–59. Hereafter referred to as the SEC Staff Report.

3. Pennsylvania Railroad, *Annual Report for 1964,* p. 19.

4. Pennsylvania Railroad, *Annual Report for 1954,* pp. 25, 34–35.

5. The Pennsylvania had taken over the bonds as part of its guarantee under the redevelopment plan.

6. *The Penn Central Failure and the Role of Financial Institutions,* Staff Report of the Committee on Banking and Currency, Jan. 3, 1972, pp. 29, 33. Hereafter referred to as the Patman Report.

7. Brief of the Interstate Commerce Commission, Bureau of Enforcement, *Investigation into the Management of the Penn Central Transportation Company . . . ,* March 8, 1972, p. 113.

8. Ibid., pp. 114–115.

9. Patman Report, p. 23.

10. Pennsylvania Railroad, *Annual Report for 1960,* pp. 2, 25.

11. Bevan Papers, memorandum from William L. Day to James Symes, May 20, 1963.

12. Bevan Papers, memorandum from Howard Butcher III to David Bevan, May 15, 1963.

13. Bevan Papers, memorandum from David Bevan to the Pennsylvania Railroad Board of Directors, written, undated, in May 1963.

14. Bevan Papers, Bevan memorandum, written, undated, in 1968.

15. Testimony of William L. Day before the Securities and Exchange Commission in the Penn Central Case in Washington, D.C., April 13, 1972, pp. 74–75.

16. Pennsylvania Railroad, *Annual Report for 1966,* p. 13.

17. Bevan Papers, Bevan memorandum, written, undated, in 1968.

18. Pennsylvania Railroad Statistical Supplement to the *Annual Report for 1966,* p. 21; Penn Central Statistical Supplement to the *Annual Report for 1967,* p. 22.

19. Pennsylvania Company, *Annual Report for 1972,* p. 10, and *Annual Report for 1975,* p. 16.

20. Patman Report, p. 44.

21.   In addition to the cash investment in the diversification program, the Pennsylvania Company issued preferred stock with a book value of more than $70 million to acquire the complete ownership of Buckeye.

22.   Patman Report, p. 28.

23.   Ibid., pp. 29, 30.

24.   Ibid., p. 30.

25.   Brief of the Interstate Commerce Commission, Bureau of Enforcement, Investigation into the Management of the Business of the Penn Central . . . , March 8, 1972, p. 113.

Chapter 6
THE DREAM OF SOLUTION THROUGH MERGER

While the Financial Department labored to reconstruct the Pennsylvania's debt and bring modern financial tools to the system, forces beyond anyone's control began to cast grave shadows over the entire American railroad industry. Early in the 1950s, the Pennsylvania Railroad appeared to prosper. The Korean conflict, which began in June 1950, brought an abrupt halt to the decline in rail traffic that had set in immediately following the end of World War II. Even the return of an uneasy peace in Korea in mid-1953 failed to depress rail revenues. For a while, it was possible to be optimistic, but in the fall of 1957, recession struck the American economy, the railroads being particularly hard-hit. *Fortune* magazine reported that rail freight movement in the fourth quarter of 1957 ran more than 10 percent below the 1956 level, and it noted that fourth-quarter railroad earnings "were the lowest in 11 years" [1]. James Symes told his stockholders that the 1957 recession "struck the Pennsylvania . . . with severe and unexpected force. What had been a moderate decline in car loadings for the first 9 months turned into a sudden and accelerating drop through the last 3 months of the year" [2]. January 1958 was worse; in that month the Pennsylvania ran a deficit of over $2,500,000, compared with a net income of $500,000 during the same month of the previous year. Low earnings undermined dividends. In 1958, the Pennsy cut its dividend to a· token 25 cents [3].

THE TRAUMA OF
EASTERN RAILROADS

The recession did not strike all railroads equally. Eastern rails could be divided into three large groups: the New England systems, the great trunk lines of the Middle Atlantic, and finally those serving the Pocahontas coal fields of Virginia and West Virginia. Symes recognized that the first two major groups were in long-term trouble. New England's roads faced the worst problems. They were heavily oriented toward passenger traffic. The New York, New Haven & Hartford, a system linking New York City with Connecticut, Rhode Island, and Massachusetts, derived a higher proportion of its revenues from passengers than any other major railroad in the United States except for the Long Island. The other large New England carrier, the Boston & Maine, which operated most of the region's trackage north of Boston, was also a significant passenger carrier. Furthermore, important economic changes had drastically altered New England, which, since 1900, had lost many of its freight-producing industries, particularly textiles, iron and steel, and heavy electrical manufacturing. At the same time, the region's homeowners and electric power generators had switched from domestic coal, which had been carried by railroads from the Middle Atlantic states, to imported oil, which arrived by sea from South America and the Middle East. Simultaneously, Massachusetts and Connecticut had embarked on massive highway construction programs that allowed trucks to drain away much of the remaining freight. All these changes wreaked havoc on New England's railroads, of which the New Haven was especially hard pressed.

The recession of 1957 devastated the New Haven line. In October of that year, the line's "net income virtually disappeared, plummeting 91 percent to $41,000" [4]. For the entire year of 1957, the New Haven reported a loss. This was only the prelude of worse to come. In January 1958, the system incurred a deficit of more than $1.2 million, or 3 times the January 1957 loss [5]. The recession year of 1957 marked the beginning of a long series of annual losses which, on July 7, 1961, again forced the company into receivership.

JAMES SYMES VIEWS THE
POCAHONTAS REGION'S PROSPERITY

As Symes viewed the Middle Atlantic railroad picture, he saw most of the region's major lines in trouble. These systems included four of the United States's most important railroads, each one a giant system linking the Atlantic seaboard at New York City with the Great Lakes at Chicago. They included Symes's own Pennsylvania, the New York Central, the Erie, and the Baltimore & Ohio. Each company reported substantial profits in January 1957, but the following January saw three of the four plunge into the red [6]. Even the smaller mid-Atlantic railroads lost money, especially the Delaware, Lackawanna, & Western and the Lehigh Valley, both of which connected New York City with Buffalo.

In sharp contrast, the three major railroads serving the Pocahontas coal fields were booming. They were the Virginian, the Norfolk & Western, and the Chesapeake & Ohio. Coal had proved a never-failing source of prosperity for these railroads. Even the decline of coal after World War II did not hurt them. Demand for steam coal to generate electricity continued strong, particularly in the Ohio Valley and the mid-Atlantic states. Also, rising European prosperity, coupled with a decline in Europe's coal reserves, especially in Germany, France, and the Low Countries, opened an export market for American coal. The Pocahontas railroads were strategically located to deliver coal for overseas markets. *Barron's* magazine estimated that in 1956 the three railroads carried over 135 million tons of coal, or slightly more than 27 percent of all the soft coal mined in the United States [7]. In addition, these railroads lacked the substantial passenger traffic that burdened the mid-Atlantic and New England systems. Consequently, the Pocahontas lines consistently produced some of the best profits in the United States. The Chesapeake & Ohio's operating ratio in 1956 was approximately 68 percent; the ratio was 69 percent on the Norfolk & Western, and 47 percent on the Virginian. Even in the depressed 1930s, these railroads had all been lucrative. The Norfolk & Western had an unbroken dividend record reaching back to 1901. The 1957 recession barely touched the Pocahontas lines. While the Middle Atlantic and New England railroads accumulated deficits in January 1958, the coal roads continued to earn profits [8].

James Symes understood that the conditions producing prosperity for the Pocahontas roads were peculiar to the region they served and did not apply to the Middle Atlantic and New England lines. He recognized that drastic measures were needed to restore health to the railroads in his region. Part of the problem was overcapacity. Between New York City and Buffalo, for example, five different railroads, the New York Central, Erie, Lehigh Valley, Pennsylvania, and Lackawanna, competed for traffic. From Buffalo west to Cleveland, the tracks of the New York, Chicago & St. Louis (the Nickel Plate) closely paralleled those of the New York Central, while just a bit further south ran the Erie. Shippers between Chicago, Pittsburgh, and Baltimore had the choice of two direct lines, the Pennsylvania and the Baltimore & Ohio. Further south, the Baltimore & Ohio, the Chesapeake & Ohio, and the Pennsylvania competed for traffic between Washington, D.C., and Chicago.

Symes felt that if the railroads in the East could be reduced through merger, substantial benefits would accrue to both the industry and the economy as a whole. He thought the merger of the Pennsylvania, in 1957 America's largest transportation enterprise, with the country's second largest transportation venture, the New York Central, was natural. Both railroads served the same regions. Symes believed a merger could eliminate duplicate trackage. The new company could choose the best and most efficient routes and abandon circuitous or mountainous lines. The railroad would save substantial property taxes by abandoning certain trackage and be able to concentrate high-quality maintenance on that retained. Symes also saw significant savings in administrative costs and in labor. Merger was the key to competing with motor carriers.

There were, of course, many obstacles to merger. The management of the New York Central and its shareholders had to be won over. Labor opposed any measures that would reduce employment. Cities and towns on lines that might be abandoned or downgraded from main-line to branch status would not favor a merger. Other eastern railroads that were not included in the merger opposed the creation of a well-financed, efficient system that would put them at a competitive disadvantage. Still other lines, such as the New Haven, would fight a plan that did not include them.

THE STORMY NEW YORK CENTRAL: ROBERT YOUNG AND ALFRED PERLMAN

Actually, the idea of merging eastern railroads was not new. It had been periodically advanced in past times when railroads had run into financial troubles. One of the most recent proponents of eastern railway mergers had been Robert R. Young, who burst onto the financial scene in the 1930s when he gained control of the Alleghany Corporation. Through the Alleghany, Young, after a bitter battle with certain Wall Street banks, gained control of the Chesapeake & Ohio.

After World War II, Young used his position in the Alleghany Corporation and Chesapeake & Ohio to attempt a takeover of the New York Central Railroad. He was opposed by the Central's management, which was backed by a number of powerful New York banks that Young had alienated in his fight for control of the Alleghany and the C&O. Young lost his battle to merge the Chesapeake & Ohio and the New York Central in May 1948 when the Interstate Commerce Commission ruled against him. He never ceased to desire the Central, for he regarded it as a more significant system than the C&O and an ideal road on which to test his ideas to improve passenger service.

In January 1954, Young resigned as a director of the Chesapeake & Ohio and caused the Alleghany Corporation to sell its interest in the railroad as well. Young's friend, the brilliant but maverick Cleveland financier Cyrus Eaton, succeeded to the chairmanship of the Chesapeake & Ohio's board. After resigning from the C&O, Young turned his full attention to capturing the New York Central. In 1952, the Central had chosen a new president, William White. In common with most other eastern railroads, the Central faltered financially after World War II, and White undertook the rebuilding of the railroad's physical and financial structure. When Young approached the Central's management for a place on its board, White, with the support of some of New York's biggest banking houses, rebuffed him. In response, Young launched the most colorful fight for the control of a corporation in Wall Street's long history. He posed as the friend of the small shareholder, "Aunt Jane," and he made lavish promises to improve both freight and passenger service while at the same time raising the railroad's dividend. At the annual meeting in June 1954, he won control of the railroad's board of directors and became the board chairman.

Although White had made some progress in the New York Central's rehabilitation, Young found that the company faced problems similar to those of its arch-rival, the Pennsylvania. Although slightly smaller in terms of both mileage and total investment, the Central served the same general region and cities and carried similar kinds of traffic. In 1955 the Pennsylvania and the New York Central were the first and second largest passenger carriers in the United States in terms of passengers carried 1 mile [9]. Both were among the nation's seven largest bituminous coal carriers, although this traffic accounted for only about 17 percent of the gross freight revenue of each system. This was strikingly different from the two largest Pocahontas roads, the Chesapeake & Ohio, where soft coal produced over 56 percent of its freight revenue, and the Norfolk & Western, where it accounted for almost 64 percent of gross freight revenue [10].

The Central, like the Pennsy, had built its fortune largely upon carrying relatively high-value manufactured commodities produced in hundreds of eastern and midwestern industrial cities and towns. This was the traffic most vulnerable to motor truck competition. It is not surprising that James C. Nelson, writing for the Brookings Institution in 1959, commented that since World War II, the New York Central and the Pennsylvania were among the railroads producing the lowest rate of return on money invested in them in the United States [11], a fact well recognized by management. In 1958, Alfred Perlman, who became the Central's president under Robert R. Young, wrote that "since 1930 [the New York Central] has shown a profit from railroad operations in only 10 years. Seven of the ten," he continued, "were war years" [12]. Like the Pennsylvania, the New York Central had outside income. It owned more than $50 million of real estate, much of it along Park Avenue in New York City above the underground tracks leading to Grand Central Terminal. The income from nonrailway sources annually exceeded $25 million and often kept the railroad afloat [13].

Although Robert Young underestimated the difficulties of rebuilding the New York Central, he knew that the task would not be easy. His first problem was to select a new manager, for the bitterness resulting from the proxy fight made White's retention impossible. For the Central's new president, Young chose Alfred Edward Perlman, who had made his mark as an operating man on western railroads. Perlman, a midwesterner, was born in St. Paul, Minnesota, in 1902, the son of a civil engineer. He went east to college, receiving a bachelor of science degree from the Massachusetts Institute of Technology in 1923. Perlman began work as a laborer on a Northern Pacific Railway track gang in Montana. He later recalled, "I thought I'd never graduate from the gandy dancer ranks" [14]. However, he had a rapid rise, quickly becoming foreman of the Northern Pacific's Rosebud Branch, and then joining the staff of the railroad's vice-president for operations. After taking a short course in railroad transportation at the Harvard Graduate School of Business Administration in 1931, Perlman returned to the Northern Pacific as roadmaster. In 1934, he left to work for the Reconstruction Finance Corporation (RFC). There Perlman made a study of the New Haven, which was striving to avoid bankruptcy through an RFC loan. After that assignment, he made several similar studies for other railroads in financial trouble, including the Denver & Rio Grande Western. In 1935 Perlman returned to private railroading, this time on the Chicago, Burlington, & Quincy's maintenance-of-way division. The following year, he went to the Rio Grande, where he became the engineer in charge of maintenance of way. In 1947, Perlman became the Rio Grande's general manager, and in 1952, the company's executive vice-president.

Perlman's experience with the Rio Grande was in engineering and technical functions. In these areas, he quickly developed a reputation for innovation. To reduce track maintenance costs, he switched track gangs from trains to motor vehicles. Perlman early advocated replacing steam locomotives with diesel-electric engines. He also organized a research laboratory, which reduced locomotive maintenance costs through using sophisticated scientific techniques. For example, when each Rio Grande diesel locomotive finished its run and went to the yard, a sample of its oil was subjected to spectrographic analysis. The results could determine the presence of impurities that resulted from "wear, corrosion, and other operating strain" [15]. This procedure enabled maintenance personnel to detect wear and tear more efficiently and to institute preventive maintenance programs that averted breakdowns.

While Perlman emphasized modern ideas, many of his managerial concepts were of a traditional operational nature. On the Rio Grande, he was responsible for the maintenance of the system's track. He liked to ride in the front of the diesel locomotive to observe conditions. He also enjoyed personally overseeing some major operational problem such as a washout, avalanche, wreck, or other disaster. Perlman believed in the direct supervision of his men. Because the Rio Grande was a small railroad with only about 2500 miles of line, he came to know every mile of it. His style, which on one hand stressed the adoption of modern scientific techniques and on the other managerial methods that avoided the delegation of authority, worked well on the Colorado system.

Perlman came to the Rio Grande shortly after the railroad entered receivership in 1935 under Section 77 of the Federal Bankruptcy Act. In April 1947, after 12 years of trusteeship, the Rio Grande emerged from bankruptcy, and Perlman received much of the credit. He came to Young's attention through a laudatory article in a periodical called *Railway Progress,* the house organ of the Federation for Railway Progress, an organization created largely to further Young's ideas. During Young's fight for the Central, many informed observers considered Perlman a logical candidate to head the railroad should Young win. On March 29, Young spoke in New York City before an association of customs brokers. He made graphic comparisons of poorly and well-managed lines. "As Young pointed to the figures on the Denver & Rio Grande charts, someone in the rear called out the question, 'Isn't Al Perlman the executive vice-president of that road?' Young thought for a moment and then responded, 'Yes, Perlman represents the progressive kind of railroad man I would like to put into the New York Central as president' " [16]. It was no surprise that one of Young's first acts after winning control of the Central was to appoint Perlman president.

The Young-Perlman team took charge of the Central amid great hopes. Young said he "could see the day . . . of the '$10 dividend,' when the Central shares would be selling for $100" [17]. For a while, things appeared to go well. Perlman's management drastically cut inventories of material and supplies, completed the switch from steam to diesel locomotives, installed centralized traffic control on some of the most heavily utilized trackage, and eliminated some surplus rail mileage. In 1955, the Central's net income reached $52.3 million, or $8.03 per share [18]. Early in 1955, Young announced that he had put the railroad on a regular $2 annual dividend, and Central stock sold for $49 a share. Initial success soon faded. In 1956, the Central had difficulty in maintaining its dividend rate and did so only by distributing as a fourth-quarter dividend the stock of the U.S. Freight Company. In 1957, a recession year, things turned sour. By midyear the Central was running at a deficit which constantly increased through December. Earnings for 1957 fell to $5.9 million, or $.91 a share, and the railroad canceled its first-quarter dividend in 1958. In January of that year, the stock traded at $15, the lowest since 1950.

In 1958, some on Wall Street began to express doubts concerning the Young-Perlman stewardship of the Central. *Barron's* magazine stated that despite initial successes, the Central's problems had not been solved. The periodical made unfavorable comparisons between the New York Central and the Pennsylvania, observing that while both lines had large passenger deficits, the Pennsylvania achieved better utilization of its equipment. In fact, *Barron's* criticized many aspects of Perlman's management. It saw the Pennsylvania as superior in the speed of handling its freight trains. It asserted that Perlman had allowed track maintenance to decline, and suggested that things were worsening for the Central. *Barron's* seized upon the transportation ratio, that is, the ratio of those costs directly involved in running trains to operating revenues. Under the White management in 1954, *Barron's* reported [19]:

> Those costs resulting directly from the moving of trains, that is, fuel, trainmen's wages, etc., was 42.4 percent, a trifle higher than the Pennsy's 41.8 percent. The latter's ought to be heavier, since its trains must chug up the Pennsylvania mountains while the water level route is famous for discreetly avoiding them. In four years, that disparity has widened. Last year, the Pennsy's ratio was 44.9 percent, the Central's 46.8 percent—against that for all major U.S. railroads of 39 percent.

PROPOSAL TO MERGE: PORTENTS OF TROUBLES TO COME

The Central's precipitous decline in 1957 coincided with similar problems on the Pennsylvania and made Young cast about for new answers. He had always favored railway mergers. It will be recalled that in 1948, he attempted to merge the Chesapeake & Ohio with the New York Central. In 1957, he again thought of marrying the Central and the C&O. This idea was doomed to failure because Walter J. Tuohy, president of the Chesapeake & Ohio, flatly opposed merging his prosperous Pocahontas railroad with the faltering Central.

While Young worried about the future of the New York Central, the Pennsylvania's Symes decided that the eastern railroads could be saved only by a large-scale merger program, the keystone of which was the union of the New York Central and the Pennsylvania. Symes made his decision in the early fall of 1957. For a reason that remains obscure, he ignored Perlman and discussed the matter directly with Young. On November 1, the managements of the New York Central and the Pennsylvania announced that they had had a series of preliminary discussions and that they were going to study the possibility of a merger of the two roads.

Symes's decision to bypass Perlman ensured the hostility of the New York Central's president. In fact, the relationship between the two men had never been cordial. Both became presidents of their respective railroads in the same year, but each came from a very different background. Symes had always been in big-time railroading, and he assumed the Pennsylvania's leadership with ease and confidence. By contrast, Perlman had never held a position higher than executive vice-president, and that was on a minor western railroad that could have been put on the sidetracks of the Pennsylvania or the New York Central. Bevan sensed that Perlman was ill at ease in dealing with the Pennsylvania, seeming to have an overpowering awe of Philadelphia and its so-called Main Line.

But for an accident of history, Perlman's views might not have mattered. On January 25, 1958, Robert Young, despondent over the New York Central's financial problems, committed suicide in the billiard room of his Palm Beach home, and Perlman became the New York Central's unchallenged leader [20]. Perlman was hostile to a merger. He, as events proved, correctly opposed a union of his system with the Pennsylvania. He saw that Walter Tuohy of the Chesapeake & Ohio was attempting to arrange a merger between his road and the Baltimore & Ohio. He wanted to be part of that arrangement, even though Tuohy wanted no accommodation with the Central. Perlman did not give up easily. He worked to terminate merger talks between the Central and the Pennsy. Symes, in the Pennsylvania's 1958 annual report to stockholders, set down his version of the story [21]:

In November, 1957, we announced the start of studies to examine the desirability of a corporate merger with the New York Central. During 1958 these studies were advanced sufficiently for both railroads to reach a decision whether or not to propose such a merger to their stockholders.

Studies presented to your Board of Directors demonstrated that the savings in expenses through improved efficiency and lower costs for the combined properties would be approximately $100 million annually after the first few years. Studies also confirmed the expectation that service would be greatly improved. . . . It is our belief that this merger, if it could have been consummated, would have been beneficial to all parties concerned including the general public. Consequently, we of the Pennsylvania Railroad did everything possible to have the Central proceed with us in the necessary steps to make it effective ultimately.

Symes reported that "the New York Central issued a statement to the newspapers on January 7, 1959, which halted any further steps toward the merger. . . . It is self-evident that a productive corporate merger can be accomplished only when all parties are enthusiastic about it. The proposed merger with the New York Central, therefore, cannot be accomplished—at least not until there is a change of attitude on their part."

The failure of merger talks between the Pennsy and the Central did not dampen Symes's enthusiasm for eastern railroad consolidation. In 1960 he moved to take over the financially troubled Lehigh Valley Railroad. The Pennsylvania already owned 44 percent of the Lehigh Valley's common stock, but the shares had been held in a voting trust by a bank. Under Interstate Commerce rules, the Pennsylvania legally could not control the Lehigh Valley or participate in its management. Symes successfully appealed to the ICC and received permission to control the line. In 1962, through an exchange of stock, the Pennsylvania acquired 97 percent of the small eastern railroad, which connected New York City with Buffalo. In vain, Bevan opposed this acquisition. The policy did not make sense financially. He maintained that the Lehigh Valley "should have been allowed to go through bankruptcy and then, if it was necessary to have it, . . . we could have acquired control of the railroad." In contrast Symes's takeover forced the Pennsy "to advance the Lehigh Valley cash that would go to pay debts which could have been eliminated if the railroad had gone through the bankruptcy procedure." But Symes "was adamant," and between the time of takeover and the bankruptcy of the Penn Central, the Lehigh Valley required an infusion of about $18 million in cash. Symes looked at the problem from a different perspective. He saw resolution of the Lehigh Valley difficulty as one step in "an overall simplification of the eastern railroad competitive situation."

Even though his initial overture to the New York Central had been rebuffed, Symes remained determined to restructure the railway system in the East, and he still considered the merger of the Pennsylvania and the New York Central as the keystone of his policy. In this light, he encouraged the Norfolk & Western, in which the Pennsylvania held a substantial investment, to merge with another profitable Pocahontas line, the Virginian. The Virginian and Norfolk & Western stockholders approved this merger in 1959 and it became effective on December 1 of that year. Symes further approved the Norfolk & Western's plans to acquire control of two midwestern railroads, the New York, Chicago & St. Louis (the Nickel Plate) and the Wabash, a system controlled by the Pennsylvania.

All this activity was on the fringe of the Pennsylvania's main interest. The real question was what the relationship would be between major eastern railway systems: the Pennsylvania, the Baltimore & Ohio, the Chesapeake & Ohio, the New York Central, and the Norfolk & Western. Perlman's concept of the alignment between the eastern railroads was very different from Symes's. In early 1959 after Perlman terminated the Central-Pennsy merger talks, he approached Chesapeake & Ohio's two leaders, Cyrus Eaton, the chairman of the board, and Walter Tuohy, the president, and also Howard Simpson, the president of the Baltimore & Ohio, and proposed a three-way merger. Tuohy objected. He maintained the Central's weak financial position would be a drain on the prosperous C&O and prevent it from continuing its $4 annual dividend [22]. Tuohy and Eaton favored a more modest plan: the merger of the Baltimore & Ohio and the Chesapeake & Ohio. On June 13,

1960, Eaton and Tuohy took the first step toward this solution when they asked the Interstate Commerce Commission for permission for the Chesapeake & Ohio to buy control of the Baltimore & Ohio's outstanding stock.

Perlman opposed the plan. The New York Central received substantial coal traffic from the Chesapeake & Ohio, and the Central's president feared that it would be diverted to the B&O should Tuohy's plans be approved. Perlman charged that Cyrus Eaton was "scheming to bring the Central to its knees, and take it over at bankruptcy prices" [23]. Perlman attempted to influence the Interstate Commerce Commission to block C&O control of the Baltimore & Ohio and, failing in this, tried vainly to interest the Baltimore & Ohio stockholders in a counter offer, which would have allowed the New York Central, rather than the Chesapeake & Ohio, to seize control of the B&O.

In all this frantic maneuvering, it was Symes, not Perlman, who held the key. After some preliminary discussions, the managements of the Chesapeake & Ohio and the Pennsylvania agreed to sit down at a railway summit and discuss the whole problem of eastern railway mergers. The purpose of this conference was to find ways to stabilize conditions and build a healthy new group of strong railroads on the ashes of the old.

Bevan remembered the summit clearly. One bright sunny summer day in 1961 he, Symes, and Fred Carpi, the Pennsy's vice-president for sales, flew to the Chesapeake & Ohio's luxury resort hotel at White Sulphur Springs, West Virginia, to meet with Walter Tuohy and John Kusik, C&O's financial vice-president. Significantly, Perlman had not been invited. The participants at White Sulphur Springs formulated a new railway alignment in the East. Walter Tuohy opposed Symes's concept of a New York Central–Pennsylvania merger. The railway executives talked most of the morning without coming to any conclusion. When the meeting seemed almost hopelessly deadlocked, Tuohy turned to "John Kusik, on whom he relied heavily, and asked him to give his honest opinion of what should be done." Kusik answered frankly that "although in theory he agreed with Tuohy's position, unless something was done quickly, all railroads in the East would be in bankruptcy." He concluded that a Pennsylvania–New York Central merger appeared to be the only practicable answer. Tuohy, like Symes, was quick to make decisions, and during luncheon he agreed to go along with two separate mergers: the combination of the C&O with the B&O, and a union of the Pennsy with the Central. The Norfolk & Western was to remain independent of these combinations.

The White Sulphur Springs accord was momentous. Although Symes seemed to get what he wanted, the price his railroad paid was large. Since the year 1900, the Pennsy had purchased a controlling interest in several important connecting railroads. They included the Wabash, of which the Pennsy owned approximately 87 percent, and the extremely prosperous Norfolk & Western, of which the Pennsy owned 35 percent. In both cases, the Pennsy had exercised its influence to name the key officers of the connecting roads, who in turn inaugurated policies that were consistent with the Pennsylvania's goals. Furthermore, the Norfolk & Western always paid a substantial dividend on its stock. In 1961 over $12.5 million flowed into the Pennsylvania's treasury from this source. In that year, it made the difference between profit and loss for the Pennsylvania Railroad, which showed a consolidated net income of only $12,333,000. For the opportunity to merge with the New York Central, the Pennsy agreed to terminate its interest in the Wabash and the Norfolk & Western. Symes, in effect, gambled that the savings from the merger of the two largest railroads of the East would more than offset the loss of the steady income derived from the Norfolk & Western stock or that a cash flow equivalent to the old investment could be generated from reinvesting proceeds from the sale of the Norfolk & Western and Wabash securities. Since these plans would take much time to accomplish, it could be years before anyone would know whether the gamble would succeed.

Meanwhile, Symes informed Stuart Saunders, then president of the Norfolk & Western, of the White Sulphur Springs agreement. Saunders was delighted with the news, for it meant that he would be freed from the Pennsylvania's influence. This could only increase his stature in the railroad industry.

In contrast, Perlman was unhappy for he had never been convinced that a merger of his company with the Pennsy made sense. Nevertheless, he agreed to renew the negotiations for the merger of the Pennsylvania and the New York Central. Actually, the Central was in such poor financial condition that he had little choice. In the fall of 1961, three New York investment banking houses, First Boston, Morgan Stanley, and Glore-Forgan, were engaged to make independent studies to fix a fair basis of exchange of the stock of the New York Central and the Pennsylvania. When it is recognized that these were the two most complex corporate structures of any businesses in America, it is surprising that all three investment bankers arrived at the same exchange ratio: 1.3 shares of Penn Central stock for each share of New York Central, each share of the Pennsylvania to represent one share of stock in the surviving company. In 1961, James Symes emerged as the architect of the railroad merger movement in the East. Without his tireless efforts in its behalf, it would have died in the struggle between Alfred Perlman of the New York Central and Walter Tuohy of the Chesapeake & Ohio.

References

1.   Edward T. Thompson, "What Hope for the Railroads?" *Fortune,* February 1958, p. 137.

2.   Pennsylvania Railroad, *Annual Report for 1957,* p. 5.

3.   Arthur Jansen, "Railroad Outlook," *Barron's*, March 24, 1958, p. 11.

4.   Arthur Jansen, "Bucking the Trend," *Barron's*, December 16, 1957, p. 11.

5.   Arthur Jansen, "Railroad Outlook," *Barron's*, March 24, 1958, p. 11.

6.   Ibid.

7.   Arthur Jansen, "Pocahontas Prosperity," *Barron's*, September 23, 1957, p. 11.

8.   Arthur Jansen, "Railroad Outlook," *Barron's*, March 24, 1958, p. 11.

9.   Pennsylvania Railroad, *Annual Report for 1956*, p. 63; New York Central, *Annual Report for 1956* (Statistical Supplement), p. 31.

10.   Joseph T. Lambie, *From Mine to Market*, New York University Press, New York, 1954, p. x.

11.   James C. Nelson, *Railroad Transportation and Public Policy*, The Brookings Institution, Washington, D.C., 1959, p. 183.

12.   New York Central Railroad, *Annual Report for 1957*, p. 7.

13.   Richard Elliott, Jr., "Wrecked Hopes: The Story of Robert R. Young and the New York Central," *Barron's*, January 27, 1958, p. 3.

14.   Pasquale L. Marranzino, "Perlman of the Rio Grande," *Railway Progress*, August 1948, p. 26.

15.   Ibid., p. 28.

16.   Joseph Borkin, *Robert R. Young, The Populist of Wall Street*, Harper & Row, New York, 1969, p. 166.

17.   Richard Elliott, Jr., "Wrecked Hopes," *Barron's*, January 27, 1958, p. 3.

18.   Ibid., p. 17.

19.   Ibid., p. 19. *Barron's* conclusions receive support from Karl Borntrager, a senior vice president during the first part of Perlman's administration (until 1958) of the NYC. Borntrager credits a dramatic improvement in the NYC's transportation ratio in the early 1950's to the policies of former President White, and credits sharp adverse results after 1956 to Young's policy which Perlman had to administer. See Karl Borntrager, *Keeping the Railroads Running: Fifty Years on the New York Central*, Hastings House, New York, 1974, pp. 181, 189, 194–195, 246.

20.   Borkin, *Robert R. Young*, op. cit., p. 224.

21.   Pennsylvania Railroad, *Annual Report for 1958*, p. 5.

22.   Gilbert Burck, "Mating Time for the Railroads," *Fortune*, January 1961, p. 119.

23.   Ibid., p. 121.

Chapter 7
TURMOIL AT THE TOP

November 1, 1959, found the Pennsylvania Railroad's executive suite in a state of shock. On that date, Bevan arrived at his office to learn that the railroad's board of directors had elevated James M. Symes to be board chairman and had named Allen Jackson Greenough as president. The 54-year old Greenough had spent almost his entire career with the Pennsylvania. A civil engineering graduate of Schenectady's Union College, he had served in the railroad's engineering department, operating department, and at the time of his election, he was the vice-president for transportation and maintenance. Greenough had not sought the presidency and was genuinely stunned at his selection. Symes delighted in this surprise, and he spoke repeatedly of it. He seemed to be unconcerned that he had not prepared Greenough for one of the toughest positions in American railroading.

ADMINISTRATIVE SHIFTS

Early in the morning in which Greenough became president, Symes called Bevan into his office. He apparently thought that Bevan wanted the railroad's presidency. Seeking to assuage Bevan's supposed disappointment, he urged him not to be upset, since the presidency was "only an operating job." He added that Bevan "had done a magnificent job for the railroad, that [he] had more friends both within the railroad and outside than any other officer," and implied that Bevan would ultimately replace Symes as chairman of the board. Bevan answered that he was not upset and that if he "had been offered the presidency, [he] would have rejected it." He went on to say that he knew "nothing about operations" and was not qualified to supervise the operating side of the railroad.

However, he added that Symes had made a mistake in selecting Greenough. He suggested the presidency should have gone to Herman Pevler, whom he considered one of the best operating men in the country. Pevler in 1959 was vice-president in charge of the Pennsylvania's northwestern region, headquartered in Chicago, but upon Bevan's recommendation had been made president of the Pennsylvania-controlled Wabash Railroad. The Wabash had been sinking financially under the administration of Arthur Atkinson, and Bevan pointed to the quick recovery that the railroad was making under Pevler. Symes did not agree and replied that Pevler could "not stand up under strain and crises." Bevan felt Symes's reasons had no substance; to this day, Bevan believes that had Pevler assumed the Pennsylvania's presidency, the tragic events of the Penn Central might never have occurred. The meeting between Bevan and Symes ended on an unhappy note. However, since they had always been frank with one another, there was no permanent rupture in their relationship.

As it turned out, Symes had no intention of giving Greenough a free hand, as the new president quickly learned. Greenough wanted to retire James P. Newell, vice-president for operations, and wrote a memorandum to Newell requesting his resignation. Newell immediately went to Symes and handed him the memorandum. Symes promptly blocked Greenough's action, and Newell held his position on the Pennsylvania until Symes's retirement in 1963. At that time, Symes used his influence to have Newell elected the president of the Trailer Train Company, a multirailroad piggy-back operation for carrying automobiles and containers on flat cars.

In the early fall of 1963, the Executive Committee of the Pennsylvania's board of directors held a meeting in Philadelphia to select James Symes's successor as chairman of the railroad's board. Philip Clarke, a Chicago financier who was then chairman of Montgomery Ward's Executive Committee and who had served on the Pennsylvania's board of directors since 1945, told Bevan his version of the events. The evening before the meeting while traveling eastward on the Pennsy's crack Broadway Limited, Clarke sketched out a recommendation that he planned to make to the committee. Clarke wanted to nominate a new two-man team to replace Greenough and Symes. Herman Pevler would run the railroad and David Bevan would supervise all nonrailroad activities. Clarke was surprised and dismayed when he arrived at the meeting and discovered Stuart Saunders in detailed discussion with other members of the Executive Committee about the terms of a proposed contract for Saunders. Things had gone too far for Clarke to change the course of events. As a result of the meeting, James Symes retired on September 30, 1963, and Stuart Saunders succeeded him as chairman of the board the following day. David Bevan, who held the position of vice-president for finance, was given new titles: he became chairman of the Finance Committee and chief financial officer on October 1, 1963.

Philip Clarke retired from the board of directors at the mandatory age, and one day in the following year when Bevan was in Chicago, the two men met for lunch. Since Clarke no longer was a Pennsylvania director, he felt free to talk. He described how he had hoped to influence the board to place Bevan and Pevler in charge of the corporation. Having said this, he gave his guest a quizzical look and made some comment about the very good earnings which the Pennsylvania had just reported. Clarke said that he had "been around too long and had too much experience to believe that any one man in such a short time could turn a company around to the extent indicated by the reported figures." During the course of the conversation, it became apparent that Clarke had concluded that a change in accounting policy must be at the root of the improved financial showing. Clarke had been used to the policy under President Symes which had been conservative in reporting earnings. At this point, Bevan commented that Saunders, as chief executive officer, "had the right to set policy and he had chosen to maximize earnings and had the support of at least some of the directors." Bevan added that as long as he was "in charge of accounting, such a policy would never be allowed to go beyond the limits of generally accepted accounting principles."

STUART SAUNDERS AT THE NORFOLK & WESTERN

Stuart Saunders was no stranger to the Pennsylvania. A native West Virginian, he had graduated from Roanoke College in 1930 and had then taken a bachelor of law degree at Harvard. In 1939 he entered the Norfolk & Western Railway's Legal Department, where he rose gradually through the ranks to become the company's general counsel in 1951. It was then that Bevan and Saunders first met. The Pennsylvania Railroad's ownership of Norfolk & Western stock was large enough to exert considerable influence on management. When Bevan joined the Pennsylvania as vice-president in charge of finance, he was also elected to the board of directors of the Norfolk & Western, and he became chairman of the Board's Finance Committee. He held this position for 12 years, when he was forced to resign, along with the other Pennsylvania directors, as part of the price for the Interstate Commerce Commission's approval of the Norfolk & Western's acquisition of the Wabash and Nickel Plate railroads.

Bevan's relationship with Stuart Saunders during the latter's Norfolk & Western days was cordial. His first memory of Saunders was "of a pudgy individual of medium height, already balding, trudging along after Bob Smith, president of the Norfolk & Western, and usually with an armful of

Smith's papers." In 1954, Saunders was named a vice-president of the Norfolk & Western, and in 1956, he became the executive vice-president. As previously noted, the Norfolk & Western under President Robert Smith was one of the most profitable United States railroads. It was solidly financed and it continually increased its earnings and dividends. The railroad was fortunate to have an excellent vice-president of operations in Harry Wyatt. Because of the Norfolk & Western's good management and excellent earnings, the duties of its Finance Committee were not demanding. Bevan noted, however, that Saunders was "aggressively seeking to put himself in the position to succeed Bob Smith on his retirement." Saunders wanted to attend the meetings at which President Smith, James Symes, and Bevan reviewed the operations and results of the Norfolk & Western preliminary to presenting them to the full board of directors. He frequently asked Bevan that he be included in these meetings. Bevan was usually able to comply.

Saunders's opportunity came in 1958, when Smith decided to retire and Harry Wyatt, the vice-president for operations, was in poor health. This situation left Saunders as the logical choice for president, and he was elected. Bevan recalls that some members of the Norfolk & Western's board of directors were worried about Saunders's lack of operating experience. These directors wanted Smith to remain in a supervisory capacity as chairman of the board. Saunders, upset, asked Bevan to help block this move. Bevan felt that Saunders should be given a free hand and discussed the matter with Symes, who agreed. Saunders was overjoyed and warmly thanked Bevan for the efforts in his behalf.

Saunders inherited the Norfolk & Western at a peak of its prosperity. The railway's annual earnings had been increasing for a number of years and reached record levels in 1956 and 1957. The year 1958, however, did not dawn auspiciously and *Barron's,* the financial magazine, reported that the prospects were "bleak for all but a few carriers" [1]. Even though the Norfolk & Western remained highly profitable, a general economic recession caused its operating gross for January 1958 to decline by 11 percent when compared with the previous year, and its net income declined slightly more than 20 percent. At this point, it hardly seemed possible that Saunders's career could outshine that of his predecessor, Robert Smith.

Yet, fate smiled on the Norfolk & Western's new president. The financial reverses of early 1958 proved temporary, and while eastern railroads struggled to make ends meet, the Norfolk & Western set new earnings records. There was improvement in almost every measure of the railroad's performance. Its operating ratio, which had been 68.8 during the record year of 1956, fell to 65.5 in 1963, the last year of Saunders's presidency. Earnings on common stock, $7.39 in 1956, rose to $8.26 in 1963, and the railroad's dividends rose accordingly, from $3.75 in 1956 to $6 in 1963 [2].

There were solid reasons for the Norfolk & Western's outstanding performance. Strong demand for Pocahontas coal continued, and it kept Norfolk & Western trains running at near-capacity. Dieselization also improved earnings. Starting with the end of World War II, the diesel rapidly replaced steam power on America's railroads. The new locomotives were more efficient because they were cheaper to run and repair. By 1958 the Norfolk & Western stood alone among all major American railroads in its refusal to dieselize. Its president, Robert Smith, felt the railroad should curry favor with its most important shippers and burn what it hauled. Since Smith was nearing retirement, the Pennsylvania put no pressure on him to change his policy. However, James Symes made it clear to Stuart Saunders that he would be expected to dieselize the Norfolk & Western rapidly. Saunders, who had no operating experience, accepted this advice and quickly phased out steam.

Another factor was Saunders's successful merger of the Norfolk & Western and the Virginian railroads. The Virginian was the smallest, yet most profitable, of the three major railroads serving the Pocahontas coal fields. It linked West Virginia with a deep-water Atlantic port at Sewall's Point in Norfolk and its rails closely paralleled those of the Norfolk & Western. With the two systems under one management, they could move coal even more efficiently and achieve substantial savings. Saunders, with Symes's encouragement, proposed merger soon after he became president. He went to Bevan for advice on how to arrange the merger, since the Norfolk & Western's president had no experience in this area. Bevan recommended that Saunders use the services of the First Boston Corporation, a New York investment banking house. George Woods, First Boston's chairman, handled the merger skillfully. In April and May of 1959 the Virginian and Norfolk & Western stockholders approved the merger. The Interstate Commerce Commission (ICC) agreed to the union on October 8, 1959, and it became effective on December 1 of that year. Particularly significant was the ICC's statement regarding the merger. It pointed out that "so long as the public has a choice of transport, the elimination of inter-railroad rivalry cannot be equated with the elimination of competition" [3]. The Virginian merger brought Saunders much favorable national publicity. *Fortune* magazine, in a feature article on railway consolidation in 1961, commented that Saunders had put the two railroads together "adroitly." *Fortune* added that Saunders, "mindful of how people opposed his company's attempt to lease the Virginian back in 1925, . . . made sure that the communities affected were behind the idea, and he also made concessions to labor and other roads. Thus the merger was consummated a year after its inception . . . " which, as the magazine demonstrated, was a remarkably short span of time [4].

As soon as the Virginian merger was assured, Saunders started work on a larger project, the merger of the Norfolk & Western with the New York, Chicago, & St. Louis (the Nickel Plate) and the Wabash railroads. This would turn the Norfolk & Western from a modestly sized Pocahontas line into a giant system, linking Norfolk with such cities as Cleveland, Buffalo, Chicago, St. Louis, and Kansas City. James Symes, the architect of eastern railroad mergers, encouraged Saunders to carry out this union. Unlike the Virginian merger, the new proposal was enormously complex because it contemplated the takeover of the independent Nickel Plate and the Pennsylvania-controlled Wabash. Under the final arrangement, the Norfolk & Western agreed to lease the Wabash and then, at a later date, to exchange the Wabash stock held by the Pennsylvania for Norfolk & Western shares. This arrangement required the Pennsylvania to cooperate at every step. Not only did the Pennsy have to approve the Wabash lease, but it also had to agree to sell its Sandusky branch, which linked Columbus and Sandusky, Ohio, so that the Norfolk & Western could physically connect with its new acquisitions. Although this complicated merger agreement was not fully consummated until October 1964 after Stuart Saunders had left the Norfolk & Western, all the work had been completed long before his departure. In view of the increase of the Norfolk & Western's profitability under Saunders and his reputation as an adroit manager of mergers, it is not surprising that the Pennsylvania's board of directors selected him to carry out James Symes's goal of merger with the New York Central.

Although Bevan always had cordial relations with Saunders as president of the Norfolk & Western, he first became aware of another side to Saunders's personality during the negotiations over the sale of the Sandusky branch. In this affair Saunders represented the Norfolk & Western and Bevan the Pennsylvania. By mutual agreement the two railroads hired an engineering firm to place a value on the Sandusky branch. The firm arrived at a figure substantially higher than Saunders had anticipated. When the report was finished, the outside consultants sent a middle-management man to discuss the findings with the two negotiators. On hearing the figures, Saunders became angry and seemed to blame the consultants. Bevan had never before experienced this side of Saunders's personality.

Bevan also learned about Saunders, the negotiator. Because a large number of operational factors were involved, Bevan asked Herman Pevler, then the Wabash's president, to counsel him during the sessions. Saunders, however, apparently never consulted anyone but carried on the talks alone. This practice gave Bevan the tactical advantage of better information as the talks progressed. Bevan felt that Saunders was too eager to make the deal. He always seemed ready to compromise, particularly if one waited. When the two reached an impasse over price, Bevan merely broke off the negotiations. Finally, Saunders capitulated and the Pennsylvania received $27 million for the 110-mile Sandusky branch. His tendency to strive for an agreement at any price unfortunately reappeared during negotiations over the merger between the Pennsylvania and the New York Central.

Ironically, when Saunders became the Pennsylvania's chief executive, Herman Pevler moved over to the Norfolk & Western as president. Later, Bevan remembered that every time he "mentioned how much the Norfolk & Western had paid for the Sandusky branch, Pevler became very unhappy. He had to be reminded constantly that he had helped to negotiate the agreement." Bevan never admitted that the price the Norfolk & Western paid was unfair. He merely noted that Saunders was not a particularly good judge of the strength of his bargaining position. Because Symes was so strongly committed to the merger movement in the East, he probably would have agreed to a price somewhat below the $27 million the Norfolk & Western paid.

NEW ERA AT THE PENNSY

Symes, committed to the idea that the salvation of the eastern railroads lay in merger, saw Saunders as possessing exactly the right talents for the Pennsy. He was a superb politician—an active Democrat who moved easily in the highest political circles in Washington. The railroad's new chief executive was friendly with Lyndon Johnson and top Democratic congressional leaders, but he also got along well with Republicans. Symes thought that Greenough, who continued as the Pennsylvania's president, was capable of handling the operational problems while Bevan was more than adequate to cope with the finances.

Bevan had a number of attractive offers of other positions and he told Symes he was thinking of resigning. Symes urged him to stay. Saunders also applied pressure. The new chairman of the board said the financial department was the best-managed function in the entire railroad and that he needed Bevan's help. Bevan took several weeks to reach a decision to remain, and then he told Saunders, "I will do everything in my power to be the best right-hand man you could possibly have." He was proud of what he had accomplished on the Pennsylvania and he felt he could continue to be effective. Furthermore, he did not want to be regarded as a quitter just because things did not go his way.

He soon discovered, however, that his relationship with Saunders had changed. When the two worked together on the Norfolk & Western, Bevan represented the majesty and power of the Pennsylvania, which through its stock ownership held powerful influence over the Norfolk & Western. Saunders recognized this strength and was cordial toward the Pennsylvania directors. When he became the Pennsylvania's chief executive officer, the situation was reversed. He was Bevan's boss, and the Pennsylvania's chief financial officer was soon to discover exactly what that meant. For him, the discovery came accidentally. Late in 1963 after a brief absence from the Pennsylvania's Philadelphia headquarters, he read an article about the railroad written by a New York investment house. It painted a rosy picture, including a prediction of startling improvements in the Pennsylvania's operating ratio for the years 1964 and 1965. Bevan believed that prophecy to be unattainable. It had been his policy that the railroad should give investment analysts only facts but should not make forecasts. He believed that although he might make an honest estimate of future results, unforeseen circumstances could quickly change any prediction. The danger was that anyone who made decisions on the basis of such a forecast might be hurt. Bevan liked to tell the analysts that he "did not want to take their jobs away from them." He provided the data and allowed the analysts to draw their own conclusions. However, in the article Bevan read, he was certain that the information had come from the railroad.

At the next staff meeting, he brought the matter up. He quoted from the article and pointed out that someone had violated policy that had existed since he became the railroad's financial vice-president in 1951. What he did not know was that the information had come directly from Stuart Saunders. The result was an acrimonious exchange. Saunders said that since he was running the railroad, he would set the policy and that he resented Bevan's criticism of him. Bevan stated that he had no idea that Saunders had released the information and added that Saunders knew the railroad's policy about the release of forecasts, and that he should have informed the officers that he was changing it. Bevan continued, saying that the Pennsylvania's "policy in the past might not have been as spectacular as some people might want, but in the long run we would build more confidence with the public by 'understating and overperforming,' and that had been our objective." On hearing this, Saunders grew even more angry and soon terminated the staff meeting. The two men left the room together and continued the discussion in the chief executive's office. Bevan told Saunders that "in times past, when he [Saunders's] had been with the Norfolk & Western, he had sought my advice, had followed it, and apparently everything had worked out to both his satisfaction and mine." Bevan stressed that he did not expect Saunders to consult him on anything but the railroad's financial affairs. In this area, he believed that as chief financial officer, his policies should be followed except under the most unusual conditions. Later, Bevan recalled that Saunders, in an angry mood, told him that their relationship was to be "on an entirely different footing now that he was chief of the Pennsylvania as against when he had been president of the Norfolk & Western, and I, chairman of the Finance Committee." Bevan discovered that time would not improve his relationship with Stuart Saunders and their deteriorating ability to work together would have devastating consequences as the railroad faced financial difficulties in the years to come.

References

1. Arthur Jansen, "Railroad Outlook," *Barron's,* March 24, 1958, p. 11.

2. Arthur Jansen, "Pocahontal Prosperity," *Barron's,* September 23, 1957, p. 11; Norfolk & Western, *Annual Report for 1966,* p. 18.

3. Gilbert Burck, "Mating Time for the Railroads," *Fortune,* January 1961, p. 116.

4. Ibid., p. 118.

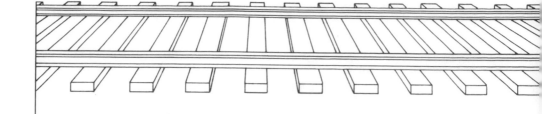

Chapter 8
COLLISION COURSE

Although it may not have been apparent at the start, David Bevan and Stuart Saunders were on a collision course. The reason was a fundamental disagreement on what was important. As the chairman of the Pennsylvania's Finance Committee and as a pillar of the nation's financial community, Bevan desired above all else to keep his company solvent. Unhappily, between 1964 and 1967 the railroad's financial fortunes began a gradual but accelerating decline. Deeply aware of the Pennsylvania's long-standing financial problems, he constantly worried about the system's long-term prospects. He attempted to communicate his fears to both Saunders and the railroad's operating men. In doing so, Bevan was the bearer of unwanted news.

Stuart Saunders had a different outlook. Hand-picked by James Symes and certain Philadelphia directors, he worked above all else to merge the Pennsylvania Railroad and the New York Central. He accepted Symes's reasoning that the union would solve many of the eastern railroads' financial problems. The board chairman's previous experience with the Pocahontas region made him optimistic. He seemed unconcerned with the details of finances and business administration. In his opinion, the money problems encountered by the Pennsylvania between 1963 and 1967 were not long-term but temporary. He worried that exposure of financial woes would derail the merger and believed that the railroad's finances should be put in the best possible light. This idea led him to change accounting policies to maximize reported earnings. At first, Saunders's steps in this direction were modest, but as the years progressed, he began to advocate what were later criticized by government investigators as questionable accounting measures [1]. Had he headed a continually expanding and profitable business, all might have gone well. It was, however, his misfortune to preside over the Pennsylvania Railroad during its darkest crisis. No amount of creative accounting could alter reality. By 1967 Bevan found himself in sharp conflict with Saunders over accounting.

While Bevan served as the railroad's chief financial officer, he created a solid, professional staff which in 1967 he considered was the finest such organization in railroading. One of his most important appointments was that of William S. Cook, a 39-year-old native of Duluth, Minnesota, who became the Pennsylvania's deputy comptroller in September 1962. In 1963, Cook moved up to the comptrollership, a position that was crucial. He supervised the railroad's accounting system, which provided the data necessary for the formulation of the income budget and cash-flow projection that Bevan regarded as the keys to financial planning. To recruit a top comptroller, Bevan searched the financial departments of some of America's best-managed large corporations. He discovered Cook at General Electric, where he was the financial manager of G.E.'s meter department in Somersworth, New Hampshire. Cook's background differed substantially from Bevan's. The new comptroller had attended a public high school in St. Paul, Minnesota, and after graduation in 1940, he had worked as a fountain and bus boy in Montgomery Ward's. After serving in World War II, Cook used his military benefits to put himself through the University of Minnesota where he earned a bachelor of business administration degree in 1948. He then went to work for General Electric, where he rose rapidly up the ladder in the fields of auditing and accounting. At the time Bevan discovered Cook, General Electric executives considered him one of their most promising young men. But they were willing to see him take a much more important and better-paid position with the Pennsylvania, since he was still 5 years away from a comparable position at G.E.

Cook brought wide experience to the railroad. With General Electric, he had served as a tax accountant, as a traveling auditor, and as the manager general and tax accountant of the company's large lamp division in Cleveland before taking the Somersworth job. In 1960, he attended General Electric's advanced management course, which exposed him to some of the most sophisticated financial thinking in American industry [2]. In Cook, Bevan recruited a competent subordinate who went on to become president of the Union Pacific.

Carl G. Sempier, who in 1966 became the manager of the Pennsylvania's business systems and information processing, was another key appointment. Sempier worked directly under Cook. Like him, Sempier had an impressive record of accomplishment in a large American business. After serving with the United States Navy as a jet fighter pilot, Sempier in 1957 joined the International Business Machines Corporation (IBM). After 2 years, he became, in Bevan's words, "manager in charge of planning and implementing data processing programs with that company." Later, Sempier worked with IBM to install the Pennsylvania's computer system. This assignment led to his becoming IBM's marketing manager of transportation in the Philadelphia area. In that role, he became totally familiar with the railroad's needs and its computer operations. Cook hired Sempier when he was "dissatisfied with the lack of forward planning demonstrated by the previous data processing manager" [3]. Sempier combined first-rate experience in the service of the leading manufacturer and installer of data processing equipment with solid knowledge of the railroad industry.

INCOME BUDGETS, CASH FLOW, AND THE CLASH OVER CAPITAL EXPENDITURES

One of Bevan's major tasks was to raise money for the Pennsylvania Railroad. To do so, he needed accurate knowledge of his corporation's income as well as of its expenses. Since joining the Pennsylvania in 1951, he had attempted to recruit to his accounting force personnel familiar with the latest business management techniques. He used the data supplied by the accounting department, which was under William Cook's supervision, to construct his major analytical tool—the income budget. The new managerial techniques, particularly the control devices program, which Bevan had Peat, Marwick, Mitchell & Company devise for the railroad in 1959, were crucial in building an accurate income budget. It will be recalled that the railroad had been divided into regions. On the managerial staff of each of these regions Peat, Marwick placed a comptroller who implemented a new accounting system that abandoned the Interstate Commerce Commission (ICC) concepts in favor of responsibility reporting.

Building the annual income budget started with the individual regions. Each manager forecast expenses for each of his divisions. He forwarded these estimates to the railroad's Philadelphia headquarters, where they were consolidated. There top management had a budget committee composed of the principal officers, the chairman of the board, the president, the chairman of the Finance Committee, and the vice-presidents for sales (traffic) and operations. Normally, a number of others, such as the comptroller and deputies to the principal officers, also took part in the Budget Committee meetings. This committee had a revenue-estimating subcommittee that reported to it.

The income budget had several important sections. It began with the operations forecast, which included the estimated income from carrying passengers, mail, express, and freight. Subtracted from this total projected income were the budget expenses forecast for transportation (wages for crew, costs of fuel and other supplies, and the like) and maintenance costs for such things as track, bridges, and buildings. After the railroad's net operating income was established (by subtracting operating expenses from operating revenues), estimates were made by various departments of interest charges, leasing costs, the repayment of debt due in that year. These charges, subtracted from the operating income, determined the railroad's projected cash flow. Furthermore, depreciation for equipment and physical plant had to be calculated. Bevan added these estimates back to "cash flow."

There was another vital part to the system. Figures provided to the accounting department from the computers enabled top management to check weekly and to determine whether the forecasts were proving accurate. This up-to-date information was crucial in helping management to plan expenditures.

Once a sound income budget and cash-flow estimate had been established, the Budget Committee could advise the railroad on its capital budget. The railroad developed its capital budget in much the same way as it worked out the income budget. It resulted from requests made by the regional vice-presidents, which were in turn consolidated at the Pennsy's Philadelphia headquarters. The capital budget had two main categories: the first dealt with equipment; the second concerned physical improvements. The requests for new capital expenditures were always larger than the resources available. The chief financial officer's responsibility was to find enough money to support necessary capital expenditures and also to aid management in determining which capital expenditures would produce the highest return on investment.

Capital expenditures could be financed by plowing earnings back into the system, by the use of depreciation cash, and by the sale of new securities. In the last instance, the options were strictly limited. Wall Street was not receptive to the stock of almost any company in the railroad industry. Therefore, if new money were to be attracted into the company, it would have to be through the creation of additional debt through either the sale of bonds or equipment trust obligations. Each time funds were raised via the creation of new debt, it placed long-term interest charges on the railroad. One of the major tasks was to keep new capital expenditures at a point where operating income could safely carry interest charges and debt maturities. Railroad earnings had to be able to carry debt service. Any other course would push the Pennsylvania system into slow liquidation or move it toward bankruptcy.

From 1951 through 1964, Bevan had some success in managing the railroad's financial affairs. He even managed to reduce the railroad's overall debt. In 1952, the Pennsylvania's total debt, including bonds, equipment obligations, and lease obligations, totaled $1,250,000,000. By December 31, 1964, this total had been reduced to $1,025,000,000, a decrease of 18 percent [4]. This significant reduction in the Pennsylvania's debt, with its corresponding lessening of interest charges, had not eliminated capital spending. Between 1955 and 1964, the Pennsylvania had poured more than

$635 million into new equipment and improvements to physical plant. During Symes's regime, top management took Bevan's advice and kept capital expenditures to amounts that could be safely financed through the use of depreciation cash, the reinvestment of retained earnings, and a conservative amount of outside financing. In addition, Bevan carefully built up the investments of the railroad's wholly owned subsidiary, the Pennsylvania Company, whose dividends became vital in carrying the railroad through lean years.

Starting in 1964, the financial picture began to change drastically. A vast capital improvement program was partially responsible. For example, in the 10 years between 1956 and 1965, the Pennsy's total capital budget had been $875 million, or $87.5 million per year. However, for 1964 through 1966, the railroad's capital expenditures were $480 million, an average of $160 million per year [5]. Bevan reluctantly supported larger capital expenditures when they began in 1964. He reasoned that because the railroad's debt had consistently decreased since 1951, it could carry a modest increase. In 1965, however, when railroad earnings did not rise dramatically and the capital budget proposals remained at a high level, Bevan began to worry.

He expressed concern in a series of letters to Stuart Saunders that spelled out the consequences. In December 1965, he wrote that as a member of the Budget Committee for the years 1964 and 1965, he "went along with an extremely high capital budget on the basis that the operating department of the railroad would realize a profit of $50 million each year." He then noted that these projections had fallen short by $21 million in 1964 and $22 million in 1965, and that as a result of capital expenditures for those 2 years, there had been a "net increase in system debt of approximately $140 million and an increase in interest charges on an annual basis of $9.3 million" [6]. Bevan warned that the new equipment program represented a radical financial departure. Whereas, previously, depreciation cash was used to meet maturing equipment obligations, these funds would no longer suffice. Equipment maturities were reaching a high level. On an annual basis, they amounted to $52 million in 1966, compared with equipment depreciation of $34.5 million, a deficit of almost $18 million. In fact, this imbalance was so large that even if the railroad's entire depreciation for both equipment and physical plant were applied to the equipment maturities alone, there would be virtually no excess cash flow. But worst of all, the railroad had seemed unable "to realize any return on the added investment."

Bevan pinpointed serious shortcomings in Pennsylvania's capital program. He noted that many new projects, such as the rebuilding of Penn Station in conjunction with the utilization of the air rights in the Madison Square Garden program, incurred large overruns. In 1965 this overrun was more than $800,000 [7]. Equally important, he discovered that the operating department proposed capital investments without carefully calculating the actual return. Bevan wrote Saunders that he had been impressed with the principles enunciated at a New York Central budget meeting that he had attended. He commented that "they will not entertain capital expenditures other than for safety where the labor savings are less than 20 percent, and if labor only is involved, less than 30 percent after consideration of attrition payments" [8]. Bevan recommended that similar rigorous standards be adopted by the Pennsylvania's operating department. He took particular aim at its 5-year equipment plan for freight cars. Under this proposal, between 1966 and 1970 the railroad would add a total of 36,400 new cars. While approving of such advance planning, he thought it lacked sophistication, charging that the operating department's historic depreciation standard of 2.07 percent a year was unrealistic. Bevan knew that this was "not a true measure of the actual depreciation" since it assumed that cars would last 45 years. He wrote, "There is no question that to the extent we use such a rate, it will be more than offset by an increase in estimated repair expenses." However, he added, "I do not believe there is anyone who sincerely believes that the economic life of . . . cars is approximately 45 years." In Bevan's opinion, a 5 percent depreciation rate would put the Pennsylvania in line with other railroads and give a better example of the true equipment costs. Furthermore, he said, the equipment plan did not consider the effects of "greater utilization of equipment through control of our computer system."

Bevan wanted the operating department to completely reformulate its program. The railroad, he argued, was "similar to an industrial manufacturing company. Our product is revenue ton miles. Our fleet should be broken down by classes of equipment and a study should be made in the case of each class as to how many revenue ton miles in the past these cars have been capable of producing and allowing a factor for increased efficiency." Bevan hoped for better car utilization each year and insisted that plans should be made to accomplish that goal. Another weakness in the proposal was that it dealt "only with the number of cars and gives no recognition to increased capacity." Bevan asserted that if the railroad developed its requirements according to the guidelines he had outlined, it would have a better gauge of its "manufacturing efficiency" and that it could "see which classes of cars are showing increases in the production of ton miles and which are showing decreases" [9].

In addition to his hard-hitting analysis of the railroad's capital spending, Bevan criticized the accounting behavior of a number of division heads. Since Stuart Saunders had assumed the Pennsylvania's leadership, he had stressed increased earnings. Several division executives apparently were trying to curry his favor by reporting earnings through accounting manipulation. In order to make earnings look better, they did not report the consumption of inventories at the time they were used. This failure to charge inventory artificially inflated results and allowed the reporting of better than actual earnings. Ultimately, systemwide audits detected these tactics; the result was sudden expense overruns. Bevan told Saunders that this practice "indicates a very serious situation." The chief financial officer pointed out that accounting irregularities had been responsible for Yale Express's troubles, a situation that had recently been analyzed in *Forbes* magazine. Bevan recommended that the *Forbes* article be made "required reading for every member of the Budget Committee and for each of the regional managers." He concluded that "this situation cannot be repeated in the future and to the extent that responsibility can be pinpointed at this time, I think that action should be taken against the personnel involved" [10].

In the last half of 1966, a crisis arose over the proposed 1967 budget. The operating department requested capital expenditures of $232 million, which included $175 million for equipment [11]. Even Saunders felt the request was too high and told the department to reduce the equipment budget to $140 million. This figure did not satisfy Bevan, who maintained that the railroad could not afford more than $85 million [12]. He cited its steadily worsening financial position. In the 3-year period between 1964 and 1966, he noted, the debt applicable to rail operations had increased by $240 million, which had raised the railroad's interest charges and depreciation by $17.5 million annually. For Bevan, the railroad had "reached a very serious danger point with respect to [its] ability to carry on new financing" [13]. He worried particularly about the equipment obligations falling due. In 1967, the railroad's maturities would amount to approximately $56 million, compared with an equipment depreciation charge of $37 million. The Pennsylvania Railroad's road depreciation was $19 million, and Bevan estimated that the company's entire depreciation would be needed to meet its 1967 equipment maturities. He explained to Saunders that this endangered the railroad's credit rating because "the usual rule-of-thumb formula used by analysts of the railroad industry is that when equipment depreciation equals equipment maturities, you are fairly well in balance, but anything above this is a danger signal" [14]. On September 23, 1966, he warned Saunders that when Moody's bond rating service saw the great disparity between the Pennsy's equipment depreciation and its equipment maturities, it would drop Pennsy's rating from A to Baa. "This would be very bad on two counts," Bevan stated. First, "it would severely restrict the size of the market" in which the railroad could sell its equipment certificates because, as a matter of policy or for legal reasons, many buyers could not or would not buy obligations with less than an A rating. Second, a lower rating would cost the railroad at least an additional percentage point in interest charges [15].

Throughout the fall of 1966, the Pennsylvania's top management heatedly debated the capital budget. David Smucker, the vice-president for operations, and Henry Large, the vice-president for traffic, strongly defended the proposal for an equipment budget in excess of $120 million, while Bevan insisted that this should be cut to $85 million. Stuart Saunders was slow to make up his mind. On October 25, the day after a particularly hot budget discussion, Bevan wrote a strong letter to Saunders in favor of containing capital costs and lashing out at the operating department. He not only criticized the equipment budget, but he came down hard on expense overruns, especially those connected with the development of high-speed passenger service in the northeast corridor between Washington and New York [16]. This project, supported by Congress and President Johnson, had started in 1965. Saunders enthusiastically backed high-speed trains for the northeast corridor—partially for political reasons. He worried that a refusal to cooperate with the federal government could have an adverse, if not a fatal, effect on the Pennsylvania–New York Central merger. Therefore, beginning in 1965, Saunders agreed on a joint venture in which the Pennsylvania was to spend $10 million to upgrade its roadbed and the federal government would provide a like amount for experimental trains. Costs on the northeast corridor project quickly escalated. Soon the railroad increased its commitment by $23 million, and in late 1966 further expenses loomed. Bevan pointed out that an initial commitment of $10 million had ballooned to between $45 and $50 million. He wanted an absolute ceiling on these expenditures, and he chided both Saunders and the operating department on having made an agreement that would not only prove unprofitable but that also failed to protect the railroad, since the government did not participate in the increased costs [17].

Saunders disagreed. He thought that Bevan was too pessimistic and that the merger would brighten the railroad's financial picture. He also apparently felt Bevan's conservative accounting practices would hamper the merger by making the Pennsylvania look bad. At this time, four operating men, Allen J. Greenough, the Pennsy's president, David Smucker, vice-president for operations, Henry Large, vice-president for traffic, and A. Paul Funkhouser, vice-president for coal and ore traffic, made a strongly worded denunciation of Bevan's position. In a memorandum to Saunders, they asserted that Bevan had raised a "number of matters, which have no relation to the 1967 capital budget and are apparently made solely for the purpose of being critical" [18]. The operating men pleaded for continuing large capital expenditures. They minimized the impact of debt on the railroad, arguing that capital obligations were "only one of many factors, such as the passenger burden, strikes, storms, and taxes affecting" the railroad's ability "to carry gross through to net in any particular year." Taking an optimistic view, the four argued:

The increases in net income from year to year ever since this company in 1963 deliberately began to revitalize and reequip itself to exploit its natural advantages have resulted from increased gross and reduced operating costs, which have more than overcome increased wages, depreciation, and interest charges.

Inevitably, we will continue to be faced with year-to-year increases in wage rates which for 1967 can be expected to amount to nearly $30 million. Such increased costs can best be met through a continuation of the strong, positive policies that have revitalized the company and succeeded during the past few years. There is no need [the operating men argued] to spell out the disadvantages of a static period, or one designed to go forward on a much more modest basis. All that one needs is to examine the results for the period 1953 to 1963, during which the debt reduction policies of the financial department overrode all other considerations and during which period of relative national prosperity, the fortunes of the company reached an all-time low, culminating in a net deficit for the 4 years 1959 to 1962, inclusive.

The operating men said that the allegedly better showing of the railroad since 1963 could "be attributed largely to the expanded capital improvement program," not to the unprecedented national prosperity that accompanied America's growing involvement in the Vietnam war. Finally, they wrote:

For some time the assets of our operating properties have been used as a cash source for large-scale diversification programs. We support this policy so long as the cash so diverted does not jeopardize the Pennsylvania Railroad. . . . We believe that the assets of the consolidated system should be regarded as indivisible, freely interchangeable, and available for optimizing the overall return on the entire enterprise.

Bevan reacted strongly to the challenge. He discussed it with an unsympathetic Saunders, who advised his chief financial officer to take some tranquilizer pills in order to keep his blood pressure down while reading the memorandum [19]. Bevan did not let the matter rest. He wrote Saunders charging that the operating men had been put up to the attack by the vice president, Basil Cole, who had actually written the paper, which was " 'rough' in words, but pathetically weak in substance." Cole, Bevan stated, "was either careless of the facts or very ignorant of them." The attack on diversification particularly annoyed Bevan, who pounced on the statement that "the assets of our operating properties have been used as a cash source for large-scale diversification programs." This, he insisted, was "manifestly incorrect." He asserted that "anyone with the most meager knowledge of our operations knows that the Pennsylvania Company in effect has subsidized the operations of the railroad for many years and this fact has been pointed out by you [Saunders] in a great many speeches" [20].

Saunders replied by accusing Bevan of "lack of respect" for his fellow officers. "I disagree," he said, "with your characterization that [the operating men's] memorandum is 'pathetically weak in substance.' On the contrary, I found it filled with substance." He also denied that the attack was the "product of one mind" and insisted that all four senior officers "participated in its preparation and subscribe unequivocally to the statements contained therein" [21].

This fracas marked the beginning of what was to become a very serious rift between Stuart Saunders and David Bevan. For Bevan, much of the debate missed the vital point that the increased debt caused by the proposed capital expenditures would raise interest charges beyond the railroad's ability to carry them. None of the operating men challenged Bevan's arithmetic, nor did they suggest how such expenditures could be financed without undermining the railroad's viability. In addition, Bevan felt the operating men did not appreciate the good record, considering the system's meager resources, made by the Pennsylvania in the area of capital expenditure.

Later, Alfred Perlman of the New York Central also claimed that the Pennsylvania had made a poor showing in its capital budgets. He liked to assert that the New York Central had outspent the Pennsy and thus came into the Penn Central in better shape. The record does not support Perlman. In 1967, Bevan summarized the capital expenditures for the Pennsylvania and the Central between 1945 and 1966 (see Appendix B, Table B-3). His summary covered four periods: postwar (1946–1966), 10 years (1957–1966), 5 years (1962–1966), and 3 years (1964–1966). In each period the Pennsylvania's capital expenditures outclassed the Central's in the areas of both road and equipment budgets. On the average, the Pennsylvania, although only 25 percent larger than the Central, outspent its rival by a ratio of nearly 2 to 1. For example, in the 5 years from 1962 through 1966, the Pennsy's average annual capital expenditures were $137.57 million, compared with $72.96 million for the Central. In the last 3 years analyzed (1964–1966), Bevan's road outspent Perlman's by an annual average of $180.84 million to $95.02 million. The record indicates that the Pennsy's capital expenditures for the railroad grew most sharply during the diversification program. In fact, the Pennsylvania's capital expenditures of $244.24 million in 1965 substantially exceeded the $209 million of cash used in the railroad's entire diversification program (see Appendix B, Table B-1).

THE CONFLICT OVER ACCOUNTING

In 1967 as the merger between the Pennsylvania and the New York Central grew near, Bevan described Stuart Saunders's concern with the railroad's poor earning record as an "obsession." Saunders's anxiety led him to use every means at his command to boost the railroad's reported earnings. On the other hand, Bevan's main worry was about cash flow, but Saunders appeared to be unmoved by the problem. To put it simply, the cash generated by the railroad's operations did not provide the funds needed to sustain these operations, pay fixed charges, and support the capital improvement programs. The railroad was becoming increasingly dependent upon the dividends from its wholly owned subsidiary, the Pennsylvania Company and, more important, upon borrowing in a money market that was growing ever tighter.

Bevan came to realize that Saunders's main worry was not cash flow but reported earnings. When these lagged behind his expectations, Saunders desired to boost the earnings record by eliminating charges against the railroad's income. There were several methods to accomplish this. One was to delay reporting the use of physical inventories in the railroad's repair and maintenance. If such charges could be postponed, the income record would be temporarily inflated. A second technique was to reduce the reserves that the railroad was required to carry for its self-insurance program for personal injuries, loss, and damage. Another method was to place a worthless asset on the books. All these and similar ideas had one thing in common. They produced no real income for the railroad; they merely delayed the day of reckoning. Besides, all were unacceptable accounting practices. Saunders seemed not to worry. Apparently he hoped the general confusion surrounding the forthcoming Pennsylvania–New York Central merger would mask these actions. He talked incessantly about the need to increase the Pennsylvania's reported income, and by the middle of 1967 Bevan noted that the pressure on his subordinates to produce results had become extreme. Those most vulnerable to his pressure were officials, such as regional managers and operating people, who had little or no knowledge of the legalities of accounting and reporting. By contrast, Bevan and his comptroller, Cook, were well-versed in accounting and reporting and they were determined to prevent illegal actions.

An example of Saunders's pressure was an attempt by A. Paul Funkhouser to aid him in increasing reported income. Funkhouser had come with Saunders to the Pennsylvania from the Norfolk & Western. He had become the Pennsylvania's vice-president for coal and ore traffic, and he discovered a dispute between the Pennsy and the New York Central over the prorating of revenues from coal traffic. In mid-June 1967, the Pennsylvania claimed it was due roughly $335,000. Funkhouser discussed this claim with Cook, who said it could not be placed on the railroad's books as an asset until the dispute was settled. Funkhouser did not agree. On June 20, he took the matter over Cook's head to Saunders by writing a confidential memorandum suggesting that the railroad place $335,000 of income on its books. He concluded, "It seems to me there should be some way to put this in our second-quarter revenues even if it had to be deleted at some later date" [22]. When Cook discovered Funkhouser's action, he was deeply angered. He complained to his boss, David Bevan. Cook sent him a copy of Funkhouser's memorandum, observing that the vice-president for coal and ore traffic had urged that even though the dispute has not been resolved and "even though we probably have no intention of taking this matter to court, we arbitrarily put this in second-quarter revenue even with the strong possibility that it will have to be deleted some time in the future." Cook's covering memo concluded, "As far as I'm concerned, this is placing a worthless asset on the books and creating imaginary income" [23]. Bevan shared Cook's views and insisted to Saunders that it would be wrong to place this disputed income on the books of the railroad until the matter had been settled, and he refused to allow it.

Saunders's tactics became very clear at the railroad's budget meetings. A short time after the Funkhouser incident, he proposed that the Pennsylvania should deliberately underestimate its per diem account (that is, its payments owed to other railroads for the use of their freight cars) until it received a rate increase, which would boost the income account. Bevan ignored this suggestion, but after the meeting, one of his subordinates in accounting, Tom Schaekel, approached him "very much disturbed and shocked and asked" if Saunders "meant this," since Bevan had specified that there was not to be any juggling in the per diem account. Bevan instructed him "to ignore the entire thing . . . and accrue per diem as accurately as possible regardless of anyone" [24].

Saunders's tactics deeply worried Bevan, who started to reflect on past events. He remembered the previous year when he had chastised some of the railroad's regional managers for deliberately understating the utilization of inventories. Then, too, Philip Clarke's admonition not to trust Stuart Saunders kept echoing in Bevan's mind. In order to protect himself and his staff, he decided to keep a diary that would record Saunders's attempts to force accounting irregularities. He also began systematically to collect letters and other documentary evidence that would support his diary. He did this without Saunders's knowledge, and the diary remained confidential until the Penn Central's collapse in 1970. Much of the following story is based on that diary, together with letters and other material in the files of the Pennsylvania Railroad. Later testimony before the SEC investigation supported Bevan's diary. [25].

In August 1967, as the accounts for the railroad's third quarter were being made up, Saunders again applied pressure to force the accounting department to inflate the railroad's earnings. Bevan discovered this on October 22 when he and Saunders were flying from New York to Philadelphia. Saunders stated that he had reviewed the third-quarter earnings and felt that it was necessary to "find an additional $5 million of revenues." Although he did not explicitly say so, Bevan feared that Saunders expected him to achieve this revenue by juggling the clearing account, that is, the account by which the Pennsylvania Railroad determined the amount it had coming from other railroads with which it did a joint business. Bevan did not reply and took no action. Later, he discovered that Saunders was trying to influence others to find $5 million. Immediately prior to lunch on Friday, August 25, one of

Bevan's subordinates, Fred Sass, came in to discuss an urgent matter. It developed that Saunders had called Sass and told him that "we had to find $5 million of additional revenues in the third quarter" [26]. Bevan expressed surprise because Sass was not in accounting but in forecasting. Bevan suggested that he ignore the incident.

Saunders applied still further pressure at a budget meeting on August 30. At that time, Bevan told him that a recent audit had indicated a deficit of $4 million in the railroad's inventory. He went on to explain that this deficit "meant that our inventories were currently overstated by $4 million and that our operating expenses for the year to date were understated by $4 million through failure to charge out the missing inventory and, therefore, our profit picture was $4 million worse than so far reported" [27]. Saunders, alarmed, stated that "we could not afford to have a charge of this magnitude made against income," and he asked his vice-president for operations, David Smucker, to investigate. Bevan noted in his diary that he had no idea what Smucker "can produce other than if the figures mentioned should contain some error or errors. However, in view of the fact that I was not sure whether the figures were firm or preliminary, I did not press the matter nor did [Smucker] ask what he was to look into."

The problem came to a major crisis at the budget meeting on Monday, November 6. William Cook, the comptroller, who usually attended these meetings, was out of town and his place was taken by a subordinate. Among those attending were Bevan, Saunders and his administrative assistant Basil Cole, Paul Funkhouser, David Smucker, and Henry Large. The issue was the earnings to be posted for the fourth and final quarter. Bevan indicated that there would be a $3-million deficit as a result of inventory shortages and also that it was necessary to increase by $2.1 million the reserve requirements for injuries to persons and for property loss and damages. This meant a total of $5.1 million to be charged against fourth-quarter earnings. Saunders had known about these items earlier and had argued that they should be postponed from the third to the fourth quarter when, he alleged, the railroad's income would improve. At this meeting, however, Bevan's diary indicates that Saunders objected to "loading everything against the fourth quarter. He said some people did not seem to realize that we were going to merge with the New York Central and whether or not we were under-accrued by several millions of dollars at the time would never be known and would make no difference." Bevan explained that the inventory deficit "represented an overstatement of earnings and had to be taken care of this year." Saunders then complained about the requirements for injuries to persons and property loss and damage. He said, "These are estimates at best and there is no reason to catch up in the fourth quarter." Bevan replied that the railroad closed its books at the end of the year and that it had to have its reserves correct at that time. Saunders, becoming angry, said, "I and nobody else will decide what we are going to charge in this connection." Bevan promptly told him, "The accounting department has reported the deficiencies. They have been reviewed by Cook and then by me." He later recalled saying that "if Saunders tried to avoid the required charges, neither Cook nor I will certify any statement made to the Interstate Commerce Commission, since this would constitute a fraud. If Saunders were forced to certify the statements, the ICC would immediately raise questions and Saunders would be on his own." The budget meeting closed on a note of tension and Bevan went off to lunch.

When Bevan returned to his office, Basil Cole, Saunders's right-hand man, was waiting. Bevan remembers that Cole expressed "great regret that there had been much hot and acrimonious disagreements at the budget meeting that morning." He argued that Saunders's viewpoint should receive every consideration because the merger was in danger. Could not Bevan see his way clear to go along with Saunders? Cole asked. He repeated the argument that "the merger would occur shortly, figures would be consolidated, and no one would know the difference." Bevan voiced surprise that Cole, as a lawyer, did not see the danger of his suggestion. The chief financial officer then cited the troubles arising in the Yale Express and the Westec cases, where company officials had been charged with reporting inflated earnings [28]. Bevan told Cole, "Neither Cook nor I [are] going to be involved in any such problems on the Pennsylvania, either directly or indirectly." He then went over the entire matter thoroughly for about a half-hour, and Cole, when he left, thanked him graciously. Cole added that "he had not really understood the situation and that he appreciated" Bevan's cooperation in explaining it.

The very next day, November 7, Basil Cole went to see Bevan's subordinate, William Cook, the comptroller. Cook recorded the incident in a memorandum. Cole told him that "Mr. Saunders wanted to see what could be done to avoid the booking of the $3 million inventory deficit in the fourth quarter of 1967." Cook "explained to Mr. Cole that nothing could be done—that the inventory was taken at the end of June and that the results had been constantly reviewed by the auditors and other accounting personnel and that this item would have to be booked in 1967." Cole argued that he "did not see where it would hurt anything to let this go until some time next year after the merger," and Cook retorted that Cole was "suggesting the same type of thing that occurred at Yale Express and Westec, which was a criminal offense and that [he] would not be a party to it" [29].

The next morning Cook told Bevan of Cole's visit. Cook had fire in his eyes. He said that he had heard about the acrimonious budget meeting on November 6, and that he would have absolutely nothing to do with what Cole and Saunders were suggesting. Bevan noted that he told Cook his position was correct and that "nobody in our department should have anything to do with it, and that for his protection . . . he should write a memorandum, put it in the file," and give Bevan a copy. Bevan suggested that the memorandum should state exactly what Cole had asked him to do. When Bevan received the memorandum, he sent for Cole, told him to sit down, and showed him a copy of Cook's statement. He then explained that at the previous meeting, he had given Cole the benefit of the doubt. Now he knew that Cole "had deliberately and surreptitiously asked Cook to manipulate the figures in the same way" that had been suggested in the previous meeting with Bevan. The chief financial officer added that "there was no longer any lingering question in [his] mind that [Cole] was willing to do anything Saunders wanted [and] that he was intellectually dishonest." Bevan told Saunders's aide that from that day forward, regardless of the fact that Cole "was on Saunders' staff, if he ever came into my department and asked anyone to perform an improper or illegal act, I would go directly to the board of directors and request his resignation." He added that in such a circumstance, if the resignation was not forthcoming, he himself "would resign on the spot."

As Cole left the interview, he met William Gerstnecker, who noted that he seemed badly shaken. Gerstnecker then came in to ask Bevan what had happened, volunteering that perhaps Bevan had been "too hard on Cole." Bevan did not go into detail, but he explained in general what had occurred and that, under the circumstances, "it would be impossible to be too hard on an individual when he had already had one warning."

Bevan never discussed his conflict with Cole directly with Saunders, but it soon became evident that Saunders must have known all. On Thursday, November 9, he telephoned Bevan to say that he was leaving for California and that "in his absence, he did not want any letters written about the accounting questions he raised at the budget meeting on Monday, the 6th of November" [30]. Bevan said he did not understand what Saunders meant, as he "did not know why or who would be writing letters dealing with that subject." Saunders hesitated, then said he really meant he did not want any written memoranda going back and forth between officers. Then, in a more conciliatory vein, he added that he wanted to sit down with Cook and Bevan and discuss the budget controversy. He reiterated that everything possible had to be done in order to improve the fourth-quarter earnings. Bevan said he understood but added that "the real problem was that the operating people were failing to meet the budget, particularly in the western region." Saunders ended the conversation by saying he would talk the matter over with Greenough. He ceased trying to force Bevan and Cook to alter accounting reports for the Pennsylvania Railroad's fourth quarter of 1967.

For Bevan, the budget contretemps of November 6 and its aftermath were the turning point. Basil Cole became Bevan's dedicated enemy. Saunders never forgave Bevan for his lack of support in what the Pennsy's chief executive thought was a real crisis. He could not fire his chief financial officer.

Bevan's reputation on Wall Street was good and a public conflict with him might fatally damage the Pennsylvania Railroad's financial reputation and thus subvert the merger. Saunders's only recourse was to pull back and patch things up until later. Bevan's position was different. He and Cook had won their argument. He hoped that Saunders had learned a lesson. He did not realize that never again would he have a cordial relationship with Saunders and that things would go from bad to worse.

For the Pennsylvania Railroad and its coming merger with the New York Central, the budget arguments had an even greater significance. Not only did they open up an irreconcilable gulf between two of the Pennsylvania's top officers, but they indicated that the system's chairman did not appreciate the fragile nature of his corporation's financial position. Worse yet, Stuart Saunders's growing estrangement from Bevan kept him from accepting his chief financial officer's advice during the crucial early months of the merged Penn Central's history while there was still time to take the steps that possibly might have avoided bankruptcy.

References

1.   See *The Financial Collapse of the Penn Central Company*, a Staff Report of the Securities and Exchange Commission to the [House of Representatives] Special Sub-Committee on Investigations, Hon. Harley O. Staggers, Chairman, Government Printing Office, Washington, D.C., August 1972, pp. 33–42.

2.   Bevan Papers, data on Cook from Cook's employment record and Cook to Bevan, June 21, 1962.

3.   W. S. Cook to Bevan, October 5, 1967.

4.   Pennsylvania Railroad, *Annual Report for 1964*, p. 7.

5.   Bevan to Saunders, August 31, 1966.

6.   Bevan to Saunders, December 17, 1965.

7.   Bevan to Saunders, October 22, 1965.

8.   Ibid.

9.   Ibid.

10.   Bevan to Saunders, December 17, 1965.

11.   Bevan to Saunders, August 31, 1966.

12.   Bevan to Saunders, December 8, 1966.

13.   Bevan to Saunders, October 25, 1966.

14.   Bevan to Saunders, August 31, 1966.

15.   Bevan to Saunders, September 23, 1966.

16.   Bevan to Saunders, October 25, 1966.

17.   Ibid., and Bevan to Saunders, October 21, 1966.

18. Greenough, Smucker, Large, and Funkhouser to Saunders, December 22, 1966.

19. Bevan to Saunders, December 28, 1966.

20. Ibid.

21. Saunders to Bevan, January 16, 1967.

22. A. Paul Funkhouser to Saunders, June 20, 1967.

23. Cook to Bevan, June 21, 1967.

24. David Bevan kept a diary outlining accounting and other irregularities at the Pennsylvania and Penn Central in 1967 and 1968. The entire diary was published in *The Financial Collapse of the Penn Central Company,* a Staff Report of the Securities and Exchange Commission to the [House of Representatives] Special Sub-Committee on Investigations, Hon. Harley O. Staggers, Chairman, Government Printing Office, Washington, D.C., August 1972, pp. 77–82. My account of Saunder's accounting policies is largely pieced together from letters Bevan wrote to Saunders at the time of the incidents. It also makes use of the Bevan diary, admittedly a self-serving document. Nevertheless, this diary has stood the test of the SEC investigators, who were very unfriendly to Bevan. These investigators remarked, *"Typical of the intense pressures to which the accounting department was subjected in the interests of reporting higher profits are those described by Bevan in the diary which he kept in 1967 and 1968, assertedly for his own protection. . . . While Bevan's credibility on some subjects, as illustrated elsewhere in this report, is open to serious question, and while he may have had his own personal reasons for keeping this permanent record of Saunders' improper activities at the same time that he was concealing so many of his own, the entries are supported by the testimony of Cook, who was the comptroller during most of the period covered by the diary. The testimony of other witnesses also support this document, although on occasion they question the tone (rather that the substance) of some of the entries"* (p. 36). The Staff Report on the Securities and Exchange Commission strongly supports the evidence in Bevan's correspondence, and the testimony of witnesses such as Cook and others before the SEC confirm the account I have constructed for this book. (See the SEC report, especially pp. 33–42.)

25. Ibid.

26. Ibid., p. 78.

27. Ibid., p. 79.

28. W. S. Cook clipped and sent to Bevan the *Wall Street Journal* articles telling of management's inflation of reported income at Westec, with the appropriate parts underlined. See copies of *The Wall Street Journal* for November 9, 10, and 15, 1967, with Cook's notations in the Bevan Papers.

29. W. S. Cook, A Memorandum of File, November 9, 1967.

30. This and the following quotations are from Bevan's diary as printed in the SEC Staff Report, p. 80.

Chapter 9
MERGING INTO CHAOS

The long-awaited merger of the New York Central with the Pennsylvania occurred on February 1, 1968. The idea had been conceived by James Symes and carried through by Stuart Saunders. David Bevan never shared the high hopes of its proponents. Even some of his most severe critics admitted that he had a clear view of a merged company's problems. "In retrospect," wrote Joseph R. Daughen and Peter Binzen in their *Wreck of the Penn Central,* "the witness whose 1962 view of this merger seems most insightful was the official whom some now blame for the Penn Central's woes—David C. Bevan" [1]. Daughen and Binzen quoted with approval Bevan's testimony concerning the merger before the Interstate Commerce Commission (ICC) in 1962. They pointed out that Bevan had "warned the ICC of the PRR's [Pennsylvania Railroad's] tremendous debt. More than $1 billion in debt would mature by 1982, he said." Bevan's testimony could have stirred little enthusiasm for the project. " 'I don't see much in the way of profits, certainly in the first 5 years,' he said, 'and if they [the PRR and the Central] go the way they are going, there won't be any profits. . . . I am just increasingly worried about the traffic trend more than anything else . . . we are going down a very tough shakedown period. . . . With the ultimate savings to be realized [from the merger], it is going to be quite a while before we get them, because we will have a great many expenses prior thereto. . . .' " Everything in the years following the 1962 testimony reinforced this judgment.

Bevan's only hope was for the creation of an administrative structure that would provide the data that the railroad's top management needed to make intelligent decisions. This requirement meant that the new Penn Central had to adopt the sophisticated reporting and accounting procedures that he had laboriously installed on the old Pennsylvania under the administration of James Symes.

TWO RAILROADS, TWO MANAGERIAL PHILOSOPHIES

The creation of an effective managerial structure for the new Penn Central was not easy. The merger of the two railroads was the largest yet attempted in American business history. On the eve of the merger, the Pennsylvania Railroad had revenues of $1.16 billion and the New York Central $819 million. The total revenues of the merged corporation would be nearly $2 billion. The assets of the Pennsylvania Railroad were $3.8 billion and the New York Central $2.5 billion for a total of $6.3 billion, and the combined debt of the two corporations exceeded $2.13 billion. The merged companies operated over 19,000 route miles of track and had more than 106,000 employees.

Statistics, however, could not provide a true measure of the magnitude of problems posed by the merger. As the Pennsylvania's comptroller, William Cook, noted, the two railroads historically had different philosophies of management. The Pennsylvania was decentralized. Its various regions operated almost as separate railroads. Its regional managers had wide authority. They not only supervised operations but they also controlled repairs and maintenance, built budgets, and developed proposals for capital expenditures. What Bevan had done was to impose a centralized, standard accounting system on the regions so they could produce uniform reports. He also had fostered the development of a standardized computer system that processed nearly all data at a central location. Thus, despite decentralization, the Pennsylvania's top management had high-quality information available to aid it in making decisions.

The New York Central had a very different managerial philosophy. It was highly centralized. As Cook observed, "Under their system, staff officers at headquarters in New York were responsible for their particular scope of overall business throughout the entire company. For example, the chief mechanical officer was responsible and held accountable for the activities in all of their car shops throughout the company, and the chief maintenance and way officer was responsible for all maintenance and way activities" [2]. Consequently, New York Central regional managers were little more than superintendents of transportation. Unlike their counterparts on the Pennsy, they did not control repairs and maintenance, nor did they have the responsibility for building budgets.

There were other basic differences between the New York Central and the Pennsylvania managerial systems. The Pennsy had deemphasized traditional Interstate Commerce Commission accounting in favor of responsibility reporting, while the New York Central, under Perlman, retained the old system. Ironically, despite its centralized managerial philosophy, the New York Central had not unified its computers. C. G. Sempier, summarizing the state of the Central's data processing in December 1967, commented that on Perlman's railroad computer, components were "spread throughout the organization. For instance, data origination and terminal management are within operations; data communications and network are within communications and signals; computer operations are within the financial department; and operations research is within the operating department. Of extreme importance," Sempier continued, "is the lack of any organizational component that is addressing itself to management reporting techniques" [3]. Sempier's report made it evident that not only were the New York Central's computers different from the Pennsylvania's, but the nature of the two organizations made it difficult, if not impossible, for top management to have at its fingertips the full range of information needed to make intelligent decisions.

The first merger study began in late 1961 soon after Symes and Perlman agreed to combine the two roads. The fruits of this work were known as the Patchell Study, and it was used as the basis for testimony in the ICC hearings on the merger in 1962. The Patchell Study was preliminary, and as the merger date grew closer, Saunders and Perlman created a group to work out an operations plan. They put one person from each road in charge of a large staff, which produced "a six-volume master operating report which they planned to present to Saunders and Perlman at a meeting in November of 1967" [4]. This report was never implemented. Minutes before the plan was to be discussed at a November 28, 1967, meeting, Perlman "ordered all copies marked 'preliminary.' The marked copies were distributed at the meeting, then gathered up, and apparently permanently laid aside" [5]. The SEC staff investigators concluded that no substitute plan was developed and the Penn Cental began life with no firm operating directives. The results were disastrous.

CRITICAL FACTORS

Actually, the Penn Central's fate was cast in the 2 years leading up to the merger. Stuart Saunders, who had inherited James Symes's mantle of leadership, presided over conflicting forces. Division rent the Pennsylvania Railroad itself. These years saw the emergence of two important contesting factions: the operating group and the financial department. The operating men had come to resent Bevan's administrative and accounting reforms, which they associated, rightly or wrongly, with what they considered a scarcity of money to improve the railroad's physical plant. The operating department looked upon the merger as an opportunity to lessen the chief financial's officer's influence. But Saunders had other problems. The New York Central's Alfred Perlman had never reconciled himself to the merger that Symes had forced upon him. Not only did he resent the Pennsylvania, but he underestimated the organizational problems involved with the merger [6]. Saunders's main task should have been to evaluate and to try and reconcile these conflicting forces. Unfortunately, of the Penn Central's three top officers, only David Bevan had a clear concept of the administrative and financial difficulties that the Penn Central would face on merger day. Bevan's activities highlight the complex forces at war with one another in the two railroads prior to their consolidation. The evidence also indicates that Saunders was warned of many of the troubles that the Penn Central would face after it became operational.

Although Bevan himself never wanted the merger, he began to prepare for it almost from the day Symes developed his proposal. It will be recalled that in the late 1950s, Bevan selected Peat, Marwick, Mitchell & Company as the Pennsylvania Railroad's auditor because that firm already was auditing the New York Central and he hoped that the accountants could help create a uniform reporting system for both railroads. In the 1960s, Bevan attempted to convince Saunders to get the operating departments of the New York Central and Pennsylvania together on their capital improvement programs. In 1965, when the Pennsylvania's operating men proposed a 5-year capital improvement program for new rolling stock, he was critical because no attempt had been made to coordinate it with the Central. Bevan wrote Saunders that he believed that "we should continue to work strenuously on the 5-year equipment program, but that this should be done in conjunction with the Central and that we develop it based upon our inventory of cars and theirs." Bevan concluded his letter to Saunders by urging that "immediate steps should be taken to get together with the Central and start developing a really sound program that will allow us to program our equipment building and financing on an even keel" [7]. Later the same year, he noted that in 1964, when the capital program for 1965 had been approved, the operations department had agreed to reduce the Pennsylvania's work force by 5000 people. He noted that nothing had been done to accomplish this and wrote Saunders thus: "Actually, I think that this is where you can use Perlman to a very great advantage and I doubt that without his help anybody else is going to do it" [8]. The advice fell on deaf ears.

While chaos in planning for operations after the merger worried Bevan, his main concern was with finance, accounting, and data processing. Saunders took no leadership in formulating a way to merge these areas. Bevan attempted to fill the void. It will be recalled that starting in 1960, the Pennsylvania developed its systemwide centralized computer operation. A key factor was a data origination system that collected both waybill and car movement information, "with error rates below 0.4 percent for movement and below 0.7 percent for waybills" [9]. The Pennsy system kept an accurate track of car loadings, revenues, and billing. This information was essential in planning, and it contributed to the accuracy of Bevan's income budgets.

It was vital that the Central's and the Pennsy's computer data origination systems be compatible. In 1965, Bevan offered the New York Central the Pennsylvania's successfully operating billing program, but Walter R. Grant, the Central's vice-president for finance, refused it. Instead, the Central started an installation in Detroit "of Univac 418, stating that they would have it completed systemwide within a year." At that point, Bevan told Grant that he would swing the Pennsy system over to the New York Central system if its installation was successful [10]. Unfortunately, the New York Central never completed its computerized billing installation. On the eve of merger, the system was only "partially operational." In addition, the Central's error rate was approximately 10 percent, or almost 20 times that of the fully operational Pennsylvania system [11]. Bevan warned Saunders "of difficulties which would ensue from the failure of the New York Central to work with us in creating compatible systems." He added, "There is no question that after the merger we are going to have . . . great difficulties in giving management the caliber of reports our people are accustomed to. This problem cannot be avoided at this late date" [12].

As the merger date grew near, Saunders still failed to provide guidance on how the Pennsylvania and the New York Central should coordinate their financial planning. Bevan became alarmed and asked both his comptroller, William Cook, and the Pennsylvania's computer specialist, C. G. Sempier, to analyze the problems facing the accounting and data processing people. Sempier's reports were thorough and made chilling reading. He pointed out that Alfred Perlman, the Central's president, was dissatisfied with data processing on his own railroad. Sempier's investigation turned up many reasons why this should be so. He wrote, "It is my considered opinion that NYC's data processing efforts operate in a highly unplanned environment. The only evidence of planning seems to be short-range reactions to immediate situations. This, in my mind, has caused the conditions recognized by Mr. Perlman . . . ." [13]. Sempier reported the Central's difficulties with car accounting and waybills, and he took particular note of the Central's lack of responsibility accounting. He added, "Until such time as responsibility reporting is completely implemented on the NYC, the only method of consolidating the merged roads is on an ICC basis" [14]. Sempier also listed other difficulties, including a poor personnel policy on the Central. He argued that it did "not have challenging career paths and marketplace competitive salary ranges for its data processing personnel" [15]. He felt this caused the extremely high turnover rate among the New York Central's data processing personnel.

In December 1967, Bevan attempted to convince Saunders that something had to be done to develop a coordinated approach to data processing and accounting on the new Penn Central. He wrote, "I have been giving a lot of thought . . . to the current status of data processing operations within the two companies and the proposed solution to make them compatible for operations after the merger." He then summarized the history of his efforts to achieve coordination thus [16]:

> At least five years ago, although we believed that the PRR was on the right track, we were fearful that unless the two companies worked closely together, that at the time of merger we would have some points of incompatibility that would give us trouble. We strongly recommended that we form a team of New York Central, Pennsylvania, IBM, and Peat, Marwick & Mitchell personnel to develop compatible systems for the two railroads. This approach was flatly rejected by the New York Central as they felt that Peat, Marwick & Mitchell were good auditors. And as you have heard Mr. Perlman say on many occasions, IBM was only a "hardware salesman." Our suggestion has been reiterated many times subsequently but has fallen on fallow ground.

Bevan then explained to Saunders the problems that would be created by the incompatible car movement and waybilling data and the difference in accounting methods. "One very basic difficulty," he stated, "is that Mr. Perlman is completely sold on ICC accounting, which he has used for many years. On numerous occasions he has insisted that reports coming to him should be in the ICC format." Perlman's preference for ICC accounting was no different than that of most top operating men who had been schooled in it since the turn of the century. Bevan told Saunders that if the Pennsylvania system were adopted, it could provide Perlman all the data he needed in its ICC format. The problem was that the New York Central system could not provide the type of information that the Pennsylvania had been accustomed to receiving. He recommended that Saunders try to get Perlman to adopt Pennsylvania's system of data processing and accounting. He also hoped that Saunders could convince Perlman to allow William Cook and Carl Sempier to "move expeditiously forward in integrating the two systems. With a unified set-up," Bevan added, "as bad as the problems are, we are satisfied that we can find satisfactory solutions within a reasonable time period. There should be no misunderstanding, however, that under ideal circumstances, at this late date these operations are going to be unsatisfactory for some time to come." Bevan stressed that action had to be taken and warned that "the longer we temporize, . . . the worse the situation will be."

SAUNDERS REFUSES TO ACT

Saunders did not follow Bevan's advice. From the perspective of hindsight, Saunders's action seems inexplicable. However, from his position in 1967, his strategy had logic. Ever since Saunders had assumed the chairmanship of the Pennsylvania, his main goal had been to merge his railroad with the New York Central. He subordinated everything to this aim. His income maximization policy had originated in his fear that a more conservative reporting of income might jeopardize the merger. Saunders, aware that Perlman had never been enthusiastic about the merger, may have feared that a confrontation with him over such vital matters as accounting and data processing might also thwart the union.

Perlman was a proud man. In the New York Central's annual reports, he had boasted of his railroad's "quiet revolution." The key was "cybernetics," which he "defined as the new science of communication and control in human beings as well as machines." On the Central, Perlman's report stated, cybernetics "provided management with more well-organized information, allowing decisions to be made rapidly on the basis of fact and logic" [17]. Perlman's use of the term "cybernetics" impressed the nation's financial and business press. However, he never explained precisely what he meant by cybernetics or exactly how the New York Central employed it. Publicly, he conveyed the idea that his railroad had advanced computer techniques equal to the best in American industry. Privately, at premerger meetings Carl Sempier observed that Perlman admitted that the New York Central had very serious trouble with its data processing [18].

Saunders was a good politician, keenly aware of the feelings of those about him. It is logical that he did not want to embarrass Perlman over data processing on the eve of merger. He also knew that Perlman strongly favored ICC accounting and had little appreciation for the systems Bevan had installed on the Pennsylvania. Saunders probably did not want to risk confrontation on these issues either. Moreover, he himself lacked a financial and accounting background and did not clearly understand the thrust and importance of Bevan's arguments. Thus, the Penn Central began its life with its data processing system and its accounting in chaos.

PENN CENTRAL'S NEW
ADMINISTRATIVE STRUCTURE

While Bevan had been attempting to develop a last-minute coordinated program for his major interests of finance, accounting, and data processing, Stuart Saunders and Alfred Perlman were busy making the final decisions about the shape of the new organization that would administer the Penn

Central. For almost a year prior to the merger, they had been considering others' advice about the new organizational structure. Seeking help, they retained an outside management consulting firm, McKinsey & Company, and they also relied on an internal committee presided over by one administrative officer from each railroad. Saunders's administrative assistant, Basil Cole, represented the Pennsylvania, and Fred Kattau, the New York Central. Perlman, Saunders, and their two advisers worked in almost total secrecy, and few people on either railroad learned the shape of the new administrative structure until the last minute. Cole later testified before the Securities and Exchange Commission that "the only people who knew what that top organization was going to be were Mr. Saunders, Mr. Perlman, Fred Kattau, and myself. The four of us did all the work and were the only ones privy to that information. Mr. Bevan didn't know what his role was going to be. Mr. Greenough, president of the Pennsylvania, didn't know what his role was going to be" [19]. Bevan, even though he was the Pennsylvania's third ranking officer and a member of its board of directors, had to be content with occasional rumors from other directors. One of his closest friends on the board, Edward J. Hanley of Pittsburgh, board chairman of the Allegheny Ludlum Steel Corporation, told the railroad's chief financial officer he would find plans for finance and accounting at the Penn Central satisfactory.

The week before Christmas 1967, Saunders called Bevan into his office to explain the Penn Central's proposed organizational structure. He told Bevan that his responsibility and authority would be different on the Penn Central than it had been on the Pennsylvania. Under the new structure, Bevan was to retain the title of chairman of the finance committee and he was to report directly to Saunders, who had the title of chairman of the board and chief executive officer in the new Penn Central. Although Bevan's title remained the same, almost everything about his position was to be altered. On the Pennsylvania, he chaired the Finance Committee of the board of directors and was a director himself. On the Penn Central, despite the fact that he would chair a committee of the board of directors, he would no longer be a member of the board. Next, he discovered that most of his jurisdiction had been stripped. He was to lose control of the comptroller's office, which included accounting and budgets. He was also to lose control over taxes, insurance, and banking operations. These functions would report to a former New York Central officer, Walter Grant, who in turn was directly responsible to the Penn Central's new president, Alfred Perlman. Bevan was also to lose data processing. The Pennsylvania's bright young computer man, Carl Sempier, was to become assistant vice-president for data systems, reporting to a New York Central man, R. G. Flannery, who in turn was to work directly under Perlman. In the new structure, Bevan's main responsibility would be raising funds for the railroad. He would also supervise the corporation's pension fund and oversee diversification.

Saunders's explanation of the new program stunned Bevan, and he immediately objected. He told Saunders that accounting should be kept separate from operations. Bevan explained that Perlman still favored the ICC accounting approach, that he did not appreciate the benefits of the Pennsylvania's accounting system, and that he would have no interest in installing it throughout the entire Penn Central. Bevan also reminded Saunders of the memorandum he had just written describing the backward state of the New York Central's data processing. He worried about placing Carl Sempier under Flannery, primarily an operating man who had little experience with computers. This would undoubtedly delay the emergence of a uniform, sophisticated data processing system for the Penn Central, Bevan argued, and would probably perpetuate the existing state of chaos in that area. He also feared that the staff he had assembled—men like Cook and Sempier—would feel uncomfortable working for a nonfinancial man like Perlman. In addition, Bevan said that Perlman, with ten vice-presidents reporting directly to him, could not possibly supervise all of them adequately. Operations alone, in Bevan's opinion, would keep Perlman fully occupied. Perlman could not possibly have time to analyze the problems of such diverse activities as accounting, data processing, research, purchasing, and management planning. But the most serious result, Bevan explained, would be that he himself would be hard pressed to do a satisfactory job without control of accounting and budgeting. He was convinced that Perlman did not believe in income budgets and cash-flow statements and that if Perlman had control of accounting and budgeting, none would be produced. Without a proper income budget, Bevan could not have accurate cash-flow data. Without them, it would be difficult for the Penn Central's management to plan capital expenditures or accurately predict the requirements for raising new money.

While Saunders may have disliked Bevan, the chief financial officer was vital to the success of the merger. In 1967, Bevan's reputation was high. The financial community gave him credit for successfully managing the Pennsylvania Railroad's large debt, and at that time, the diversification program showed every sign of success. In fact, the railroad's stockholdings in the Great Southwest were appreciating rapidly, and by mid-1969 they had a market value of more than $1 billion. Bevan's connections with the banking community made it easy for him to raise the money needed to see the Penn Central through merger and the years thereafter. His departure would seriously undermine the trust of the financial community in the new venture.

At the end of the interview in which Saunders had explained the Penn Central's new structure, Bevan said that "the organizational structure was not only impossible to operate but that [he] would not remain as a figurehead with an empty title regardless of the salary." Moreover, he "intended to resign." Saunders, aware of his chief financial officer's importance, kept insisting that Bevan had a "very responsible position, and that everything would be fine."

BEVAN CONSIDERS RESIGNATION

Immediately after the interview, Bevan called his friend Edward Hanley and told him that "my worst fears have been confirmed." He said he was going to resign and he asked Allegheny Ludlum's chairman "why he had not sufficient courage to tell me the truth, but let me find it out for myself at a very late date." Hanley told Bevan that he "was utterly surprised" and urged him "not to take any precipitous action."

The next morning, Bevan called his close friend Richard Mellon, the Pennsylvania Railroad's senior director, saying that he wanted to fly to Pittsburgh to discuss an urgent matter. Mellon explained that he was not feeling well, that he was leaving in 10 minutes to attend a board meeting and then flying south. It would not be possible for him to see Bevan. He added that "he knew what the problem was. He had heard it the previous evening from Hanley and that he had been walking the floor since 4 o'clock that morning." Bevan told him that he "wanted to embarrass no one" and that he wanted to resign only because he had been put "in an impossible position by Saunders and Perlman." It would be "extremely difficult, if not impossible, to work with them," he said, adding that in his opinion, the new organization would not work. Bevan concluded that "he did not wish to be involved in a failure as complete as [he] thought this one would be." Mellon's answering words seared themselves into Bevan's mind. "Dave," he said, "this is the worst double-cross I have ever experienced in my corporate career. I am sick about it. I have never asked you to do me a personal favor before, but I am going to now. I have worked years to bring about this merger, and if you pull out now, Perlman, who does not want it anyway, may cause a collapse of the whole plan. Please, as a personal favor, grit your teeth, say nothing, go through with the merger, and as soon thereafter as possible, I will insist that all the things that are wrong be corrected. I do agree with you that it is an impossible situation."

Bevan reluctantly agreed to stay through the merger. He had an ironic relationship with Mellon who, in 1951, had offered him the presidency of the Mellon National Bank. As was noted earlier, Bevan had refused and had instead joined the Pennsylvania. This decision was a serious error. In 1967, Mellon pleaded with him to stay with the railroad. This time, he did as Mellon wished. This turned out to be an even greater mistake [20].

Later the same day, Hanley called Bevan to say that he had discussed the whole problem further with Mellon and that both agreed they would talk to Saunders and try to get the Pennsylvania's chief executive officer to make some immediate changes. Mellon reiterated his pledge to set matters right after the merger. Unfortunately, he never acted. After Christmas, he became seriously ill and he never attended another board meeting. Mellon died in June 1970. Bevan remained certain that had Mellon retained his health and lived, changes would have been made in the Penn Central's organization that might have slowed or ended the march toward disaster.

Hanley told Bevan to expect a call from Saunders. It came the day before Christmas while Bevan was having lunch with two of his staff. He offered to go to the chief executive's office, but Saunders preferred to come to him. The discussion involved the appointment of a new treasurer. This office was important to Bevan because the treasurer supervised the railroad's bank deposits. Bevan would find it very difficult to borrow massively from financial institutions if he did not control deposits. The treasurer was crucial to Bevan's duties in raising money for the railroad. In planning the Penn Central's new organization, Perlman and Saunders did not even consult Bevan about the treasurer's position or who should fill it. He was astounded when Saunders told him that the new treasurer would be a New York Central man who reputedly did not want the position, who wished to handle investments for which he had inadequate experience and training, and who refused to leave New York. Further, he was to report to Walter Grant, who worked for Perlman. At the December 24 meeting, Bevan explained to Saunders that it would be nearly impossible to raise funds without handling the relationship with banks. Saunders confessed that he had not understood the significance of this function, and he agreed that the new treasurer would report to Bevan's right-hand man, W. R. Gerstnecker, who was to become the Penn Central's vice-president for corporate affairs. Bevan did insist, although most of them would no longer work for him, that Gerstnecker, Cook, Warner, Fox, and Haslett be made vice-presidents, since they deserved the title.

Bevan recognized that Saunders would not concede further points without considerable pressure from Richard Mellon. Having every confidence that this pressure would be forthcoming rapidly after the merger, he reluctantly agreed to formalize the Penn Central's new structure. Under this arrangement, Walter R. Grant, the New York Central's vice-president for finance, became an executive vice-president on the Penn Central and assumed responsibility for many of the departments that had formerly been Bevan's. Grant maintained his office in New York City and reported directly to the Penn Central's new president, Alfred Perlman. He took over supervision of the comptroller, William S. Cook, whose office remained in Philadelphia. Budgeting and controls became the responsibility of J. J. McTernan, Jr., a New York Central officer who had never prepared an income budget or an annual cash-flow statement at the Central. In fact, under Perlman, income budgets and annual cash-flow projections were never made.

Other key men in finance lost out. This was particularly true of Cook's lieutenants. It was Cook, as the reader may recall, who had installed General Electric's accounting and managerial system on the Pennsylvania and recruited a number of bright young men directly from G.E. to implement this system. Among them was Bruce Relyea, who became the Pennsylvania's budget manager. In addition, Thomas Meehan, a highly capable certified public accountant and a lawyer, was made the Pennsy's general auditor. Cook's well-trained men became subordinate to New York Central men; Bruce Relyea worked for McTernan, as did Thomas Meehan, the auditor. Meehan's position particularly alarmed Bevan. On the Pennsylvania, the auditor had high status; he reported directly to both Cook, the comptroller, and Bevan. Under this system, his prestige enabled him to use his office to uncover equipment shortages, fraud, and other serious shortcomings. To bury the auditor at the low level proposed by Perlman and Saunders drastically weakened his effectiveness.

THE SIDETRACKING OF DAVID BEVAN

Saunders did not discuss with Bevan the reasons for organizational changes introduced at the time of merger. Among the most important of the changes was the removal of accounting and auditing from Bevan's control. Saunders merely stated that he had given the matter careful thought and would not change his mind. Later evidence makes it clear that both Saunders and Bevan disliked each other. It should also be added, however, that some of the Pennsylvania's operating men undoubtedly hoped that placing accounting and budgeting under the control of Perlman, an operating man, would result in more generous capital outlays.

Years later, Saunders outlined some of his reasons for removing accounting from Bevan's control. The occasion was the presentation of testimony on August 29, 1972, in connection with the Penn Central's securities litigation. In these proceedings, Edwin P. Rome, special counsel to the trustees of the bankrupt Penn Central Transportation Company, cross-examined Saunders. The testimony makes interesting reading. During the day, Saunders testified that he had not been satisfied with the performance of the Pennsylvania Railroad's accounting department immediately preceding the merger. He placed much of the blame on Bevan. Rome questioned the former chief executive officer in detail [21].

Q.   And when did you first have an experience learning that his [Bevan's] estimates were wrong?

A.   Oh, particularly in '67, '68. That's one of the reasons that I wasn't getting the type of information that I wanted. I mean, that I thought was accurate. There were such large variances that I just wasn't satisfied with the reports.

Q. May I inquire, Mr. Saunders, whether you ever sent Mr. Bevan any sort of memorandum or writing in which you told him that you were dissatisfied with his estimates or any other aspect of his performance?

A. I don't recall sending him anything in writing, no.

Q. Did you not think it appropriate to communicate your dissatisfaction to him in writing?

A. No. It wasn't necessary. I talked to him.

Q. And you talked to him as early as '67 or '68?

A. I don't recall exactly when I talked to him but he was well aware of my dissatisfaction. That was one of the reasons we took accounting away from him.

Q. And you took accounting away from him incident to consummation of the merger?——————

A. That's right.

Q. And you took it away from him then, at least for one reason, because you were already dissatisfied with his performance?——————

A. Well, that was partially the reason but there were others, as I have already explained in my testimony.

Q. You have referred to "others," Mr. Saunders, but I do not believe you have specified what they were and I would like to ask you to do so now, sir.

A. I thought I had but I am glad to do it.——————

Q. ... With the decision to take away the accounting area from Mr. Bevan, who participated in and made that judgment and decision?

A. The Board of Directors; they approved it.

Q. Are you suggesting that it was done by the Board of Directors on their own initiative?

A. No.

Q. Who suggested it to the Board?

A. Well we had been working for months and trying to divide up, to set up the organization structure—not for months—but for a year or more before the merger; and the decision was based upon advice that we received from McKinsey & Company and also the advice we received from the staff that was working on the organizational set-up; and Mr. Perlman and I made the decision as to the division of authority and we recommended it to the Board.

Q. Your recollection is that McKinsey & Company made the recommendation to take accounting away from Mr. Bevan.

A. I don't know whether they did or not but they were consulted about the whole organizational structure. I don't know whether they made any—

I didn't have any personal dealings with them. That was handled by staff———

Q. When you say staff, to whom do you refer, individuals?

A. Well, it's primarily Mr. Cole in the Penn Central—I mean from the Pennsylvania, and Mr. Kattau from the New York Central.———

Q. Now am I correct in believing that your testimony is, accounting was taken away from Mr. Bevan because, among other reasons, you did not find his estimates accurate and reliable?

A. I didn't say that. That's too strong. I was dissatisfied with his estimates and I thought they varied too much within a short period of time, and these weren't necessarily his own estimates. Some of them weren't, I think they were prepared by the accounting department, but we thought we'd get better results.

Q. You're going to get better results if the accounting department . . . [prepared] the estimates that you found inaccurate?

A. I didn't say they were inaccurate. I just said they varied too much.———

Q. Now when accounting was taken away from Mr. Bevan did you thereafter find the estimates were more to your liking and your satisfaction?

A. I haven't said anything about my liking—all I wanted was the facts.

Q. Did you find that after accounting was taken away from Mr. Bevan that the estimates were more factual?

A. I don't know what I can say that they—there was some improvement, but we still had problems, because of the complex set-up of the organization, getting figures, getting the two properties nailed together, but they were adequate.

Q. Were they to your satisfaction?

A. I don't know what you mean "to my satisfaction." It wasn't a matter of my satisfaction other than to get the facts upon which we could work.

Q. I used the words, Mr. Saunders, because you used the words earlier with regard to the estimates that Mr. Bevan presented to you as not being to your satisfaction.

A. I didn't say that; at least I didn't mean to. I was talking about Mr. Bevan generally, and my dissatisfaction with him.

Q. With what?

A. Well, with his whole approach to the organizational set-up.

Q. Now you hadn't mentioned that before, Mr. Saunders. Would you please explain what you mean with your dissatisfaction with Mr. Bevan's whole approach to the organizational set-up.

A. Well, I think you have to know the man. You just can't think about these things in a vacuum. You have got to———

Q. I'm trying not to. That is why I ask you to fill in the vacuum?

A. You have to deal with personalities.

Q. Well, would you explain, sir?

A. What do you mean, 'explain.'

Q. Will you fill in the vacuum that you tell me exists in my state of knowledge?

A. I didn't say that. I think I have explained my position as well as I can.

Q. ——You have now referred to an element of your dissatisfaction being Mr. Bevan's whole approach to the organization set-up, and I am asking you to explain what you mean by that.

A. Well, I can explain. Mr. Bevan never wanted me on the Pennsylvania Railroad.

Q. Sir?

A. Mr. Bevan never wanted me on the Pennsylvania Railroad. He was highly dissatisfied because he didn't get the job as Chairman of the Board and he never got it.

Q. It is—is it your conclusion from that that thereby his approach to the organizational set-up was colored in some way?

A. I think it speaks for itself.

While Bevan went along with the new organization, he wanted to make his position crystal clear. He wrote his friend Edward Hanley, then a senior Penn Central director, and enclosed a copy of the understanding he had finally reached with Saunders on December 26. In describing his feelings, he wrote [22]:

Despite our individual opinions as to the soundness of the overall organization, we have both agreed to do our best to make it work. However, I do not want S.T.S. [Stuart Saunders] or anyone else at the next board meeting or any subsequent meeting to indicate in any way whatsoever that I am in accord with the proposed organizational set-up. I do not think the responsibilities are properly allocated, nor in certain cases do I believe the proper man is heading the department. . . . Further, it is to me totally impractical to have certain heads of departments located in New York with the departments themselves in Philadelphia.

Bevan then went on to emphasize the problems facing the railroad's accounting:

I also had the benefit of seeing how bad the accounting operation can be when it is not kept completely separate from operations per se. I believe accounting should be kept separate from operations but constitute a service organization to all departments of the railroad. When I took over accounting in 1958, it had been subjected for a long period of years to the domination of the operating department and I never saw a more badly or more disorganized or worse operation. I believe that both accounting and data processing should be part of the financial set-up and I also believe, at least for the time-being, data processing should continue to be part of the accounting organization.

To emphasize his point, Bevan included in the letter to Hanley an organizational chart that stressed the changes he felt were necessary. This chart placed accounting, the treasury, investments, diversification, data processing, taxes, real estate, and employee benefits and insurance all under the supervision of the chairman of the Finance Committee. Bevan felt that the railroad's new president, Perlman, would have more than enough to do with labor relations, operations (including maintenance of way and structures, maintenance of equipment, engineering, transportation, and so on), marketing, research and development, and sales. Cook, the Pennsylvania's comptroller, seconded Bevan's fears about the future of accounting and management on the new Penn Central. He wrote, "Although I believe the accounting department has been one of the strongest organizations [on the Pennsylvania Railroad] principally because of the infusion of the highly skilled people from other industries, it is in real danger of reverting to its former position."

Cook told Bevan that many of the key people that had come to the Pennsylvania in accounting felt uneasy with the new organization and were looking for jobs elsewhere. Their restiveness was motivated, Cook argued, "by the feeling that the New York Central philosophy will prevail in accounting and, as you know, the Central has done essentially nothing in the area of managerial controls. Our people suspect that the progress that we have made will come to a halt and that the accounting organization will revert to its former bookkeeping role" [23]. Cook also stated that it was "imperative that a common accounting system be installed on the merged company as rapidly as possible." He felt that even though the plans called for establishing the Pennsylvania's responsibility reporting system throughout the former New York Central by October 1968, this was going to be difficult. Cook concluded regretfully that he did "not believe that our management even realizes that a common information and control system is one of the most important problems with which it is faced." Given what lay ahead of the Penn Central, these words were prophetic indeed.

References

1. Joseph R. Daughen and Peter Binzen, *The Wreck of the Penn Central,* Little, Brown & Co., Boston, 1971, pp. 62–63.

2.   Cook to Bevan, March 29, 1968. The citations for this chapter are either corporate letters or memoranda preserved in the Bevan Papers.

3.   Sempier to Cook, December 5, 1967.

4.   *The Financial Collapse of the Penn Central Company*, a Staff Report of the Securities and Exchange Commission to the [House of Representatives] Special Sub-Committee on Investigations, Hon. Harley O. Staggers, Chairman, Government Printing Office, Washington, D.C., August 1972, p. 19.

5.   Ibid., p. 20

6.   For another survey of the operational problems resulting from lack of planning, see Richard Saunders, *The Railroad Mergers and the Coming of Conrail*, Greenwood Press, Westport, Conn., 1978, pp. 262–269. Saunders and I have used the same ICC developed material, but have selected different incidents to illustrate the lack of planning at the operational level.

7.   Bevan to Saunders, October 22, 1965.

8.   Bevan to Saunders, December 17, 1965.

9.   Sempier to Cook, December 5, 1967.

10.   Bevan to Saunders, December 8, 1967.

11.   Sempier to R. G. Flannery, F. J. Lesh, R. E. Mann, R. C. Karvwatt, and J. McCrain, December 1, 1967.

12.   Bevan to Saunders, December 8, 1967.

13.   Sempier to Cook, December 5, 1967.

14.   Sempier to Flannery et al., December 1, 1967.

15.   Sempier to Cook, December 5, 1967.

16.   Bevan to Saunders, December 8, 1967.

17.   New York Central Railroad, *Annual Report for 1965,* p. 5.

18.   Sempier to Cook, December 5, 1967.

19.   Testimony of Basil Cole before the Securities and Exchange Commission in Washington, D.C., May 2, 1972, p. 154.

20.   Bevan's account of his relationship with Mellon and Mellon's request for Bevan to stay with the Penn Central is supported in a report Director Edward Hanley made to the Penn Central directors on September 24, 1969. This is quoted in full in Chapter 11, footnote 19, p. 168.

21.   From Saunders's deposition in the Penn Central Securities Litigation M. D. L. Docket No. 56, All Cases, in the U. S. District Court for the Eastern District of Pennsylvania. Fourth Day of Testimony in Philadelphia, August 29, 1972, Paul J. McGowan and George Lennox, Official Court Reporters.

22.   Bevan to Hanley, January 4, 1968.

23.   Cook to Bevan, March 29, 1968.

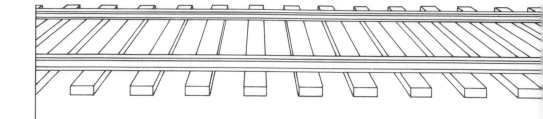

Chapter 10
TOWARD DISASTER: OPERATING FAILURE

The Penn Central had a short life. It began amid the founders' high hopes on February 1, 1968; and on June 21, 1970, less than 2½ years later, it became the biggest business failure in the history of the United States. A great many explanations have been offered for the Penn Central's collapse. Some have blamed Bevan's diversification program for much of the trouble. Others have targeted the Penn Central's liberal dividend policy. Still others have focused on the major costs associated with the merger itself, particularly the agreement with labor and the inclusion of the New York, New Haven & Hartford Railroad in the final system. All these explanations have diverted attention from the most important factor in the Penn Central's demise—the unprecedented breakdown of operations in the merged company.

The real question is, why should two railroads that had a long history of small but manageable operations losses suddenly, after merger, develop uncontrollable losses? The answer lies partly in the management style of the two top men at the Penn Central: Stuart Saunders and Alfred Perlman. Saunders, as the Penn Central's chairman of the board and chief executive officer, must be held largely responsible. From the day Saunders arrived at the Pennsylvania, he seemed singlemindedly fixed on one goal: the merger of the Pennsylvania and the New York Central. He subordinated everything to that goal. Perlman's outlook was different. He had never wanted to merge his New York Central with the Pennsylvania and did so only when James Symes's maneuvers left no alternative. Throughout the long merger negotiations, Perlman accepted the merger reluctantly. Stuart Saunders, excellent politician that he was, sensed Perlman's attitude and in the premerger planning was afraid to push the chief executive of the New York Central too far for fear that he might thus derail the merger. In addition, Saunders lacked the needed operational and financial expertise and underestimated the extreme complexity of putting two corporations the size of the Pennsylvania and the New York Central together. He seemed to feel that once the merger had been accomplished, things would go more smoothly.

THE PROBLEM OF CASH FLOW

The best place to begin the explanation of the disaster is with the Penn Central's cash-flow problems. The trouble was that more money flowed out than in. A loss because of railroad operations was nothing new for either the New York Central or the Pennsylvania Railroad. For example, between 1964 and 1967, the Pennsylvania lost $20.4 million on operations and the New York Central $7.6 million, for a total of $28 million, or approximately $7 million annually for the combined railroads [1]. Fortunately, during the premerger era the Central and the Pennsylvania could offset railroad losses with income derived from other investments. Starting with the merger, the railroads' losses increased dramatically—to $140 million in 1968, $220 million in 1969, and $100 million during the first 3 months of 1970. Thus, in slightly more than 2 years, railroad operations drained more than $460 million in cash from the Penn Central, or a yearly average of more than $230 million. Worst of all, the losses began at a high level and escalated rapidly. The trend was worse in 1970.

It is true that causes other than rail operations drained the Penn Central cash. In 1972, a report prepared for the Senate Committee on Commerce summarized some of them [2]. For example, as previously recounted, the Pennsylvania Railroad, largely prior to the merger, engaged in a large-scale diversification program and the New York Central made some small outside investments. The report concluded that the cash outlay for diversifications before and after the merger was $203.2 million. "Of that, the Pennsylvania Railroad (largely through its subsidiary, the Pennsylvania Company) paid out $172.1 million, the Central $21.4 million, and the Penn Central, $9.18 million." However, the report noted that "after offsetting the cash received for the Norfolk & Western and Long Island liquidation," there was a final net cash outflow of $41.8 million. "This," the report concluded, "is an important sum in absolute terms but not of great significance by itself." When matched against the Penn Central Railroad's operating losses, cash drained by diversification was minor. In fact, the entire cash invested in the diversification program would not have covered the Penn Central's operating losses for 1969 alone. Nor was diversification an important factor in denying the railroad funds for capital improvement. The Senate's Commerce Committee Report found that from "1959 through 1967, $1.5 billion was reinvested in the railroad; nearly ten times the amount put in diversification during 1963 through 1970."

The cash loss through the Penn Central's dividend payments was larger. In 1968, they amounted to $55.4 million and in 1969, $43.4 million, for a total of $98.8 million [3]. In retrospect, David Bevan agreed that any Penn Central dividend payments were unwise, but he noted that even if the cash had been retained in the corporation's treasury, the bankruptcy could not have been avoided; it would have merely been postponed about 3 months. He also noted that a cessation of dividends might not have saved money because it would have undermined confidence in the railroad, pushing up the cost of financing the almost $1 billion borrowed in the years 1968 and 1969 by more than the cash paid to stockholders.

The New Haven inclusion also had cash-flow implications. It has been previously noted that New Haven was in the worst financial shape of any major eastern railroad. It had been operating at a loss since 1957; it had been bankrupt since 1961; and it was in wretched physical condition. Bevan, in his 1962 testimony before the Interstate Commerce Commission (ICC), strongly opposed the inclusion of the New England road in a New York Central–Pennsylvania merger. Alfred Perlman held similar views. But Stuart Saunders had too easily agreed to take over the New Haven as a condition for government approval. Because of a dispute as to the price the Penn Central would pay for the New Haven, the railroad was not included in the merger until December 31, 1968, or 11 months after the creation of the Penn Central. ICC Auditor Stanley G. Jordan estimated that the Penn Central had to spend $29 million in cash to rehabilitate the decrepit New Haven, in addition to its cash loss of $11 million on 1969 operations [4].

From this it is clear that the slightly more than $41-million cash drain due to the New Haven inclusion was only a small part of the Penn Central's operating losses. However, the long-term implications of the New Haven inclusion were very serious. Under the agreement made by Saunders, the Penn Central was expected to pay the trustees of the New Haven for the dubious privilege of taking over their railroad. The ICC set a price of $140.6 million, which the New Haven trustees disputed. The matter went to the United States Supreme Court, which handed down its decision 8 days after the Penn Central's own bankruptcy. The Supreme Court raised the price of the New Haven by $28.9 million, which would have been an outlay in excess of $168 million for the Penn Central had it survived as a solvent corporation. This amount was in addition to the annual operating losses incurred by the New Haven and further large capital investments that were necessary to refurbish the line [5].

Labor represented another cash drain. On May 20, 1964, the Pennsy entered into an agreement with the various railroad unions that gave protection to any member discharged, laid off, or downgraded as a result of the merger. The unions exacted this agreement as a price for their support of the merger. The estimated cost to the Penn Central was approximately $78.2 million, all of which would accrue within 8 years after the merger date [6]. Incomprehensively, Saunders never consulted his labor relations staff on the agreement. He negotiated alone without expert advice.

With the cash drain caused by diversification, dividends, the New Haven inclusion, and the labor agreements, the total amounted to nearly $260 million. While this sum is very large, it is still relatively small compared with the $460-million railroad operating loss. Furthermore, the cash drain from diversification, labor, and dividends comprised one-time charges. Moreover, the cash drain caused by diversification took place entirely prior to the Penn Central merger, and dividends stopped in 1969. The drain caused by labor agreements would, it is true, have continued for some time. In contrast, the railroad's operating losses increased rapidly as the Penn Central aged. In fact, even bankruptcy and reorganization did not stop the operating losses. The record of the trustees who inherited the Penn Central after its 1970 collapse demonstrates this. From 1971 to 1974, Penn Central Railroad operating losses ranged from a high of $179.8 million in 1971 to a low of $92.6 million in 1973 [7]. These figures do not even include the cost of other items, including fixed charges. The deficits occurred despite Amtrak's absorption of all long-haul passenger service and substantial increases by local authorities in the support of commuter trains. In addition, the trustees had the advantages of lower real estate taxes and certain other benefits accorded to bankrupt railroads.

On April 1, 1976, a new government-backed corporation, Consolidated Rail (Conrail), took over the Penn Central and five other bankrupt northeastern railroads. Losses have continued unabated on the Conrail system. During its first 9 months, ending on December 31, 1976, Conrail, according to its own statistics, lost $205.5 million. Admittedly, these figures are not comparable with those of the old Penn Central, since they include five smaller railroads, but, ironically, Conrail reports its earnings and losses using an accounting system that would have aroused Stuart Saunders's envy. *The Wall Street Journal* reported that "Conrail's loss . . . is based on an accounting method under which its extensive spending for long-term track and structure rehabilitation is capitalized rather than charged against current income. During its first nine months, Conrail capitalized $232.9 million in this manner. If Conrail reported according to the ICC standards, its nine months' loss would have been $418.8 million rather than the $205.5 million which it reported" [8]. Also, these losses exclude long-haul passenger and commuter deficits absorbed by Amtrak and local authorities in Pennsylvania, New Jersey, New York, Connecticut, and Massachusetts.

PERLMAN AND THE CONSOLIDATION
OF PERSONNEL

While Perlman did not block the merger, his behavior indicated that he always remained a New York Central man and never at heart became a Penn Central man. The problem for Perlman as the Penn Central's president and chief operating officer was to create a team out of a staff that came from two separate railroads with dramatically different histories and administrative traditions. Even under the best of circumstances, this would not have been easy, but Perlman did not help matters.

His immediate deputy was David E. Smucker, executive vice-president for operations. Smucker was a Pennsylvania man. He had come to the Pennsy from its subsidiary, the Detroit, Toledo, & Ironton Railroad in 1963, and he had served under the Pennsylvania's president, Allen Greenough, as vice-president for operations. After the merger, his title should have made him the primary operating authority on the new system. However, this was not to be. From the very beginning, Perlman made it clear that all was wrong on the Pennsylvania and right on the Central [9]. It was bruited around the Penn Central's Philadelphia headquarters that Perlman would not even allow Smucker to visit some portions of the former New York Central Railroad. Whether this was true or not, Bevan witnessed striking indications of Perlman's hostility toward Smucker. By mid-1969, Perlman and Smucker were not on speaking terms, and Perlman constantly "issued orders directly to the field without informing his vice-president for operations." This made Smucker's position untenable. Stuart Saunders's reaction to this contretemps was revealing. Smucker wanted to quit. Saunders did not want him to, for fear that such an action would alert the Penn Central's board of directors to key personnel problems. Therefore, Saunders spent most of a weekend in 1969 urging Smucker not to retire early but to move upstairs on the staff of the chairman of the board. Smucker did so but, soon tiring of a job with nothing to do, retired early in 1970.

Perlman did not confine his hostility to Smucker, but feuded openly with many ex-Pennsylvania men. Bevan recalls one case clearly. It occurred at a staff meeting where Perlman sarcastically criticized poor track conditions that slowed trains across the Penn Central. He reserved some of his harshest words for George C. Vaughan, former general manager of the Pennsy's eastern region who had become the Penn Central's vice-president for engineering and equipment. Vaughan could take only so much; then he quietly replied to Perlman, "I think that you should know that most of these [slow] orders are on the New York Central and not on the Pennsylvania."

Perlman's attitude spread throughout much of the Penn Central and made effective teamwork difficult, if not impossible. After the Penn Central's collapse, John R. Michael of the ICC's Bureau of Operations examined the

Penn Central's Indianapolis region and "found the relationship . . . between the employees of the former Penn[sylvania] and the former Central to be strained and suspicious." Wherever Michael checked, he always heard "derogatory comments about employees of the other 'side'." He found that the policy of "mixing" officers forced former Pennsylvania men to report to former New York Central men or vice versa. "Since the management philosophy of the two railroads was so different," he observed, "these people did not understand one another, or if they did, they were frequently at odds with the instructions or the methods involved." This lack of rapport caused supervisors to bypass their immediate superiors to get the ear of a friend in a higher position who was from "their" railroad. The result was frequent countermanding of orders and much ill feeling [10]. Burke A. Tracey and Nicholas G. Sotor, ICC men who examined the Penn Central's Chicago region, found much the same story. They concluded, "A final and most serious aspect of the merger study . . . is the almost complete failure to consolidate the personnel into a single company. In spite of denials, there is still a red [Pennsylvania] and a green [NYC] railroad and the employees of each remain steadfast in their loyalty to the old railroad and are deeply resentful of the other." The ICC examiners laid much of the blame on Perlman. "Even Mr. Perlman," they observed, "has expressed such feeling publicly and his remarks were received with approval by former NYC personnel and disapproval by the former PRR personnel" [11]. Another examiner described the situation in Pittsburgh thus: "On the surface there appears to be an amiable feeling between former NYC and PRR employees. However, even though regional personnel are virtually 100 percent PRR, you cannot help but detect in office conversations a feeling of animosity toward the two former NYC officials in the region. There is no outward show of contempt, but it is there" [12].

BREAKDOWN IN OPERATIONS

The ill-feelings between the former Pennsy and Central personnel were only part of the story. At the heart of the problem was the decision to integrate the two railroads immediately. In embarking on this course, wrote Daughen and Binzen, "Saunders and Perlman had taken a calculated risk" [13]. Daughen and Binzen observed that the Penn Central could have followed the precedent of the B&O and C&O where after the union, each "continued to function separately but with a single top management" [14]. But the Penn Central tried to capture merger savings immediately [15]. However, poor planning prevented the realization of any savings. It will be recalled that prior to the merger, Perlman had all copies of a proposed operating plan marked "preliminary" and then suppressed. No other plan was prepared and the operating breakdown stemmed from that fact. The evidence for this is overwhelming. After the Penn Central's collapse in 1970, the Interstate Commerce Commission undertook a detailed survey of the entire railroad. While conditions varied from region to region, they were inevitably bad where the Pennsylvania and the New York Central came together and coordination was necessary. ICC's Arnold Barter described the situation at St. Louis, where he found conditions chaotic. "The reason for congestion, delays, etc.," he wrote, "appeared to be a lack of planning at the local level. A great deal of planning went on at the top level of management regarding policy, management jurisdiction, accounting and the like, but very little thought was given to training of employees, consolidation of systems and procedures, etc., necessary to consolidate two different systems into one without serious disruption of service" [16].

John Michael, the ICC investigator at Indianapolis, found similar conditions. He wrote, "Perhaps I am excessively sensitive to the area of advanced planning and coordination in the matter of train operation because of my prior railroad experience, but it was here that I believe the greatest deficiencies existed after the merger." Michael explained that two different systems existed for control of trains. He observed that "neither system was completely adopted upon merger, but rather a mixture of both. The lines of authority became muddled and fuzzy, with former NYC people trying to operate under their system, while at the same time former PRR people were operating under their system. This often resulted in cross purposes" [17]. George Finn of ICC discovered that at Buffalo "for the first several months following the merger, there was considerable difficulty experienced in routing traffic because of the unfamiliarity of the former PRR personnel with the NYC routing and vice versa" [18]. Investigators Burke A. Tracey and Nicholas G. Sotor blamed a similar planning lack in Chicago for poor service. They noted that no training had been given to classification clerks and that they were "not qualified to handle the responsibility of new territories suddenly thrust upon them. The result was a high percentage of misrouting" and there were many cars with missing waybills. Large numbers of cars were lost and "delays were compounded by the differences in the Pennsylvania and New York Central car accounting systems. For some time immediately after the merger, car tracing was all but impossible" [19]. Poor planning resulted in seriously congested terminals, a striking increase in derailments, particularly in yards, with corresponding delays, vast numbers of cars misrouted or sent out without waybills, the inability to trace cars when lost, numerous incorrect bills sent to those customers fortunate enough to receive their cars, and a sharp increase in goods damaged in transit.

The operations breakdown had a very unfavorable impact on the railroad's volume of traffic. The ICC survey indicated adverse effects occurred most severely in the Midwest, particularly in the St. Louis, Chicago,

Indianapolis, Cincinnati, and Buffalo regions. Conditions were better in the regions in which there was little need to intertwine the Pennsylvania and the New York Central. But even in the East, conditions were bad.

LOST BUSINESS

Traffic losses in the Midwest were a severe blow. The Interstate Commerce Commission interviewed many major shippers, and their comments illustrate the problems. Gail Coff, the traffic manager of National Starch of Indianapolis, remarked that before the merger, the Pennsylvania "had the best customer relations and the poorest service, while the New York Central had the better service and the poorer customer relations. In the merger, they managed to get the worst of the two systems." Coff said that prior to the merger, National Starch moved 65 percent or more of its traffic on either the Pennsylvania or the Central. Since the merger, however, the Penn Central moved less than 50 percent of National Starch's traffic, and Coff asserted that he would divert more if it were possible [20]. Nick Brown, Central Soya's traffic manager, reported that the Penn Central's service was "extremely poor." He noted that it took 10 days just to get a car out of Indianapolis and 17 days to move that car to Louisville, which was only 115 miles away. The result was that Central Soya had diverted to other railroads 85 percent of its inbound traffic and 100 percent of its outbound traffic. The story was the same for the Indianapolis Grain Cooperative. Prior to the merger, almost all its traffic moved on either the New York Central or the Pennsylvania; however, "because of poor service, lack of car supply, and arbitrary claim policy of the Penn Central, all traffic possible has been diverted from their line." Robert Decker, Indianapolis Grain's traffic manager, reported that a typical movement of grain from Indianapolis to Chicago amounted to 290 cars. Of this, 202 went by the Norfolk & Western and only 88 by the Penn Central. The Cooperative was planning to install a 100-car-unit train to move grain to Baltimore and was routing this on the Baltimore & Ohio rather than the Penn Central [21].

The Penn Central's breakdown had a long-term impact on traffic. Corporations planning new plants often decided to build them near other railroads. For example, Stokely–Van Camp, a major food processor, shipped in 1969 over 2000 cars of canned goods from Indianapolis alone. Stokely had a number of serious incidents. One example was the gross mishandling of a car of fruit shipped to Indianapolis from the West Coast. C. H. Schmidt, Stokely–Van Camp's traffic manager, reported that before the car had been placed for unloading on the company's siding, it somehow "started back to the West Coast as an empty, and got all the way back to California before the error was discovered" [22]. Stokely–Van Camp had originally decided to build a

2½-million-case warehouse distribution center on the Penn Central. However, because of the poor service, it located the warehouse on the Norfolk & Western at Tipton, Indiana. Schmidt estimated that between 1500 and 2000 carloads per year were handled by that warehouse, all of which were lost to the Penn Central.

Poor Penn Central service forced shippers to use other methods of transportation. For example, C. C. Cline, traffic manager for the Kroger Company, a supermarket chain, reported the difficulty he had with perishable freight. Kroger's Indianapolis office had to use seven man-hours a day just tracing cars. Cline reported that "often we will call four or five PC officers just to find and make sure a placement will be made on a carload of freight." Often the chain was seriously inconvenienced. One week Kroger advertised a cantaloupe sale based on its expectation that a car would arrive via the Penn Central. The car "went to Pittsburgh instead of Indianapolis, and the sale was over" before it arrived filled with rotten melons. The Penn Central service drove Kroger to consider every possible alternative. The same was true for Cuneo Press, located at Kokomo, Indiana. Max Knuby, Cuneo's traffic manager, explained that his firm's principal business was magazine printing and that it had to meet publication dates. He had found that the former Pennsylvania Railroad was service-minded. After the merger, however, "the attitude and service changed." Frequently, he said, "we were hard pressed to meet a deadline and would make special efforts to get a car out on time, only to discover the next day that the car was still in Kokomo because the Penn Central had annulled the scheduled pickup because of no power, no crews, or whatever." Cuneo stayed with railroads for traffic west of Kansas City, diverted cars destined for New England and the mid-Atlantic to the Norfolk & Western and moved everything going less than 500 miles by motor truck [23].

The weight of the ICC testimony indicated the majority of shippers found that Penn Central service was substantially worse than that provided either by the New York Central or the Pennsylvania. Almost all who could do so shifted their traffic either to other railroads or to other modes of transport. Many of these changes, once made, became permanent, especially when corporations invested in trucks or built new plants or facilities on other railroads, as did Stokely–Van Camp. This permanent diversion of traffic was one explanation of the long-term nature of Penn Central's deficits.

Not only did the Penn Central lose business; it also lost money on much of the traffic that it did carry. One reason was a breakdown of billing and collections, a situation which Cook and Sempier had predicted. The ICC investigation revealed that billing was slow and that bills took, on the average, almost 19 days to reach the customers after they had shipped a car. Bills for inbound shipments took even longer to arrive. The cash impact of this problem on the railroad was staggering. For example, in June 1968, the Penn

Central had over $57.6 million of freight bills outstanding, of which $14.5 million had been due more than 30 days. As the railroad moved toward bankruptcy, the situation worsened. In March 1970, the railroad had $100.5 million of bills outstanding, with $34.6 million due more than 30 days. Along with this backlog went a dramatic rise in accounts of doubtful collection. The year end of 1969 saw doubtful accounts amounting to $22.7 million; this figure contrasted sharply with doubtful accounts of only $2.6 million for the combined accounts of the New York Central and the Pennsylvania for the year immediately preceding the merger, 1967 [24].

In addition to the money lost on traffic diversion and a breakdown in billing and collections, poor planning often resulted in increasing the operations expenses. John Michael explained how the Penn Central failed to properly utilize merged facilities in the Indianapolis region. Writing of Terre Haute, he said, "It is difficult to imagine how one could implement a more unworkable consolidation of facilities than was employed" there. In the railroad's attempt to eliminate duplicate yards, Michael discovered, it had made arrangements that increased the number of man-hours devoted to switching and making up trains [25]. Another ICC investigator, Ray Tankersley, discovered that an attempt to divert traffic to Toledo's obsolete Stanley Yard had resulted in a serious derailment problem: from May 1969 through April 1970, the year averaged 50 derailments per month, with costs in excess of $8800. Tankersley noted this figure did not include man-hours or material necessary to repair damaged trains, track, or structures [26]. All these troubles are ironic because the theory behind the merger was that operating costs would fall, not increase. It is a double irony because, while Penn Central Railroad service was deteriorating, the corporation engaged in a massive program of capital improvements allegedly designed to make the Penn Central into an efficient, low-cost transportation enterprise.

While the full magnitude of the Penn Central's operations breakdown is apparent now, it was perceived only dimly at the time it occurred. Problems were real for the individuals involved, but there was no mechanism to collect the data and make them readily available either to the public or more important, to the Penn Central's top management. The experience of David Bevan indicates why this was so.

References

1. United States Senate, Committee on Commerce, *The Penn Central and Other Railroads, A Report to the Committee on Commerce,* prepared at the direction of Warren G. Magnuson, Chairman, Government Printing Office, December 1972, p. 73. Hereafter cited as *The Penn Central and Other Railroads.*

2. Ibid., p. 15. For the examples and following quotations and statistical data.

3. Ibid., p. 63.

4. Interstate Commerce Commission, Brief of the Bureau of Enforcement before the Interstate Commission, Docket No. 35291, The Investigation into the Management of the Business of the Penn Central Transportation Company and Affiliated Companies, March 8, 1972, p. 85. Hereafter cited as ICC Brief, March 8, 1972.

5. *The Penn Central and Other Railroads,* p. 331.

6. Ibid., p. 332.

7. Moody's *Transportation Manual,* 1976, p. 239.

8. *The Wall Street Journal,* April 1, 1977, p. 2.

9. Most secondary accounts of the Penn Central's crisis have agreed that Perlman had a very low opinion of the Pennsylvania and its operations personnel. Daughen and Binzen said in their *Wreck of the Penn Central*: "Almost from the opening day Perlman was out to get his two executive vice presidents [Henry Large and David Smucker] . . . One of Saunders' closest associates said 'Perlman had been after Saunders to let him get rid of Smucker. Saunders wouldn't do it . . . The feud between Perlman and Smucker did more than anything else to set up the red-green [Pennsy-NYC] rivalry.' " (See Joseph R. Daughen and Peter Binzen, *The Wreck of the Penn Central*, The New Mentor Executive Library edition, Signet Books, 1973, pp. 97-98.) Richard Saunders (no relation to Stuart Saunders) in his *The Railroad Mergers and the Coming of Conrail* Greenwood Press, Westport, Conn., 1978, pp. 280–281) wrote "Perlman didn't get along with another Red Team senior vice president, David Smucker, described as an aristocratic PRR traditionalist, known as 'Mother Smucker' to some of his subordinates. The two men apparently just hated each other." Rush Loving, Jr. in "The Penn Central Bankruptcy Express" (*Fortune*, August 1970, p. 108) had a generally sympathetic view of Perlman. Yet even Loving commented on the ill-feeling between Perlman and Smucker. Wrote Loving, "Perlman was unhappy with his executive vice president for operations, a former Pennsylvania man named David E. Smucker . . . On the other side Perlman's open disdain of the Pennsy's stodginess hadn't endeared him to Smucker. 'You run a wooden-wheeled railroad,' he had told Smucker before the merger, thus adding a few more lightning bolts to their relationship." Bevan's personal recollections of the Smucker affair, which I quote here, support the above sources.

10. Interstate Commerce Commission, Bureau of Enforcement, ICC Docket No. 35291, Verified Statement 16, pp. 27–28.

11. Ibid., Verified Statement 18, p. 7.

12. Ibid., Verified Statement 21, p. 8.

13. Daughen and Binzen, *The Wreck of the Penn Central*, p. 92.

14. Ibid.

15. See also Richard Saunders, *The Railroad Mergers and the Coming of Conrail*, Greenwood Press, Westport, Conn., 1978, p. 263.

16. Interstate Commerce Commission, Bureau of Enforcement, ICC Docket No. 35291, Verified Statement 15, p. 2.

17. Ibid., Verified Statement 16, pp. 14–15.

18. Ibid., Verified Statement 26, p. 12.

19. Ibid., Verified Statement 18, p. 4.

20. Ibid., Verified Statement 16, p. 30.

21. Ibid., p. 31.

22. Ibid., p. 34.

23. Ibid., p. 35.

24. ICC Brief, March 8, 1972, pp. 58, 61.

25. Interstate Commerce Commission, Bureau of Enforcement, Docket No. 35291, Verified Statement 16, pp. 2–3.

26. Ibid., Verified Statement 19, p. 9.

Chapter 11
TOWARD DISASTER: MOUNTING CHAOS AT THE TOP

As we have seen, David Bevan began his work on the new Penn Central in a difficult position. Stripped of his authority over accounting, auditing, and data processing, he found it increasingly hard to obtain the information that he needed for his remaining responsibilities as the company's chief financial officer. Although he had sat on the board of directors of the Pennsylvania Railroad since 1951, he was not a member of the Penn Central's board, even though, curiously enough, he sat as the chairman of the board's Finance Committee. While this position gave Bevan access to the company's directors, it became clear from the first that the board made many important decisions without his advice or knowledge.

UNDERMINING OF BEVAN'S STAFF

Typical of such actions was the selection of the Penn Central's treasurer. Bevan did not attend the organization meeting of the Penn Central's board of directors. Afterward, Saunders informed him that the board had decided that the treasurer was to be Raymond McCron, who had held the same office on the New York Central. It will be recalled that the organizational plan originally proposed by Saunders had placed the treasurer under Perlman, but in a last-minute compromise, Saunders returned the treasurership to Bevan's jurisdiction. Unfortunately,

McCron's appointment added to the merger confusion. Bevan immediately talked to him and discovered that the new appointee would not move to Philadelphia, had no real interest in the treasurer's duties, and wanted to manage the Penn Central's investments. Bevan explained to McCron that Robert Haslett was to be the Penn Central's full-time investment officer. Haslett had performed this function on the old Pennsylvania in an outstanding manner. Bevan pointed out that McCron had managed only a small portfolio for the New York Central, its contingent compensation fund (a fund set up to pay deferred compensation to the railroad's management after retirement). Under McCron's management, the Central's fund had a market value at the time of merger that was below its cost. In contrast, Haslett had managed the larger Pennsylvania contingent compensation investments and had produced very substantial appreciation from the outset. He was also in day-to-day charge of the very large supplemental pension fund and various other investment operations.

Bevan put McCron in charge of simplifying the Penn Central's corporate structure by reducing the number of subsidiaries and affiliated companies. According to Bevan, when McCron made no progress in this effort, he fired him. The treasurer's position then went to John Shaffer, former Pennsylvania treasurer, who served very ably until his retirement in 1972.

The confusion and dislocation in the treasurer's office was mild compared with what went on in those areas of Bevan's former responsibilities that had been shifted over to Perlman. Bevan had predicted that the staff he had assembled would probably leave. Regrettably, Bevan's forecasts started to come true almost immediately. Within weeks after the merger date, William S. Cook, the new company's vice-president for accounting, announced his resignation. He had been the driving force behind the modernization of the Pennsylvania's accounting and auditing, and his steadfast integrity had helped Bevan stand firm against the serious accounting abuses proposed by Saunders. Cook, after a brief stint outside the railroad industry, joined the management of the Union Pacific where he became vice-president of finance, and in 1977, president. Replacing Cook at the Penn Central was Charles S. Hill, who had come up through the Pennsylvania's accounting department.

Cook's departure was quickly followed by those of two other key employees, Tom Meehan, director of auditing, and Bruce Relyea, formerly the budget manager of the Pennsylvania who had become the assistant budget manager on the Penn Central. Auditor Meehan felt from the day of the merger that his position had been undermined. It will be recalled that under Saunders's organization plan for the Penn Central, the auditor, who, on the Pennsylvania, had reported directly to the comptroller and the chairman of the Finance Committee (the chief financial officer), now reported at a low level to the budget manager, J. J. McTernan. As soon as Meehan started in his new position, he was warned not to be too aggressive in his audits. He went to Bevan with his complaints. Bevan had no authority to act but, in April 1968, discussed the matter with Saunders. He explained Meehan's value, stressing that he had uncovered "very substantial areas of fraud." Bevan recommended that Saunders change the organization plan to allow Meehan to report directly to the comptroller and executive vice-president, Walter Grant, on Perlman's staff. Saunders said that he agreed with Bevan and would take action. However, several weeks went by and nothing happened. Then, on Monday, May 20, Bevan got a call from Charles Hill, the new comptroller, who told him that Meehan was extremely upset, had an appointment with Saunders, and was probably going to quit. Bevan immediately called Meehan and "tried to calm him down." In his diary, Bevan reported Meehan's saying that "there never had been any problem so long as he reported to W. S. Cook and me, but things were unsatisfactory now and he had gone too far to reverse himself and stay." Furthermore, Meehan thought he had been "deliberately undercut by his new superiors, that he had lost his effectiveness, and that he thought our auditing department was disintegrating very rapidly." Later the same day, Basil Cole told Bevan that Saunders had failed to change Meehan's mind. Cole added that if Saunders "had an opportunity to get into this earlier" he was sure Saunders "could have persuaded him to stay." [1].

Later in May, Bevan heard rumors that Bruce Relyea was leaving. Disturbed, he invited Relyea for a talk, wherein he urged him to ride out the difficulties and keep his position. Relyea told him that the morale of the Pennsylvania men in accounting was bad, and that he considered his superior, McTernan, the budget manager, a bright person, but lazy and "only willing to take the course of least resistance." He said, "McTiernan [sic] was not interested in developing true costs throughout the railroad but was satisfied with something far less than what was potentially possible and desirable." Relyea felt that he would waste his time if he stayed and then added that many of the regional comptrollers who were former Pennsylvania men were also leaving "because they thought we were going to lapse into the former NYC bookkeeping approach rather than a modern scientific accounting approach that had prevailed on the Pennsylvania prior to the merger" [2].

CONFUSION IN ACCOUNTING AND BUDGETING

Bevan's lack of authority, and the disintegration of the staff he had built in auditing and accounting, ensured that he could not get the data he needed as chief financial officer. Ironically, after the Penn Central's collapse Perlman maintained that he really had no authority over the comptroller and the functions of auditing and accounting. He liked to refer to the merger as a "takeover" of the New York Central, and he asserted that he had little real authority and power. After the debacle, the ICC interviewed many of the Penn Central's chief officers. They asked Charles Hill, "Was the accounting department under Perlman?" Hill answered that, "sometime Perlman is going to have to accept the fact that accounting and operations were under his control until he was relieved as President. I was on his staff and attended his staff meetings. When O'Herron came in July, 1969, he was also under Perlman. Perlman had accounting responsibility while he was President" [3]. In the face of organization charts and the testimony of key Penn Central officials, Perlman did not dare deny he had control of the comptroller's functions. When the ICC investigators asked him if he had the responsibility for accounting, he answered, "Yes, supposedly, but not in reality. They instituted the cost controls and the accounting system of the Pennsylvania Railroad. . . . At a staff meeting, I asked Hill for certain figures and in front of all my staff, he said, 'I am proscribed from giving you those figures.' I asked Saunders what that meant but he wouldn't answer" [4]. The Interstate Commerce investigators asked Saunders's lieutenant, Basil Cole, about his view of the matter [5].

Q. From the date of the merger until he became vice-chairman, Mr. Perlman was in charge of the accounting function. Was there any doubt in anybody's mind that Mr. Perlman was in fact in charge of the accounting?

A. No, no question about it. Perlman was in charge of the accounting from the date of the merger until O'Herron came in. [Actually, even O'Herron worked directly for Perlman until September 1969, when he became financial vice-president.]

Q. Are you aware of any effort on anyone's part to withhold accounting or financial information from Mr. Perlman?

A. Absolutely not. I've heard Perlman say it but it's not so. Perlman did not always use the information but it was there.

Q. Did you hear or ever become aware of an incident at one of Mr. Perlman's staff meetings where Mr. Perlman requested certain figures from Mr. Hill and was denied such figures by the response, 'I am proscribed from giving you those figures'?

A. I was not there but I've talked to others who were. Charlie Hill wanted to disseminate all information to everyone in the company through his monthly financial review. After the "Butcher affair," Mr. Saunders thought that excessive information would get to outsiders who might use it improperly so the financial review was limited in its distribution. At the noted staff meeting, Perlman asked for confidential information which was not to be given to his whole staff. However, Perlman himself already had the figures which he was denied by Hill.

Saunders's testimony agreed with Cole's version. In response to the statement, "It is our understanding that Mr. Perlman had responsibility for the
accounting function. Is that correct?" Saunders said, "Yes. Prior to the
merger Bevan had the financial and accounting functions. His counterpart on
the Central was Walter Grant. Mr. Bevan and Mr. Grant could not get along,
so Mr. Grant took over the taxes and accounting under Perlman and Mr.
Bevan took charge of the financial department." When asked whether he was
aware of "any effort on anyone's part to withhold accounting information
from Mr. Perlman," Saunders said, "I don't know of any. I really can't
answer that. Mr. Perlman got all of the information I got." The ICC investigators questioned Saunders about the staff meeting where Hill refused to
give Perlman accounting information. "Did Mr. Perlman talk to you about
this incident?" they asked. Saunders said "He may have but I don't recall
it" [6].

Bevan attempted to perform his duties on the Penn Central in the same
manner that he had on the Pennsylvania. This meant the construction of an
accurate income budget and cash-flow projection. His worst fears were
confirmed after discussion of these matters with Perlman. The Penn Central's
president told Bevan that he did not feel that an income budget was practical
on a railroad. It also became evident that Perlman did not appreciate a
financial man's concept of cash flow nor did he place a high importance on
projecting it. Perlman's attitude toward financial planning was a major factor
in Cook's decision to leave. Charles Hill, Cook's replacement, testifying to
the ICC examiners about Perlman's philosophy of financial management,
said, "It appeared that Perlman's view was that earnings followed day-to-day
operations without planning. After some things [sic] was done, you just
added up the score." When asked whether Perlman prepared income budgets, Hill replied, "No, Perlman declined to plan ahead. There were just
estimates of the results" [7].

The lack of cooperation and the chaos in accounting and auditing forced
Bevan to fall back on the resources of his own financial department. Without
a tight income budget, however, it was impossible to project accurate cash-
flow statements.

Unfortunately, under Perlman, accounting and auditing became so confused that neither Bevan nor anyone else had access to figures that indicated
the massive breakdown in the Penn Central's operations. This point is crucial.
Bevan had long experience with the poor earnings record on the rail operations of the Pennsylvania. He knew of the similar conditions on the Central
and expected them to continue on the new Penn Central. He knew that the
two railroads suffered a combined loss from rail operations during the period
1954 through 1967 of approximately $7 million a year. Bevan thought this
would continue for a while. In addition, he recognized that there would be
sizable costs associated with the merger. Bevan also knew that it would take

time for the merger to operate smoothly and he expected a considerable amount of confusion. While his letters to Saunders about poor merger planning, especially in accounting, warned of trouble, nothing prepared him for an almost total breakdown in the railroad's operations.

BEVAN, PERLMAN, AND THE CAPITAL EXTRAVAGANZA

As Bevan began his duties on the new Penn Central, the problems he faced seemed similar to those he was familiar with on the old Pennsylvania, except they were larger in magnitude. Nothing better illustrates his view of the Penn Central than his holding of its shares. As an executive officer coming to the Pennsylvania Railroad, he had continually exercised his stock options so that by the time of merger, he held more than 30,000 shares, more than any other railroad officer except Stuart Saunders, who held 45,000 [8]. At the time of the merger, Bevan's stock represented about two-thirds of his $2 million of total assets. In March 1968 he routinely exercised another stock option and bought 3600 additional shares, making a total of 33,904. While expecting rough going for the first year or two of the merger, he had confidence that ultimately the railroad's losses would be brought under control and that the gains from his diversification program would make the Penn Central a profitable venture. His decision to reduce his Penn Central stock holdings in 1969 had nothing to do with the railroad's fortunes. Actually, the Penn Central's future still looked good to him. Although the rail operations had problems, Great Southwest's value was rapidly rising and exceeded $1 billion in mid-1969. Furthermore, Bevan had arranged financing that he felt would sustain the Penn Central through the difficult period of rail losses. To enable the exercise of stock options, Bevan had negotiated an unsecured loan in excess of $650,000 at the Mellon National Bank. He testified before the Securities and Exchange Commission that at the time he arranged the loan in 1965, he planned to pay it off by the date of his retirement in 1971. In order to repay the loan, he decided to liquidate approximately one-half his Penn Central stock in January 1969, and he ordered the stock sold according to a pattern in blocks of 3000 shares. This was done by June 25, 1969, and the proceeds, coming to about $835,000, allowed him to pay his capital gains tax and the Mellon Bank loan [9]. After this, he retained the rest of his Penn Central holdings of 18,546 shares until after he was dismissed as the Penn Central's chief financial officer at the time of the corporation's collapse in 1970. With the exception of Stuart Saunders, Bevan still remained the largest shareholder of any officer in the corporation. When he sold the first half of his shares, the price of Penn Central stock ranged between $50 and $66 a share. When he disposed of his remaining shares after his dismissal, the price had sunk to $11.50 for the first 4900 shares and between $6.25 and $6.08 for the final 8142 shares, sold on July 2, 1970. Bevan lost $233,000 on his remaining stock [10].

The Penn Central began life with a serious shortage of working capital and a projected cash shortage. On February 1, 1968, the merger date, the Penn Central's working cash was $13.3 million, an amount Bevan considered "totally inadequate" [11]. As on the old Pennsylvania, he worried about the possibility of large new capital expenditures that would further aggravate the Penn Central's weak cash position. In the forefront of his mind was the memory of the struggle he had waged with the operating department to trim the Pennsylvania's capital expenditures to affordable amounts. In his battles to restrain the Pennsylvania's capital expenditures, he had a very effective tool: the 1961 merger agreement under which the Pennsylvania had consented to a debt limitation of $100 million above the company's debt at the time the agreement was signed. Although this restriction was later raised to $195 million, he could always exercise a considerable influence on Saunders by pointing to the debt limitation and indicating that if it were exceeded, the New York Central might exercise its option to back away from the merger. Unfortunately, on the new Penn Central there existed no debt limitation, a fact he came to regret.

Although Perlman spurned income budgets, he favored capital budgets. He developed capital spending proposals at meetings, held in New York City, that generally lasted 2 or 3 days. In those sessions, various railroad officials conferred and the final programs were adopted. Although Bevan seldom attended Perlman's capital budget sessions, representatives of the financial department were always there. High on the list of Perlman's preferred projects were classification yards. He had built several of them on the New York Central, and he proposed the construction of two massive facilities on the new Penn Central, a $29-million computer-controlled yard at Selkirk, near Albany, New York, which was started prior to the merger and which became known as the Perlman Yard, and a $26-million installation at Columbus, Ohio [12]. Many Pennsylvania operating men insisted that the Perlman Yard should not have been built and that a nearby facility could have been easily expanded in its stead. To buttress their argument, the Pennsylvania officers pointed out that one year after Perlman had closed the old yard, it had to be reactivated because the Perlman Yard could not handle the traffic and that many of the employees who had received severance pay upon closing of the old yard were rehired. Bevan felt the same way about Columbus. He later noted that James Symes, then a Penn Central director, remarked that "if there was any place on the Pennsylvania Railroad he knew anything about, it was the operation in and around Columbus, and he said it was nonessential and foolhardy to spend the amount of money Perlman insisted on using at that point and at that time." Operating vice-president

Smucker told Bevan he agreed with Symes. To make matters worse, Perlman overran his budget at Columbus by more than $10 million, and the final cost was approximately $36 million.

Perlman held his first capital budget meeting almost immediately after the merger. Although Bevan did not attend, his representatives reported that expenditures of $300 million or more had been proposed. On hearing this, he had a talk with Walter Grant, the former New York Central vice-president for finance who had become executive vice-president in charge of accounting on the Penn Central. Saunders asserted that Bevan could not get along with Grant. Later, Bevan insisted that this was not true. He remembered that both he and Grant shared a common concern about the Penn Central's cash-flow problem and agreed on many other things as well. In this case, he told Grant that he just did not know how he could finance a $300-million capital program. Grant agreed and said that "he had talked to Perlman, he would talk to Perlman further, and he was sure that in the last analysis, the program would not be anywhere that magnitude."

Much to Bevan's surprise, at the next board meeting the directors approved almost without comment a $300-million capital program. Bevan "did not even know that it was coming up at that meeting, no one had asked [him] how it was to be financed, informed [him] at what rate funds were to be expended, or any of the necessary and essential facts necessary to formulate a financial program for a company already having problems with cash." Deeply concerned, he determined to talk Perlman out of the program. He went to New York and invited Perlman to lunch. The meeting was cordial. Perlman "talked constantly of how he had revamped the small Denver & Rio Grande; how he had come into the New York Central when it was on the verge of bankruptcy, and completely rebuilt it." Bevan seized upon this approach and "expressed pleasure that [he] was going to be associated with an operating man who had so much background in working out problems despite financial difficulties." He explained that the Penn Central faced an even more serious financial squeeze than that of the New York Central when Perlman became president. Bevan warned Perlman not only about the cash crisis but also about the Penn Central's heavy borrowing. Suggesting that during the company's shakedown period, it was particularly unwise to propose a $300-million capital budget, he urged Perlman to find ways to reduce it. The lunch was pleasant but Bevan felt he had not made his point. Later, he dropped by to see Walter Grant, who related Perlman's version of the luncheon. Bevan's worst fears were confirmed, and it was evident that he would have to find some way to finance the new capital program.

The Penn Central's directors must collectively take a considerable amount of responsibility for pushing the railroad rapidly down the road to bankruptcy. They gave the new corporation a board of directors that did not include the railroad's top financial executive. They approved an impossible capital budget that doubled the rate of such expenditures on the railroad without consultation with its financial authorities. They did so even though a cursory reading of the railroad's own annual reports would have indicated that the transportation part of the Penn Central's business was unprofitable even before merger. Bevan was in a difficult position. He had alerted the railroad's two ranking officers, Perlman and Saunders, who were also directors, to the grave consequences of the large capital expenditures. To have appealed over their heads to the directors would have ended in his resignation. In retrospect, this is the action he should have taken. Given Bevan's perception of the railroad's mounting crisis, it is difficult to understand why he avoided confrontation at this point.

DESPERATION MOVES

Bevan's problem was how to find more cash. His options were limited. Wall Street was unreceptive to a new issue of Penn Central's stock. A new bond issue was not feasible at that time. Furthermore, not only was the railroad's position difficult, but the state of the nation's economy hindered all large-scale fundraising. The last part of Lyndon Johnson's second term saw the increasing escalation of both the Vietnam war and government expenditures. Accompanying inflation began to push interest rates higher. In 1968 the prime interest rate, that is, the rate at which the banks' best customers could borrow money from them stood at 6 percent. To Bevan, this seemed high. Worse was yet to come. When Richard Nixon became President in 1969, he faced an ever-increasing inflation, and his administration fought back by contracting the money supply and increasing the interest rates. Starting in January 1969, the prime rate began to climb; in June it hit a peak of 8½ percent, where it remained throughout the rest of the year [13]. Never in Bevan's long experience in finance had interest rates been so high or money so tight. The Penn Central could not have picked a worse time to attempt to raise capital.

Bevan recognized that new initiatives were needed to meet the Penn Central's capital needs. In March 1968, he had a discussion with Gustave Levy, managing partner of the New York investment banking house of Goldman Sachs." Bevan's friendship with Levy dated from the late 1940s when the former had served with New York Life. He arranged with Levy for the Penn Central to issue commercial paper. This type of obligation is a short-term unsecured promissory note which usually runs for 90 to 270 days. Commercial paper is routinely issued by large industrial and retail corporations and is generally used to finance short-term inventory requirements, but many larger companies constantly roll it over, since they have continuing short-term needs. Prior to Bevan's arrangement, however, commercial paper was foreign to railroads, except for a few isolated small issues. There were good reasons for this. Commercial paper is ideal as a means of supplying working capital for industrial or retail corporations, since such capital is usually in the form of assets that can quickly be liquidated. By contrast, Bevan used commercial paper to supply money for long-term capital needs, hoping to replace it at a later date with long-term borrowing. This would take time to accomplish and would depend on an improved bond market and a turn-around of Penn Central's earnings picture. The great risk in Bevan's strategy was that the railroad might have a large issue of commercial paper suddenly come due and be unable to roll it over. Goldman Sachs recognized this danger and suggested that the Penn Central try to cover itself by securing lines of credit from banks equal to half the face value of the issued commercial paper. Bevan took this advice. Under the circumstances, he had virtually no choice in his methods of finance, but he later recognized that the commercial paper triggered the railroad's bankruptcy. However, at first all seemed to go well. Bevan applied to the Interstate Commerce Commission for authority to issue commercial paper. The ICC approved the issuance of $100 million at first, another $50 million in early 1969, and then still a further $50 million, so that at the end of 1969 the Penn Central had issued $200 million of the unsecured notes [14].

The commercial paper did not supply enough cash. Bevan had to negotiate with banks to borrow more money. It will be recalled that in 1954 Bevan concluded a revolving bank credit of $50 million. At the time of merger, this had been increased to $100 million. Early in 1969 Bevan arranged to expand this revolving credit to $300 million. The revolving loan was a considerable improvement over the commercial paper, since the Penn Central had the right to draw down any or all of the credit prior to December 1970, after which date it would become a 5-year term loan. In order to back up the Penn Central's commercial paper, Bevan withheld borrowing $50 million of the revolving loan and then obtained an additional $50-million confirmed bank line to support the paper. Bevan tried to get still further confirmed bank lines by borrowing in the Eurodollar market, but he was unsuccessful.

At the time Bevan made the new revolving credit arrangements, both Perlman and Saunders agreed that this financing would last the company through 1970. Such was not to be. Despite the loss of $140 million because of railroad operations in 1968, Perlman convinced Saunders and the company's board of directors that another $300 million of capital expenditures was necessary. In Bevan's recollection, in 1968 and 1969 the financial department under his supervision raised approximately $950 million for the railroad. This included lease agreements for new equipment as well as commercial paper and the revolving credit. He summarized that "of this amount, about $560 million was used for capital expenditures—approximately $379 million for equipment and $181 million for road expenditures. Of the balance, about $245 million was applied against debt maturities," with the remainder going to finance operating deficits. Bevan thought about the critical state of the railroad's finances for weeks, and finally came to the conclusion that he had fulfilled whatever obligation he had to Richard Mellon. He was certain that he had done everything in his power to save the company and that his only choice, in view of Saunders's and Perlman's policies, was to resign. Bevan hoped that his action would force the matter to the attention of the railroad's board of directors and result in new policies.

On June 22, Bevan went to see Saunders, taking with him a letter of resignation. This was two days before a Penn Central board meeting, after which Saunders planned a short European trip. Bevan dated his letter June 23, 1969. It read:

Dear Stuart:

It has become increasingly evident to me that I should take early retirement. Since the innumerable factors influencing my decision are well known to you, it would be superfluous to detail them in this letter.

However, for the record, and to preclude the possibility of misunderstanding or misinterpretation on the part of anyone, my reasons can be summarized very simply. In my position as Chairman of the Finance Committee, and Chief Financial Officer of the system, the situation has become exceedingly awkward. Having the responsibility for the financial welfare of the company, but given neither the power nor the opportunity either to influence or to remedy unsound financial practices, my position has become wholly untenable. Finally, virtually my entire staff, the finest in the industry, has left as a consequence of the unsound structuring of the financial organization at the time of the merger, an organizational setup that I strongly opposed. This fact, in itself, would make it impractical for me to continue.

Under the circumstances, I would like to make my retirement effective as of March 1, 1970. Also, I wish to announce my retirement in the near future at a time and in a manner which will cause the company no embarrassment.

Obviously I have given this matter intensive and prolonged thought before reaching my decision. In submitting this letter I extend every good wish to the company and to the Board of Directors for the future development and success of the entire system. Towards this objective I offer complete assurance of my fullest cooperation and assistance whenever and wherever it may be possible to provide it.

Sincerely,

David C. Bevan

In later years, Bevan vividly remembered Saunders's reaction. Saunders became "very excited" and told Bevan that he had "performed brilliantly" and that his resignation would be "upsetting to the public as well as to our stockholders." He also stated that "it would be catastrophic as far as the banks were concerned" and that Bevan had an obligation to stay and try to work things out. Furthermore, Saunders had finally decided to fire Perlman as chief operating officer, and that when he returned from Europe, he would do so. He offered to increase Bevan's salary to $200,000 if he would remain. Bevan refused to stay, emphasizing that an increase in salary was not his objective. He told Saunders that he was "satisfied that the operation would never be successful under the current management and that . . . he wanted out now, even more than . . . he did at the time of the merger." When Saunders asked Bevan what he wanted, he replied, "Nothing," then corrected himself by adding, "except to start sleeping again at night, which I have not done for almost 2 years." Saunders brushed that aside with the remark that "he never had been able to sleep at night." Bevan replied that "irrespective of what he [Saunders] had or had not been able to do previously, I had always been able to get a good night's sleep and I wanted to return to that routine."

Saunders again asked Bevan to withdraw his resignation, at least temporarily, since Saunders wanted to delay this matter until after his European trip. He then asked whether, if any director should raise the issue with him, he could say that Bevan had no thought of resigning. Bevan said that Saunders could not make such a statement, but added that he did not "believe there was much of a chance between Monday and Wednesday of any officer or director raising the question." Saunders answered that one director had already heard rumors that Bevan was going to take early retirement. Bevan replied that he had never talked to the director in question about the matter and that his information was based upon pure gossip. Finally he agreed that nothing more would be said about the resignation until after Saunders's return from Europe. Bevan pointed out that the letter gave Saunders the opportunity of picking the time to announce the resignation since the designated date was still 9 months away. Before the meeting ended, Saunders asked Bevan if he would join the Penn Central's board of directors and its executive committee. Bevan refused, stating that this action would make no sense with his resignation imminent. In retrospect, Bevan recognized that it was a serious mistake not to announce his resignation publicly before Saunders's departure. Had he done so, he might have been spared much of the ordeal he endured as a result of the Penn Central's collapse.

GORMAN REPLACES PERLMAN

Stuart Saunders arrived back in Philadelphia from his brief European trip determined to find a replacement for Alfred Perlman. Neither Saunders nor Bevan fully appreciated the magnitude of the Penn Central's operations collapse, but both recognized that things could not go on as they had been. In fact, Saunders had begun to panic. Earlier in 1969 when Perlman had forced Smucker's resignation as chief operating officer, Saunders had lost his temper. In an unguarded moment, he revealed his true state of mind. He told Smucker, "I'll be rid of Perlman within 90 days; he's the worst enemy I've ever had in my life; he's cost me untold millions of dollars; I didn't want him in the first place and I'll get rid of him; you can have my word on it; I'll get rid of him in 90 days" [15]. Although Saunders also clearly disliked Bevan, he was not yet ready to lose him. When he met his chief financial officer, the conversation turned to his impending resignation. Saunders asked him if he would not change his mind and go on the Penn Central's board of directors. Bevan declined. Saunders then asked him to help search for a new president. Bevan agreed, commenting that as long as he was on the payroll, he would "do anything in the line of duty that was required." Saunders then asked Bevan's opinion of Louis Menk, who was then president of the Northern Pacific Railroad. Bevan replied that Menk's reputation was one of the best in the industry, but that, aside from Menk and Herman Pevler, there were few men, if any, in railroading equal to the Penn Central's challenge. Saunders then asked Bevan to furnish a list of presidential candidates.

Bevan thought long about the kind of man who should succeed Perlman. Finally, he picked Richard Terrell, a General Motors executive who had come up through that corporation's Electromotive Division. Bevan liked Terrell's experience in the manufacture of railway locomotives as well as the managerial training he had received at GM. Unfortunately, when the chief financial officer checked Terrell's compensation and his "rapid rise in the General Motors organization, it became clear that under no circumstances could the Penn Central entice him away from General Motors." Terrell was never approached.

Saunders had no better luck in hiring Menk. Over a number of weeks he did talk with Menk, and he told Bevan that Menk and his wife spent one weekend in Philadelphia at Saunders's home. He found that "Menk was under a long-term contract" with the Northern Pacific and that it was impossible to break it.

The successful candidate to replace Perlman came from an unexpected source. During the summer of 1969, Charles Hodge, chairman of the Executive Committee of the New York brokerage firm of Glore Forgan, was apparently thinking in terms of some sort of takeover of the Penn Central or at least becoming more influential in its affairs. He thought the stock, then selling in the 50s, was unduly depressed. Hodge had long been a close friend of David Bevan, and had helped the Pennsylvania in its diversification program. Saunders discovered Hodge's plans before they had advanced very far, and the two met to discuss the Penn Central's future. During this meeting, Saunders told Hodge that Perlman was being replaced. Later, Hodge submitted a list of potential candidates for Perlman's position. At the top was Paul Gorman, then president of Western Electric.

In early August, Hodge arranged a meeting in his New York office between Gorman, Saunders, and himself. At the last minute, Saunders asked Bevan to attend. Discussion lasted an hour or two, and Saunders did most of the talking. Gorman asked a few questions and Bevan's only role was to supply information dealing with fringe benefits given by the Penn Central to its executives. Bevan "liked Gorman's clean-cut appearance." He was happy to learn that Gorman had been trained in accounting, "was very strong for strict cost controls, precise budgets, and that he had a reputation for cost cutting." However, Bevan worried that Gorman had spent his entire life in the telephone industry, "most of it under the wing of the parent company, where he had all possible resources at his command, and where revenues and income could be forecast fairly accurately, which made budgeting and forward planning not too difficult." He also was not enthusiastic about Gorman's age of 63, which he felt was too old. In his opinion, the Penn Central "needed someone much younger, who could stay in office for 10 to 15 years and really become knowledgeable about the company."

After the initial meeting, Saunders carried out all the negotiations with Gorman. As these went on, Bevan thought it important that either Hodge or Saunders advise Gorman that he had submitted his resignation. He did not consider himself "indispensable," but wanted Gorman to have "full knowledge of the situation." Bevan "did not want to be placed in a false position, and seem to walk out, because a new man was brought in as president." Later he found out that nothing had ever been said to Gorman about the chief financial officer's proposed resignation.

Saunders completed the arrangements with Gorman toward the end of August, and at a meeting on the twenty-sixth, the Penn Central's board of directors elected him president. Gorman later claimed that he had no real conception of the problems existing at the Penn Central. While Bevan long retained a high opinion of Gorman's integrity, he distinctly remembered a telephone conversation with the president-elect immediately after he agreed to take the office. Gorman called to explain "that it was impossible to get a waiver from a provision in an overall agreement in Western Electric, that no one could resign, or leave, without 90 days' notice. He explained that this meant he could not come to the railroad before December 1. Did [Bevan] not think it would be a good idea if [he] just waited until January 1?" Bevan's exact words to Gorman at that time were, "Paul, if you are coming, the quicker, the sooner, the better!" Gorman replied, "Are things that bad?" Bevan said, "No, they are worse." Thus it was that Gorman did not take active control of the Penn Central's management until more than 3 months after he had been appointed president.

ORDEAL IN THE FINANCIAL SUITE

During August 1969, Saunders subjected Bevan to continuing pressure to reverse his decision to resign. Part of Bevan's reluctance to stay was based on his stormy relationship with Saunders. The Penn Central's board chairman had never forgiven Bevan for blocking the accounting manipulation on the Pennsylvania just prior to the merger. At one point, Bevan remembered, Saunders in a fit of anger had told him that "he was out to get him." Certainly Saunders would have liked to remove Bevan if it could be done in the right way, and the right way for Saunders was for Bevan to be dismissed in disgrace —not to resign of his own choosing. Saunders's problem was that he needed Bevan. The chief financial officer's standing on Wall Street and in the banking community remained high. Saunders appreciated Bevan's crucial role in raising money to see the Penn Central through the cash crisis that followed the merger. He feared that if Bevan left in anger, it would reflect badly on the Penn Central's board chairman and undermine the railroad's relationship with the money market. Even Bevan's departure in disgrace held peril for the Penn Central's ability to raise capital.

Bevan remembered a very curious incident that took place in early 1969. Shortly after the turn of the year, his deputy and alter ego, William R. Gerstnecker, announced that he was resigning as of July 1969 in order to take a position as vice-chairman of Philadelphia's Provident National Bank. He told Bevan that he had no confidence in Saunders, did not want to report to him directly after Bevan retired, and just wanted to get away from the Penn Central and start a new career. About a month later, Bevan dropped in to tell Saunders about the negotiations in progress to increase the railroad's revolving credit from $100 million to $300 million. He remembered that Saunders was "extravagant in his praise" of the chief financial officer's efforts on behalf of the railroad. Ironically, however, just one hour later while Bevan was traveling to New York, Saunders called Gerstnecker and allegedly offered him Bevan's position if he would withdraw his resignation from the Penn Central. Saunders promised to return to the financial department a number of functions that had been stripped from it at the time of merger. Gerstnecker refused to change his mind. Then Saunders tried "to get Gerstnecker to say he was leaving because of a personality clash" with Bevan. Gerstnecker had no desire to undermine Bevan, who had early recognized his talents and rapidly promoted him up the corporate ladder on the old Pennsylvania. He ended the interview by stating that he had an excellent relationship with his boss.

When Bevan arrived back in Philadelphia, Gerstnecker told him what Saunders had said. When Bevan confronted Saunders with what Gerstnecker had told him, the board chairman "denied it" and "attempted to wriggle out of the situation" by claiming that he was "only talking to Gerstnecker in terms of gradually taking ever-increased responsibilities." Since Bevan would be 65, the Penn Central's mandatory retirement age, in August 1971, Saunders's machinations were more of an annoyance than a threat.

In the middle of 1969, Bevan also came to an open break with his long-time friend, Charles Hodge. Bevan had accepted several acquisitions submitted by Hodge of Glore Forgan in the railroad's diversification program. Hodge actually knew very little about the operation of the railroad, and when the Penn Central's price began to fall in mid-1969, he decided that it would be a good time to form an investment group to buy into the corporation. While Bevan was helping Saunders search for a new president, Hodge moved. He came to Bevan and told him that with the stock down to between $40 and $50, it would be a propitious time to put a large group of investors together who would buy into what he termed "the greatest railroad in the world." Hodge asserted that the investors would do well financially and, although he did not say so, Bevan "gained the impression that in reality he was thinking in terms of obtaining control of the company."

Bevan tried to discourage Hodge. He pointed out that the Penn Central had a serious management problem and that, so far, the costs of the railroad were not under control. Although he thought that the Penn Central ultimately would be a good investment, he believed that its current problems would continue for some time and that it was impossible to predict the future course of the company's stock prices. Bevan said it would be a disservice to bring in a large number of new stockholders under these conditions. If, Bevan argued, the stockholders became unhappy, their discontent would merely create a new problem for the Penn Central's management in addition to those associated with the merger. Hodge became upset at Bevan's attitude, and especially so when Bevan said that even knowledge of a plan such as Hodge's could be misinterpreted. Bevan "wanted no part of joining in what might be considered or actually represent a takeover move," since he was part of management. He also told Hodge he had submitted his resignation and was planning to make a clean break. After Hodge left, Bevan told Gerstnecker about the proposed takeover. Gerstnecker suggested that he himself might be able to discourage Hodge, but when he discussed the matter with the stockbroker, all he received was "an expression of dissatisfaction as to Bevan's attitude." Hodge stated that "Bevan was becoming increasingly hard to deal with and irritable." Bevan knew this feeling marked a real break in what had been a close and friendly association.

A little later, Hodge mentioned his plan to a friend of Perlman. Hearing about it in this manner, Perlman became worried. He immediately told Saunders that Bevan was involved in a planned takeover of the company. Bevan assumed that Perlman came to this conclusion because he knew of the close relationship that existed between Hodge and himself. Saunders promptly questioned Bevan, who told him the entire story and suggested that "he call Hodge and talk to him directly." Hodge immediately agreed to talk with Saunders. Hodge told him that "all he wanted to do was to be helpful and back up management as far as possible, but that he was of the opinion that Perlman should be retired." The relationship between Hodge and Saunders became friendly, and the New York stockbroker injected himself into the search for the Penn Central's new president.

While the search was in progress, Hodge introduced a new major investor to the Penn Central: Clayton Gengras, who was the chief executive officer of Hartford's Security Insurance Company. Hodge set up a meeting with Saunders and Gengras in New York. At the last minute, Saunders again invited Bevan along. At the meeting, Gengras inquired whether or not, "if he were part of a group buying into the Penn Central, it would be possible for him to become a director." Saunders encouraged him. Shortly after the meeting, Security Insurance purchased 200,400 shares of Penn Central's stock through Glore Forgan [16]. Saunders then nominated Gengras to become a member of the Penn Central's board.

Despite Hodge's worsening relationship with Bevan, he recognized that it was important that the Penn Central's chief financial officer continue to serve during the period of the railroad's cash crisis. Saunders and Hodge discussed the matter, and finally the Penn Central's board chairman asked Hodge to urge Bevan to agree at least to discuss staying with the company. Bevan reluctantly agreed to go this far, thinking that "only a fool would refuse to listen." But at the time, he had no intention of changing his mind. He stated flatly that "he would not enter into any negotiations" and instructed Hodge to tell Saunders that. Nevertheless, when the meeting took place, Saunders "immediately started to bargain." Bevan explained that he had explicitly "only agreed to sit down and listen." Saunders assured him that "so far as he was concerned, he would stop interfering in financial affairs, would virtually rubber stamp [Bevan's] recommendations, and that the financial department would be set up exactly as" Bevan wished it. While not committing himself, Bevan told Saunders that he thought that John O'Herron, who had come into the Penn Central from Buckeye Pipeline as the vice-president of accounting, "should immediately be built up in stature by being made financial vice-president, with both accounting and finance under his supervision." Bevan also said it was essential that accounting come under the jurisdiction of the financial department, where it had been on the Pennsylvania immediately before merger. He stressed that "the accounting department should act as a service organization, acting as the eyes of the operating department, ferreting out weaknesses in operations, through analysis of figures. Beyond that, it should be free to record the actual results attained, leaving no one in a position to distort the results in any way." However, he recommended that data processing stay in the operating department even though, prior to the merger, it had been in the financial department. Saunders seemed surprised at this advice, but Bevan explained that "with Gorman's background, it appeared that he was better qualified to oversee its operations." Saunders then asked whether Bevan would remain with the company if all Bevan's recommendations were put into effect, and if so, what salary did he want? Bevan responded "that salary was one subject that [he] had never discussed, that [he] would not in this instance negotiate salary because [he] did not want [his] motives in any way to be misunderstood; this was a matter for him and the board to decide." After considerable pressure from Saunders, Hodge and a number of the directors, Bevan finally agreed to remain with the Penn Central until his normal retirement date. He also agreed to go back on the board of directors and its executive committee. In effect, Bevan agreed to delay his departure from the company from March 1, 1970, to his normal retirement date of August 31, 1971, or approximately 18 additional months. Saunders told him that he would ask the board to approve a raise in Bevan's salary from $165,000 to $200,000 a year. Bevan reiterated that as far as he was concerned, salary was not an important matter.

The Penn Central's directors met on August 26 to confirm Paul Gorman's nomination to the presidency and Bevan's return to the board. The day before the meeting, Saunders telephoned Bevan asking for a memorandum covering administrative changes that Bevan desired. Bevan knew this was not necessary because Saunders had taken very careful notes at their meeting. He told Saunders that he "could not afford to place a memorandum in his hands which he might represent to the board as demands on [his] part." He emphasized that the administrative revisions he proposed were essential to the Penn Central whether he stayed or not. He also insisted that "he preferred early retirement and was only reluctantly agreeing to continue for a period of months and if the organization was sufficiently revised to give it a chance to work."

Bevan attended the first part of the August 26 board meeting, when the board discussed Executive Jet Aviation (EJA), in which the Penn Central had an investment. One of the points mentioned was a suit brought by a former Executive Jet officer, John Kunkel, against Executive Jet, Penn Central, Glore Forgan and Company, General Olbert F. Lassiter (Executive Jet's president), Charles Hodge, and David Bevan [17]. Then Bevan left the meeting prior to the discussion of his appointment.

At the luncheon following the meeting, Saunders told Bevan that the proposed reorganization that he had recommended had been approved and that he had been elected to the board. Saunders added, however, that he could get Bevan a salary of only $185,000, not the $200,000 he had proposed. Bevan repeated that he would not discuss salary and had made no request for an increase. Finally, almost as an afterthought, Saunders said the board had appointed a committee, to be chaired by Edward J. Hanley, to investigate the Executive Jet problem. Bevan sensed "trickery of some sort," but he tried not to show his feelings and inquired what the committee was to investigate. Saunders brushed this question aside by saying the investigation was routine and that the directors wanted to determine what the Penn Central's liability in the Kunkel suit might be. Bevan pointed out that this was a problem more for the Penn Central's legal department than for a committee of the board. He felt that Saunders was evasive in describing the scope of the committee's assignment. He then told Saunders that he proposed to call Hanley and find out "the truth of the matter."

That evening Bevan telephoned Hanley. During their lengthy conversation, Hanley told him that the request for an investigation into Executive Jet came as the meeting drew to a close and the directors actually had started to leave the room. At the very last minute, Stewart Rauch, president of the Philadelphia Savings Fund Society and a close friend of Saunders, proposed that the directors create a committee to investigate the handling of the Executive Jet investment. Bevan told Hanley that as far as he "personally was concerned, they could investigate EJA to their hearts' content and that [he] would gladly cooperate 100 percent with the committee." However, Bevan considered this proposed investigation "a vote of 'no confidence' by the board." He said that his patience was at an end and that he would submit his resignation to Saunders the next morning. Hanley asked Bevan to wait, saying that he had confidence in him, his judgment, and his integrity. Hanley pointed out that the entire action had been taken so hurriedly that no one had much time to think about it. Bevan suspected that Saunders had arranged with Rauch to make the motion at the very end of the meeting when everyone was in a hurry to leave. To Bevan, this was just one more of Saunders's steps to undermine him in the eyes of the board members so that he could be forced out at an appropriate time. Another fact reinforced this opinion. Bevan learned that at the directors' meeting, Rauch had asked why Bevan should receive any salary increase while the Kunkel suit was pending. Saunders answered that he needed Bevan's cooperation in the months ahead.

Saunders did not want Bevan's immediate departure. When Hanley told Saunders about Bevan's intention to resign immediately, the Penn Central's board chairman sprang into action. He talked to John Seabrook, another director, to enlist his support to retain Bevan. Seabrook later testified about the conversation [18].

Q. Did Mr. Saunders indicate that he wanted to keep Mr. Bevan?

A. He surely did.

Q. Had you understood that there was any animosity between Mr. Bevan and Mr. Saunders?

A. Yes, I didn't think that they were fond of each other at all.

Q. Well, did you see any reason why this was not a good time for Mr. Saunders to accept Mr. Bevan's resignation?

A. Well, keep in mind that timing, August, was two months before we passed the cash dividend and he regarded Bevan as a wizard at raising cash and so I think he didn't want to lose his services at the time.

Saunders also told Rauch to call Bevan. Rauch did so on September 3. The call was awkward, but Rauch was convinced that Bevan's services were essential and that he should stay. In the following days, a large group of the directors visited or called Bevan asking him not to retire. Nearly all emphasized that the resolution to investigate the EJA investment had been hasty, and they expressed confidence in the chief financial officer. Bevan made a serious error in judgment; he agreed to stay. Hanley worked out the compromise. The board of directors expunged the resolution on EJA, and Bevan submitted, at the board's next meeting, a written report covering Executive Jet that had been reviewed by the Penn Central's legal department as well as by Covington and Burling, the Washington law firm handling the matter for the railroad [19].

References

1. Bevan Diary, quoted in *The Financial Collapse of the Penn Central Company*, a Staff Report of the Securities and Exchange Commission to the [House of Representatives] Special Sub-Committee on Investigations, Hon. Harley O. Staggers, Chairman, Government Printing Office, Washington, D.C., August, 1972, p. 81. Hereafter referred to as the SEC Staff Report.

2. Ibid., p. 82.

3. Interstate Commerce Commission, Brief of the Bureau of Enforcement before the Interstate Commerce Commission, Docket No. 35291, The Investigation into the Management of the Business of the Penn Central Transportation Company and Affiliated Companies, March 8, 1972, p. 129.

4. Ibid., p. 130.

5. Ibid., p. 132.

6. Ibid., pp. 132–133. Bevan, after the bankruptcy, stated that as far as he was concerned, it was not true that he could not get along with Grant. He admitted that he and Grant had some sharp exchanges prior to the merger, but they worked together. When Grant left the Penn Central, Bevan was sorry to see him go and openly said so, because Grant seemed to be the only officer on Perlman's staff who recognized the seriousness of the Penn Central's position.

7. Ibid., p. 130.

8. By contrast, the other major officer, Penn Central President Alfred Perlman, had little stake in the company. The SEC Staff Report summarized Perlman's position

as follows: "Prior to the February 1968 merger, Perlman had exercised options granted to him (these grants had been made before 1964) and had sold 32,890 of these shares. As of February 1968, Perlman reported his ownership of stock at 2860 shares. His only transactions in 1968 and 1969 were disposing of 960 shares as gifts. On April 1, 1970, he sold 500 shares and held the remaining balance of 1400 shares until after bankruptcy." SEC Staff Report, p. 259.

9.   There is considerable controversy over Bevan's decision to sell part of his shares. Bevan received a letter in December 1968 from Spencer R. Hackett, a vice-president of the Mellon Bank, suggesting that Bevan liquidate his loan. Hackett admitted writing the letter but, later, testified under oath that Bevan had asked him to write such a letter. Bevan also testified under oath that he did not ask Hackett to write this letter. See SEC Staff Report, p. 248. Hackett's letter to Bevan made no mention of a telephone call or any other communication between the two. Hackett's letter clearly indicated that the desire to reduce Bevan's loan originated at the Mellon Bank.

10.   SEC Staff Report, pp. 244–249; Staff Report of the Committee on Banking and Currency, House of Representatives, *The Penn Central Failure and the Role of Financial Institutions,* Washington, D.C., January 3, 1972, p. 341; also undated memoranda in the Bevan Papers detailing sales of Bevan's stock and the prices he received.

11.   Bevan to Saunders, August 30, 1968.

12.   Cost data from *Annual Report* of the Penn Central Company, 1968, p. 11. It is interesting to note that Pennsylvania men were not alone in criticizing Perlman because of his building of yards. Karl A. Borntrager, who spent 50 years on the New York Central and served Perlman as a senior vice president, wrote of his first meeting with Perlman in June 1954 that "Mr. Perlman said he thought our [NY Central's] greatest weakness was our poor yards. He felt that we needed to construct about five or six large modern yards to replace yards that he considered obsolete. Now I had worked practically all the NYC—much of it on yard studies—and did not think our Yard situation pressing. Mr. White [former NYC President] a hard-bitten railroader, didn't think so either." (Karl A. Borntrager, *Keeping the Railroads Running: Fifty Years on the New York Central*, Hastings House, New York, 1974, pp. 185–186.) Later in his book, Borntrager is critical of Perlman's decision to spend resources building new yards (p. 188).

13.   Data on prime rates from *Newsweek,* April 6, 1970, p. 67.

14.   SEC Staff Report, pp. 271, 277.

15.   Ibid., p. 24.

16.   Ibid., p. 164.

17.   Promptly after the filing of the suit, Bevan obtained copies of the complaint and sent them to both the Counsel for the Penn Central and Saunders. No papers in this suit were ever served on Bevan.

18.   SEC Staff Report, p. 160.

19.   The following copy of a report, dated September 24, 1969, that Penn Central Director Edward Hanley presented to the board of directors clarifies Bevan's position on the Kunkel investigation.

Mr. Chairman:

I think it would be well if my report did not become part of the minutes of this meeting. However, I expect to keep a copy of this report in my own files and to give Mr. Bevan a copy for his personal files. Both he and Mr. Saunders are familiar with the contents of this report. In fairness to everyone concerned, I believe the board should have the benefit of the following facts:

Prior to the merger Mr. Bevan strongly objected both internally and to me personally in regard to the proposed organization of the merged company. He stated it was unsound both from the standpoint of structuring and capabilities of the personnel involved. It was only after some changes had been made in this and at the personal request of General Mellon and myself that he agreed to continue on with the merged company. Unfortunately his judgment has been substantiated by the loss of a number of key personnel, particularly in the financial area, for reasons which he had anticipated.

Since the merger he has also been in serious disagreement with respect to the way some things were being handled. Finally, on June 23 in a letter addressed to the Chairman he requested early retirement. However, he acceded to Mr. Saunders' request to hold it in abeyance until after Mr. Saunders returned from Europe. On the day before our last board meeting, he finally agreed to stay on in light of changed conditions provided the organizational setup of the Financial Department be put on what he considered a proper and sound basis, and that Jonathan O'Herron also be made Vice-President, Finance. He made no request for increased compensation and, as a matter of fact, refused to even discuss this.

If you will recall, Mr. Bevan was out of the room when a committee was created to investigate the EJA situation and he was not informed of this until after the meeting. That evening he called me in my capacity as Chairman to determine what the scope and purpose of this committee was. When I explained the situation to him he was very shocked. He stated that he did not question the right of the board to carry on any investigation it desired, and in this instance he would welcome it, but since this action had been taken after he had tried to give the board as detailed an explanation as possible of a very complex situation, he did not believe he had any alternative but to request the Chairman to activate his early retirement letter of June 23, but that he would extend the fullest cooperation to the committee in any investigation they cared to carry on. He said he planned to request a meeting with Mr. Saunders the following morning and so advise him.

It is the unanimous opinion of my committee that its creation was ill-advised, a mistake, and that it should be dissolved. Furthermore, the action creating the committee should be stricken from the minutes and the minutes of the last board meeting should be amended to read that the board authorized the

Chairman of the Board and the Chairman of the Finance Committee, with advice of counsel, to take whatever action seemed best with respect to the consent decree.

I want to make it very clear at this time that at no time has Mr. Bevan questioned the right of the board to investigate nor has he attempted to block an investigation. He stands ready to answer any questions that any director might have in regard to the whole matter.

If the report of this committee is accepted, Mr. Saunders and I believe that Mr. Bevan will consent to continue at least for the time being in view of the seriousness of the financial problems confronting the company.

I think we should also take official cognizance that under the supervision of Mr. Bevan the diversification program has been outstandingly successful.

One final thing—some opinion was expressed at the last board meeting that the board had not been kept properly informed regarding EJA. I am advised that a report has been made to the board at least once in each year since its inception, and so far in 1969, twice. When it is realized that this is an investment and not a subsidiary or affiliated company and that the amount involved was very small until recently, it appears to the committee that we have been kept informed.

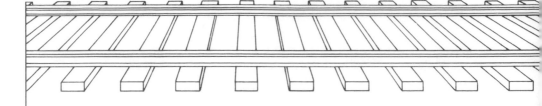

Chapter 12
DISASTER

In September 1969 Bevan came back with renewed power. One of his first assignments to Jonathan O'Herron, the new financial vice-president who replaced Gerstnecker, was to develop a "capital budget, an income budget, and a cash-flow statement" for 1970. However, while Bevan's office undertook these tasks and before Gorman began his duties as the Penn Central's new president, the Penn Central omitted its dividend. As previously noted, the Penn Central was severely criticized for paying dividends, and subsequently the staff reports of two congressional committees blamed the payouts for contributing to the bankruptcy. In its short career, the Penn Central paid nearly $100 million in dividends, representing quarterly dividends in all of 1968 and three quarters in 1969. Bevan admitted that in retrospect, dividends should have been dropped earlier. He also said that it would be nice to be on record as opposing dividend payments, which he did not. He observed, as noted earlier, that even had the Penn Central paid no dividends in 1968 and 1969, the bankruptcy would have been delayed by only 2 or 3 months at best.

In any case, Bevan did not set the dividend rates. Each payment was approved both by the board of directors' Finance Committee of which Bevan was chairman and by the board of directors as a whole. Bevan explained that although he presided at Finance Committee meetings, during Stuart Saunders's tenure as chief executive officer, Bevan turned the meeting over to him. Saunders always discussed the Penn Central's "results of earnings, prospective earnings, and various background material and then [made] the recommendation as to the dividend" [1]. Saunders also made the dividend recommendation to the board as a whole. In all cases, he decided upon the amount. Perlman later told a senate committee chaired by Vance Hartke that he had opposed dividends. This may be true, but Perlman's opposition is not recorded in the minutes of the meetings where the decisions were made until the directors unanimously voted to pass the dividend in November 1969. Until June 24, 1969, the records of the Finance Committee and the board of directors show that no one questioned any of Saunders's recommendations. Discussion did occur at that June directors' meeting when Saunders proposed a regular 60-cent quarterly dividend, payable in late September. Several directors suggested that in view of the railroad's poor financial results, it would be better to defer consideration of the dividend until a later time. Bevan later remembered some of his thoughts at the time. He favored dividends in the mistaken belief that the railroad's costs could be controlled. He was aware that the Penn Central's predecessor, the Pennsylvania Railroad, had paid dividends since 1847 and that stopping them would indicate "a lack of confidence on the part of management in its ability to get the costs of the railroad under control." Bevan feared that an omission might have an unfavorable impact upon the railroad's interest rates, particularly in the short-term money market, and thereby would add to the company's financial woes. As he put it, he believed that by discontinuing dividends the increased "interest paid on our ever-mounting debt would offset, in the form of higher interest rates, much of the cash retention by the discontinuance of dividends." The board of directors settled the question by declaring a dividend payable September 26, and this information was released to the press [2]. By November 26, the railroad's financial condition had deteriorated so substantially that the board did omit the final-quarter dividend.

BEVAN'S STRATEGY TO SAVE THE PENN CENTRAL

Despite the cash crisis in December 1969, Bevan remained optimistic that the railroad could be turned around. He based his hopes on Perlman's replacement by Gorman. The chief financial officer was certain that modern corporate managerial techniques would work. He saw his main task as buying time for the Pennsy's new president. He did not expect miracles nor did he even think the rail operations would become immediately profitable. He merely thought that management could lower the losses to the point where the Penn Central's other investments could carry the company, as indeed the Pennsylvania Company in the past had often rescued the old Pennsylvania Railroad.

When Bevan reassumed many of his old powers, he found the budget-making department, accounting, and data processing in such disarray that he could not immediately construct a reliable income budget or cash-flow statement. He tried to compensate by building a conservative income budget. He felt under no condition could the railroad project results for 1970 better than those obtained in 1969. His operating budget for 1970 assumed a railroad operating loss of $56 million. After careful consultation with Gorman and Saunders, he agreed to a capital budget that assumed the infusion of $170 million of new money, including $70 million for equipment and $100 million for improvements to the physical plant. This meant a net projected cash outflow of $226 million for 1970, which the financial department would have to raise.

When Bevan presented these plans to Saunders, the board chairman was horrified. He said that improved service and efficiency in 1970 would be better than Bevan's estimates. Furthermore, he argued that a projected loss of $56 million would "scare the directors to death." Bevan, remaining adamant, said financial planning would have to be done on the basis of his projected income budget and cash-flow figures. Saunders attempted to salvage some optimism by creating a management target that projected profit of somewhere between $25 million and $50 million. Bevan knew this figure was unrealistic, but since his planning was based on what he considered a bedrock income budget and cash-flow projection, he went along with Saunders's creation of a management target budget.

In January 1970, Bevan and Saunders presented their budgets first to the Finance Committee and then to the entire board of directors, who unanimously approved them. According to Bevan, director Stewart Rauch commented upon the wide disparity between his income budget for financial planning and Saunders's management target budget. Bevan recalled Rauch's statement "that we should really look into the budget operations and tighten up our procedures." It was obvious to Bevan that this director "had so little concept of what had been going on that he failed to realize that this was the first income budget that had been presented to the board since merger."

The afternoon following the board meeting, Bevan received a call from Gorman asking if he "was now free to go ahead and operate on the basis of these budgets." Bevan said yes. Commenting that he "had heard a great deal about the problems with budgeting in the past with Mr. Perlman," Gorman then promised that he "would move heaven and earth to see that these budgets were met."

Bevan got an early start on his plans. He quickly placed $70 million of equipment financing. This meant he had to raise only $156 million more to see the Penn Central through 1970. He proposed to accomplish this by floating a $100-million loan backed by the assets of the Pennsylvania Company. He planned to raise the remaining amount by borrowing either from banks in the United States or abroad in the Eurodollar market.

THE COMMERCIAL PAPER CRISIS

Bevan's whole financial program depended upon keeping railroad losses to a level no higher than that experienced during 1969. Any rapid increase in railroad losses could trigger the time bomb that hung over the Penn Central. In early 1970, Bevan had $200 million of commercial paper outstanding. Adverse financial news about the Penn Central would make it difficult for Goldman Sachs, the railroad's commercial paper dealer, to roll it over. Bevan felt partially secure against such a crisis because he had $100 million of bank credit to use in an emergency. This arrangement, in theory, would enable the railroad to withstand the withdrawal of $100 million of commercial paper from the market. Things did not work that way.

Bevan faced his first major crisis on February 5, 1970. That morning, press releases announced that the railroad had sustained an operating loss of $56 million for the year 1969 and that it had written off $126 million invested in long-haul passenger service. The financial papers also stated that the Penn Central's consolidated income for 1969 (which included the railroad and its other interests) amounted to only $4.38 million, compared with $87.8 million for the previous year. Robert G. Wilson, head of Goldman Sachs's commercial paper department, read about Penn Central's poor financial performance in 1969 and immediately called John O'Herron. He told the Penn Central's vice-president for finance that "the news will have an adverse effect on . . . [the] sale of [commercial paper] and we may not be able to keep out $200 million of their notes." Wilson urged that Penn Central increase its backup for commercial paper with an additional $100 million in standby bank credit [3]. The next day Gustav Levy, Goldman Sachs's managing partner, and Wilson had lunch with Bevan and O'Herron. Bevan thoroughly explained the income budget and cash-flow projections he had made for the railroad for 1970. According to his estimate, the railroad would need to raise $226 million in 1970, which would allow for a $56-million loss on the railroad and $170 million of capital expenditures. Bevan had already raised $70 million of this amount through equipment financing, and he told the Goldman Sachs representative about his plans to raise an additional $100 million through the sale of long-term bonds of the Pennsylvania Company. He stressed that "for the first time since the Pennsylvania Railroad and the New York Central merged, [he had] confidence in the budgets." In his opinion, Gorman was "a top nonrailroad, cost-conscious, cost-controlled businessman" [4]. The Goldman Sachs officials seemed satisfied with Bevan's explanation, but they stressed that the railroad should try and get $100 million more in confirmed bank lines to cover 100 percent of the outstanding commercial paper. Wilson predicted that, at the very least, Penn Central's commercial paper could run down by $50 to $100 million [5]. The Goldman Sachs men also stated that they would not carry so much unsold Penn Central paper in their inventory. Prior to February, the New York investment house had carried as much as $15 million, but hereafter, Wilson said, $5 million would be their limit.

Unfortunately, even Bevan's projections of the railroad's operating loss proved greatly in error. Winter weather caused part of the problem. Severe snowstorms in late January and throughout February tied up Penn Central trains for weeks at a time. Not only did the railroad lose revenue, but it incurred massive expenses for snow removal. In addition, Bevan grossly underestimated the railroad's operating collapse and the losses resulted from 2 years of poor service.

While Bevan worked to reassure the sellers of Penn Central's commercial paper, he struggled to provide the new money necessary to meet the income budget he established for the year 1970. In December 1969, he collaborated with the First Boston Corporation, Glore Forgan, William R. Staats, and Morgan Stanley to have the Pennsylvania Company issue $50 million of debentures, which were exchangeable for shares of Norfolk & Western common stock [6]. Bevan planned to have the Pennsylvania Company issue another $100 million of debentures at a propitious time in 1970. However, in order to supply Penn Central's need for cash prior to the next Pennsylvania debenture issue, he sought a $50-million "bridge" loan from New York City banks on the credit of the Pennsylvania Company. Bevan initially went to the First National City Bank of New York (later renamed Citibank), which had taken the lead in establishing the Penn Central's $300 million of revolving credit. But the First City Bank had already begun to worry about the size of the Penn Central's borrowing and the railroad's losses. City Bank tried to use Bevan's new loan request to get further security for the previous loans. This Bevan was unwilling to provide. Consequently, he went to New York's Chemical Bank and described his problems with City Bank. The Chemical then took the lead in a consortium of banks that supplied the needed $50 million [7]. Bevan's next step was to initiate a new $100-million debenture offering of the Pennsylvania Company, a move which he had told Wilson of Goldman Sachs was critical in meeting the Penn Central's capital budget.

The railroad's legal and financial staffs started to work on the preparation of the Pennsylvania Company's debenture offering in February 1970. Because the Pennsylvania Company's assets were large and its debt relatively small, the underwriters were at first confident of their ability to sell a $100-million issue. Prospects quickly turned sour. The parent railroad's poor financial announcements and a sharp fall in the value of a Pennsylvania Company subsidiary, Great Southwest, made the outlook dubious. Bevan had already used the Pennsylvania Company as a vehicle to pump money into the faltering railroad. He had pledged Penn Central's ownership of Pennsylvania common stock as security for the $300-million revolving credit. As previously noted, Bevan pledged some of the Pennsylvania's unencumbered

Norfolk & Western shares in order to back $50 million of debentures issued in December 1969. The Pennsylvania Company's greatest unpledged asset was its holding of 25 million shares in the Great Southwest Corporation. In May 1969, this stock had sold above $40 a share and had a market value in excess of $1 billion. Unfortunately, the tight money situation which the Nixon administration instituted to combat the inflation inspired by the Vietnam war began to have a serious impact upon the Great Southwest, since tight money and high interest rates slowed its operations. The corporation's stock started to fall in value; it sold at $16 a share at the end of 1969, fell to $14 a share in March 1970, and plunged to $6 a share in May of that year. In order to secure funds, the Great Southwest borrowed overseas; yet its fortunes were inexorably linked with its parent company, the Penn Central. The rapid decline of Great Southwest's value made it difficult for Bevan to launch a new issue of debentures based on the Pennsylvania Company's assets. This stumbling block caused him to delay.

THE DILEMMA OF RESPONSIBLE REPORTING

After the Penn Central's collapse in June 1970, Bevan received much criticism, particularly from congressional committees, for two aspects of his behavior during his final year with the railroad. One charge accused him of failing to disclose, both to the Penn Central's shareholders and to the holders and potential holders of its debts, the company's precarious financial predicament. The second accusation claimed that he deliberately attempted to hide railroad losses by submerging them in the consolidated reports that included the results of both the railroad and its diversified subsidiaries. In retrospect, these charges seem unreasonable.

To the staffs of the congressional committees that investigated the Penn Central, its collapse seemed obvious from the date of the merger. This assertion is based on hindsight and almost no one, including Bevan, recognized the magnitude of the shortcomings in the Pennsylvania's, and then in the Penn Central's, management. Bevan foresaw the problems that developed in data processing and in accounting, and he recognized that the Penn Central was in for serious financial problems if managerial deficiencies were not corrected. However, he believed that once the company improved its management, it would succeed. Bevan saw such improvement in Gorman's rise to the presidency in 1969. When he reassumed most of his old duties at the Penn Central in the fall of 1969, he faced a serious dilemma. On one hand, he had to be honest about the serious financial problems the Penn Central faced. On the other hand, because he believed the corporation would eventually work its way out of its difficulties, he could not afford to be too pessimistic in his public statements. Bevan had never forgotten his experiences during the Great Depression following the stock market crash of 1929. He had seen many bank managements panic, causing runs on their institutions, and close their doors even though they had ample assets to ride out the crisis. On the other side, there were occasions where bank managements had acted too optimistically when they should have closed. Bevan recognized that Penn Central was in a similar position. Throughout the early part of 1970, he thought his major duty was that of buying time so that Gorman could institute the necessary reforms to turn the railroad around. He tried to avoid any statement or action that might deny Gorman this opportunity. Bevan was aware that a misstep might inadvertently raise the cost of borrowings needed by the railroad or precipitate a run on the Penn Central commercial paper. He knew that panic on his part could destroy the shareholders' investment, imperil the security of loans already made to the railroad, and in addition, have a severe impact upon the nation's commercial paper market. It is significant that even after the collapse of the Penn Central, the Pennsylvania Company, which controlled the diversified interests, remained a sound and profitable business. This stability supports Bevan's assertion that if the railroad costs could have been brought under control, all would have worked out well. What Bevan did not know and could not have known, given the confusion in accounting and data processing, was the depth and permanency of the railroad's collapse. Unfortunately, this became clear only in the years following the Penn Central's bankruptcy.

The charge that Bevan obscured the railroad's financial problems is not true. Nothing better illustrates this fact than the Penn Central's annual report, issued in March 1970. Pages 16 and 17 of this document present a statement of consolidated earnings that lumped together the railroad and the diversified enterprises. This is immediately followed by a two-page summary (on pages 18 and 19) of earnings and retained earnings and of the balance sheet of the railroad only. The report clearly indicates that the railroad lost $5.15 million in 1968 and $56.33 million in 1969, prior to the extraordinary loss of $126 million caused by the write-off of long-haul passenger service. Not all financial analysts have been critical of the Penn Central's reporting. David Macey, a lecturer in finance in Boston's Northeastern University, wrote in *The Boston Globe* [8] that "a brief and unsophisticated examination of Penn Central's 1969 annual report, the last one issued, makes one wonder why the firm's failure caught investors by such surprise, and more importantly, why there are so many lawsuits, the SEC's included." Macey pointed out that the annual report (on page 7) showed that the Penn Central "only earned 0.2 of 1 percent . . . on total sales, an absolutely rotten performance for any kind of company." Furthermore, on page 14 a "numeric and pictorial presentation of the sources of funds at Penn Central for 1969" showed that "of the total funds used in the business during 1969, 82 percent were borrowed and that only one-half of 1 percent came from earnings from operations." Macey asked how many firms had to "borrow 82 percent of the funds they need in order to keep operating." Footnote 7 contained "a tabulation showing the annual principal payments due on the firm's long-term debt for the 1970–1974 period." Macey noted that during these years, $986 million would come due. "What more indications of pending cash problems did the world need?" The Penn Central's annual report had been audited by Peat, Marwick, Mitchell & Co., which also received severe criticism for not alerting the financial community to the Penn Central's problems. "What was [Peat, Marwick, Mitchell & Co.] supposed to do back in 1969? Print 'B-A-N-K-R-U-P-T' in red ink on the cover of the Penn Central's report for the benefit of those investors who were either too lazy or too stupid to see all the warning flags?" asked Macey. One might excuse smaller shareholders for failing to read the annual report thoroughly, but ironically, some of the biggest losers were sophisticated financial people, such as major bank officers, and investment houses, such as Goldman Sachs.

Lee J. Seidler, professor of accounting at New York University's Graduate School of Business Administration, took a similar tack in an earlier article in the *Commercial and Financial Chronicle* [9]. He pointed out the weakness of the charges made by the Securities and Exchange Commission. Commenting on the SEC's report, Seidler said that a new era had blossomed that might be called, "Get the Accountant." When a company goes bankrupt, "a writer armed with 20-20 hindsight proceeds to unearth all the 'facts' which were earlier omitted (or concealed by the company and its auditors). He then places the blame for the debacle on the hapless accountant." The heart of the SEC's complaint was that the 1969 income statement obscured losses of the railroad because it indicated " 'loss from ordinary operations' of only $56,328,000." Later the railroad admitted to losses of $193,215,000 for the same period. According to the SEC, this last figure seemed to indicate that railroad losses had been understated by $137 million. Did the annual report actually do this? asked Seidler. He continued:

True, the "loss from ordinary operations" is shown as $56,328,000. A glance at the revenue section showed the first item to be, "railway operating revenues . . . $1.652 billion." Immediately below that are five other revenue items such as "dividends and interest" and "net gain on sales on properties and investments." Does it take a financial expert to know that these items are not part of running a railroad? To find the railway loss figure, why not add them back to the $56 million ordinary loss, which was clearly not labeled railway losses. Not surprisingly, the total loss comes to $193,215,000, precisely the figure [the SEC later found to be so revealing].

Seidler concluded that the annual report of the Penn Central, prepared by Bevan's staff and certified by Peat, Marwick gave ample warning of the company's severe financial troubles.

What no one knew in 1969 and early 1970 was the long-term and severe nature of the collapse of the northeastern railroads. Of course, it was evident that the Pennsylvania and the New York Central had long been marginal enterprises. It was also clear these railroads suffered from the general decline of the Northeast and were further damaged by Eisenhower's massive highway program, which diverted much of the high-value traffic still remaining in the region. Hindsight tells us that the operating failure created large operating losses. Also, it accelerated the decline by forcing railroad customers to find other means of transportation. Once they did so, the damage proved permanent. Many people even in the railroad industry did not understand this. One such man was John Barriger, who had long been president of the Pittsburgh & Lake Erie Railroad before his retirement in 1964. Then, however, he achieved a substantial reputation as a doctor for sick railroads. Shortly after Penn Central's bankruptcy, Barringer proclaimed that if a competent management were placed in charge, the Penn Central would at the end of the year be operating at a profit. Time has not sustained his view.

In any case, the Penn Central's annual reports indicated the corporation had very serious financial problems and that an investment in the firm entailed grave risk. Even so, Bevan continued to believe that railroad losses could be cut to the point where they could be offset by income from diversification. When the results of the railroad's operations for the first quarter of 1970 came out, he began to lose his confidence that the railroad could be turned around in time.

THE FINAL CRISIS

Bevan long remembered the first months of 1970. The first quarter of each year was traditionally poor for the railroad, and he had budgeted a loss of $49 million for it. He knew the revenues had been off severely because of the bad winter weather in January and February. Yet the Penn Central sales department indicated that there was a huge backlog of business waiting and that March would be a good month. The operating people, also optimistic, said there would be a substantial reduction in operating expenses in March. Both departments were wrong and the operating loss for the first 3 months of 1970 totaled $79 million. Bevan and Saunders were sitting side by side at a budget committee meeting when the preliminary results were presented. Bevan "was absolutely stunned." He noted that "Saunders took one look at my face and said, 'Do you think this will affect your $100-million financing in the Pennsylvania Company?' " He said, "Stuart, I am so shocked that I am speechless, and I am unable to think or predict what effect this will have on our financial plans."

On April 14, before any outsider had the preliminary estimates, John O'Herron warned Goldman Sachs's Wilson to expect that the Penn Central's first-quarter railroad losses would be "staggering." At 5 o'clock that afternoon, Wilson and Vogel of Goldman Sachs met with O'Herron and Bevan and discussed the Penn Central's plight. At that moment, Bevan could not tell the exact amount of the first-quarter losses, but he explained that they would be substantially greater than the $12- to $13-million loss in the comparable 1969 quarter. He pointed out that the railroad accrued $20 million in extra expenses because of the severe winter weather and that a retroactive wage increase would cost the Penn Central an additional $18 million. At that moment, Bevan still was uncertain as to what course he was going to take. He emphasized Gorman's cost-cutting program. He also explained that in an emergency, the railroad could raise cash through such methods as the sale of its holdings in Madison Square Garden, the sale of a portion of its Great Southwest stock, the sale of the Arvida Company, which was not yet pledged, or money raised through the very profitable Penn Central subsidiary, the Pittsburgh & Lake Erie Railroad, which he believed could issue $50 million to $100 million of its bonds, since it was debt-free. Bevan stressed that he would not raise money by selling the Pennsy's extremely valuable Park Avenue holdings because these properties were encumbered by several layers of mortgages, and additionally, it would be unwise to sell these assets until litigation over the price of the New Haven Railroad had been settled. Wilson emphasized that the inevitable public announcement of the Penn Central's first-quarter losses might trigger a runoff in the commercial paper regardless of Bevan's statements or Goldman Sachs's views [10]. Robert Wilson had considered stopping the sale of the Penn Central's commercial paper, but as a result of the meeting with Bevan, Goldman Sachs agreed to continue selling the notes [11].

Wilson's prediction proved accurate. On April 26, the Penn Central announced the results of the railroad's first quarter, and the first indication of a run on the railroad's commercial paper began. However, Bevan thought that if the backup bank credit of $100 million was used, the market for the Penn Central's commercial paper would stabilize. For a brief time, the situation did seem to ease. Bevan spent many sleepless nights trying to decide what should be done. Finally, he came to the conclusion that things were almost beyond control, and he told Saunders that the time had come to seek government aid. Saunders arranged an appointment with Nixon's Secretary of the Treasury, a former Chicago banker, David Kennedy, on May 19. Bevan explained that the Penn Central was facing a serious run on its commercial paper. At that point, the railroad had been forced to retire $50 million of its notes from the market and it was about to have to turn to the

$50 million of its revolving credit, which it had held in reserve to back the paper. Bevan, foreseeing that this would not suffice, pointed out that $100 million of the notes were not backed up by confirmed bank lines. He suggested that the implications went far beyond the Penn Central. Altogether, there were between $36 billion and $38 billion of commercial paper outstanding, and the failure of such a prominent company as the Penn Central might start a nationwide liquidity crisis. Bevan recalled that upon hearing this, the Secretary of the Treasury "paled perceptibly." Kennedy told Saunders and Bevan that he did not know what powers he had, but he "understood the problem and everything possible would be done" to help. They all agreed that the Penn Central should tell both the commercial and investment bankers of the problem.

On May 21, Bevan met with representatives of the First National City Bank and the Chemical Bank in the latter's offices. He explained his meeting with Kennedy and announced that the Penn Central was withdrawing its attempt to sell a $100-million debenture offering through the Pennsylvania Company. To meet the continuing run on its commercial paper, the Penn Central was going to draw down the remaining $50 million on its $300-million revolving loan. Bevan and the bankers agreed that all the banks in the $300-million consortium should be told of the situation, and Bevan promised to delay the final $50-million drawdown until a meeting with all the banks had been held. He asked the bankers to join the Penn Central in requesting government aid. The meeting ended with nothing decided [12]. During the next week, Bevan participated in a series of frantic meetings with leading bankers. On Thursday, May 28, he met with representatives of the nearly 90 commercial banks doing business with the company. The meeting was not happy; in the end, the representatives of the First National City and Chemical Banks congratulated him on a detailed and precise presentation and on his frankness in answering their questions. Later the same day, he met with the investment bankers, and they decided to announce publicly Penn Central's abandonment of its Pennsylvania Company bond issue.

For Bevan, the major problem now was to negotiate terms of government support. For many years, his relationship with the banks had been cordial and cooperative. Now the situation had changed. He understood that few bankers are "ever happy about discovering that they have a bad or slow loan." Nevertheless, he felt that some of the banks took an unrealistic position. They wanted Penn Central to put up the rest of its unpledged assets to secure loans already made. Bevan pointed out that this was contrary to customary procedures for dealing with new money coming into financially troubled corporations. Traditionally, fresh capital came in on a priority basis. Furthermore, Bevan recognized that the government faced a delicate political problem and that it would be subject to embarrassing questions if it got no security for its loans. Throughout the difficult negotiations, Bevan "reiterated time and time again that it was not a question of negotiating the terms of the loan with [himself]." As far as he was concerned, he recognized that he was in a difficult situation. As far as he and the Penn Central were concerned, he would recommend to the Finance Committee and the company's board of directors any package that made available all the railroad's remaining collateral and would agree to divide this up "in whatever way the government and the banks decided was fair and equitable in order to obtain . . . the essential guaranteed [government] loan." Despite what seemed like endless negotiations, no progress could be made.

COLLAPSE: THE OUSTER OF SAUNDERS, PERLMAN, AND BEVAN

On Thursday, June 4, Saunders telephoned Bevan to say that he and Gorman had been called to New York to review the Penn Central's financial troubles with Walter Wriston, the chairman of the board of the First National City Bank. Bevan expressed surprise that Wriston had not consulted the company's chief financial officer, as had been the standard practice in all previous instances. He suggested that he should accompany Saunders to New York, but Saunders rejected the suggestion. From what Bevan later learned, he came to believe that Saunders, not Wriston, had initiated the meeting. Bevan suspected that Saunders wanted an opportunity to place blame for the trouble squarely on his chief financial officer.

The meeting took place on the morning of Friday, June 5; that afternoon, Saunders told Bevan that he was calling the Penn Central's board together on Monday. Bevan said that there was still no word from Washington about the terms of a proposed $225-million guaranteed loan, and that he did not know what there was to tell the board. Saunders retorted that, nevertheless, he wanted to discuss the entire situation with the Penn Central's directors. At about 11 P.M. on Friday, Bevan received yet another telephone call from Saunders. This time, the board chairman warned him that Wriston had "been highly critical" of him and that Saunders was going to repeat this criticism to the board. Bevan asked for the exact nature of Wriston's remarks, but Saunders refused to discuss the matter further.

Prior to the fateful board meeting on Monday, June 8, Saunders, Gorman, Bevan, and the Penn Central's special counsel, Robert Guthrie, met in Saunders's office and talked about the proposed $225-million government guaranteed loan. Everyone thought the loan would still be forthcoming, although no one knew what the terms would be. Bevan remembered Guthrie's stating that "in his opinion, nothing should be done at this particular meeting with the board." On this note, all four went into the boardroom, where Saunders brought the directors up to date on the events of the past few days. Bevan also told the directors about his meetings with the bankers. Surprisingly, Saunders said nothing about Wriston's criticism of Bevan. Then, to Bevan's surprise, Saunders suggested that Perlman, Gorman, and Bevan should withdraw from the meeting in order to allow an informal and frank discussion by the outside directors.

Bevan returned to his office. Several hours later, he heard by the grapevine that a committee of the board, composed of Gengris, Hanley, and Seabrook, was visiting Stuart Saunders. He thought that this might mean that although Saunders would be retained as chairman, he would be a figurehead without authority. Bevan assumed that Gorman would emerge as chief executive officer and that, since Perlman had no real duties, he would be ignored.

Bevan later learned that the directors' visitation caught Saunders unprepared. Saunders apparently thought that he had been successful in placing the blame for the Penn Central's crisis on Bevan. Therefore, the board chairman was stunned when the directors told him that he had been relieved of all his duties and that his association with the Penn Central was at an end.

As Bevan pieced information together, he concluded that Saunders must have convinced Wriston that Bevan was to blame for the Penn Central's problems and had persuaded the New York banker to insist on Bevan's ouster by the board. This conclusion explained Saunders's eagerness to call a special meeting of the directors. However, apparently a snag developed Sunday evening during a series of telephone calls between some of the leading bankers involved. Bevan learned that at least one tried to persuade Wriston that he should not be dismissed, but to no avail. Thereupon, the banker insisted that if Bevan went, Saunders had to go as well.

After the directors' committee dismissed Saunders, its members went to Perlman and told him that he had been relieved of all duties with the Penn Central. Next, they came to Bevan's office and gave him a similar message. Trying to take the news quietly, he inquired about the basis on which he was to be retired. The committee answered that "under the terms of the merger agreement" he was entitled to "full salary for one year," and that this arrangement would take him up to his normal retirement date. The committee said that if Bevan thought any injustice was being done, the directors would be glad to discuss the matter further. The committee gave him no reason for its actions and he didn't ask for any.

Bevan spent the rest of the afternoon in his office with several of his loyal staff members. During the course of the day, some of the directors dropped in to express regrets at what had happened. He tried to take it all philosophically, pointing out that, as the old saying went, "If you lose the war, the generals' heads are all chopped off." He felt that this had happened in his case, since he had been dragged down by the mismanagement of Saunders and Perlman. Some of the directors agreed with him. One of his friends, Frank Lunding, chairman of Penn Central's Executive Committee, stopped by to say, "Dave, I consider this action, as far as you are concerned, an absolute outrage. The worst decision you ever made was when you reluctantly agreed to withdraw your June resignation. I feel particularly guilty since I was one of those who put the most pressure on you to stay, but I thought it was necessary if we were going to bring this merger out successfully." Bevan replied that he had "no bitterness," that he was unhappy that the merger had not been successful, and that he had been unable to "contribute enough to stabilize the situation, but the odds had just been too great."

Director William Day came in shortly thereafter, and made a comment that took Bevan by surprise. Bevan asked, "Don't you realize that from the day of the merger I had nothing to do with accounting, budget administration, and no real voice in the control of the expenditures in the railroad until last fall?" Bevan recollected that, in a very weak and puzzled voice, Day said, "That had never filtered up the ladder to the board of directors." Bevan replied, "You were present at the first board meeting after the merger, and all you had to do was to look at the organization chart, and you would have known just what the organizational structure was. It now appears that you never had any concept of the fact that I was stripped of virtually all my responsibilities and authority until late in the fall of 1969." Day "just shook his head and said 'I never realized that'."

The firing of the Penn Central's three top managers failed to save the company. The banks continued to insist that they should receive additional security for the outstanding loans they had made to the firm. Furthermore, the Nixon administration began to have second thoughts, particularly since the move to bail out the company met strong resistance from Representative Wright Patman, chairman of the House of Representatives Banking and Currency Committee, and other key congressional leaders. Part of the problem lay in the administration's rescue strategy of trying to funnel aid through the Department of Defense. Several key members of Congress advised Defense Secretary Melvin Laird that they thought the proposed loan guarantee was illegal. The growing congressional opposition forced the Nixon administration to withdraw its support for the loan guarantee and on June 21, 1970, the Penn Central filed a bankruptcy petition.

References

1. "Answers of David C. Bevan in the Bevan Papers," undated.

2. *The Financial Collapse of the Penn Central Company*, a Staff Report of the Securities and Exchange Commission to the [House of Representatives] Special Sub-Committee on Investigations, Hon. Harley O. Staggers, Chairman, Government Printing Office, Washington, D.C., August 1972, p. 158. Hereafter referred to as the SEC Staff Report.

3. Bevan Papers, Robert G. Wilson, Confidential Memorandum on the Penn Central Transportation Company, February 5, 1970.

4. Bevan Papers, Robert G. Wilson, Confidential Memorandum on the Penn Central Transportation Company, February 6, 1970.

5. Ibid.

6. These shares held their value even after the Penn Central's bankruptcy since they were backed by the valuable Norfolk & Western stock. See SEC Staff Report, pp. 108–09.

7. Ibid., p. 100.

8. David Macey, "Accountants Should Get 'Clean' Bill on Pennsy," *Boston Evening Globe,* June 25, 1974.

9. Lee J. Seidler, "Don't Blame the Auditors," *Commercial and Financial Chronicle,* December 7, 1972.

10. Jack A. Vogel, Very Confidential Report on the Penn Central Transportation Co., April 14, 1970. *Note:* Since bankruptcy, the trustees have refused an offer of approximately $100 million for the Pittsburgh & Lake Erie.

11. Robert G. Wilson, Memorandum on the Penn Central, April 14, 1970; Wilson Confidential Memorandum, April 15, 1970.

12. SEC Staff Report, p. 103.

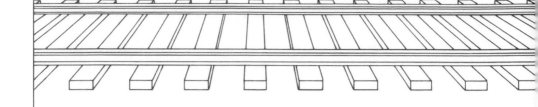

Chapter 13
A TASK UNFINISHED

The Penn Central was the biggest business failure in the history of the United States and much is to be learned from it. Unfortunately, the headline-catching, scandal-focused government investigations that followed the collapse diverted attention from the important issues. This focus made it difficult to understand the railroad crisis that even now grips the northeastern United States. It is vital to pull together all the various complex strands of the Penn Central story so that the real issues may stand out clearly from the mass of detail.

David Bevan is significant because he devoted his entire career at the railroad trying to overcome the basic problems that eventually caused the bankruptcy. In retrospect, the issues emerge clearly.

When Bevan joined the Pennsylvania in 1951, the company had serious financial challenges. The railroad, for all its glorious history, was marginal. The Pennsylvania had one of the lowest rates of return on rail operations of any major American railroad. This record was especially ominous because the entire rail industry was depressed. As previously illustrated, the Pennsylvania, in common with its arch-rival, the New York Central, during some post-World War II years actually sustained losses on its rail operations, and the company remained solvent only because of substantial revenue from outside investments. The railroad faced a second major threat—low cash resources. Bevan found, soon after he became financial vice-president, that the Pennsy had one of the most unfavorable ratios of working capital to gross operating revenues of any major American corporation, worse even than the chronically depressed steel companies. Finally, the Pennsy had a massive debt, which in 1951 considerably exceeded a billion dollars.

The triple problems of low earnings, inadequate cash, and large debt caused Bevan deep concern from the very first. The challenges fell into three separate areas. The first was beyond Bevan's control and he could have little, if any, impact on it. This area consisted of outside forces operating on the railroad with relentless pressure: government policies that favored trucks, waterways, and airlines; high state and local real estate taxes; industrial decline in the Northeast; America's shift from coal to oil, with the resulting loss of traffic; the political and social forces that required the continued operation of money-losing passenger trains; the unresponsiveness of Interstate Commerce Commission rate regulations to the company's needs; collective bargaining procedures that routinely required the payment of large retroactive wage increases; and strong labor unions that kept antiquated work rules and crew requirements.

The second major challenge, the problem of debt management, was internal and within Bevan's area of responsibility. Until Stuart Saunders arrived, Bevan had striking success with the debt. He restructured it to make refinancing easier when the time came to roll it over, and by 1963 he had reduced the debt 30 percent. Here the railroad's top operating men and its chief executives, despite Bevan's attempt to explain the situation, did not understand what was happening. Much of the cash used to retire debt came from the sale of real estate and other assets the Pennsy had accumulated in its more than a century of existence. In this case, debt reduction was a form of slow liquidation, a fact that Bevan pointed out to the Interstate Commerce Commission and the railroad's operating men at every opportunity.

The third area of challenge that Bevan found was the railroad's managerial structure and practice. Here, reform was only partially within his area of responsibility and control. The Pennsylvania, in common with most other railroads, including the New York Central, had long been run by operating men who did not understand and sometimes explicitly rejected modern managerial techniques. Consequently, the company in 1951 lacked such elementary financial tools as an income budget, cash-flow projections, responsibility accounting, and cost and profit analysis geared to enable top management to make intelligent decisions about the allocation of scarce corporate resources. One of Bevan's major tasks was to attempt to make improvements to the railroad's administration. He began with the corporation's accounting system. He brought into the railroad top executives who were familiar with accounting and financial management in the most advanced American industries.

Bevan's new team, headed by Cook and Sempier and aided by outside consultants such as the accounting firm of Peat, Marwick, Mitchell & Company, abandoned reliance on the traditional Interstate Commerce Commission accounting system used by the operating men. They substituted for it the kind of financial management typical of advanced American corporations. This system included responsibility accounting, which allowed management to evaluate the performance of each segment of the business and of the people in charge. Furthermore, Sempier, in conjunction with IBM and Peat, Marwick, worked to install a sophisticated, centralized, data processing system that Bevan used to build income budgets and cash-flow projections. His results helped the management to plan realistic operating and capital budgets.

Unfortunately, the top operating men did not view the railroad from a business executive's perspective. Their chief goal was to move cars rapidly and effectively along the tracks, but they did not systematically collect information that would enable them to analyze whether cars moved profitably. The Pennsy's top management had never assessed with any degree of accuracy which traffic was most profitable. The railroad traditionally made investment decisions on the basis of traffic volume rather than revenue. Even here, management used, not hard data, but seat-of-the-pants estimates made by division managers. Bevan attempted to change this practice by applying his information system and his budgets.

Bevan's ideas and practices conflicted with long-established traditions followed by the railroad's powerful operating department, and in the mid-1960s, he clashed sharply with operating men during debates over the adoption of the company's capital budgets. He repeatedly criticized proposals that he considered were not carefully made and that failed to estimate such things as return on capital investment, realistic depreciation charges, and potential utilization. These debates in part isolated Bevan and his financial team from the operating segment of the railroad, and they may have been in some measure responsible for Saunders's decision to shunt him aside at the time of merger.

Through the administrations of Walter Franklin and James Symes, Bevan found support for his policies at the highest level. Both company presidents appreciated Bevan's successful program of debt reduction. However, Symes did not really understand the implications of his new accounting systems, data processing, and budget making. Symes sought salvation for the railroad in another direction: merger with the New York Central. In theory, merger offered much; in practice, it was fraught with almost insurmountable difficulties. The biggest obstacles were the very large size of both the Pennsy and the Central, the fundamental difference in the organization of each company, and the almost negligible cash resources. When the union finally occurred in 1968, the New York Central had only $7.6 million of cash in the bank, and the Pennsylvania, $5.5 million. There was absolutely no margin for error.

The merger might have succeeded in spite of all, had certain elements been present. These were an enthusiasm and deep commitment to the concept on the part of all the top management; an understanding on the part of the railroad's leaders of the importance of organization; a recognition by

Perlman and Saunders of the merged company's financial limitations; and finally, careful, detailed, and sophisticated advance planning at all levels. But none of these conditions existed.

The immediate key to the Penn Central's failure is to be found in the leading executives in the new company, Stuart Saunders, the chief executive officer, and Alfred Perlman, the president and chief operating officer. As the Penn Central's top man, Saunders bears the most responsibility for what happened. He came to the railroad unprepared for the role he was to play. He had inadequate experience in railroad operations, a poor understanding of the significance of corporate organization, a naivete about the importance of advance planning, and a dangerous ignorance of finance and accounting. His main assets were his steadfast enthusiasm for, and faith in, the merger, and a political ability that, among other things, allowed him to secure its approval from reluctant quarters, such as government and labor.

Saunders's record in the areas of finance and accounting is revealing. It had been the view of Peat, Marwick that in 1965 the Pennsy had installed the most sophisticated budgeting program in the railroad industry. The program had started under Symes but was just reaching its peak under Saunders. One of the budget's values was its ability to monitor and forecast railroad operating revenues and operating costs. Each year the budget became more accurate. In 1964, the first full year of Saunders's administration, the actual operating revenues varied from the budget by 5.2 percent; the discrepancy was 1.5 percent in 1965 and only 0.9 of 1 percent in 1966 [1]. The budget figures for operating costs were equally reliable. All this precision was essential in predicting the railroad's cash flow and in determining the amount of money that would be available for capital improvements.

During Saunders's regime, two contradictory but very important trends began to emerge on the Pennsylvania. The cash flow from railroad operations started to decline, and spending on railroad capital improvements rose sharply. The cash generated from rail operations could not carry the capital improvements and the difference had to be borrowed. The problems that faced the merged New York Central and the Pennsylvania from the very first were accelerating railroad operating losses and rapidly growing capital expenditures. This situation led to massive borrowing, and unless it could be reversed, it was the certain road to bankruptcy.

No one can say that Stuart Saunders was not warned. Bevan, because the budget system he implemented was so precise, quickly recognized what was happening and tried to communicate his fears to Saunders, who apparently ignored the important difference between reported net income and cash flow. In vain Bevan tried to convince him, writing in November 1966 that "a policy may be instituted of attempting . . . to keep net income and cash flow as closely together as possible without regard to what the immediate effect is on earnings. Up to several years ago this was basically the policy pursued by the Pennsylvania Railroad." In contrast, Bevan explained, "the policy may be instituted of maximizing earnings to the greatest extent possible within the limits of good accounting practices. In the last several years this has been done on the Pennsylvania in accordance with your [Saunders's] expressed desires. It does mean, however, that we tend to create a wider and wider difference between reported income and cash flow." Bevan then pointed out that the Pennsylvania's consolidated income figures were not an accurate indication of cash flow because the subsidiary companies had "their own requirements for the ploughback of money" [2]. In short, all the income produced by the subsidiaries could not be channeled to railway operations to make up a cash shortage there.

Bevan tried constantly to keep the railroad's cash problems before Saunders. In October 1966 he informed the company's chief executive that the cash drain from rail operations during 1964 through 1966 had been $97 million. He added, "As has been pointed out many times in the past 3 years, we have rapidly reached a very serious danger point with respect to our ability to carry on new financing" [3]. Conditions worsened, and in September 1967 he told Saunders that "because of our presently extremely low cash position, it is imperative that we plan carefully for the balance of the year and for 1968. . . ." Bevan warned that "we cannot get through October and November of 1967 when our cash is reduced by the end of those months to $13 million and $6 million, respectively. On top of this, based on present estimates and historical results, we are faced with a decline in cash between the end of this year and the first quarter of 1968 of $25 million" [4]. One solution, the chief financial officer suggested, was for the Pennsylvania Company to issue $50 million of debenture bonds. This was a short-term measure. Someday, cash outflow from the railway would have to be balanced with cash inflow from earnings.

The information Bevan sent to Saunders indicated that the most serious single problem facing the Pennsylvania was the cash hemorrhage caused by the railroad. On the Pennsylvania, these losses had been manageable only because they were offset by the earnings from the outside investments. However, the increasing capital expenditures for the railroad business made it harder and harder for the company as a whole to maintain a positive cash flow. One might have assumed that this problem would have been foremost in Saunders's mind when he considered the merger, especially since the New York Central was confronted with the same difficulty. It might also have been expected that Saunders would have appreciated the sophisticated and accurate budget operation which Bevan had created since it was potentially management's most valuable tool in bringing cash outgo in line with income.

But that was not Saunders's only merger problem. Compounding all was the radical difference of nearly everything about the organization and operation of the Pennsy and the Central. As demonstrated earlier, the Pennsylvania had a decentralized organization. Each region operated almost as a minicompany, with its own chief executive and functional officers for such duties as operations, maintenance, and traffic. In contrast, Perlman's railroad was highly centralized. That meant, for example, that maintenance people in one of the Central's regions reported to a top boss at the company's New York headquarters, not to a regional office. This was only the most obvious difference. The railroads used different accounting systems. The Pennsylvania had advanced responsibility accounting and the Central the old Interstate Commerce Commission bookkeeping. The New York Central did not even have an income budget or a cash-flow estimate. Much has been made of the fact that the two companies used different computer hardware and software, but this disparity was not the real problem. The Pennsylvania's former head of data processing, Carl Sempier, in an interview with the author, explained that it was a relatively simple matter to hook the two systems together so that they could talk to each other. The difficulty arose because each company had a different philosophy about the use of the computer. Ironically, the Pennsy's data processing was highly centralized, with data for billing, car tracing, car movements, and other information all going into one highly reliable system. On the Central, however, not only was the information fed into the computers unreliable, but there was a separate, unconnected set of hardware for each function. Differences between the railroads extended down to operations and equipment. Pennsylvania engines could not run on the Central's tracks and vice versa because the two companies had different automatic train-stopping equipment. And there were still other problems. In every city where the two railroads came together, each company had separate terminals and yards. This was true in dozens of places as far flung as Chicago, St. Louis, Indianapolis, Pittsburgh, Cleveland, Buffalo, New York, Columbus, Erie, and Cincinnati. When the two companies became the Penn Central, to which yard would a car routed to one of these cities go? To the one formerly belonging to the Central, or to that which had been the Pennsy's?

In view of these questions, one would have expected advance planning to be extensive and all important decisions to have been made prior to the merger date. Again Saunders was warned. As pointed out, Bevan had originally retained Peat, Marwick as an adviser on organization and data processing because that firm already audited the New York Central. He tried to coordinate the Pennsy's data processing system with the Central's but could get little cooperation from the New York Central. During the latter half of 1967, he and members of his staff brought the many problems associated with data processing and accounting to Saunders's attention and urged that decisions be made.

The failure to mesh the Pennsy with the Central bears testimony to the backgrounds from which Saunder's and Perlman came. Saunders clearly did not appreciate the importance of organization. This was true even after the railroad failed. In August 1972 Edwin Rome, counsel for the Penn Central's trustees, asked Saunders, "Was there any problem with regard to a basic difference of approach on the part of the Pennsylvania Railroad's philosophy of operation as contrasted with the New York Central's philosophy, to wit, centralization versus decentralization?" The former ex-Penn Central chief executive replied, "Well, it developed later on that there was some problem there, but basically I don't think that had anything serious to do with the reorganization. . . . They were what I call 'fringe problems'." [5]. This answer typified Saunders's whole approach to the merger.

It is impossible not to be impressed by the extremely casual way in which the Penn Central was put together. The top organization was determined by a committee of four, consisting of Saunders, Perlman, and two junior staff members. These men kept secret the final selection of officers for the top positions almost until merger day. Worse yet, before the merger, few decisions were made on any of the major issues. Alfred Perlman even scrapped most of the advance planning done in operations when he marked a report that had been especially prepared as "preliminary" and had it put away in a safe, never to be used. After the collapse, he explained his viewpoint to the Securities and Exchange Commission. The Penn Central's former president was asked, "Had there been any attempt to indoctrinate or to instruct shippers or connecting lines as to ways in which it could draw up waybills or make up their designations in routing and traffic?" Perlman answered, "No, it hadn't even been decided . . . what system of accounting we would use. It hadn't been decided what waybills we would use because, as I said, we didn't know when we were going to merge and all these things would have cost a lot of money and we weren't about to spend all that money until we knew that we had to" [6].

At the last minute, Saunders decided to remove accounting and data processing from Bevan's control and to place them under a former New York Central official, Walter Grant, who reported to Perlman. This decision scrapped all the progress that had been made in these areas. The New York Central operated on the ICC accounting system. In vain, Bevan tried to explain the problem to Saunders. Immediately prior to the merger in January 1968, he again alerted Saunders that the Pennsylvania's carefully planned budget system could not be used to assess the results of the merged companies. Bevan wrote, "We have been informed by the NYC that they have no budget figures for the first quarter and only make them up on a month-to-month basis" [7]. The financial officer urged Saunders to ask Perlman to produce a first-quarter budget, but Perlman did not act. After the merger, Bevan continued to warn Saunders of what was happening. Typical was his

July 1968 message that "in the absence of an income budget for the year 1968, we have not been able to make a detailed cash-flow estimate for the year" [8].

The merger brought into operation three different factors, each of which played a major part in destroying the Penn Central. First, lack of planning caused an immediate operations breakdown. Saunders and Perlman might have been able to avoid this had they merged only the top administrations of the two railroads but left the operating units intact with their separate organizations and identities. This approach would have allowed time to develop a detailed operating plan that could integrate operations over a number of years. This was the method adopted by the Chesapeake & Ohio and the Baltimore & Ohio in their successful merger. But Perlman tried to accomplish operational union immediately. The inevitable result was tens of thousands of lost cars and missing waybills, crews that could not work together, motive power breakdowns and shortages—in effect, chaos.

The second force for bankruptcy resulted from Saunders's transfer of accounting and data processing to Perlman. The former New York Central president did not feel that railroads needed income budgets or cash-flow estimates. Perlman favored primary reliance on Interstate Commerce Commission accounting. At the same time, there was a massive increase in capital spending. Always before on the Pennsylvania, Bevan had had reliable information on its cash position, and he had exercised enough influence to keep capital expenditures down to a point where they could be carried. On the new Penn Central, he had little influence on the capital budget, which Perlman set at $300 million for the first year. Worse yet, the operating department made large commitments for capital expenses in advance of notifying the railroad's financial side. In exasperation, Bevan brought the practice to Saunders's attention. In April 1969, he wrote, "I was informed this morning that bids are out for $30 million of diesels with delivery starting on May 20." He continued, "It is very difficult for me to understand or believe that this kind of procedure can be adopted when facing the kind of a money market we are in. I just cannot see when or how these diesels are going to be financed" [9].

The third force contributing to the bankruptcy was the almost-total breakdown of reliable information on the general state of the railroad and its finances. This failing stemmed directly from the confusion in both data processing and accounting. The lack of reliable information permitted Saunders and Perlman to recommend adoption of record capital-spending programs at the same time as the railroad was experiencing record cash losses.

Despite inaccurate information that masked the extent of the disaster, Bevan recognized that the Penn Central was headed for trouble. On August 30, 1968, some 7 months after the merger, he told Saunders that "in my judgment, we are faced with the most serious problem, from a financial viewpoint, that I have encountered since I have been with the railroad." This problem was caused by a severe cash shortage. On merger date, the railroad had "combined working cash of $13.3 million . . . inadequate for the operation of a corporation our size. . . . Coupled with this, a capital budget for over $300 million was approved for the year 1968. All these factors combined created a very difficult situation" both from the standpoint of cash and financing. Furthermore, Bevan estimated that rail operations drained a total of at least $136 million during the company's first 7 months of existence. He recommended that the Penn Central "stop all capital expenditures which represent a cash drain until such time as we can reestablish a positive cash flow" [10]. Saunders, unimpressed, rejected Bevan's advice and yielded to Perlman's proposals for still another capital budget of $300 million for the year 1969!

In the face of all these signals, why did Saunders refuse to act? The inescapable conclusion is that he never really understood the issues. That he did not fully comprehend accounting or cash flow even after the railroad's collapse is plain enough. Edwin Rome's cross-examination of Saunders reveals the confused thinking about accounting of the Penn Central's former chief executive. In answer to the question, "Did the company have a budget?" Saunders replied, "I don't know what you mean by a budget. . . . At the beginning of every [year], we prepare[d] earnings projections or revenue projections, cost, operating projections. . . . There were limitations set on how much could be spent on capital improvements, things of that sort." Rome then asked, "Was that the same kind of budget after the merger as it had been before?" Saunders replied, "Well, I can't answer that question. I don't know." When asked, "Was the budget used or followed within Penn Central in the same manner that it had been used and followed within the Pennsylvania?" Saunders said, "Some people disagreed about that. In my judgment, yes."

At another time, Rome asked Saunders whether there was an income budget for the Penn Central in 1968. Saunders replied, "I said yesterday that we had what I regarded as an income budget. Some people may not have regarded it as such." Later, Rome asked, "Have you any recollection of having discussed with Mr. Bevan at about the period of July 25, 1968, the problem of cash-flow estimates . . . ?" Said Saunders, "I discussed this matter, yes, [and an] income budget with Mr. Bevan from time to time. I know his views." Saunders subsequently commented that "Mr. Bevan was not satisfied with the statements that we had and he wanted to improve them, which I have no objection to, but at this time . . . Mr. Perlman told me . . . it couldn't be done." Later, Rome enquired, "Did you ever ask Mr. Perlman to get up an income budget?" Saunders replied, "Oh, yes, a number of times. . . . He said that he couldn't do it at that time" [11].

Thus we have the true picture of accounting at the Penn Central. Saunders, the chief executive, claimed that the company had an income budget; Perlman, the president, insisted he could not produce one; and Bevan, the chief of finance, knew that it didn't have one. Perlman might be excused— he was an operating man. Saunders had no such retreat. As the top executive, it was his responsibility to see that competent people were assigned to each task, and when things went wrong, he was supposed to act. No one can claim that he was not warned.

The result was predictable. The Penn Central failed not because of Bevan's diversification program, or even because of the agreements Saunders made to placate labor or buy the support of the federal or local governments, but because of an operational breakdown combined with management's loss of control over accounting, data processing, and most of all, the budget. These two factors led to the fatal mixture of both record capital expenditures and record losses from operations. In the background there were the long-term problems that had cast dark shadows over the eastern railroads since the 1930s. With another chief executive and another president, the story might have been different. Railroad losses might have been kept to a point where the outside investments could have carried them. But there was no margin for error. Saunders never seemed to grasp this last condition.

There were several important things to be said about the Penn Central's debacle. At the core, there was the immediate operational failure. It had long-term consequences because it forced many customers to find alternative means of transportation. In some cases, the railroad lost business forever as shippers located new factories on other systems or purchased fleets of trucks and switched permanently to highway transportation. Most of the public attention that was not diverted to David Bevan went to the elementary operational breakdown. There was an equally, if not more important, problem, on the Penn Central. This was the explicit rejection of the modern managerial techniques that Bevan and his financial team had installed on the Pennsylvania. The outflow of the key personnel from the Penn Central's finance, accounting, and data processing departments symbolized this rejection.

One of the myths of the Penn Central's collapse is that the railroad was starved for funds. A related myth is that diversification had drained its assets. Actually, in the less-than-2 years of Perlman's presidency, the Penn Central adopted capital budgets that authorized the expenditure of $600 million— more than double the previous highest combined capital budgets of the old New York Central and Pennsylvania Railroads. This massive infusion of new money, which Bevan borrowed, in some cases pledging the firm's nonrail assets, had no visible impact upon the Penn Central's earning power. Under Perlman—as under the trustees who followed him and Conrail, which took over from the trustees—the railroad had a consistent record of poor service and large financial losses. Much of the problem lay with traditional concepts of budgeting and accounting that had characterized railroads since the ICC had started to control ratemaking. Most operating men believed that a railroad's primary duty was to move cars from one point to another. Perlman, although he believed in a strong sales effort, like his predecessors on both the Pennsy and the Central made investment decisions on a seat-of-the-pants judgment. The data at his command did not even give him an accurate picture of traffic volume, let alone profitability.

The main thrust of Bevan's career at the Penn Central was his attempt to introduce modern managerial and analytical techniques. When Saunders yielded to the operating men, he undermined Bevan's work and drove away the key personnel who could have taken part in a resurrection after the Penn Central failed. The experience of Conrail, which took over the Penn Central's railroad assets, indicates that many of the same problems that had brought down the Penn Central were at work in the new corporation. In November 1977, *The Wall Street Journal* reported that the Interstate Commerce Commission had issued "an early warning report" on Conrail's financial problems, stating that the railroad's losses exceeded expectations. The ICC emphasized that Conrail had experienced "a deterioration" in freight car utilization during its first year of operation, and asserted that while Conrail's "massive" track rehabilitation program was supposed to reduce transportation costs, it had not done so.

In retrospect, Bevan could look back on his railroad career at certain bright spots. The first was the supplemental pension plan. When he joined the Pennsylvania, he found the plan managed in an outmoded manner; many of its obligations were unfunded and nearly 90 percent of its assets were in fixed income securities, many of which were oriented to the railroad. Under Bevan's stewardship, the pension fund prospered, and when the Penn Central collapsed, the fund was independent, strong, and able to meet its obligations. The second bright spot turned out to be the much criticized diversification program. In March 1978 the bankruptcy court accepted a reorganization plan for the Penn Central. The nation's financial press is optimistic that the company will again be profitable, and it bases its conclusions largely on the strength of the companies that Bevan acquired in the diversification program: Buckeye, Arvida, and Great Southwest. These conclusions are still further evidence that had Stuart Saunders made different decisions, the Penn Central might never have failed.

In addition, Bevan, more than any other individual, was responsible for Penn Center, a highly successful and profitable rehabilitation in the heart of Philadelphia's central city. Finally, Bevan created Trailer Train, a company that now serves the entire railroad industry in its highly successful piggy-back operation. It represents one of the few areas in which an industrywide cooperative effort was made to work.

Bevan's experience after the Penn Central's failure throws a bright light upon the changing relationship between government and American business. The investigations demonstrated that major company officials must assume that their every act must stand up to possible public scrutiny. Big business, especially since the 1930s, has lost much of its private character and has become largely public. Corporate officers, as well as government officials, must guard especially against possible conflicts of interest and must recognize that investigators will probably interpret behavior in the worst possible light. A key factor shaping the Penn Central investigations was the rivalry between governmental bodies and agencies at every level. Even within the federal government, sharp competition existed, particularly between the House of Representatives Banking and Currency Committee, chaired by Wright Patman, the Securities and Exchange Commission, and the Interstate Commerce Commission. The American political system guaranteed that the Penn Central's collapse would become a political issue with large payoffs to those who could exploit it. Wright Patman used the railroad's collapse to protect his position of power within the Congress. The bureaucrats in the Securities and Exchange Commission seized upon the Penn Central's troubles to undermine the Interstate Commerce Commission and to bring railroads under SEC regulation. Competition between various governmental authorities led to a battle for news media publicity that ensured an emphasis on the lurid and the spectacular.

The individual citizen caught in the center of a major business failure finds it almost impossible to receive a fair hearing. Soon after the Penn Central went into receivership, no fewer than five government agencies were conducting detailed investigations of Bevan's record. Their activity was in addition to private legal actions launched by the railroad's trustees, various stockholders, and the criminal proceedings undertaken by the Philadelphia District Attorney and the federal government's Justice Department. How could any individual, even someone of Bevan's wealth and stature, stand against such overwhelming force? That some actions, such as District Attorney Specter's charges, were frivolous did not lessen Bevan's problem. All investigations, lawsuits, and criminal charges had to be taken seriously, and there was no guarantee that once an investigation or action had been concluded by one body, it would not be re-opened at a later time by another.

Bevan's experience suggests that in cases of national importance, such as that of the Penn Central, the public as well as the other interests involved would best be served by an investigation conducted by a single body especially appointed for the occasion. A suitable model might be the Royal Commission used for investigations in the United Kingdom. A single commission would eliminate competition, reduce expenses, and be more likely to lead to a fair result. If such an investigation should produce evidence of criminal behavior, the information could be turned over to a federal prosecutor, who could present it before a federal judge, who would have the power to bind over the accused for trial.

Bevan's experience indicates serious shortcomings in the present federal legal procedure. Despite the massive investigation by congressional committees, the SEC, the ICC, and the trustees of the Penn Central, the Justice Department acted slowly and under much political pressure, especially from Wright Patman. The government did not even present the results of its investigation to a grand jury until 1974, about 4 years after the railroad's collapse and more than 3 years after most of the facts had surfaced. Federal attorney Oliver Burt's behavior in the prosecution of Bevan for the alleged theft of $4 million raises serious questions about the grand jury system of indictment [12]. The evidence that emerged at Bevan's trial indicates that the grand jury acted largely in response to unsworn testimony read into the record by a federal investigator. This "evidence" proved so weak that the prosecutor dared not present it before the judge and jury at the actual trial. The trouble stemmed from the nature of the grand juries, which operate in secret. Grand jury witnesses testify without legal representation and are not subject to cross-examination. The inevitable results are indictments that cannot stand before a judge and jury. Such indictments cause enormous costs for both the prosecution and the defense. In fact, the defense costs are becoming so great that only the very rich and very determined have a chance to defeat government action.

The government's behavior in the case of the Penn Central was not unique. Rather, it is becoming typical in cases that capture the national attention. This argument is not to say that investigations ought not to be conducted or that prosecution ought not to be launched, but only that they should be undertaken in an orderly fashion by a single authority and in a single trial. The rights of the public must always be balanced against the individual's right to self-protection.

The investigation and legal overkill in the Penn Central affair make the assumption of a top-management post increasingly less attractive for anyone of high talent. For the corporation executive, failure may now mean not only financial loss, but also a destroyed reputation with little hope of redress. These risks are compounded by the length of the various investigations and legal actions. Bevan's experience points to the need for reform—not only of railway managerial practices—but also of the procedures the United States uses to investigate and analyze major corporate failures.

References

1.   Bevan to Saunders, Greenough, Smucker, Large, Jones, and Funkhouser, June 8, 1967.

2.   Bevan to Saunders, November 21, 1966.

3.   Bevan to Saunders, October 25, 1966.

4.   Bevan to Saunders, September 8, 1967, quoted in *The Financial Collapse of the Penn Central Company*, a Staff Report of the Securities and Exchange Commission to the [House of Representatives] Special Sub-Committee on Investigations, Hon. Harley O. Staggers, Chairman, Government Printing Office, Washington, D.C., August 1972, p. 92.

5.   Stuart T. Saunders's Deposition in the Penn Central Securities Litigation: M.D.C. Docket No. 56. All Cases in the U.S. District Court for the Eastern District of Pennsylvania, first day of litigation, August 21, pp. 107–108. Hereafter cited as Saunders Deposition.

6.   Testimony of Alfred Perlman before the Securities and Exchange Commission in its investigation into the financial collapse of the Penn Central, February 4, 1972, p. 65.

7.   Bevan to Saunders, January 18, 1968. Long before Perlman became associated with the Penn Central, Karl Borntrager noted Perlman's lack of appreciation for modern accounting methods. Borntrager was a New York Central official who in 1958 retired as senior vice president. Before serving under Perlman, Borntrager had worked with the Central's former president, Willian White. One of Borntrager's projects had been the development of a new budgeting procedure to control transportation expenses, especially labor costs. White encouraged Borntrager, and the latter felt the new "transportation budget" proved itself by producing very favorable results during Perlman's first years as president. Unfortunately, Borntrager discovered that Perlman showed no interest in the program and made appointments that undermined it. This may be one reason that transportation ratio, after a brief period of improving started to become unfavorable again, especially after 1956. See Karl A. Borntrager, *Keeping the Railroads Running: Fifty Years on the New York Central*, Hastings House, New York, 1974, pp. 187–188, 196.

8.   Bevan to Saunders, July 25, 1968.

9.   Bevan to Saunders, April 11, 1969.

10.   Bevan to Saunders, August 30, 1968.

11.   Saunders Deposition, August 22, 1972, pp. 199, 200, 201, 211.

12.   The story of the alleged theft of the $4 million and the trial is told in Chapters 18 and 19.

Part 2
FALSE ALLEGATIONS CONCERNING CAUSES OF THE PENN CENTRAL BANKRUPTCY

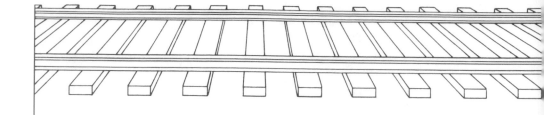

Chapter 14
SCAPEGOAT

June 8, 1970, the date of David Bevan's dismissal, marked the real beginning of his troubles. The next 18 months saw him emerge as a major villain in the Penn Central's collapse. For a few weeks the chaos that followed the railroad's bankruptcy prevented the formation of any firm conclusions. By summer's end, Bevan was on the defensive. His critics blamed him for diverting the railroad's attention toward diversification and draining its cash. Some observers alleged that Bevan's motives were dishonest or corrupt. They also claimed that he managed the railroad's investments and its pension funds to favor his own rather than the railroad's interests.

THE PATMAN VENDETTA

Democratic Senator Vance Hartke of Indiana provided an early indication of the treatment Bevan would receive. Hartke became involved because the Penn Central's trustees needed a large amount of new cash, and they asked for an emergency federal loan. Senator Hartke chaired a Senate subcommittee that held hearings on a Nixon administration bill to provide $750 million of loans to financially troubled railroads, including the Penn Central. Hartke's committee systematically called the railroad's former top executives to testify. Alfred Perlman appeared prior to Bevan and *The Wall Street Journal* observed that Hartke handled him gently. The *Journal* observed that Hartke repeatedly attempted to get the former Penn Central president to say that the railroad's operations had been "financially starved by real estate and other nonrail investments." The *Journal* reported that Perlman would not "entirely go along." He said, "I don't think too much was diverted to outside acquisitions." Rather, Perlman blamed the Penn Central's collapse on "basic" problems inherent in the railroad industry [1].

Bevan appeared before the congressional committee on August 6 and read a twenty-four–page statement recommending changes in the railroad industry. Unlike Perlman, he did not receive a warm welcome. Hartke criticized the former chief financial officer for the Penn Central's investments in Executive Jet Aviation and the Great Southwest Corporation, hinting that Bevan "pushed [the] airline venture for personal gain" [2]. Looking back, Bevan felt that Hartke's attitude was almost favorable by comparison with what came later.

The real key to Bevan's trouble lay in the hands of a Texas Democrat, Representative Wright Patman, who chaired the House Committee on Banking and Currency. Patman had been elected to Congress in 1928 and had spent a lifetime as a populist attacking banks and other financial institutions. Patman had long criticized the way banks loaned money. He once said, "Bankers are the only people who can manufacture money without going to the penitentiary." At one time, Patman showed his contempt for the banking system by posing for photographers with a giant pair of foam-rubber dice, which he claimed were "loaded . . . and that's just what you come up against when you deal with the Federal Reserve System—loaded dice" [3]. Bevan, who had served as director of the Federal Reserve Bank of Philadelphia, was the kind of person Patman had spent a lifetime attacking.

Patman saw the Penn Central's collapse as a perfect example of big corporations' and banks' misuse of power and other people's money, and he immediately set his staff to investigate. The Texas congressman quickly concluded that "some officers and directors of the giant railroad were involved in 'serious conflict of interest situations' with their personal financial transactions." He then had the House Banking and Currency Committee expand the investigation to include the widespread use of subpoenas to produce information. Although the probe lasted months and did not produce a final report until January 3, 1972, Patman began systematically to release segments of the findings in November 1970 [4]. Patman's strategy was to dribble out information, thus keeping the railroad's problems in the headlines for more than a year. In almost all Patman's releases, Bevan was the major villain.

Patman started his attack on the first of November, 1970. In a well-attended press conference, he asserted that Penn Central's "real estate and other investments drained it of 'at least $175 million' " in cash critically needed by the railroad. He argued that "this is in direct contradiction to the claim put forward by David C. Bevan, the former chief financial officer of the Penn Central, that the diversification provided benefits and income for the operation of the railroad" [5].

Patman's most stinging attack came several weeks later. In mid-December he blamed Bevan for all that had gone wrong with the Penn Central subsidiary, Executive Jet Aviation, and the disclosures proved irresistible for the newspapers [6]. The *Philadelphia Inquirer* displayed the headline, "Probers Link Sex Deals to Penn Central's Losses." In a lead paragraph to the story, the newspaper explained that "Congressional investigators have linked suggestions of sex and possible blackmail to a $21-million business loss that helped push the Penn Central into bankruptcy."

In February 1971, Patman announced his staff's finding on Bevan's participation in Penphil, a private investment club. The *Philadelphia Evening Bulletin* covered Patman's disclosures in a story headlined "Bevan's Deals Called Harmful to Pennsy." The *Bulletin* then said that the staff report "charged that David C. Bevan, fired June 8 from his $132,000-a-year post with the Penn Central, and Charles J. Hodge, a partner in the firm of E. I. du Pont–Glore Forgan, Inc., used railroad money to boost the profits of Penphil Corp., an investment club they formed." Patman specifically claimed that Bevan and Hodge "manipulated the financial resources, the assets, and the credit of the nation's sixth largest corporation for the benefit of an investment company, Penphil" [7].

Next, Patman portrayed Bevan as a central figure in the theft of $4 million from the Penn Central. The Banking and Currency Committee staff reported that Bevan borrowed $10 million in Europe for the Penn Central, part of which was placed in a Liechtenstein trust account. The staff indicated that a European industrialist, Fidel Goetz, who "had been involved with Penn Central in the ill-fated attempt to turn Executive Jet Aviation Corp. into a worldwide transportation system," had stolen the money. Patman remarked that this episode illustrated "how tangled the personal, financial, and corporate affairs of Penn Central and its management became, thus contributing ultimately to the collapse of the Penn Central." While Patman admitted that there was no evidence that Penn Central officers personally profited from Goetz's action, he implied that "the misappropriation" could not have happened without Bevan's help [8].

INTRAGOVERNMENTAL RIVALRY FOR THE PENN CENTRAL STORY

Patman's allegations were only part of Bevan's ordeal. He was also a major figure in three other full-scale investigations launched by either Congress or government agencies. Senator Hartke, chairman of the Senate Committee on Commerce's Sub-Committee on Surface Transportation, oversaw an inquiry, the results of which were finally published in December of 1972 [9]. The Interstate Commerce Commission and the Securities and Exchange Commission each launched separate probes that proceeded simultaneously. Bevan often found himself shuffling from one government inquiry to another. The competition between government and congressional agencies over the Penn Central story encouraged the investigators to hold press conferences in which each tried to outdo the other in their revelations. The Interstate Commerce Commission (ICC) moved more slowly than Patman and its focus tended to be on the Penn Central's operational breakdown, a subject which received scant attention from the Banking and Currency Committee investigators. Nevertheless, the ICC devoted considerable attention to alleged financial irregularities in the Penn Central. On December 20, 1971, it charged that David Bevan and his staff had probably "been guilty of a conflict of interest when they invested funds from the [railroad's] employee pension plan" [10]. The ICC argued that David Bevan often purchased shares for his personal account in firms in which he was investing for the pension funds. As an example of this supposed conflict of interest, the ICC pointed to parallel investments in CBK Industries, a stock on which the railroad pension fund, as of 1970, had a substantial loss.

William Vance, a reporter for the *Philadelphia Inquirer*'s Washington bureau, wrote that the ICC disclosures provoked sharp conflict between its investigators and Wright Patman. Vance observed that the ICC's study rehashed much of what had already been covered by Patman's staff. However, he noted that it "zeroed in on at least one aspect the House Committee was working feverishly to develop: the alleged misuse of employee pension funds for personal profit by David C. Bevan." Patman was angry because the ICC's exposé "took the edge off the House Committee's review of the same subject two weeks later." Patman did not lose gracefully. He struck out, saying "of all the government regulatory agencies involved in the Penn Central fiasco, the ICC stands out as the most inefficient and ineffective of them all." He continued, "On the basis of this 1760 pages of rehash, one would think that the ICC was a branch of the National Archives." In the same article, Vance reported asking the ICC about Patman's criticisms. Warner Baylor, a Commission spokesman, declined specific comment but "suggested that cooperation with the House Committee has been a one-way street." Said Baylor, "By law we have to cooperate. Whatever we do we must make available and we have. They don't and have not" [11].

The Securities and Exchange Commission (SEC) did not make its report until early August 1972. It retraced much of the terrain already covered by Patman and the ICC. Still, it had an emphasis of its own. The SEC explored the Pennsylvania's accounting policies, and quoted in its entirety David Bevan's diary about Stuart Saunders's ill-fated efforts to maximize the railroad's income. Bevan's role in the last stages of the Penn Central's financing, particularly his use of commercial paper, received much criticism. The Commission censured him, along with other Penn Central officials, for their sale of Penn Central stock. Furthermore, both Bevan and Saunders were castigated for failing to disclose to investors the Penn Central's financial difficulties [12].

CRIMINAL AND CIVIL CHARGES

The many investigations into the Penn Central's collapse resulted in criminal charges against Bevan. Philadelphia County's District Attorney Arlen Specter acted first. Specter read Patman's disclosures about Executive Jet Aviation and on January 4, 1972, called a press conference and announced that he was obtaining warrants "charging former Penn Central Finance Chairman David C. Bevan and two of his associates with illegally diverting more than $21 million from the railroad" [13]. Codefendants with Bevan were Charles J. Hodge and retired Brigadier General Olbert F. Lassiter, who had been Executive Jet's founder and its president.

Federal authorities moved more cautiously than the Philadelphia district attorney, but they were under strong pressure from Wright Patman to do something. On January 10, 1972, *The Wall Street Journal* noted that Justice Department officials were "fully aware of the interest of Rep. Wright Patman (D., Texas) House Banking and Currency Committee Chairman, in pressing the investigation. . . . Departmental officials said that they expect to inform Mr. Patman as soon as the entire matter is under investigation." Within 2 weeks the nation's business press reported that the Federal Bureau of Investigation had entered the case, and that it seemed likely that the government might take its evidence before a grand jury for criminal indictment [14]. In May the federal government convened a 23-member strike force grand jury to investigate the Penn Central's collapse. Assistant United States District Attorney C. Oliver Burt directed the Justice Department's probe, which eventually resulted in an indictment of five men who were accused of siphoning $4 million from a Penn Central trust account in Liechtenstein. These included two railroad officials, David Bevan and former Vice-President William R. Gerstnecker, two Washington lawyers, Francis N. Rosenbaum and Joseph H. Rosenbaum, and a German financier, Fidel Goetz. The grand jury named no other Penn Central officials [15].

Bevan, in common with other former Penn Central top management and directors, also was subject to a large number of civil suits. Many of them came from disgruntled stockholders who charged mismanagement. By July 1971, at least fourteen such suits had been filed in various state and federal courts [16]. Furthermore, the trustees of the bankrupt Penn Central, in April 1971, filed a suit against Bevan, Gerstnecker, and Hodge, charging that they had entered into "an unlawful combination and conspiracy" to use the railroad "for their own personal profit." The trustees alleged that "it was one of

208 FALSE ALLEGATIONS—CAUSES OF BANKRUPTCY

the purposes of the conspiracy, by the exploitation of Penn Central's resources, to build Penphil into a large worldwide conglomerate by making Penphil a recipient of all advantages, gains, benefits, profits, and unjust enrichments which were intended to result from the conspiracy" [17].

Shortly afterward, the trustees asked the United States District Court to "suspend without prejudice" a portion of David Bevan's retirement benefits. Bevan, in common with other former Penn Central top executives who had been dismissed at the time of the company's collapse, had been allowed to collect the pension to which he was entitled. Soon after the trustees took over control of the railroad, Judge John P. Fullam ordered that no retirement benefits in excess of $50,000 a year be paid. Saunders was entitled to an annual pension of $114,000, Perlman to $94,140, and Bevan to $78,112 [18]. The trustees' decision in addition prevented any of the top three officers from receiving any benefits from the contingent compensation fund. Under the contingent compensation plan, a portion of each top executive's salary was deducted, invested by the fund, and then paid after retirement. The purpose was to delay taxes until retirement when personal earnings would drop substantially. Bevan always took a large portion of his salary in deferred compensation and his stake in the fund at one point exceeded $1 million.

INTERPRETING THE PENN CENTRAL'S COLLAPSE

Why was David Bevan, the Penn Central's former chief financial officer, at the center of the investigations into the corporation's bankruptcy? The question is intriguing because all evidence indicates that the railroad's trouble was not financial but operational. Even two of Bevan's most severe critics, Joseph R. Daughen and Peter Binzen, recognized this. In their book *The Wreck of the Penn Central,* they discussed the various theories about whether or not diversification through the Pennsylvania Company had drained cash from the railroad and helped it to collapse. They wrote [19]:

> The Pennsylvania Company, because it used the railroad's money and was in turn used by the railroad, did figure in the collapse, but it was not the decisive factor. Once the railroad failed, Pennco preferred stockholders and bondholders filed suits charging that the railroad had milked the investment company. Congressional leaders and the Interstate Commerce Commission maintained that Pennco was responsible for draining cash *away* from the railroad. . . . There is evidence to support both positions. In the final analysis, however, it was the railroad that failed and it is to the railroad and the nature of its operations that one must turn for answers.

Others found the Penn Central investigations less than satisfying. Robert J. Samuelson, writing in the *Washington Post* 2 years after the corporation's collapse, commented that investigations had been "as titillating as . . . enlightening" and that "it may only be a matter of time before someone decides to turn it into a full-length motion picture. Unfortunately," continued Samuelson, "the plethora of well-documented government reports has had some unintended side-effects. By popularizing the Penn Central blunders, it has left the impression that the railroad collapsed primarily as a result of human frailties and failings. Except for the postmortems on these pitiful characters then, the Penn Central affair was closed." Samuelson, however, commented that Penn Central's case was far from over in 1972, since the railroad was still in bankruptcy and was defying the best efforts of new management to restore it to profitability [20].

Because the Penn Central's bankruptcy was the failure of the largest United States transportation enterprise, the public had an important interest in finding out the real reasons behind the collapse. The record indicates that railroads in the northeastern United States had been generally unprofitable since the Great Depression of the 1930s. The evidence is overwhelming. Almost all other northeastern railroads either preceded or followed the Penn Central into bankruptcy. They included the Reading, the Central of New Jersey, the New York, New Haven & Hartford, the Erie-Lackawanna, the Boston & Maine, the Pennsylvania-Reading Seashore Lines, the Lehigh Valley, and the New York, Ontario & Western. One commentator observed that every railroad entering the state of New Jersey had gone into receivership by 1972. As far back as 1962, Bevan had testified before the Interstate Commerce Commission that the Pennsy had been in slow liquidation since World War II. He was certain that it, too, would have gone bankrupt prior to 1968 had it not been for a very substantial income that it received from outside investments, notably the Wabash and the highly profitable Norfolk & Western.

In the same manner, the New York Central's Park Avenue real estate kept it afloat after the transportation business turned downward. In retrospect, it is apparent that mismanagement of the merged New York Central and Pennsylvania condensed into $2\frac{1}{2}$ years what would probably have occurred over 10 years.

Investigations into the Penn Central's collapse diverted attention from the real crisis facing railroads. They delayed Congress and the government from getting on with the task of finding a solution to the Northeast's transportation problems. Even when investigators found genuine mismanagement of the Penn Central, they often—deliberately or otherwise—missed the point. An example is Patman's reaction to the many internal memoranda that David Bevan had written to Saunders about the premerger computer systems of the

Pennsylvania and the New York Central. It will be recalled that Bevan warned Saunders of the problems that the Penn Central would face in accounting and data processing. His points were vital. One of his most significant accomplishments had been to bring modern managerial techniques in the use of accounting to the Pennsylvania Railroad. Bevan, with the help of the comptroller, William Cook, moved the Pennsylvania from a backward-looking Interstate Commerce Commission bookkeeping system to a program of responsibility reporting and cost accounting. Patman released Bevan's memoranda in a way that obscured the issues, and the newspapers followed the lead. The *Philadelphia Evening Bulletin* of May 23, 1972, entitled an article summarizing Bevan's memoranda as "More Backbiting with Penn Central Disclosed by Patman." The article started with the observation [21]:

> Fresh evidence of the executive suite warfare that plagued the Penn Central transportation has been turned up by the House Committee on Banking and Currency. Internal documents obtained by Wright Patman, Committee chairman, indicate that corporate backbiting began even before the Pennsylvania and New York Central railroads merged on February 1, 1968. . . . Material gathered by Patman discloses that high Pennsylvania officials sniped at Alfred E. Perlman, former Central head who became president of the merged line, and Robert G. (Mike) Flannery, a Perlman protegé who became Penn Central's vice-president for operations.

As usual, Bevan was the villain, but more important, the public was denied the opportunity to understand the real nature of the managerial problems that were facing American railroads as they attempted to cope with the economic challenges of the mid-twentieth century.

Since the real issues behind the Penn Central's operating collapse were both fascinating and important, certainly worthy of disclosure by a congressional committee, one might ask why the investigations took the form they did. Wright Patman was the key to the Penn Central investigations. His staff appeared in Philadelphia more quickly than the others, and he stage-managed the disclosures, beating all other investigators to the punch. The Securities and Exchange Commission staff report mostly followed Patman's lead. The much more voluminous investigation of the Interstate Commerce Commission received almost no media attention compared with either those of Patman's committee or the Securities and Exchange Commission. In fact, the ICC found itself continually on the defensive against attacks, not only from Patman's staff, but also from the Securities and Exchange Commission, which resented the fact that railroads operating under the ICC escaped SEC regulation. Actually, much of the SEC's staff report tried to convince Congress that railroads should be made subject to the SEC. While the Interstate Commerce Commission may be subject to heavy criticism for its activities prior to the collapse of the Penn Central, no one can read the results of its investigation without recognizing that it was far more impartial and enlightening than either the SEC or Patman's staff. Significantly, the report issued for the Senate Commerce Committee, which came last of all in December 1972, and which on the whole was quite objective, received hardly any press notice [22]. By that time the Penn Central's collapse was old news and the public interest had waned.

WHY A SCAPEGOAT?

Bevan quickly recognized the importance of Patman's investigation. Shortly after the first staff reports were released, he thought of launching a counterattack. He discussed this idea with his lawyer, Edward C. German, who represented him in the cases arising out of the railroad's failure. Bevan proposed to go to Washington and to call a press conference at which he would deny categorically Patman's statements. German opposed this idea, saying that the odds were with Patman. To prove the point, German arranged an appointment with Representative William A. Barrett, a Philadelphia Democrat, the second ranking member on Patman's Committee on Banking and Currency. Barrett supported German, arguing that Bevan's proposal would allow Patman to stay in the headlines for several extra months and put Bevan "through the meat grinder."

Barrett then told how and why Patman started the investigation. The Philadelphia congressman explained that Patman's opposition had scuttled a last-minute federal bail-out of the Penn Central. In committee, Patman had argued that the banks were so deeply committed to Penn Central that they would save the railroad regardless of whether the government acted. He had long opposed the large New York banks, and saw federal aid to the Penn Central as merely disguised aid to them. Barrett pointed out that Patman's analysis had been wrong. When the government did not act, the banks refused to continue to support the railroad, and it collapsed with consequences reaching far beyond the financial community. Barrett observed that Patman was particularly anxious not to be held responsible for any of the problems associated with the Penn Central's downfall. Barrett said that Patman sent investigators to Philadelphia to "find a scapegoat." Bevan asked Barrett, "But why me? Was it because I was once a banker, or because I served for 5 years as a member of the board of directors of the Federal Reserve Bank of Philadelphia?" Barrett answered that none of that made any difference to Patman, that he just wanted a scapegoat, and that the Penn Central had provided him with one—David Bevan.

When asked what he meant, the congressman replied that he did not want to name names but that he would describe the Penn Central officer who had supplied the ammunition against Bevan. He indicated that if Bevan were half as smart as his reputation, he would have no trouble in identifying the person involved. Bevan had none. The man was Stuart Saunders's administrative assistant, Basil Cole [23].

However, the issue was not so clear cut. Two Philadelphia lawyers very knowledgeable with the Penn Central's collapse did not agree with Congressman Barrett. They were Stewart Dalzell and Raymond Denworth, partners of the firm of Drinker, Biddle and Reath. They served as counsel for the Penn Central's outside directors in the many suits launched against them after the railroad's demise. Both lawyers thought Bevan was a scapegoat. They described the Penn Central's management as "a troika consisting of Stuart Saunders, chairman of the board, Alfred Perlman, president and responsible for operations, and David Bevan, responsible for finances." The lawyers agreed that Bevan did his job "extremely well." Denworth emphasized that the Penn Central's collapse was an operational failure. He stressed that Perlman was not equal to the task of accounting, organization, or the delegation of authority. The lawyers regarded Perlman's failure to develop and follow any plan to guide the merger as one of the main factors that resulted in the operational chaos [24].

Neither lawyer was surprised that the investigation of the House Banking and Currency Committee focused on Bevan rather than Perlman. Nor did the lawyers feel that Patman needed encouragement in making Bevan the scapegoat. They saw Patman in his populist role—as a diehard opponent of the eastern banking establishment. Bevan, they agreed, was the kind of person Patman liked to hate. Furthermore, Dalzell observed, Bevan's behavior appeared arrogant to many members of Congress. The Penn Central's former chief financial officer faced his critics without the slightest bit of contrition. He refused to admit any errors and defended his actions. Both lawyers thought that Bevan's attitude angered Patman. Moreover, they felt that the Penn Central's trustees went along with Patman's approach for strategic reasons. They had inherited a bankrupt railroad desperately in need of government aid. They found it convenient to blame the financial department, not operations, for the collapse. To have admitted an operations failure would have risked a lengthy investigation into the railroad itself, which might delay essential aid [25].

REFERENCES

1. *The Wall Street Journal,* July 30, 1970.

2. Ibid., August 7, 1970; *The New York Times,* August 7, 1970.

3. *Philadelphia Inquirer,* March 8, 1976.

4. *Washington Post,* September 16, 1970. While Patman was enthusiastic about the work of his staff, many of the members of the House Banking and Currency Committee did not share his view. He tried to get the Committee to endorse the report, but failed. He had to add to the letter of transmittal of the report the statement, "The views and conclusions found in this report do not necessarily express the views of the Committee or any of its individual members."

5. *Philadelphia Inquirer,* November 2, 1970.

6. For the story on Executive Jet Aviation, see *Philadelphia Inquirer*, December 21, 1970.

7. *Philadelphia Evening Bulletin,* February 15, 1971. Note the Patman Committee quote saying that the Penn Central was the ninth, not the sixth, largest corporation. See Patman Report, p. 254.

8. Philadelphia *Evening Bulletin,* March 10, 1970.

9. *The Penn Central and Other Railroads, A Report to the Senate Committee on Commerce,* prepared at the direction of the Honorable Warren G. Magnuson, Chairman, for the use of the Committee on Commerce, United States Senate, December 1972.

10. *The New York Times,* December 21, 1971.

11. *Philadelphia Inquirer,* December 31, 1971.

12. *Philadelphia Inquirer,* August 7, 1972; also *The Financial Collapse of the Penn Central Company,* Staff Report of the Securities and Exchange Commission to the Special Sub-Committee on Investigations, Hon. Harley O. Staggers, Chairman (with comments on H.R. 12128 by the SEC and ICC [the Interstate Commerce Commission]), Government Printing Office, Washington, D.C., August 1972.

13. *Philadelphia Evening Bulletin,* January 4, 1972.

14. *Journal of Commerce,* January 24, 1972.

15. See the *Philadelphia Inquirer,* May 18, 1972.

16. Ibid.

17. *Philadelphia Inquirer*, April 9, 1971.

18. Ibid., May 12, 1971, for Saunders's and Perlman's retirement entitlement; Bevan's records, for his own.

19. Joseph R. Daughen and Peter Binzen, *The Wreck of the Penn Central,* Little, Brown and Co., Boston, 1971, p. 208.

20. Robert J. Samuelson, "Penn Central's Wayward Track," *Washington Post,* June 18, 1972.

21. *Philadelphia Evening Bulletin,* May 23, 1972. In actual fact, Bevan had a high regard for Robert Flannery as an operating man and the two had a friendly relationship.

22. *The Penn Central and Other Railroads, A Report to the Senate Committee on Commerce*, prepared at the direction of the Honorable Warren G. Magnuson, Chairman, for the use of the Commerce Committee.

23. As told to author by David Bevan, and confirmed in author's interview with Edward German.

24. Author's interview with Raymond Denworth and Stewart Dalzell, May 23, 1977, in the offices of Drinker, Biddle and Reath, Philadelphia.

25. Ibid.

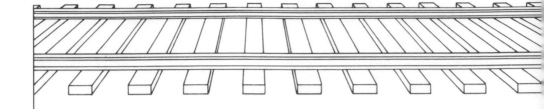

Chapter 15
PENPHIL

THE CHARGES

Almost all David Bevan's troubles can be traced to his participation in two separate corporations, Penphil and Executive Jet Aviation. Penphil was a small private investment club which Bevan and some of his close friends founded in 1962. Few activities of the Penn Central and its executives have been more fully investigated. Both the staff of Wright Patman's House of Representatives Banking and Currency Committee and the Securities and Exchange Commission made the club the subject of full-scale inquiries. Together, they probed almost all aspects of Penphil. They traced its every security purchase and the parallel investments made for the private accounts of Penphil members, as well as the relevant investment decisions made by the Pennsylvania Railroad, the Penn Central, and their various accounts. Despite an assertion to the contrary by Patman's staff, there is very little "mystery" to Penphil [1]. Patman's staff left no doubt about its stand [2]:

> The story of Penphil constitutes a classic example of the use of corporate power for personal profits. In fact, it is the chronicle of how two men, David C. Bevan, the former chief financial officer of the Penn Central, and Charles J. Hodge, the former chief investment adviser of the railroad, manipulated the financial resources, the assets and the credit of the nation's ninth largest corporation for the benefit of an investment company, Penphil, which they established and directed. The ultimate goal of Bevan and Hodge was to create a large conglomerate operating and holding company while orchestrating Penn Central investments in a way that would serve the interests of Penphil. In an overall sense, the history of Penphil is not only the story of monumental disservice to the Penn

Central, the nation's largest transportation system; it is a detailed record of activities which distorts our concept of the democratic free enterprise system.

The investigators made a number of specific claims. They said Bevan used his railroad position to get special privileges from banks, that he manipulated railroad investments in order to boost Penphil securities, that his activities posed an inherent conflict of interest with the railroad, that he used inside information to further his private investments, and finally, that he made big profits from Penphil.

Most of the charges centered on Bevan's supposed misuse of his power to control the railroad pension funds and his role in the Pennsylvania's diversification program. However, the investigators' reports are interesting for the charges they did not make. Although Bevan was alleged to have used the railroad's bank deposits as a lever to extract loans for Penphil, no one claimed that such loans were unsound or could not be repaid. Moreover, the investigators never asserted that pension funds or other trust accounts under Bevan's stewardship lost large amounts of money. It is true that Patman's staff did find the Supplemental Pension Fund had a substantial loss at that time from its holdings of the securities of one firm, CBK Industries. Ironically, CBK had no connection with Penphil and was only one of several hundred pension fund investments. Even here, the accusation proved worse than reality. All stocks, as well as other investments, fluctuate in price. In this case, if the pension fund had continued to hold CBK, on several occasions subsequent to Patman's report the fund would have had an opportunity to sell its shares at a profit. It is significant that the investigators never claimed the overall pension fund investment record was bad, or even that the Penn Central's funds had a low average return when compared with similar trusts. In fact, there was no effort to compare Penn Central's funds with those of any other company. There is a good reason for this: the railroad funds did exceptionally well under Bevan's supervision and the results of such a comparison would have undermined the investigators' case [3].

PENPHIL: THE CLUB
AND ITS FOUNDERS

The facts about Penphil are simple enough. Its founding in the summer of 1962 had nothing to do with the railroad. It was the idea of seven friends associated in a fishing club; all were top financial men, most were investment bankers. The seven were Warren Bodman and Carroll Seward, partners in the Philadelphia firm of Yarnall, Biddle, & Company; Lawrence Stevens, a partner in Hemphill Noyes & Company; John Acuff of Sheridan, Bogan & Company; Francis Cannon, administrative vice-president of the First Boston

Corporation; Charles Hodge, chairman of the Executive Committee of Glore Forgan; and David Bevan. Penphil's founders sought a lawyer to do the necessary legal work, and they agreed upon David Bevan's brother Thomas, who was a partner in the Philadelphia law firm of Duane, Morris, & Heckscher. Thomas Bevan remembered that it was not his brother who had invited him to join Penphil, but Warren Bodman, a friend whom Thomas had known for 20 years and who had handled his personal investments and those of his aunt and uncle. Thomas Bevan told Bodman that he hesitated to join such a club because he feared he could not afford to invest on the same scale as the others. Bodman assured him that the club would operate on a relatively small scale, which it did. The initial contribution turned out to be $1000, with $500 more required every 6 months thereafter. Altogether, the founding members had invested $16,500 each by the time of the railroad's collapse in 1970.

By the time Thomas filed the incorporation papers, the club had added eight members, including himself. They were Benjamin Sawin, president of the Provident National Bank; Frederick Holmes, sales manager of the Glatfelter Paper Company; Edward D. Meanor, an independent investment broker with a seat on the Philadelphia Stock Exchange; William Gerstnecker, David Bevan's assistant vice-president on the Pennsylvania Railroad; Robert Haslett, also a member of Bevan's staff; and two other railroad employees, Paul D. Fox and Theodore K. Warner. Wright Patman insisted that Penphil was a club dominated by David Bevan and his fellow railroad associates. Thomas Bevan later observed that this was not true and that the Penphil members never thought of their club as being railroad-related. Of the original seven founders, only one, David Bevan, worked for the Pennsylvania, and of the first fifteen, only five were railroad men. The club was composed largely of investment bankers and their friends. David Bevan never served as a Penphil officer; he was not a member of its investment committee, nor did he recommend any of its investments. The club's officers reflected its nonrailroad orientation. Bodman served as Penphil's first president, Stevens as its treasurer, and Thomas Bevan as its secretary. Thomas Bevan thought it "highly significant" that in the minds of Penphil's members, the club had nothing to do with the railroad. Consequently, he said, "when we were asked if we didn't know that the railroad was investing in similar stocks, the answer is not only that we didn't know, but *we had no occasion or reason* to ask what the railroad was investing in, any more than we would have had reason to ask what was Glatfelter Paper Co., Provident National Bank, Yarnall, Biddle & Co., Hemphill Noyes, or Glore Forgan, or their pension funds invested in" [4].

In addition to the original fifteen, another fourteen joined Penphil between its founding and February 1969. Few of them had any connection with the Pennsylvania. The new members included some executives of firms in which Penphil invested, such as Fred H. Billups, president of Tropical Gas; Thomas F. Fleming of First Bancshares of Florida; and Herbert Fisher, chairman of the board of Kaneb. Others were friends or business associates of the club's founders, such as Olbert F. Lassiter, president of Executive Jet Aviation; Leslie Cassidy, former chairman of the board of Johns-Manville; Vincent G. Kling, a Philadelphia architect; and H. C. Ramsey, retired chairman of the board of Worthington Corporation and a limited partner of Glore Forgan.

Along with Bevan, Charles J. Hodge, partner in the brokerage firm of Glore Forgan, bore the brunt of the investigators' wrath. Hodge, a year younger than Bevan, had been born in Washington, D.C. In the late twenties he studied at Georgetown University's Foreign Service School. Later, after moving to New Jersey, he attended New York University in 1939. Hodge joined the New Jersey National Guard on the eve of World War II, and during that conflict he served in Europe. He retired from the Guard with the rank of brigadier general and returned to civilian life as an investment banker with Glore Forgan. In that capacity he met Bevan. The various investigations and the newspapers often portrayed Hodge as the Penn Central's or the Pennsylvania's chief investment adviser, implying that he held an official position with the Pennsy. Actually, Hodge had no such relationship.

The railroad managed two important funds. Of these the largest was the Supplemental Pension Plan which in December 1969, encompassed about 21,700 active Penn Central employees and 15,200 retired workers. The total value of this fund in that year was approximately $330 million [5]. Effective control of this fund rested with a Penn Central board committee.

Bevan reported on pension fund business directly to this committee. In practice, Robert Haslett had charge of the fund on a day-to-day basis. At the plan's inception in 1938 and for many years after, the Philadelphia investment banking firm of Drexel and Company served as adviser. When Paul Miller, president of Drexel, resigned and formed his own investment counseling firm, it became the plan's adviser.

Robert Haslett made the pension plan's individual investments; most of the time he bought and sold on his own initiative, and at other times, after consultation with Bevan or Drexel and Company. Haslett occasionally asked Bevan's advice. Later, the former Penn Central chief financial officer remembered that the tenor of such conversations was more on policy than on actual cases. Hodge and Glore Forgan were in the same category as every other stockbroker in the United States. All were free to make suggestions. As a matter of policy, the broker who made the recommendation usually received the order. This arrangement encouraged all brokers to come to the Penn Central. The Supplementary Pension Fund purchased hundreds of different issues of stocks and bonds and Glore Forgan recommended relatively few of them. The railroad's smaller fund, the Contingent Compensation Fund, was to provide deferred compensation for the Penn Central's top executives. Bevan had a large personal stake in this fund, but he delegated the day-to-day management of it to Haslett, who ran it in the same manner as the Supplemental Pension Fund.

While Charles Hodge was unimportant in the activities of the pension funds, he did play a more substantial part in the Pennsylvania Railroad's diversification program, recommending the acquisitions of four companies of which the railroad bought control: Buckeye Pipeline, Arvida, Great Southwest, and Executive Jet. During the late fifties and early sixties, Bevan had great confidence in Hodge. Yet the two were quite different. Bevan was all hard work and serious purpose, giving almost his entire time to his job. He maintained a correct, but formal, relationship with his employees. He did not mix easily with people outside his own circle. When Bevan was not working, which was seldom, he spent most of his days at home, where he relaxed with his family. He did belong to Merion Golf Club where he occasionally played a round of golf with his old Haverford friends. But his main hobby was gardening and he prided himself on his large rhododendron collection. By contrast, Hodge was outgoing and ebullient. Although his close friends called him Charlie, he enjoyed the title of General. Bevan disapproved of the reference to military rank in civilian life but out of courtesy said nothing. Hodge liked parties and mixed in a broad circle. Despite his close association with Bevan, the two had very different financial outlooks. Bevan, who started his career at the bottom of the Depression, was cautious and conservative. His entire thrust at the Pennsylvania Railroad was an effort to restrain management from overcommitting itself. In contrast, Hodge took his cue from the boom that followed World War II. He was a stock market bull, ever optimistic about America's growth.

The friendship between Bevan and Hodge cooled as the 1960s wore on. This was especially so in 1968 when Bevan discovered that Hodge had been involved in a series of misadventures to the detriment of Penn Central's investment in Executive Jet Aviation [6]. Then, in mid-1969, Hodge came to Bevan with a plan that might have involved taking control of the Penn Central itself. Bevan was shocked and, as previously recounted, tried to explain that the railroad's poor financial position made it inadvisable to bring in new investors. Hodge refused to listen to Bevan, and this resistance marked a serious break in their friendship. But the relationship between Charles Hodge and David Bevan was never as close as the investigating committee or the newspapers intimated. Even in Penphil, Charles Hodge was not the sole adviser. The investment club made some stock purchases through firms other than Glore Forgan, and at times Hodge's views were not even solicited.

Wright Patman made much out of Bevan's intention to turn Penphil into a conglomerate. He based his accusations on a letter that Bevan wrote to

Charles Hodge in 1967, saying: "The following letter is just for your information and to give you some idea as to the current thinking of some of us and no specific action is requested until we get along a little further." Bevan then explained how he hoped to broaden Penphil's equity base. In the long run, he thought there would be "an excellent opportunity . . . to acquire a small mutual fund and if we are able to do this, we will hold it as a subsidiary of Penphil, giving out Penphil stock in exchange." Bevan continued [7]:

> You can see this will gradually broaden the equity base of Penphil if we are successful and substantially increase the number of shares outstanding. If we follow this program we will eliminate all limitations on the right of sale of Penphil stock, and actually we are thinking in terms of having a large number of shares of Penphil outstanding and going, you might say, public ultimately with Penphil and turn[ing] it at the same time into an aggressive acquirer of other companies so that we can build it up into a very substantial conglomerate holding and operating company.

Bevan later maintained that he wrote this letter thinking about the opportunities that would open to him and others upon their approaching retirements. Bevan's brother Thomas observed, "That's the way Dave thought. As chief financial officer of the railroad, he was dealing with the big picture and it was just natural that he would do that at Penphil too." No matter what Bevan's thoughts were for Penphil in the distant future, the Penn Central kept him too busy to act. As Thomas Bevan put it, "He just didn't have the time needed to expand the scope of Penphil" [8]. Not only did the club stay small in number of investors, never having as many as thirty at one time; it also remained small in terms of its total capital. When the railroad collapsed, Penphil's assets amounted to slightly more than $3 million. Patman argued that Penphil's original members did well, since in 1970 they each could claim a paper profit of $83,500 on their subscription of $16,500. While this sounds large, it was relatively insignificant for the men involved. Penphil's activities occurred over an 8-year period and all profits were reinvested. Had the Penphil return been in cash, which it was not, Bevan's share of the profits would have been approximately $10,400 a year. This was a modest sum compared with his annual salary of $134,000. Bevan's Penphil holdings were minuscule compared with his Penn Central stock, which had a value of approximately $2 million in 1969. In point of fact, neither Bevan nor any other Penphil investor received any income from the firm between 1962 and 1970, since all dividends and other profits were ploughed back into the club.

Patman's investigators could easily trace Penphil's activities because they were so few. In the 8 years while Bevan was at the railroad, Penphil purchased an interest in only nine companies, an average of about one stock each year. Moreover, once Penphil made an investment, it usually kept it. Penphil did not trade in and out and thus provided very little stock market activity.

PENPHIL'S INVESTMENTS

In order to understand the nature of the charges made against Bevan and Penphil, it is necessary to take a detailed look at the firm's portfolio. Penphil made five investments that were parallel to those made by the railroad. These were in Kaneb, Great Southwest, Tropical Gas, Continental Mortgage, and Symington Wayne. Penphil made four other investments in firms in which the railroad had no interest: National Homes, the First Bank and Trust Company and University National Bank (both in Boca Raton, Florida), and Holiday International Tours.

Penphil's investments had several common characteristics. They were, with few exceptions, special situations that had long-term prospects for capital gains. Some were listed, not on the New York Stock Exchange, but on other markets, such as the Midwest, American, and Over-the-Counter exchanges. In most cases, Penphil invested in companies that some member knew well. Bevan and several other members served as directors of Kaneb and Tropical Gas. For his personal portfolio, Bevan bought shares in Kaneb, Great Southwest, and Tropical Gas. Penphil made its investment in the Florida banks on the recommendation of Benjamin Sawin; they were located in southern Florida where he vacationed. Moreover, the railroad's subsidiary, Arvida, had interests in southern Florida. While Bevan was modern in his application of accounting to business management, his investment ideas were conservative. He, with other Penphil members, preferred personal knowledge and shunned unfamiliar situations. While Bevan's strategy did not always work, his decisions were right far more often than they were wrong. His judgment was one reason why the Penn Central's pension fund did well. It also helps explain why the Pennsylvania Company, the vehicle that Bevan used for the railroad's diversification program, survived the Penn Central's crash as a solvent, secure corporation and has since become a focus around which a new Penn Central is emerging.

The most important criticisms made of Bevan and Penphil were that he used the club to achieve control of other corporations, that Penphil conflicted with the interests of his primary railroad responsibilities, and finally, that he profited from the unethical use of inside information. For the purpose of analysis, it is useful to group Penphil stock purchases in three broad categories. The first includes the three Penphil investments which the investigators claimed were made to allow Bevan to control outside corporations. These were Kaneb, Tropical Gas, and Great Southwest. The second category were parallel investments of Penphil and the railroad where, the investigators agreed, Bevan was not attempting to control. These were Continental Mortgage, National Homes, and Symington Wayne. The third category consisted of Penphil investments in which the railroad did not participate. Patman maintained that Bevan used the railroad to aid these firms—the two Florida banks and Holiday International Tours.

PENPHIL'S PARALLEL INVESTMENTS IN KANEB, TROPICAL GAS, AND GREAT SOUTHWEST

Penphil's first investment was Kaneb, a Houston-based pipeline that operated in Kansas and Nebraska. Penphil made two purchases, a single order for slightly more than 22,000 shares in 1962, followed by another 5000-share order in February 1963. The investment club held Kaneb until well after the Penn Central's bankruptcy. The railroad began to buy Kaneb in November of 1960 and made a number of additional purchases for the pension fund through December 1968. At the time of the collapse, the fund held 122,500 Kaneb shares. Bevan also bought slightly more than 3000 shares for his own account and additional purchases were made by other members. None of the investigators ever claimed that Kaneb was a bad investment either for Penphil or the railroad. The Securities and Exchange Commission staff found that Penphil paid $155,000 for its Kaneb shares, which, on April 20, 1972, had market value in excess of $1,820,000. The SEC did not record Penn Central's profit, but it is clear from the investigator's own evidence that pension fund gains were substantial [9].

Patman claimed that Bevan wanted to control Kaneb and based his assertion on the interlock between Penphil and the pipeline. In 1963 Herbert E. Fisher, Kaneb's board chairman, became a Penphil stockholder, and Bevan went on Kaneb's board. Patman produced a table that he said demonstrated how Bevan used Penphil to control Kaneb. The table listed the combined holdings of Penn Central, Penphil, Bevan, and other Penphil members as 271,528 shares, or 21.56 percent of Kaneb's total. (See Appendix C.)

The question that immediately arises from these data is, why did Bevan need Penphil? Of the total of 271,528 shares, the Penn Central held 122,500 and Penphil only 30,488. The remainder were owned by Bevan (3044), and Herbert Fisher, Kaneb's board chairman (115,496). Actually, the table in Appendix C understates Fisher's interest, since he controlled trusts that collectively owned 24,835 shares, giving him the authority to vote 140,000 shares, or almost as much as Penn Central and Penphil combined. Patman's staff assumed that Fisher's interests ran with Bevan's. But is it logical for Fisher to turn over decision making in the corporation which he founded to outsiders such as Penphil or Bevan? Even assuming that Fisher would do so, why did Bevan need Penphil? The investment club held a mere 30,488 shares. If Bevan had really wanted to control Kaneb, and Patman produced no evidence that he did, he could easily have had the railroad pension fund purchase another hundred thousand or so Kaneb shares. This purchase would have allowed Bevan to achieve even greater influence at Kaneb without risking his own capital and without using a cumbersome device such as an investment club in which Bevan's holdings amounted to less than 5 percent and in which Hodge and others had a voice. What seems more likely is that Bevan saw Kaneb for what it was, a highly profitable investment opportunity in which he, Penphil, and the Penn Central could share.

The Securities and Exchange Commission criticism took a different tack, asserting that Bevan himself purchased shares on the basis of his inside knowledge and urged others, including Penphil, to do the same [10]. While the use of inside information is dishonest and criminal, the problem is one of how to define "inside information." The typical case involves a corporate executive who uses privileged knowledge gained in the course of duty as a basis for buying or selling company shares. An example is the director who sells his or her stock immediately prior to the public release of an unfavorable earnings report. Inside information is almost always associated with a quick sale or purchase, and with "in-and-out trading." Executives of a firm who buy and hold for the long term are seldom accused of misusing inside information. Bevan's relationship with Kaneb does not fit a pattern of quick gain from inside knowledge. One of the SEC's bits of alleged inside information concerned a possible acquisition in 1962 of Kaneb by another company, which in fact did not occur. Another SEC example of inside information was a worksheet outline entitled "Estimated earnings and cash flow for Kaneb over the next ten years," also dated 1962. While this worksheet may have come from the inside, the stock market pays little attention to 10-year income projections. This is not the type of information that would or did lead to a quick price rise for Kaneb stock. The Securities and Exchange Commission staff provided no evidence that this document led to the profits Bevan, Penphil, and the railroad enjoyed from Kaneb.

Tropical Gas, headquartered in Coral Gables, Florida, was the second parallel investment of the railroad and Penphil. Tropical sold propane gas in the Caribbean and Central American market. In August 1963 Penphil purchased 10,000 shares in the firm. This was the investment club's only purchase of Tropical shares and they were held until the gas company was acquired by United States Freight. Penphil held U.S. Freight until late in 1970 and then sold the shares to reduce bank loans. The Pennsylvania Railroad started to purchase Tropical stock in 1960 and continued until 1968, when the various funds held a total of 89,400 shares. Together, Penphil and Penn Central held about 9 percent of Tropical. This was far from a controlling interest, since three institutional investors, Boston's State Street

Investment Corporation, Harvard College, and Yale University, together held more than 300,000 shares. Nevertheless, there was considerable interlock between Penn Central, Penphil, and Glore Forgan. Charles Hodge had been on Tropical's board of directors since 1954. Fred H. Billups, Tropical's president, became a Penphil member in July 1963, immediately prior to Penphil's purchase of Tropical shares. Bevan went on Tropical's board in 1964.

Patman's committee said Bevan's role in Tropical conflicted with his interests in the Penn Central. Patman pointed out that in June 1968, Tropical's board considered expanding the company's common stock by 230,000 shares in order to raise fresh capital. In September 1968, Penn Central's pension fund, supervised by Robert Haslett, used Glore Forgan to buy 35,000 Tropical shares. Patman asked why the railroad purchased this stock when "the chief financial officer and chief investment adviser of Penn Central, namely Bevan and Hodge, knew well beforehand that Tropical would be making a large capital stock offering shortly after which would, at least initially, dilute earnings and voting strength of all previous shares outstanding, including stock already held by the Penn Central itself" [11]. Patman's investigators quizzed Haslett as to whether Bevan knew about Penn Central's order. "Normally," said Haslett, "Dave Bevan was aware of Penn Central's Tropical stock purchases, but I'm not sure if he was in this instance" [12]. When Patman's men asked Haslett whether Bevan or Hodge should have warned the Penn Central's investment officer about the sale of 230,000 additional Tropical shares, Haslett said, "Would not that be inside information?"

The Patman charges raise two separate issues. The first is whether this action harmed Penn Central. The answer is that it did not, because Tropical never went through with its public offering. Furthermore, although a new stock issue might temporarily have depressed Tropical's prices, the price drop would matter little to an institution that planned to hold the shares over a long period because the new capital was meant to increase earning power.

The second issue involved conflict of interest. Here Bevan was more vulnerable. Haslett recognized this when he told the investigators that if Bevan had advised him of the proposed stock issue, that would be passing on inside information. Continuing the same session, Patman's staff asked Haslett whether he thought "Bevan's responsibility to protect the interests of the Penn Central railroad was greater than his responsibility to Tropical." Haslett said, "I don't know which one he had a responsibility to first. I just can't answer that." The irony of this is that it had nothing to do at all with Penphil but arose from a problem that radiates through American business —that of interlocking directorships. Bevan's outside directorships were not unusual. Just by running down the list of Penn Central's directors, it is possible to postulate a number of potential conflicts far more serious than

Bevan's position with Tropical Gas. William L. Day, chairman of the board of the Pennsylvania Banking and Trust Company, headed a firm in which the Penn Central kept large deposits and from which it borrowed money. John T. Dorrance, Jr., chief executive of Camden's Campbell Soup Company, was a large Penn Central shipper vitally interested in freight rates and service. He was also a director of Morgan Guaranty, which held Penn Central deposits and lent it funds. Edward J. Hanley, chief executive of Pittsburgh's Allegheny Ludlum Steel Corporation, was a major rail shipper. Seymour H. Knox's Midland Marine and Trust Company was a Penn Central depository. Walter A. Marting's Hanna Mining Company of Cleveland was a major shipper. R. George Rincliffe's Philadelphia Electric Company supplied electric power to the railroad's vast Philadelphia network. This partial list illuminates only some obvious potential conflicts of interest between the directors of the Penn Central and other companies with which they were concerned. In this respect, the Penn Central did not differ from any other major corporation in the United States. David Bevan maintained that he followed a standard policy developed within the financial and business community to deal with potential conflicts of interest situations. This policy was that a director of a firm should never disclose confidential information to unauthorized persons. This expressly prohibited the flow of information from one company to another. David Rockefeller, chairman of the board of the Chase Manhattan Bank, told the Patman Committee that his institution had a similar policy to stop the "flow or incidental communication of inside information from the commercial departments or division of the Bank to the Investment Department or to the Pension or Personal Trust Divisions of the Trust Department" [13].

Another Patman charge was that Bevan supported Tropical's management in its successful attempt to fight off a takeover by the Mapco Corporation. Patman asserted that Tropical's merger with Mapco would reduce Penphil's and hence Bevan's alleged control over Tropical. The takeover fight took place in 1968. Ironically, in October 1969 Tropical Gas merged with United States Freight, and Penphil received 8900 shares of U.S. Freight and Penn Central 79,566 shares of the same company. The combined Penphil and Penn Central holdings in U.S. Freight represented less than 1.3 percent of that company's outstanding stock, making it impossible for Bevan, Penphil, and the Penn Central to exercise much influence on that company through stock ownership. Tropical's merger with U.S. Freight had the full support of Tropical's management. Bevan took no action to stop the takeover. This was strange behavior for a man allegedly dedicated to gaining and keeping control of Tropical [14].

The most controversial parallel investment by Penphil and the railroad was the Great Southwest Corporation. It will be recalled that Great Southwest started out as a Texas real estate venture and eventually became a large-scale operator of amusement parks. Penn Central began buying Great Southwest in 1963. Penphil made only one purchase of Great Southwest, a single block of 10,000 shares acquired in 1963. At that time, the company was a joint venture of the Wynne and Rockefeller families. Bevan points out that in 1963 it was not possible to know that the controlling interest in the firm would come on the market a year later. Toddy Wynne, Sr., told Bevan and Saunders how this came about. The Wynne and Rockefeller families had an agreement that if the Wynne family ever sold, the Rockefellers wanted to sell also, "since the Wynnes were managing the company and the Rockefellers, for their own reasons, did not wish the task of management, if the Wynnes withdrew from the company." In late spring, 1964, a rift developed within the Wynne family, and Toddy Wynne, Sr. explained that it brought about the sale of combined Wynne-Rockefeller holdings, amounting to 42 percent of Great Southwest and thus constituting working control of the firm. In 1964 the Pennsylvania Company, the wholly owned subsidiary of Pennsylvania Railroad, purchased this block of stock. At this point, Penphil was the owner of a small block of stock in a company controlled by the Pennsylvania Railroad. This placed Bevan in a potentially troublesome conflict of interest. For reasons that Bevan could not explain, he delayed taking action for 17 months. Bevan himself recognized that this delay was wrong, and he could offer no excuse other than that his mind was occupied with other, more pressing business. Finally, in December 1965 the Pennsylvania Company was busily engaged in large-scale purchases of Great Southwest stock so that it could acquire 80 percent control to bring the firm under the railroad's tax shelter. Then the conflict of interest between Bevan, Penphil, and the Pennsylvania became embarrassingly clear. Bevan told the Penphil investors that Great Southwest "was an excellent company, but that when we had originally bought it, none of us had any way of knowing Pennsylvania would acquire a controlling interest, and participate in the management of the company." He recommended the immediate sale of Penphil's Great Southwest to avoid conflict of interest at some future date. Although some members were not "too happy about disposing of it," Bevan recalled, "since they were enthusiastic about the future prospects of the company, everyone consulted finally agreed, and the stock was sold." Bevan explained to several of his friends "that Penphil either had to get out of Great Southwest, or I had to get out of Penphil."

The major controversy involved the price that Penphil received for its holdings. Penphil had purchased its stock at $16.50 per share and sold it at $37.75, which netted the investment company a $212,500 profit. This was a 130 percent gain for Penphil, although it meant less than $10,000 for any individual member, including Bevan. Staff investigators were critical because the purchaser of Penphil's shares was the Pennsylvania Company. Bevan and his critics sharply disagreed as to whether the desire for profit motivated

Penphil's sale. The Securities and Exchange Commission charged that Penphil held onto its Great Southwest shares, knowing that the Pennsylvania Company would purchase more and drive up the price. The SEC agreed with Patman that Penphil sold, not for Bevan's stated reasons, but to make a quick profit. The investigators noted that the price of Great Southwest plunged dramatically in 1970 and that the Pennsylvania Company ended up with stock that was worth less than it had cost to buy. Bevan stated that Penphil made a great sacrifice in its sale of Great Southwest. He noted that Penphil sold for $37.75 a share in 1965, which compared with the all-time high for Great Southwest of $443 a share reached in May 1969.

All evidence indicates that in 1965 Bevan was very enthusiastic about Great Southwest. There is every reason to believe that he expected a large appreciation in the firm's shares and would not have sold them if he had not been afraid of a possible conflict of interest. Furthermore, Bevan blamed Great Southwest's collapse directly on the railroad's failure, insisting that Penn Central's collapse in a tight money market destroyed Great Southwest's credit, which in turn disrupted the plans for the development of its valuable real estate holdings in California's Orange County. He felt the change in Penn Central's management after the collapse operated against Great Southwest. In one move, the trustees swept away everyone who had knowledge of Great Southwest operations, and when the company encountered financial problems in the summer of 1970, the trustees panicked and forced the liquidation of some of Southwest's most valuable assets, including much of the California real estate. If Great Southwest had managed to hold on a bit longer, it would have come out better than it did. For, starting in 1973, Southern California, and especially Orange County, started to experience one of the most explosive real estate booms of any part of the United States since World War II.

PENPHIL'S PARALLEL INVESTMENTS IN CMI, NATIONAL HOMES, AND SYMINGTON WAYNE

There were three other cases of parallel investments on the part of Penphil and the railroad. These were Continental Mortgage Investors (CMI), National Homes, and Symington Wayne. Bevan was involved in the management of none of these companies and Glore Forgan had no interest in two of them. In 1964 Penphil, on Lawrence Stevens's recommendation, purchased a single order of 10,000 shares of Continental Mortgage Investors, the largest real estate trust in the United States. Hemphill Noyes was the investment banker for Continental and handled the orders through its partner, Stevens. Penphil held its shares until well after the railroad's collapse.

It paid $19.68 per share and its original investment was worth $196,800. As of June 21, 1971, this appreciated to $1,267,500. The Pennsylvania Railroad purchased CMI shares over a period of 8 years, starting in April 1962. The railroad's investment appreciated just as did Penphil's, and as of June 1971, both firms gained substantially from their CMI holdings. Interestingly enough, the Securities and Exchange Commission staff did not calculate Penn Central's profit [15]. The major criticism directed at Penphil's investment in Continental Mortgage was that the club may have benefited from inside information. The alleged source was a memorandum prepared by Julius Jensen III, a Hemphill Noyes partner who in 1964 projected appreciation on CMI shares over the next 3 fiscal years. As in the case of the alleged information that Penphil used for its investment in Kaneb, it is difficult to see that Jensen's long-term projections, even if they had been made public, could have substantially influenced the market for CMI. In terms of control, combined holdings of Penphil and Penn Central amounted to less than 2.2 percent of Continental Mortgage's outstanding stock. Even Wright Patman admitted that neither Bevan nor Glore Forgan controlled the company [16].

In June 1968, Penphil bought 5000 shares in National Homes Corporation, an Indiana manufacturer of prefabricated houses. Here again the investment club acted on Lawrence Stevens's recommendation. The same year, Penn Central purchased 10,000 shares of the same company for its account. The Securities and Exchange Commission found no fault in this investment, stating that, "Unlike most of Penphil's investments, there does not appear to have been any interlocking relationship between Penphil's shareholders and National. Neither the PRR, Penphil, nor Penphil stockholders owned shares of the stock of National prior to June 1968" [17]. As in the case of CMI, Hemphill Noyes acted as broker for both Penphil and the Pennsylvania Railroad. Patman's committee found combined Penn Central and Penphil investment in National Homes represented only 0.31 percent of stock of that corporation. An interesting sidelight to the National Homes investment was a complaint from Charles Hodge that he did not know about the purchase until after it was made. Hodge wrote to Bevan [18]:

> I was notified after the fact this morning that Penphil has bought 5000 shares of National Homes. Larry [Stevens] called me and explained that it was an oversight that I was not notified, and this oversight is understandable and I am certainly not put out. However, I must go on record, while this will be a popular and fast-moving stock, I do not agree with the fundamental purpose, nor do I agree with the management of the Price brothers who have not demonstrated any ability in this field. I am confident that stockmarketwise we will probably make some money in it, but would like to go on record that this is not one to hold blindly.

Interestingly, this was one investment that did not work out well for the Penn Central. The railroad purchased 9700 shares in December 1968 at 28⅛ and sold 5200 of them in September 1969 at prices ranging from 18¾ to 19¾. Penphil did not hold these shares long either, disposing of them in late 1970 at 16¾, a modest profit of $9000 [19].

Symington Wayne was the final stock in the second category of parallel investments. The Patman Committee was apparently unaware of this transaction or considered that Bevan's behavior was blameless because it wrote nothing about it. The SEC report, however, was critical. Symington Wayne was a small corporation in Salisbury, Maryland, which manufactured gasoline pumps, other service-station equipment, and railroad supplies. On June 27, 1967, Penphil bought 1000 shares of Symington Wayne at a total cost of $33,875. A month earlier, Haslett had started to purchase shares of the same stock at a similar price for Penn Central through the brokerage house of Yarnall, Biddle & Company. Other Penphil members acquired minor amounts of Symington Wayne, including David Bevan and his brother Thomas, Vincent Kling, and Charles Hodge. The SEC assertion, which was contested by all involved, was that all purchasers acted on a tip from Hodge, which indicated a forthcoming merger of Symington Wayne and Dresser Industries. In April 1968, Dresser did merge with Symington Wayne and paid $40 a share for the stock, providing Penphil, the various individual investors, and the Penn Central all with a modest profit [20].

PENPHIL'S FLORIDA INVESTMENTS

The third category of Penphil investments involved firms in which the Pennsylvania Railroad held no interest. Between January 1967 and the end of 1968, Penphil made an investment in Holiday International Tours [21] and also in two Florida banks, the First Bank and Trust Company of Boca Raton and the University Bank in the same city. Regarding the banks, Penphil's commitment amounted to slightly more than $427,000 and was valued on September 1, 1970, at $1,244,000. Benjamin F. Sawin directed Penphil's attention to Florida banking. He was a member of Penphil, a close friend of many of its members, including Bevan, and a shrewd banker who had long been associated with Philadelphia's Provident National. The Florida banks' only possible connection with Penn Central was that Arvida, which became a subsidiary of the Penn Central, had real estate interests in Boca Raton. Patman's committee argued that the two banks owed much of their success to Boca Raton's rapid growth, which it claimed was related to Arvida's developments. The investigators backed this idea with general data, which merely traced the increase of the two banks' deposits and their position in regional banking [22]. While Patman's men proved a dramatic growth in

Boca Raton's banking, they provided not one bit of specific evidence that such trends were linked to real estate development. Following World War II, Florida was one of the nation's fastest growing states. Few people would argue that Arvida—or any other real estate firm—caused that growth. What seems more likely is that both Penphil's banks and Arvida benefited from long-term economic forces operating in Florida's favor. In any case, it is difficult to see how Penphil's Florida banking investments damaged the railroad or influenced it in any manner. The railroad purchased Arvida only after a year-long study had indicated that south Florida had a bright future.

PENPHIL'S IMPLICATIONS AND LESSONS

In summary, Penphil's investments during the period reviewed by the various congressional and other government investigators produced a paper profit. The club had increases on eight out of nine stocks. The one exception was Holiday International Tours, in which Penphil lost all the $65,000 ventured. While not all the parallel investments made by the Pennsylvania Railroad and Penn Central funds were profitable, the losses to the pension fund were small and overbalanced by the profits on the successful shares. Furthermore, Penn Central's losses had no relation to Penphil's stock market activity or investment decisions. The losses resulted from independent decisions reached by Penn Central's investment manager, Robert Haslett.

Great Southwest was a special case. It was not purchased by Penn Central's pension fund but as part of the railroad's diversification program. As previously noted, the money invested in Great Southwest came not from the railroad but from the reinvestment of the Pennsylvania Company's interests, such as the Norfolk & Western stock. The money put into Great Southwest was not enough to stem the railroad's decline even had it been totally used for rail operations. Although Great Southwest did encounter financial difficulties, they occurred primarily after Penn Central's collapse, and were exacerbated by the railroad's operational failure. It is significant that even after the Penn Central's trustees liquidated in panic many of Great Southwest's assets, the company underwent a successful reorganization and, as of 1980, showed every prospect of becoming a cornerstone on which a new Penn Central would be built [23].

Since the Penn Central's pension fund remained solvent and prospered under Bevan's stewardship, it is clear that Penphil had no detrimental effect on it. Bevan himself stated that he had done nothing wrong. He emphasized that Penphil was not a "go-go" trading fund. "With one minor exception," he said, "all investments made were on a long-term basis, and the investment club did not engage in trading in the market." He pointed out that "despite charges to the contrary, there is not a single instance where either Penphil or Penphil and Penn Central together ever approached control or even amounted to as much as 15 percent of the stock outstanding in any given company." Bevan did not find parallel investments unusual since "in its various funds Penn Central probably had investments in 400 or 500 different companies. Bearing this in mind," Bevan said, "it is not surprising that in several instances Penphil and Penn Central had investments in the same companies. This is particularly true if it is realized that Penphil was primarily interested in capital gains, and the Penn Central had several similar types of funds." In an interview with the author, Bevan argued that there was no conflict of interest between his role in Penphil and the Penn Central. He pointed out,

> In the past, no one has ever raised any question of wrongdoing being involved in parallel investments, provided there has been no market manipulation, inside trading, or a corporation deprived of an investment opportunity. If it were otherwise, then no investment house managing a mutual fund could buy any of the securities that were bought in the mutual fund, no head of a trust department could buy for himself, or for any other fund in which he was interested, securities being purchased in his trust department. No officer of a life insurance company buying certain securities could buy identical securities for himself. If so-called parallel investments cannot be made in the future [Bevan maintained], there will have to be a complete revision of our whole approach to regulations surrounding investments in the financial community. It will virtually be impossible to get officers and directors for many financial organizations. It is tantamount to saying that officers, and perhaps directors, of any financial institution, would be virtually barred from buying securities.

Bevan also noted that in the case of Kaneb and Tropical Gas, his personal holdings were public knowledge. At the very least, the Pennsylvania board members who were on the Pension Committee knew Bevan was a director in those companies. His affiliations were on file in the office of the railroad's secretary. Directors are supposed to own stock in the companies they supervise. In each case, Bevan's direct holdings exceeded his interest in the same companies through Penphil. At the time, no one ever raised a question about Bevan's directorships.

The author of this book interviewed several Philadelphia attorneys who had been involved in the suits that followed the Penn Central's collapse and had a different opinion about Bevan's activities. These included Edwin P. Rome, partner in the firm of Blank, Rome, Klaus & Comisky, and Raymond Denworth and Stewart Dalzell, both of the firm of Drinker, Biddle and Reath. Edwin Rome represented the Penn Central trustees in their suit against the former Penn Central executives and others in an action against Penphil launched after the Patman disclosures. Dalzell and Denworth were retained by the outside directors (whose interests were separate from the management, which included Perlman, Saunders, and Bevan) in the many legal conflicts after the railroad's bankruptcy. Rome found that there was no evidence to support the argument that Bevan's activities in Penphil caused the Penn Central's collapse. Nor did he feel that Bevan manipulated the railroad for Penphil's benefit. Dalzell and Denworth came to similar conclusions. They specifically rejected Patman's implications that Bevan used his position with the Pennsylvania to aid Penphil. Both felt that Bevan consistently placed his obligations to the railroad above all outside interests.

Nevertheless, all three lawyers were critical of Bevan's participation in Penphil. While Edwin Rome did not oppose the concept of parallel investments, he did not like the manner in which Penphil and Penn Central made them. It was one thing for parallel investments to be made in broadly based corporations traded on the New York Stock Exchange. In Rome's view, it was quite another thing to make parallel investments in narrowly based corporations in which Bevan had a managerial interest. This was especially so in such ventures as Kaneb, Tropical Gas, and Great Southwest. Rome felt such investments were bound to produce a potential conflict of interest. The Patman Committee reported on one possible conflict in the case of Tropical Gas's proposed 1968 stock offering. Another conflict arose in the case of Great Southwest when the railroad gained control of it. Rome did not consider that Bevan used his position in the various corporations to Penn Central's detriment. Rather, he disapproved only of Bevan's participation in Penphil in principle.

Both Denworth and Dalzell agreed with Rome. They deemed Bevan's role in Penphil unwise, and singled out the parallel investments in Great Southwest, Tropical, and Kaneb as errors. While neither opposed the concept of parallel investments, both stressed that they should not be made by financial managers in small, closely held corporations where the financial manager had an interest in the firms. Again Dalzell and Denworth stressed that their objections to Bevan and Penphil were on the basis of principle rather than practice.

The three Philadelphia lawyers' views followed views encountered in antitrust decisions by the United States Supreme Court. For example, the du Pont Company was made to divest itself of its controlling holdings in General Motors. The Court required this divestiture not because it found du Pont had abused its position by forcing General Motors to buy du Pont products, but rather, because the mere fact that du Pont held a controlling interest in General Motors gave it power to behave contrary to law. In Bevan's case, the lawyers felt that Bevan had made a mistake by placing himself in a position where he *could* take an active part in the management of two corporations with interlocking interests [24]. However, interlocking directorships remain common in the American financial and business world, and Bevan, who had grown up in this world, saw nothing wrong with it as long as the individuals did not abuse their position.

So, too, Bevan thought that merely occupying a position where interests could conflict, such as through interlocking directorships, was not wrong provided the person did not use his or her power to favor one interest over another. As the 1960s wore on, the definition of conflict of interest became progressively broader. In actual business practice, however, things seemed much the same. The new ethics emerged in cases of dramatic failure and were the product of stockholders' suits and congressional investigations. In this sense, the Penn Central is significant because it highlighted and pushed forward the new trend of business morality.

Yet the implications of the Patman and the Securities and Exchange staff investigations hold serious problems for the investment community. Most might agree now, with the virtue of hindsight, that Bevan made a mistake by becoming a director in a corporation such as Tropical and simultaneously participating in a private investment club that purchased those shares while the railway's pension fund also bought stock in the same firm. But do pension fund participants want their money invested by persons who have no interest in the investments? Recently, *Forbes* magazine analyzed the performance of mutual funds and other investment trusts and postulated, half facetiously, the dartboard theory of investment. The magazine's point was that fund managers might do as well by pasting a copy of a New York Stock Exchange listing on a board, throwing darts at it, and picking the stocks where the darts landed. *Forbes* even went so far as to compare the results of a dartboard fund with a hypothetical fund managed by its own financial experts. Most investors continue to have greater confidence in selections made on the basis of human intelligence than chance.

But how are investment managers to make decisions about stock purchases? A careful reading of the criticism leveled against Bevan and others in the Penphil affair indicates how broadly the investigators defined inside information. The case of Lawrence M. Stevens of the Philadelphia office of Hemphill Noyes & Company illustrates this. The SEC criticized Stevens for recommending Penphil's purchase of Continental Mortgage because of a letter that Stevens wrote detailing a number of new financial arrangements that CMI was making through Hemphill Noyes. Stevens advised Penphil [25]:

Incidentally and confidentially, the company has a bank line of approximately $20 million at the prime rate (4½ percent). These loans require a compensating balance, however, whereas the present financing will permit 100 percent use of the funds derived. As far as additional common stock is concerned, it would represent only quite minor dilution and would not, in my opinion, represent a material factor.

Following this financing the company plans to announce, as you may note on one of the enclosed sheets, that no further debt or equity financing is contemplated at the present time. A quite substantial portion of the $10 million of notes and stock has been reserved for one of the large New York City companies. One other institution has indicated that it will take a substantial amount of notes and stock and, in addition to that, two or three other institutions have the proposal under consideration.

Dividend payments for the 1963 fiscal year were $1.10. We expect that dividend payments for the 1964 year will amount to $1.35 per share. At a price of 17¾ for the stock, this would afford a yield of about 7.6 percent.

May I again reiterate that some portions of the enclosed are confidential in nature.

Every large mutual fund in the United States that makes investments in growth stocks sends representatives to companies in which it proposes to invest. These representatives talk to management and receive confidential information that is not available to the small investors. Major banks and trust funds use the same tactics. Any fund or bank that did not attempt to accumulate this kind of information would be derelict in its responsibilities. If the Patman criticisms that were leveled against Penphil and its participation were taken seriously by the investment industry, the resulting doctrine would materially hamper the current operational practices of almost every Wall Street financial institution. The main losers would be the millions of Americans who have money invested either in pension funds or in mutual funds. Furthermore, it is doubtful that even if the kind of information Stevens gave to Penphil was made generally available, the small investors would be able to make more intelligent decisions. In fact, most of Stevens' "confidential" data were probably well-known on Wall Street by those interested in CMI.

While it is clear that Penphil had nothing to do with the Penn Central's collapse, the investment club's experience contains an important lesson for all executives of pension funds or other major financial institutions. The current climate of legal and political opinion runs against any parallel investments made for institutional and personal accounts. The Penphil case indicates that such investments are particularly dangerous when they involve small, closely held corporations not generally traded in a market like the New York Stock Exchange. Managers who ignore the Penphil experience will be particularly vulnerable if the fund or corporation in which they are involved runs into problems, even if the trouble has no relationship to the parallel investments. This doctrine, if rigorously applied, will inhibit fund managers from making personal investments. The end result may deprive some funds of significant opportunities for substantial gain. In their investigations of small companies, investment managers will be forced to choose between making institutional investments and personal investments. In some cases, the prohibition of personal and institutional investments in the same small companies may cause large institutional investors to avoid small firms altogether, thereby inhibiting the emergence of new enterprises. Thus the Patman staff might be causing the exact opposite effect of what they intend.

REFERENCES

1.   *The Penn Central Failure and the Role of Financial Institutions,* Staff Report of the Committee on Banking and Currency, 92d Congress, First Session, House of Representatives, January 3, 1972, pp. 207–210. Hereafter referred to as the Patman Report.

2.   Ibid., p. 254.

3.   For data on CBK Industries, see ibid., pp. 294–311. An analysis of Bevan's management of the pension funds is presented in Appendix A of this book.

4.   Thomas Bevan, "Penphil Memorandum" to R. K. Stevens, August 1, 1972. Other Penphil members were Angus Wynne, Jr., president of Great Southwest; Edwin B. Horner, First Colony Life Insurance; Samuel Breene, attorney in Oil City, Penna.; Joseph Davin, V. P. Stockton, Whatley, Davin & Co.; Alfonso Manero, retired partner of Glore Forgan; Harry F. Ortlip, Box Hill Realty; Brown Whatley, president of Arvida; and Cornelius Dorsey, assistant to Robert Haslett of the Pennsylvania Railroad.

5.   Patman Report, pp. 287–293.

6.   This story is told in Chapters 16 and 17 on Executive Jet.

7.   Patman Report, Bevan to Hodge, July 31, 1967, pp. 245–246.

8.   Ibid., p. 245.

9.   One wonders why the investigators omitted these data. Was it because the good showing of the Penn Central pension funds would have reflected favorably on Bevan? See *The Financial Collapse of the Penn Central Company,* a Staff Report of the Securities and Exchange Commission to the [House of Representatives] Special Sub-Committee on Investigations, Hon. Harley O. Staggers, Chairman, Government Printing Office, Washington, D.C., August 1972, p. 312. Hereafter referred to as the SEC Staff Report.

10.   SEC Staff Report, p. 311.

11.   Patman Report, p. 222.

12.   Ibid., p. 224.

13.   Ibid., p. 350.

14.   Ibid., p. 229.

15.   SEC Staff Report, p. 319. Again the question arises as to whether the railroad's earnings from CMI stock were omitted because they reflected favorably on Bevan's investment record. Later, CMI shares, in common with many real estate investment trust shares, collapsed, and Penphil, which continued to hold the securities, suffered an overall loss. Whether the railroad's pension fund continued to hold the shares is

unknown. It should be noted that Bevan had no influence on railroad pension fund decisions after June 8, 1970, and also no influence in Penphil's decision to retain CMI.

16.   Patman Report, p. 213.

17.   SEC Staff Report, pp. 328–329.

18.   Patman Report, p. 215.

19.   SEC Staff Report, p. 329. In this case, where the railroad sustained a loss on its shares, much more specific information is given than when it made a profit. This may reflect the bias of the writers of the SEC Staff Report.

20.   Ibid., pp. 323–328. In this case the SEC Staff Report indicates that the Penn Central fund made a profit of $40,000 from Symington Wayne stock; Penphil's profit was $8,125; David Bevan's, $10,450.38; Hodge's, $13,293.52; Thomas Bevan's, $756.00; and Kling's, $4,159.89.

21.   The Holiday International Tours story fits in with the Executive Jet story and will be covered in Chapter 17.

22.   Patman Report, p. 231.

23.   See Pennsylvania Company, *Annual Report, 1976,* pp. 1, 25. The Pennsylvania Company lists four companies as its mainstays of profitable operation since the Penn Central's bankruptcy. Three, Buckeye, Arvida, and Great Southwest, were acquired by Bevan. The Report states, "During the past 6 years, particularly 1975 and 1976, Great Southwest has been emerging from the shadow of negative net worth and has developed into a successful business entity."

24.   These data are from author's separate interviews with Edwin Rome, Raymond Denworth, and Stewart Dalzell in Philadelphia on May 23, 1977.

25.   SEC Staff Report, p. 318.

Chapter 16
EXECUTIVE JET AVIATION:
THE FIRST PHASE

EXECUTIVE JET AVIATION:
THE FIRST PHASE

Executive Jet Aviation was a minor venture both in the history of the Penn Central and in David Bevan's business career. The approximately $21 million the railroad lost on the airline investment was minuscule compared with the more than $460-million cash loss from rail operations incurred by the Penn Central during the first 2 years of its life. Executive Jet Aviation (EJA) was also the smallest of the Pennsylvania's diversification efforts that took place under Bevan's tenure at the railroad. The failure of a new venture, such as EJA, is not unique in American business and there is little doubt that had not the Penn Central collapsed, the airline would have been routinely written off. Such was not the fate of Executive Jet. Wright Patman saw to that. His staff report on the Penn Central's failure devoted 94 pages, or one-quarter of its 375 pages, to Executive Jet.

Patman's Report is a model of incompetent and shoddy investigation. As will be seen, almost none of his allegations stands up to scrutiny when tested against the abundant documentation on EJA that exists in Penn Central's files. Patman's investigation was unfortunate for a number of reasons. By placing Executive Jet out of all proportion to its importance, it diverted attention from the real causes of the railroad's failure. And Patman's Report had other equally serious defects. It asserted that Bevan and other railroad officials deliberately set out to engage in an illegal attempt to have the Pennsylvania enter the airline business. By focusing on alleged law violations, Patman missed the real significance of the EJA story. This is not to say that Bevan and other railroad officers never erred in their business judgments—far from it. Rather, the EJA story is not one of corruption, but of the problems and risks of dealing with the American regulatory system, in this case the Civil Aeronautics Board. The issues raised in EJA involve fundamental questions in the nation's economy: those of competition and the entry of new firms. This chapter and the following one attempt to set the record straight. They demonstrate the extreme and complex hazards encountered by even the most experienced business executives and lawyers when they attempt to promote new enterprise in the transportation area.

THE RICCIARDI AFFAIR

Executive Jet Aviation was the most controversial element of David Bevan's career. It ended disastrously for Bevan, for its founder, Brigadier General Olbert F. Lassiter, for its investment banker, Charles J. Hodge, and for the railroad. Nobody came to appreciate this fact more than Bevan. Shortly after the railroad's collapse, Senator Hartke told Bevan that Executive Jet "was a terrible investment as far as I'm concerned." Bevan responded, "I agree with you, if I had to do it all over again, I wouldn't do it" [1].

Executive Jet was a newspaper reporter's dream and a bonanza for the congressional investigators. As Wayne W. Parrish, writing for the magazine *American Aviation,* observed, "The plot is right out of a story book. The case of characters is right out of Hollywood, including international finance, ex-Air Force generals, TV and radio figures, a big railroad, and entanglements that only Philadelphia lawyers can unravel" [2]. The company's board of directors included former Air Force Chief of Staff General Curtis LeMay, movie star James Stewart, radio and television personality Arthur Godfrey, former board chairman of the Standard Oil Company of New Jersey, M. J. Rathbone, and former Assistant Secretary of the Navy James Hopkins Smith.

A minor event catapulted Executive Jet into the headlines and kept it there: the Ricciardi affair. Olbert F. Lassiter, Executive Jet's president, was known as a "swinger." In 1964 he met Joseph H. Ricciardi on the latter's Miami, Florida, houseboat. Ricciardi was involved in a number of Florida businesses. At one time or another, he was a real estate broker, the owner of a finance company, the proprietor of a slenderizing salon, and the holder of ten Arthur Murray dance studio franchises. Ricciardi knew lots of women and had a way of life that meshed easily with Lassiter's.

In mid-1967 Lassiter hired Ricciardi to do public relations work for the airline, but the job was short-lived. After serving briefly in New York and Fort Lauderdale, Ricciardi was fired by Lassiter in December 1967. Shortly afterward, Ricciardi claimed Executive Jet owed him large sums of money in back pay. Lassiter told Elihu Inselbuch, Executive Jet's New York attorney, what had happened [3]:

> There were many telephone calls from Ricciardi. . . . Ricciardi started making demands, using threatening overtones. It appeared to me that he was having financial difficulties and saw a possible opportunity for a shakedown. He started talking about $1000 a week for every week that he worked for us and threatened me by saying that if he were not paid, he would disclose to the press certain social arrangements that he had made. His comments were irrational, almost as if he were losing his mind. Finally, I would not accept any of his calls. He went to Charles Hodge and started the same tactics there. Hodge intimated to Ricciardi that he would ask me to settle with him and somehow had gotten up to $5000. When Hodge called me, I told him that I would settle with him for exactly what I thought he was worth and that would be paid expenses for the days that he had contributed something to the company. Finally, he annoyed Hodge and myself so much that I contacted an attorney in Florida, Judge Harold Van, who referred me to the former district attorney of Miami, Max B. Kogan.

Later, Patman's staff interviewed Ricciardi and reported his admission that "he threatened to call a press conference and detail the 'social arrangements'." In fact, Ricciardi did file suit against Executive Jet Aviation for $42,000, which he alleged was for salary and expenses owed him. He made a deposition asserting that Lassiter had hired him to provide women for David Bevan and Charles Hodge. This litigation was settled in February 1969 for $13,000; both Lassiter and Bevan later denied making any cent of payment.

All this conflict might have passed unnoticed except for the Penn Central's collapse, which coincided with Executive Jet's own financial troubles. After the railroad's failure, EJA went through a hard-fought managerial change. In 1968 the railroad had put its interest in EJA in trust, to be held by the Detroit Bank & Trust Company. In late June 1970, Bruce G. Sundlun, Executive Jet's counsel, convinced the trustees that Olbert F. Lassiter should be replaced. Sundlun, acting for the trustees, forcibly took charge of Executive Jet's Columbus, Ohio, headquarters on July 1, 1970. Soon afterward, he discovered a file of color photographs showing General Lassiter "in the company of various young women, all of them very pretty and amply endowed" [4]. This material, along with the Ricciardi deposition, went to the Patman staff.

Wright Patman used the Ricciardi affair to support his thesis that Bevan had funneled money into Executive Jet in order to avoid embarrassing disclosures about his personal life. Patman's press releases made sensational newspaper reading. The *Philadelphia Bulletin*'s lead story on December 21,

1970, proclaimed, "Bevan Blamed in Huge Penn Central Loss," with the subheadline reading, "House Ties 'Dates' to 'Dealing'." On the same day, the *Philadelphia Inquirer* quoted Patman as saying this was "one of the most sordid pictures of the American business community that has ever been revealed in official documents." Many of the revelations involved Miss Linda Vaughn. Lassiter had a picture taken of himself and Miss Vaughn clad in swimming suits sitting beside a swimming pool. This photograph was published in the November 9 issue of *Newsweek* magazine, and later appeared in the *Philadelphia Evening Bulletin* of December 21, 1970. It then found its way into Daughen and Binzen's *The Wreck of the Penn Central.* Miss Vaughn worked for Hurst Performance, Inc., a Warminster, Pennsylvania, auto accessory company whose products were designed for use in auto racing. Miss Vaughn promoted them by riding around racetracks "on a large replica of a floor-mounted automobile gearshift lever" [5]. Her professional name was Miss Hurst Golden Shifter.

Patman's revelations provided lively copy for Philadelphia's newspapers. The December 22 *Inquirer* ran an article entitled " 'Miss Golden Shifter' Puts Pennsy Probe into High Gear." The *Evening Bulletin* of January 10, 1971, headed a feature article "Beauty Denies Helping Penn Central Go Bust." That article, describing the Golden Shifter episode, provides an example of how headlines were more titillating than the facts. The *Philadelphia Sunday Bulletin*'s Sandy Grady interviewed Miss Vaughn and discovered that she had not even met General Lassiter until after Ricciardi had been fired. Said Miss Vaughn, "I didn't know anything about Dick Lassiter's business. I never met Bevan. I met Hodge once at an airport. All that stuff with Ricciardi must have happened before I was engaged to Dick." Miss Vaughn then told of being visited in the fall of 1970 by Phil McMartin, an investigator for Patman's Committee on Banking and Currency. She said, "I told him [Patman's investigator] everything I've told you." The response of Patman's investigator was revealing. "After I was through," recalled Miss Vaughn, "he [McMartin] said, 'Linda, you're not what we're looking for. You didn't even know Bevan or Hodge.' "

All Patman's data about Bevan in this area came from a single source, the Ricciardi deposition in his suit against Executive Jet. Immediately after Patman's disclosures, Bevan said, "Without qualification, I deny all charges of personal misconduct. The Staff Report of the Patman Committee incorporates statements by a disgruntled employee several years ago in a suit later withdrawn. As far as I am personally concerned, these statements are untrue and unfounded" [6]. But Bevan found it extremely difficult to correct the record. His main hope, he and his lawyer believed, was to put Ricciardi on the stand and to subject him to rigorous cross-examination under oath. This opportunity did not occur until a year later in January 1972, when Philadelphia County's District Attorney Arlen Specter, acting at Patman's instigation, had Bevan, Hodge, and Lassiter arraigned. At the preliminary hearing before Judge Ethan Allen Doty, the district attorney's office called Ricciardi as a witness. He had earlier claimed that Lassiter had asked him to provide some young women who would join Hodge and Bevan on a 1967 trip to Las Vegas. It so happened that Bevan and Hodge were going from Philadelphia to the West Coast for a board of directors' meeting of Macco, a Penn Central subsidiary, and planned to stop in Nevada to examine some real estate. Executive Jet had just purchased a Jet Star that lacked sufficient flight hours to be placed in commercial service. Lassiter, because of Bevan's and Hodge's interest in the airline, wished them to see the new plane and invited them to travel to Los Angeles on a shakedown cruise. Bevan and Hodge combined the shakedown flight with their trip to the West Coast. When the plane arrived in Philadelphia to pick them up, Bevan found a group already on board. The group included several officers, technicians, and pilots from Lockheed, the plane's builder, a couple of EJA pilots who were there to familiarize themselves with the aircraft, Lassiter, Hodge, Ricciardi, and a couple of women who had arranged with Lassiter to hitch a ride west. Bevan knew nothing of any arrangements made by Ricciardi, nor did he show any interest in the women. For Bevan, this was strictly a business trip, as Edward German, his lawyer, brought out in the cross-examination. On January 14, 1972, the *Evening Bulletin* reported the testimony thus:

> [Ricciardi said] "Lassiter and 'his girlfriend,' Hodge, Bevan, 'a young lady named Beth Green, myself, and another young lady' flew to Las Vegas." He said Bevan and Hodge went to Wyoming to look at a ranch there during the day and returned that evening to Las Vegas. "Mr. Hodge got ill and somebody had to put him in his bed and Mr. Bevan retired and went to bed by himself," Ricciardi testified. "Didn't Mr. Bevan fall asleep at the table?" German [Bevan's attorney] asked. Ricciardi confirmed that Bevan fell asleep "during the show."

The *Evening Bulletin* headlined this story, "Bevan and Hodge Described as Party Poopers at Vegas Night Club." The *Philadelphia Daily News* of April 6, 1972, used a slightly different headline, "Vegas Trip Dull, Says EX-PC Duo." Later on, Ricciardi, under cross-examination, could not show that he ever got a date for Bevan in his life, but this news was so boring that the papers didn't bother to print it at all [7].

PATMAN'S CONCEPT OF EXECUTIVE JET

Besides the sensational accusations made in the Ricciardi deposition, Patman's staff made numerous other charges against Bevan. They closely followed a report that Basil Cole had prepared with Stuart Saunders's approval in the spring of 1970. Patman asserted [8]:

> There was an astonishing lack of both fiduciary concern and control by the Pennsylvania Railroad (PRR) board of directors over the $21 million that was poured into EJA. The decisions which eventually provided this total investment in the air service were made almost exclusively by David Bevan, chairman of the PRR Finance Committee, and his protégé, William Gerstnecker, PRR treasurer. They did not request nor did they receive board approval for the EJA investments. In fact, $5 million had been funneled into EJA before the board even knew PRR investments were being made in EJA.

Patman's investigators claimed that

> the investment in EJA was aimed at providing entry by PRR into the air passenger and air cargo transportation industry on a worldwide basis. This project was initiated with the full realization on the part of Bevan that a railroad's control of an air carrier without CAB approval was in direct violation of the law. Indeed, awareness of the illegal nature of the project was dramatized by repeated efforts to conceal from the CAB the control over EJA exercised by PRR. This deception included two attempts by the PRR to appear to divest itself of control of the EJA while in fact its domination of the company remained virtually intact. Some $6 million in unsecured PRR investments were made in the EJA after the CAB order to the railroad to divest itself of its air carrier interest. This illegal control over EJA along with EJA's illegal foreign activities cost the PRR and EJA a total of $70,000 in fines levied by the CAB, the largest fine ever levied by the CAB in a single case.

Patman further maintained that Executive Jet drained money from the railroad and was a major factor in its collapse. He reiterated his assertion on Bevan's responsibility for Executive Jet. His report concluded:

> It was essentially the decision of one man, David Bevan, to continue to pump money into EJA when even a modicum of business judgment would have counseled for a complete divestment. That the EJA investment was doomed to failure and that its president, General O. F. Lassiter, was not the man to lead the Pennsylvania Railroad into the air transport field should have been apparent to anyone with a minimum of business judgment.

THE PENNSY'S INITIAL INVOLVEMENT IN EXECUTIVE JET

Fortunately, a vast quantity of Executive Jet and railroad records have been preserved. They do not substantiate Patman's thesis. The answer that emerges as to the question of why Executive Jet failed is complex but clear.

Executive Jet Aviation was the creation of Brigadier General Olbert F. Lassiter. In the Air Force, General Lassiter commanded a pool of small, passenger-carrying Jet Stars headquartered at Washington D.C.'s Andrews Air Force Base that furnished a taxi service for high military officials. The general's performance and his spotless military record impressed Air Force Chief of Staff General Curtis LeMay. Lassiter decided that after his retirement he would organize a similar service for private industry. In 1963 the jet revolution had already overtaken most of America's scheduled passenger airlines, but had yet to arrive at the corporations that owned small private planes to transport their executives. Lassiter well knew the reasons corporations used piston-driven aircraft. The capital cost of jets was large and the planes required specially trained pilots and a high level of maintenance. He saw that the problems that kept corporations from using the new technology could be solved by an air-taxi operation. It was he who seized the opportunity and Executive Jet was his creation, not Hodge's or Bevan's or anyone else's. Lassiter himself carefully picked the firm's illustrious, but well-rounded, board of directors [9]. The board also reflected General Lassiter's character. He was a hard-driving, extremely ambitious man who wanted to associate himself with the nation's industrial and financial elite.

At the time of Lassiter's retirement, he already had a considerable reputation in American industry. Bevan remembered that when the Executive Jet investment came before the Pennsylvania Railroad's board in December 1964, Richard King Mellon was particularly enthusiastic. After the meeting, he took Bevan aside and praised the idea of Executive Jet. Mellon, a major general in the Army Reserve, said that although he had never met Lassiter, he understood that he had a record so brilliant that if the Air Force "had wanted to give Lassiter another decoration, they would have had to create a new one, because he had been awarded practically every decoration the Air Force had to offer."

Lassiter started to organize his company before he retired from the service. He sought help from Bruce G. Sundlun, a reserve Air Force officer who was also a Washington attorney experienced in aviation law. Sundlun brought the idea to Glore Forgan, and together he and Lassiter convinced Charles Hodge that it was sound.

Hodge took Executive Jet to the Pennsylvania Railroad in the fall of 1964 while Bevan was in Europe. He and Lassiter made a presentation to Bevan's assistant, William R. Gerstnecker. When Bevan first heard about it, he was not enthusiastic. He believed "that the risks involved in going into any new venture were above average," and that at that point in the Pennsylvania's diversification program, he was "not convinced of the wisdom of taking such a step." However, Stuart Saunders had also learned of the airline and wanted more information. Bevan therefore went with Saunders to a briefing. Bevan well remembered the meeting, which took place in the Pennsylvania Railroad's staff room on the eighteenth floor of the company's Philadelphia headquarters. It was attended also by Gerstnecker, Hodge, General Lassiter, General Perry Hoisington, and Bruce Sundlun. After listening, Bevan reversed his position and gradually became enthusiastic about Executive Jet.

Saunders was particularly intrigued. The Penn Central's chief executive officer championed the concept of a well-rounded transportation enterprise. He felt that it was only a matter of time before railroads would be allowed to control a thoroughly integrated transportation system that would mix trucks, pipelines, ships, inland barges, and trains. To the north in Canada, the Canadian Pacific Railroad already did exactly that. In the West, Southern Pacific was coordinating trucks and pipelines with its rail operations. In the past, prior to World War II, the Pennsylvania Railroad itself had been instrumental in founding TAT (the predecessor of TWA), an airline that carried transcontinental passengers by day, placing them on railway Pullmans at night. The Pennsy's initial foray into air transportation had been thwarted by federal regulations that a land carrier could not control and operate an airline. Other railroads had attempted to circumvent this ruling, including the New York Central, which for a time owned some securities of an air freight carrier, Flying Tiger. Despite the failure of other railroads to retain a foothold in the airline business, Saunders was convinced that, through proper political maneuvering, a way would be found for the Pennsylvania to succeed. He saw Executive Jet as a possible entrée into air transportation.

Saunders knew that a change in the nation's policy toward railroad ownership of airlines was still in the future. The immediate question was, could the Pennsylvania invest in a company like Executive Jet? A second question was whether Lassiter's concept was sound. A third uncertainty was, could Executive Jet Aviation put its plan into operation? Patman asserted that the railroad, led by David Bevan, made its investment in Executive Jet without due consideration. He said that Bevan hid the railroad's airline investment in a small subsidiary, called the American Contract Company, to prevent knowledge about Executive Jet from reaching the railroad's board of directors, Stuart Saunders, and the Civil Aeronautics Board. The record supports none of these charges.

After the meeting of Executive Jet's promoters and the railroad's officials, Bevan examined the documentation furnished by investment banker Charles Hodge. In late 1964, Bevan and Saunders decided that the matter looked favorable enough to present the idea at the railroad's December directors' meeting. It was then that Richard K. Mellon suggested that Bevan should double-check his data. The Pittsburgh industrialist told Bevan that Pan American Airways, several years previously, had considered a similar type of service. Mellon, a good friend and former college roommate of Pan American's president, Juan Trippe, felt that Pan American would be glad to evaluate the concept.

In early February 1965, Bevan wrote Stuart Saunders a five-page letter detailing the railroad's involvement with Executive Jet Aviation. Bevan reported "a very satisfactory interview" with James B. Taylor, vice-president of Business Jets, a division of Pan American World Airways. Taylor said that when Pan American had examined an air-taxi system, its executives proposed to use piston-driven aircraft and "considered as their potential market only top executives and large companies." Pan American "found there was great resistance on the part of firmly entrenched pilots already with the companies whom they were trying to sell." Taylor observed that jets and their increased cost made Executive Jet more attractive than Pan American's original idea. Bevan sent Saunders a copy of a letter from Taylor supporting the soundness of Executive Jet. He also told Saunders that EJA "planned to start out with ten Lear Jets to be followed thereafter with additional jets of other makes as they become available." He noted that General Lassiter was an experienced test pilot, thoroughly familiar with the Lear Jet, completely sold on it, and in "a position to get a number of Lear Jets quickly in order to give his company a jump on any possible competitors."

Bevan gave Saunders a detailed outline of EJA's financial needs and the railroad's financial commitment. The new airline needed a total of $8.5 million to pay for a Lear demonstrator and ten air taxis, an operational Falcon, together with maintenance, equipment, and spare parts. "Up to this point," Bevan wrote, "we have either advanced, or committed to advance, $1.6 million. . . . We believe if we advance another $3.9 million, the additional $3 million can be raised without guarantee by us by giving banks a senior lien. The advances to date have been made by American Contract Company, and if further commitments are approved, they will also be handled through that company." Bevan stressed that American Contract was a fully owned subsidiary of the Pennsylvania and that its directors were all Pennsylvania Railroad officers. Finally, he stated that Executive Jet "is worth the risks involved, but in order to handle the matter in the most conservative manner, we suggest until such time as the company and the Lear Jets have proved themselves beyond any question, that we agree to advance an additional $3.9 million on a debt basis and agree then to raise $3 million from the banks for a total of $8.5 million required. It would be provided that any time within 36 months we shall have the right to receive upon request 60 percent of the stock of the company, this amount to be placed in escrow." Bevan explained that "if things do not work out, American Contract will only be a creditor of Executive Jet Airways. If the project is successful, we can, when that is determined, acquire a controlling interest in a company that may be outstandingly successful" [10].

From the first, Saunders was enthusiastic about Executive Jet and followed its progress carefully. On March 8, 1965, he wrote Bevan to inquire about the delivery of Lear Jets. "How many do they have in operation now? Are these planes being fully utilized? Also, I would like to know how many firm contracts they have signed up and something as to the terms of each one." He suggested "the Pennsy should start studying promptly the possibilities of Executive Jet going into the air cargo business."

Bevan urged caution. "To go into the cargo business in a real way involves a completely different concept and entirely different equipment. Also a different type of certification and varying legal problems, the latter being looked into at the present time." He wanted EJA to "get itself well started in its present concept," and concluded that "we should confine our thinking" to air taxis "until we see how things go, and this involves, then, Lear Jets, one Falcon and one Viscount" [11]. Earlier, at the February 19 Pennsylvania board meeting, Bevan explained to the directors that the treasurer's report included an item of $3.7 million advanced to American Contract Company to reimburse it for funds advanced to EJA [12].

The Pennsylvania's files show that the railroad made a thorough study of the legal aspects of Executive Jet and meticulously followed the best advice obtainable. Within days after Charles Hodge had proposed that the Pennsy should invest in an airline, William Gerstnecker, Bevan's chief assistant, referred the matter to David L. Wilson, the Pennsy's assistant general counsel. This was prior to any financial commitment. Wilson examined Executive Jet from the aspect of the federal antitrust legislation and the rules of the two federal bureaus regulating the aviation industry, the Federal Aviation Agency (FAA) and the Civil Aeronautics Board (CAB). He urged a lengthy study. Gerstnecker also referred the question of federal aviation regulation to Executive Jet's counsel, Bruce Sundlun, who found that current CAB rules exempted certain kinds of air-taxi services from regulation. He told Gerstnecker, "We have checked the question of whether any permission or authority must be made of the Civil Aeronautics Board in the event that Executive Jet Airways is owned 60 percent by the PRR [Pennsylvania Railroad]. We are advised by CAB counsel that no such permission or authority is required under any circumstances if we operate aircraft 12,000 lbs or less (the Lear Jet). The only thing that is required is a certificate from the Federal Aviation Agency evidencing safety, a routine matter" [13].

Bevan, wanting a second opinion, conveyed his concern to Stuart Saunders, who recommended the retention of the prestigious Washington firm of Covington & Burling, of which President Truman's former Secretary of State, Dean G. Acheson, was a partner. In March 1965, Hugh B. Cox, a Covington & Burling partner, began a thorough investigation of the federal law as it applied to a Pennsy investment in EJA. He advised Wilson that "the principal question that arises under the Federal Aviation Act is whether Part 298 of the Economic Regulations of the Civil Aeronautics

Board, which relieves air-taxi operators from a number of regulatory provisions of the Federal Aviation Act, would exempt an acquisition of control of EJA by the Pennsylvania from the Provisions of Section 408 of the statute." Cox concluded that the matter was a gray area, but warned that under certain interpretations it might be possible that Sundlun's opinion was incorrect [14].

Cox's finding brought on a thorough review. Bevan discussed the matter with Wilson, Gerstnecker, Lassiter, and Sundlun, and then suggested that Sundlun and Wilson confer with the Covington & Burling firm and see how the Pennsylvania's participation in EJA could be put on the strongest legal grounds [15]. The result was a new approach. Under the initial scheme put forward by Hodge, the railroad was to become an outright owner of as much as 60 percent of the airline. Executive Jet would have become a Pennsy subsidiary. Under the new arrangement, Executive Jet's charter was to be amended, creating two classes of stock, voting and nonvoting. The railroad was to take only the nonvoting shares, which would deny it the power to elect directors or to choose management. But, "with respect to dividends in any form and distributions upon dissolution or otherwise, the class B shares (nonvoting)" would have "absolute equality" with the class A shares. This provision allowed the railroad to invest in Executive Jet and share in its profits, but it prohibited the Pennsylvania's participation in the firm's management [16]. Hugh Cox reviewed the new proposal in a nine-page letter of June 1965 and concluded that if the railroad invested in EJA under the new terms, it did not need to seek prior CAB approval. He further said if the CAB did examine the issue, it would be "unlikely" that "the Pennsylvania would be found to violate Section 408 of the Federal Aviation Act [17]. Later, Cox suggested that the safest course "would be to provide that the class B stock should have no right to vote on any matter coming before the shareholders [18].

The restructuring of the Executive Jet charter followed Cox's advice, and the railroad, from that moment, effectively gave up any hope of real control of Executive Jet. No railroad official was ever elected to EJA's board of directors nor did any attend the directors' meetings [19]. In retrospect, the new terms of the Pennsylvania Railroad's participation in Executive Jet turned out to be a disaster for all concerned. David Bevan, conscious of the railroad's necessity to not control Executive Jet, was forced to allow the corporation's management to have a free hand. The railroad was also prevented from subjecting Executive Jet to the Pennsylvania's auditing and control procedures, which permitted the airline's management to make important decisions without the knowledge of the railroad.

After the railroad's collapse, Bevan recognized that the Pennsy should have ended its relationship with Executive Jet at this point. To be perfectly honest, [he later wrote to the author], the major mistake in connection with EJA made by top management of the railroad, and in this I must share responsibility, was in going ahead with the investment in EJA after various counsel had decided it could only be done on the basis of a nonparticipation in the management of the affairs of EJA. This placed the railroad in the position equivalent to that of a minority stockholder or worse. Company after company has found that to have a minority interest tends to place you at a distinct disadvantage. Such was the case in this instance, since we were unable to control management, when we saw occasion for changes, or different courses of action, should have been followed.

Along with Bevan, Stuart Saunders, the railroad's board chairman, knew about, and approved, every aspect of the new arrangement with Executive Jet, and the Pennsylvania's board of directors was also informed [20]. All continued to have enthusiasm for Executive Jet for a number of years.

The Pennsylvania Railroad's files do not support the Patman Committee's assertion that Bevan had deliberately gone ahead with an investment that violated the Federal Aviation Agency's regulations and used the American Contract Company to hide the Pennsy's involvement with the airline. The railroad's annual reports on American Contract, filed with the Securities and Exchange Commission, showed it as a wholly owned subsidiary and made no secret of the relationship between Executive Jet and American Contract. The Civil Aeronautics Board knew about the line almost from the beginning. In July 1965, Robert Burstein, director of the CAB's Bureau of Enforcement, wrote to the Pennsylvania's president, A. J. Greenough, and raised a question as to whether the railroad's financing of EJA's purchase of ten Lear Jets through American Contract had violated Section 408 of the Federal Aviation Act of 1958 by establishing an "unapproved control relationship" [21].

Bevan attended a conference in New York on July 21 to discuss the railroad's response to Burstein. There it was decided to arrange an informal meeting with the CAB to allow the Pennsylvania's Washington law firm of Covington & Burling to acquaint the federal authorities with "the many complex background facts in connection with the PRR-EJA relationship" [22]. The results confirmed the wisdom of Covington & Burling's recommendations. On November 3, 1965, Burstein wrote the president of Executive Jet, "With regard to the matter of financing arrangements between Executive Jet Aviation and American Contract Company, this is to advise you that our file has been closed, and no enforcement action has been instituted." David Wilson commented that "this is about as near as we can get to a clean bill of health on the legal question of the relationships between PRR and EJA" [23].

A CHANGE IN DIRECTION: THE MOVE
TO PURCHASE THE JOHNSON FLYING
SERVICE

In July 1966, Executive Jet Aviation, with the full knowledge of the Pennsylvania Railroad, decided to alter its status by the purchase of a supplemental air carrier, the Johnson Flying Service. The purpose was to obtain the Johnson's supplemental air certificate allowing the operation of large aircraft in either freight or passenger service anywhere in the United States. This acquisition would convert EJA from a small private-contract taxi service to a potentially large airline flying nonscheduled freight and passenger runs. It would move a giant step forward toward fulfilling Saunders's dream of making Executive Jet a major freight carrier.

The decision to buy the Johnson Flying Service was neither hastily nor secretly conceived. Partly it stemmed from enthusiasm within the Pennsylvania Railroad for expanding Executive Jet. Henry Large, the Pennsy's vice-president in charge of traffic, noted that "air freight and express volume [was] exploding," and urged that the railroad "undertake a study . . . to see whether EJA might fit into a plan for PRR-NYC Transportation Company entry into this field" [24]. At the same time, General Curtis LeMay recommended that Executive Jet purchase large aircraft and enter the freight business [25].

Executive Jet spent much time determining exactly how it could enter the air freight market and finally concluded that the best way was to purchase a carrier with a supplemental air certificate. At one time the federal government had issued as many as 200 of these certificates, but they had dwindled to 13 in 1966. The rapid escalation of the Vietnam war quickly used up the military airlift capacity and the remaining supplemental air carriers chartered planes for trans-Pacific troop movements. Certificates that once sold for as little as $25,000 rose in price to between $500,000 and $750,000 [26].

Executive Jet officials quickly discovered that few supplemental air certificates were on the market. One exception was that of the Johnson Flying Service, an airline that owned only thirty-seven aircraft operating out of Missoula, Montana, largely under contract to the United States Forest Service and engaged principally in firefighting activities. It was for sale because its founder-owner, 72-year-old Robert R. Johnson, was nearing retirement [27].

Everyone recognized that Executive Jet needed the Civil Aeronautics Board's permission to purchase the Johnson Flying Service. David Wilson, the Pennsylvania's counsel, observed that the CAB would be likely to make "a much more formal and fuller investigation" than it had on the application for the air-taxi license and concluded that "there would be a distinct possibility that the question of PRR relationship would come up" [28]. Wilson foresaw the type of opposition likely to arise, warning Bevan that "any competitor of EJA, or any other firm having substantial interest in the matter," could appear before the CAB. But he felt optimistic that a "sound defense" of the PRR's role could be made [29].

On July 20, 1966, Executive Jet agreed to acquire Johnson Flying Service subject to CAB approval, and both the Pennsylvania's regular counsel, David Wilson, and its special counsel, Covington & Burling, prepared to defend the railroad's association with Executive Jet in the coming CAB hearings [30].

Stuart Saunders closely followed Executive Jet's progress. On Monday, July 24, he hosted a meeting in his office, attended by David Bevan, General Lassiter, R. E. Hage, a vice-president of McDonnell Aircraft, James Redway, chief representative of the Washington office of McDonnell Aircraft Corp., and E. R. Quesada, the former administrator of the Federal Aviation Agency, to discuss Executive Jet's future [31]. Later, Bevan explained to Saunders how EJA had attempted to pave the way for a positive CAB ruling through informal meetings between Bruce Sundlun and the federal agency. Sundlun sent back encouraging reports indicating that CAB officials would approve the Johnson purchase [32]. Bevan did not rely on Sundlun, but told Saunders that he had "talked the matter over carefully with the legal department" and Covington & Burling's Hugh Cox. Howard Westwood, one of Cox's partners and a "highly recommended authority on aviation matters," represented the railroad at the hearings.

THE FIRST CAB RULING ON THE JOHNSON FLYING SERVICE

The Civil Aeronautics Board assigned Examiner Milton H. Shapiro to the case. The hearings continued for several months, and it was not until April 11, 1967, that Shapiro issued his initial decision. It was a curious document that, although it found against the railroad, did not call for the elimination of the Pennsylvania's investment in Executive Jet. Examiner Shapiro's decision is worth quoting in part because its complexity and ambiguity allowed the railroad to hope that if it took relatively minor steps, it could retain a great portion of its investment [33]. Even though Examiner Shapiro found Executive Jet had at times violated Civil Aeronautics Board regulations, his tone was conciliatory. He said [34]:

> EJA has tried to avoid becoming a common carrier but that the growth of its business conferred such status. According to BOR [CAB's Bureau of Enforcement], EJA's application for and receipt from FAA of a Part 121 operator's

certificate, together with FAA's opinion that the contract service did not require board approval, evidence EJA's good faith and tend to refute any suggestion that EJA intentionally and willfully set out to violate the law. It finds further
evidence of good faith in the fact that EJA has operated a great majority of its
services with aircraft covered by the Part 298 exemption. BOR urges, therefore, that the violation [using Falcon aircraft not covered by the Part 298
exemption] should not disqualify EJA as an applicant herein.

Later, the examiner stated that "to the extent that EJA has conducted
common carriage with Falcon aircraft, it has been in violation of the Act
[Federal Aviation Act of 1958]. On the other hand, the evidence does not
warrant a further finding that this violation was willful and flagrant, and
therefore of a character to require withholding the relief EJA requests in its
application" [35].

Throughout the report Shapiro encouraged Executive Jet to continue its
efforts to acquire the Johnson Flying Service [JFS], saying that" [36]

> If EJA can rejuvenate the JFS charter service and convert it into an energetic
> and aggressive competitor for civil charter traffic, while at the same time enlarg-
> ing the total capacity of both the supplemental air carrier industry and the
> military airlift, acquisition of control by EJA would be in the public interest.
> Basically, EJA's ability to improve the fortune of JFS depends on the caliber
> of management which EJA will provide for JFS and its capacity to pump new
> funds into JFS and enlarge its fleet with the latest model passenger aircraft. The
> competence of the EJA management has not been questioned. The directors
> and officers have substantial backgrounds in aviation, business or both and the
> company's personnel are rich in jet flying experience.

The examiner further stated, "On the basis of all the foregoing and all the
evidence of record, it is found that if there is a satisfactory refinancing of EJA,
it will be able to carry out its plans to put JFS to work as a robust participant
in both civil and military air charter services and, therefore, that EJA's
acquisition of control of JFS will be in the public interest" [37].

Shapiro discussed the meaning of control. The CAB's concept of control
was not easy to understand or clear-cut. Shapiro argued [38]:

> It is a long and well-established rule of the board that the existence of "control"
> within the meaning of Section 408 of the Act is a question of fact to be
> determined by weighing all the evidence in each case, and drawing reasonable
> inferences and conclusions therefrom in the light of the objective and the
> purposes of the Act. Moreover, the board has also long held that control does
> not necessarily depend on ownership of any specific minimum percentage of
> stock, or other ownership rights, but on whether there exists "as a matter of
> fact, a power to dominate, or an actual domination, of one legal personality by

another." And since control may be exercised through means other than voting stock, it is clear that it is not necessarily tied to the incidence of legal title or the power to vote stock. A debtor-creditor relationship may be enough in itself to establish the existence of control.

Later, Shapiro outlined his lenient position:

But BOR . . . goes on to urge that since EJA's acquisition of control of JFS would be in the public interest, the board should defer decision on the applications herein in order to afford EJA a reasonable opportunity to extricate itself from PRR's control.

Specifically, BOR suggests that the board defer the decision for a period of 6 months so that EJA may arrange the new financing and submit the actual terms thereof to the board for approval. It also would have the board inform possible investors that it would approve the acquisition if it received and approved a firm refinancing plan which negatives PRR's control. BOR states that it would not take such a position if EJA were not already on the threshold of arranging new financing which would nullify PRR's control of EJA. Under this proposal once the board concludes at the end of the period of deferral that PRR's control has been effectually eliminated, it would issue an order approving EJA's acquisition of control of JFS and the resulting interlocking relationships, and granting EJA the requested exemption.

Since it has been found [Shapiro continued] that it would be in the public interest to activate and expand the almost dormant supplemental air carrier part of JFS's operations, the objective of the Bureau's recommendations are considered sound and desirable.

The examiner then commented,

Despite the loopholes in the case for deferral of this decision, short of approval of the applications, deferral appears to be the quickest and least troublesome route open to the ultimate fulfillment of the EJA and JFS plans and to the benefits the plans are expected to bring to the travelling public. Perhaps the most important argument for deferral of the decision is the fact that the interim agreement and refinancing plan evidences PRR's readiness to divest itself of control. The thought and planning already devoted to these matters should shorten the time otherwise needed to complete a decontrol program. Therefore, the stage is already set for nullifying PRR's control.

Later, the examiner pointed out that the Pennsylvania did not have to eliminate its entire connection with Executive Jet. He said:

Divestment of PRR's control of EJA will satisfy the requirement of Section 408 in this case. No particular benefit can be discerned in requiring complete divestment of PRR's interest. Though the probable effect of total divestment on EJA's refinancing plan is necessarily a matter of speculation, it is fair to say that it would impair the chances of success; indeed, it might even sound the knell for EJA's hopes of refinancing. Therefore, all that should be required as a condition of approval of EJA's applications is divestment of PRR's power to control.

This was an open invitation for the Pennsylvania to present a new, but continuing, relationship with Executive Jet that would allow the airline to move forward in its acquisition of the Johnson Flying Service. Examiner Shapiro recognized that Pennsylvania's continued support of Executive Jet was probably essential, and he seemed almost to invite it. Finally, Shapiro approved of EJA's concept, writing that

the EJA concept is still an experiment, but one which the record indicates has promise. It seems to have a reasonable chance of succeeding by satisfying a special need of the business community. Therefore, the public interest would be well served by allowing the concept to take root and thrive, particularly because, in the context of the application, it does not threaten the certificated route or supplemental air carriers.

The railroad saw Examiner Shapiro's ruling as confusing and unclear. David Wilson told Bevan that "from the standpoint of EJA alone [it was] a generally favorable decision which finds that EJA is qualified to take over Johnson," and that the action was "consistent with the public interest." Wilson was not so clear about the railroad's position. Here the major thrust seemed to be that EJA should not be allowed to control Johnson until the railroad took "more effective measures to remove the ties between EJA and PRR" [39]. Wilson singled out four evidences of "control relationships" which had to be terminated. First, the debtor-creditor position that enabled the Pennsylvania Railroad to be involved in EJA's financial affairs had to be altered. Second, the railroad must reduce its equity position in EJA. Third, Shapiro objected to the presence on Executive Jet's board of two Glore Forgan partners, Charles Hodge and Samuel Hartwell, Jr. The CAB examiner made much of the long and close relationship between Glore Forgan and the Pennsylvania and asserted that even though the railroad had no directors on Executive Jet's board, it was effectively represented by Hodge and Hartwell. Finally, the CAB saw potential railroad control through EJA's treasurer, A. B. Estes, who had formerly been in the Pennsylvania's accounting department. But Shapiro's criticisms were gentle. He observed, "The record does not show that Mr. Estes considers himself responsible to PRR since his employment at EJA. Nor is there any evidence that PRR has tried to exercise its influence on him as an EJA employee. But he has apparently participated in the informal day-to-day relationship with PRR which have characterized the interchanges on most matters relating to the financial side of EJA" [40]. Wilson advised Bevan that the CAB's ruling was "vague and imprecise" and suggested that this "may be favorable in the sense that some flexibility is allowed us, but it is unfavorable in the sense that we cannot now say precisely what we must do to terminate the control relationship" [41]. Wilson complained that he was not even certain whether Examiner Shapiro demanded that every element of the Pennsylvania Railroad's alleged control had to be ended.

In the following weeks, lawyers worked out a program that had two main features. First, it tried to eliminate the Pennsylvania Railroad's areas of control specified by Examiner Shapiro. The plan's second, equally important, aspect was designed to facilitate an orderly restructuring of EJA's finances so that the airline could attract the fresh money needed to purchase the Johnson Flying Service and the new aircraft essential to its operation. All recognized the Pennsy's hasty withdrawal might jeopardize Executive Jet. This was one of the reasons why Examiner Shapiro did not require the railroad to sever all its relationships. It was not until August that the lawyers worked out a plan that Bevan explained to Stuart Saunders thus:

> In summary, General Hodge and Sam Hartwell [one of Glore Forgan's partners] will resign from the Executive Jet board and Glore Forgan's class A stock, which is now voting stock, will be exchanged for class B nonvoting stock. Both of these moves will meet objections raised by the CAB examiner and eliminate any possible claim that Hodge and Hartwell are "tools" of ours and eliminate their stock from any vote in the affairs of Executive Jet.

Bevan then enumerated the financial problems and plans of Executive Jet [42]:

> The total cash requirement is approximately $45 million. Under the plan, $23 million will be raised through senior financing in the form of lease arrangements for the two 727s and the two 707s [aircraft that Executive Jet needed to purchase in order to operate Johnson Flying Service]. Leasing of one of the 707s has been consummated and we have attractive leases available for the other three. The balance of $22 million will be required primarily for working capital, down payments on the four airplanes, spare parts, and repayment of loans made by us to Executive Jet since the first of this year. This $22 million would be raised through the sale of $11 million of debentures and $11 million of common stock.
>
> Under the plan, we will receive approximately $8.5 million of debentures similar to those which are to be sold to the public, and approximately $4.5 million of additional nonvoting stock at a value of $10 per share in exchange for the debt Executive Jet owed us at the end of last year, amounting to approximately $13 million. About $2.5 million will come back to us in cash.
>
> As a result . . . we would own initially about 39 percent of the company after the financing and Glore Forgan would own 4 percent, or a total of 43 percent. It is believed by Howard Westwood of Covington & Burling and by Bruce

Sundlun that such total percentage holding by us and Glore Forgan of nonvoting stock would meet the requirements of the CAB primarily because it would mean that our total ownership would be equivalent to the amount of stock being sold to new investors.

Bevan asked Saunders to let him "know as soon as possible if you are satisfied to proceed along these lines." Saunders responded immediately with a handwritten note across the top of Bevan's memorandum, saying, "This arrangement has my approval" [43].

Bevan also briefed the railroad's directors on EJA's progress. On April 28, 1967, soon after Examiner Shapiro's initial decision, Bevan explained the issues to the board, stating that although the Civil Aeronautics Board would "approve the application by Executive Jet Aviation to acquire stock control of Johnson Flying Service, Inc.," this was "on condition that there be filed in not less than 6 months with the CAB a satisfactory plan for the divestiture of control of EJA" [44]. Bevan reported the views of the railroad's various lawyers in much the same way he had in his correspondence with Saunders.

At this point, it is important to summarize the position of the Pennsylvania Railroad and Executive Jet in the summer of 1967. The record documents that the investment in Executive Jet stemmed, not from the clandestine activities of Bevan or Gerstnecker, but from the enthusiastic support of the railroad's Board Chairman Stuart Saunders and other top railroad officials. Moreover, through Bevan's advice, the Pennsy retained highly competent independent legal counsel who at every point monitored the railroad's relationship with the government. At no time did the railroad attempt to cover its activity or hide it from the Civil Aeronautics Board. Quite the contrary; the CAB was aware of the Pennsy's relationship with Executive Jet Aviation almost from the first. In the summer of 1967, the railroad's investment in EJA amounted to approximately $15,649,000 [45]. Stuart Saunders continually supervised this growing investment, and the minutes of the railroad's board of directors indicate that they were also informed. After the Penn Central's bankruptcy, Joseph R. Daughen and Peter Binzen, in their *The Wreck of the Penn Central,* quoted a former company director, E. Clayton Gengras, as saying that, in "this Executive Jet Aircraft deal, they sucked $25 million out of Penn Central before anybody knew what was happening" [46]. The statement was inaccurate in almost every respect. The total railroad loss was $21 million, not $25 million. The railroad directors knew of $15.6 million invested in EJA by the summer of 1967. Gengras had never been a Pennsylvania Railroad director, nor had he been a Penn Central director until the fall of 1969 when Charles Hodge maneuvered him onto the board. Gengras could not speak with authority on meetings he did not attend, nor did he bother to examine the Pennsylvania Railroad directors' minutes, which would have detailed for him the step-by-step PRR involvement in EJA. As a first-hand observer of that involvement, Gengras's testimony is worthless, but unfortunately it was given wide circulation and has become part of the mythology of Executive Jet. Finally, it should be evident that the bulk of the railroad's investment in EJA occurred prior to Ricciardi's employment with the airline and before Bevan and Ricciardi had met. It is difficult to argue that the Pennsylvania's investment in Executive Jet was for any other purpose than business reasons.

REFERENCES

1. *The New York Times,* August 7, 1970.

2. Wayne W. Parrish, "IAB: Aviation's Big Whodunit," *American Aviation,* December 23, 1968, p. 11.

3. *The Penn Central Failure and the Role of Financial Institutions,* Staff Report of the Committee on Banking and Currency, 92d Congress, First Session, House of Representatives, January 3, 1972, p. 137. Hereinafter, called the Patman Report.

4. Joseph R. Daughen and Peter Binzen, *The Wreck of the Penn Central,* Little, Brown & Co., Boston, 1971, p. 176.

5. Patman Report, p. 115.

6. Philadelphia *Bulletin,* December 21, 1970.

7. See complete transcript of testimony in Judge Doty's Court. A copy is in the Bevan Papers.

8. Patman Report, pp. 55–57.

9. EJA's board consisted of Lassiter; Curtis LeMay; Charles Hodge; Samuel Hartwell, a Glore Forgan partner; F. H. Billups, president of Tropical Gas; M. J. Rathbone, former board chairman of Standard Oil of New Jersey; former Assistant Secretary of the Navy, James Hopkins Smith; Arthur Godfrey; James Stewart; Air Force Major General (Ret.) Perry M. Hoisington; and Bruce Sundlun.

10. Bevan to Saunders, February 2, 1965; also James B. Taylor (of Pan American) to Bevan, January 7, 1965.

11. Bevan to Saunders, March 18, 1965.

12. This item noted on the Docket to the Pennsylvania Railroad board of directors' meeting, February 19, 1965.

13. Bevan Papers, notes of a telephone conversation between Sundlun and Gerstnecker's office, November 3, 1964.

14. Cox to Wilson, March 31, 1965.

15. Wilson, Memorandum for File, May 5, 1965.

16. Wilson to Gerstnecker, June 2, 1965.

17. Cox to Wilson, June 5, 1965.

18. Cox to Wilson, June 8, 1965.

19.   At this point Executive Jet also changed the firm's name from Executive Jet Airways to Executive Jet Aviation to emphasize that it was not an airline and to reinforce its case that it was a taxi service not subject to CAB regulation.

20.   Minutes of Pennsylvania Railroad Company, July 23, 1965.

21.   Burstein letter to Greenough, July 13, 1965.

22.   Wilson, Memorandum for File, July 23, 1965.

23.   Wilson to Gerstnecker, November 10, 1965.

24.   Large to Bevan, June 24, 1966, also Large to Bevan July 1, 1966.

25.   Wilson, Memorandum for File, July 19, 1966.

26.   Ibid.

27.   Sundlun to Wilson, August 3, 1966.

28.   Wilson to Gerstnecker, July 19, 1966.

29.   Wilson to Bevan, July 27, 1966.

30.   Cox to Wilson, August 4, 1966.

31.   Memorandum, signed "Jane," reminding Saunders of meeting on July 19, 1966 (included in Gorman report).

32.   Bevan to Saunders, August 9, 1966.

33.   U.S. Civil Aeronautics Board, Washington, D.C., Executive Jet Aviation, Inc. Docket 17657, et al. Initial Decision of Examiner Milton H. Shapiro, Served April 11, 1967.

34.   Ibid., pp. 12–13. Note Falcon Jets exceeded 12,500 lb, the CAB's maximum weight for air-taxi service.

35.   Ibid., p. 21.

36.   Ibid., pp. 23–24.

37.   Ibid., pp. 26–27.

38.   Ibid., pp. 28–29. The ensuing quotes are from pp. 46–50, 62–63, passim.

39.   Wilson to Bevan, April 12, 1967.

40.   Examiner Shapiro's Initial Decision, Served April 11, 1967, p. 39.

41.   Wilson to Bevan, April 12, 1967.

42.   Bevan to Saunders, August 9, 1967.

43.   Note by Saunders dated August 10, 1967, on Bevan letter to Saunders, August 9, 1967.

44.   Pennsylvania Railroad Company, board of directors' minutes, April 28, 1967.

45.   As of April 30, 1967, the Pennsylvania Railroad had loaned Executive Jet Aviation $15,320,000. (Source: Executive Jet Aviation, Inc., Financing Plan, produced by Glore Forgan, William R. Staats, Inc., June 12, 1967. These figures were checked for accuracy by the railroad's Accounting Department and the law firm of Covington & Burling before being submitted to the Civil Aeronautics Board.) The August 9, 1967, letter from Bevan to Saunders, who wrote across the top in his own

hand, "Advised DCB by telephone thru Harry Yohn that this arrangement has my approval 8/10," indicated that the PRR had an investment of $15.5 million in EJA. Under the new plan of financing that was to be presented to the CAB to meet the divestiture requirements, the PRR's interest was to be reduced to $13 million ($8.5 million in debentures and $4.5 million in nonvoting stock). Had the plan gone through, which it did not, the railroad would have received back $2.5 million in cash. Later, Saunders tried to maintain, even in the face of overwhelming documentary evidence to the contrary, that he was aware only of an EJA investment of around $13 million. See Civil Action No. 71–358, John Basil Thomas Bird, et al., *Plaintiffs, vs. Penn Central et al.,* defendants Civil Action in the U.S. District Court for the Eastern District of Pennsylvania, Testimony of S. Saunders, January 23, 1973, pp. 168 ff.

46.   Joeseph R. Daughen and Peter Binzen, *The Wreck of the Penn Central,* Mentor Executive Library Edition, New York, 1973, p. 152.

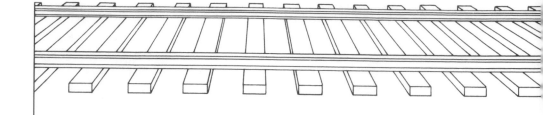

Chapter 17
THE FAILURE OF EXECUTIVE JET

A FATAL ERROR

In September 1966, the management of Executive Jet Aviation (EJA) made a serious error, that more than anything else, led to its downfall. In anticipation that the Civil Aeronautics Board (CAB) would allow the purchase of the Johnson Flying Service, EJA's directors took action leading to the acquisition of four new large jet aircraft from the Boeing Company, two 707s and two 727s. These planes, with the necessary spare parts, cost approximately $30 million, almost all of which had to be borrowed. The risk occurred because Executive Jet had no use for the aircraft should the CAB block the takeover of the Johnson Flying Service. Moreover, annual interest of almost $1.8 million on the borrowed capital necessitated either using them in the Johnson Flying Service or finding other employment for them, since EJA's air-taxi service did not produce enough revenue to carry the interest payments on the large jets.

Executive Jet's management thought that the CAB would act quickly on the Johnson Flying Service, and it wanted to be able to seize this opportunity immediately thereafter. The executives' optimism stemmed from the private conferences that Executive Jet's counsel, Bruce Sundlun, had had with the CAB's Bureau of Enforcement. Examiner Shapiro's decision in April reinforced this optimism because it appeared to clear the way, after some minor adjustments in the Pennsylvania's relationship with the airline, for the control of the supplementary carrier.

Despite EJA's enthusiasm, the CAB moved extremely slowly and the hearings extended over almost 2 years. This forced Executive Jet to find other uses for its aircraft, and the solutions that it worked out proved unsatisfactory. In retrospect, had EJA waited to purchase the Boeings until after the CAB approved the Johnson takeover, the airline might never have had a financial crisis and the Penn Central might not have lost its investment.

From the vantage point of 1978, David Bevan recognized that buying the Boeing aircraft was a serious error. He pointed out that the decision was not the Pennsylvania's but was made solely by Executive Jet's independent board, particularly Generals Lassiter and LeMay and Bruce Sundlun. The railroad, Bevan said, had no way to overrule the airline's board on this question, especially since it was asserting before the Civil Aeronautics Board that it did not control the air-taxi service. The record is clear that the decision to purchase the Boeing aircraft was made independently by EJA's board of directors [1]. The Pennsylvania's management was on the horns of a dilemma. If it had attempted to reverse the action, it would have been guilty of interfering in the airline's management, which it was not allowed to do. It is uncertain what the railroad's position would have been had it been a free agent. But David Bevan observed that Bruce Sundlun, EJA's counsel, made a convincing argument for the Boeing airplanes. Sundlun told EJA's directors in January, 1967, that the airline's application before the CAB to purchase the Johnson Flying Service was predicated on its ability to operate a supplemental air-charter line, and the contract to buy the Boeings was solid evidence of its capability to do so. "To cancel the Boeing contracts will pull out one of the major planks of EJA's case," said Sundlun [2].

Starting in 1969, everything about EJA started to go sour. Executive Jet had seriously concerned the railroad officials since the end of 1967 when the Civil Aeronautics Board had indicated that the Pennsylvania Railroad probably should divest itself of the airline. The railroad's response to the CAB's ruling was a decision to sell its interest in EJA. During the next 2 years, Bevan and other railroad officials worked hard to accomplish this but were unsuccessful. In August 1969 the matter reached a crisis. Penn Central had been unable to sell Executive Jet, and that month a minority shareholder and discharged officer of the airline, John Kunkel, brought suit against the railroad, American Contract Company (one of its subsidiaries), Glore Forgan, Brigadier General Lassiter, Charles Hodge, and David Bevan. Kunkel charged that the defendants were violating a Civil Aeronautics Board ruling by still actively attempting to control the airline [3]. It will be recalled that details of Kunkel's action emerged at the Penn Central directors' meeting of August 1969 and precipitated a move to investigate Bevan. After this step, the situation deteriorated still further, and EJA teetered on the edge of bankruptcy. By March 1970 it appeared that the Penn Central might lose its entire $21-million investment.

Stuart Saunders observed Executive Jet's rapid fall and had his assistant, Basil Cole, a lawyer, look into the matter and advise him. On March 8, Cole summarized his view of Saunders's position in a memorandum marked "Confidential." Cole told his boss [4]:

Based on a quick and incomplete review of board minutes and the files readily available in our office, I am convinced that it will be necessary to act promptly and decisively in the Executive Jet matter if you and the other directors wish to avoid personal liability in the event of a stockholder action to recover any loss which may occur.

The central issue, as I see it, is whether the board exercised due diligence in protecting the interests and assets of the stockholders *after mid-1967,* when PRR was ordered to cease economic domination of EJA, by permitting Bevan et al. to use $5 million to $7 million of company funds to finance the illegal "world operating rights" and other questionable activities of EJA. It seems quite clear that neither you nor the other directors had a clear knowledge of any of this until it was disclosed by the CAB consent order last summer, and this probably would have provided an adequate defense. But what can be said to justify nonaction during the last 6 to 8 months?

The only thing that occurs to me is that the board believed that Bevan and the others had been acting in good faith (albeit without authorization and secretly), and failed to act at that time because they further believed Bevan's representations that EJA was well worth our investment; that he had any number of anxious buyers and that we might turn in a profit. If that could be established (and I recall something along that line having been said but find no written evidence of it), it might be argued that it would have jeopardized the investment to move against him, or against EJA at that time.

But what about now? It should be clear by now that no one is willing to take over our position and Mr. Bevan apparently admitted last week the probability of a loss in EJA sometime this year, suggesting Wabash gains be used as an offset. Indeed, if rumors are true, EJA is not meeting its current fuel bills, one of the big New York banks is calling a $2-million loan within the next 10 days, and Lassiter has been diverting funds for some enterprise of his own.

Cole said that he was not certain just what could be done but suggested the following steps. First, Saunders should "ascertain the facts about current status of EJA." Second, Saunders should request that Bevan give him a a memorandum "tomorrow" covering "everything he knows."

Saunders, taking the advice, wrote a memorandum apparently designed to protect himself from any forthcoming investigation. The day after he received Cole's summary, he addressed a personal memorandum to Bevan. It said [5]:

Several days ago you spoke to me about a possible loss in connection with the disposition of our interests in Executive Jet. Within the last day or so, Jonathan

O'Herron [Penn Central's financial vice-president] mentioned something about Executive Jet securing a 30-day loan extension from the First City National Bank [sic]. These were the first indications that I have had that Executive Jet is faced with such financial difficulties.

Won't you please let me have a memorandum as soon as you can conveniently do so setting forth the current financial situation of Executive Jet. I also would like to know the status of negotiations for disposing of our interests.

Executive Jet had been losing money steadily for 3 years; it had been discussed by the Penn Central's board of directors; and it had been the subject of a number of newspaper and periodical stories. Bevan thought it strange for Saunders to write, "These were the first indications I had that Executive Jet is faced with such financial difficulties." Other Penn Central directors seemed to have been very much aware of Executive Jet's trouble. On March 8, R. Walter Graham wrote Bevan about the airline, saying, "One does not hit a home run every time he comes to bat, but by and large, your record has been most creditable. I wait with interest to learn how you will bail us out of Executive Jet; I feel confident that you will" [6].

Bevan knew nothing of Basil Coles's maneuverings nor of his recommendation of March 8. When Bevan received Saunders's March 9 memorandum, he did not understand its implications but was suspicious of Saunders's motives. In any case, the chief financial officer did not have much time to think about them because he was almost totally occupied with the difficulties that had beset the parent Penn Central. His main concern in March 1970 was not the fate of a small affiliated enterprise, but the solvency of the entire Penn Central organization. He responded to Saunders by saying that the legal department, in view of the Kunkel suit, had advised that Penn Central executives should put as little in writing as possible. Bevan told Saunders that almost all the relevant facts had been passed along to him, but added that if there were any questions, he would be glad to answer them. Later, Bevan remembered the incident well because Saunders insisted for about a quarter of an hour that his chief financial officer should make a written statement, claiming he needed it for the railroad's board of directors. Bevan replied that he would be happy to make an oral report to the directors, and he did so at their April meeting.

Saunders was unhappy; as a safeguard, the Penn Central's board chairman apparently ordered Cole to prepare a defense. The result was a nineteen-page confidential document dated March 20, 1970, entitled "Executive Jet Aviation," which became known as the Cole Report. Cole's conclusions must have pleased Saunders; they were highly complimentary to the Penn Central's chief executive and held Bevan responsible for most of the trouble. Cole stated. [7]:

There is nothing to indicate that Mr. Saunders or any other directors had actual knowledge of anything that happened between August 1967 and August 1969 which deviated from the divestiture plan which Mr. Bevan reported to the board from time to time—including the "world operating rights program," Penphil, the $5 to $8 million additional investment in EJA, and similar activities. Of course, the ought-to-have-known argument can always be made but, all things considered, it would find very little factual support until these matters were disclosed by the CAB Consent Order and the Kunkel suit.

By contrast, Cole found that Bevan's activities were open to serious question. In the same document he asserted that

[The] procedures by which funds were authorized and channeled for investment in EJA seem highly unusual, to say the least, and, while probably not actionable, they would certainly be criticized if brought to light. Rules governing the purchase of one $21,000 freight car can require a dozen interdepartmental approvals, as well as formal board authority, but a couple of minor supervisory employees in the financial department can pump $21 million of company funds into an unaffiliated and highly speculative business venture without so much as a by-your-leave.

Neither Saunders nor Cole released the report but put it in the files to use at the proper time. The Penn Central's failure momentarily eclipsed Executive Jet's troubles. By the time the airline was sold at a nominal price, neither Saunders nor Bevan was a Penn Central employee.

Cole's memorandum was eventually placed in the hands of Patman's investigators, who used it extensively. In fact, it was Patman's staff that christened the document the "Cole Report" [8].

The first time that either Bevan or his counsel, Edward German, heard of the Cole Report was when they read about it in the staff studies released by Patman's Banking and Currency Committee. German asked Saunders's lawyer if he could produce a copy of the report. Saunders's counsel said that he would have to talk to the former chief executive of the Penn Central. When he called back, he said that Saunders did not know of the report, had not seen it, and had not authorized it. Later, under oath, Cole said that Saunders had not only seen the report but had authorized it.

The so-called Cole Report was not the only document that was passed to Patman's investigators. Others included a Cole memorandum of February 6, covering Penphil and Executive Jet, Cole's memorandum to Saunders of March 8, Saunders's memorandum to Bevan of March 9, and another Cole communication to Saunders on March 13.

Cole's memoranda provided Patman with a ready-made villain—David Bevan. Patman's whole analysis of the Penn Central's problems with Executive Jet came almost unchanged out of the Cole Report. Because Bevan was, for Patman, such an attractive target, the congressman felt he had to look no further. Unfortunately, Cole's data obscured what really happened after EJA's fateful decision to change its business from an air-taxi service to a nonscheduled charter service. The evidence indicates that Saunders, Bevan, and even the railroad's lawyers never really understood the complex nature of the forces facing them in the EJA experiment.

EJA'S NEW OPPOSITION

Saunders, Bevan, and Hodge, even less than those expert in the field of aviation such as Bruce Sundlun, Howard Westwood, Lassiter, and LeMay, failed to understand the character of the opposition that Executive Jet had triggered. In 1966 several of the thirteen surviving supplemental air carriers, particularly World Airways, Capitol International Airways, and Saturn Airways, were deeply involved in moving military traffic to Vietnam. They had used government contracts, together with their supplemental certificates, as leverage for bank loans to buy or lease substantial fleets of large jet aircraft. Not only had the supplementals become significant military carriers, but they also offered low-cost charter services that competed directly with such scheduled airlines as United and TWA.

Pan American too benefited directly from the Vietnam War, since the line held the certificate for regular international flights between the Pacific Coast of the United States and Saigon. From 1964 onward, Pan American also built up a considerable business carrying troops and cargo on both its regular and charter flights.

Executive Jet's bid for a supplemental air certificate posed a direct threat to both the supplemental carriers and Pan American, especially since EJA, through its Air Force directors, had an unsurpassed entrée to the military officers who awarded trans-Pacific contracts. Lassiter boasted of this opportunity in a letter to Bevan: "In a Thursday, January 19, meeting with Gen. Bill Redell, Dir. of Material, Military Airlift Command, he assured our representative Mr. Thompson that as soon as we put our May aircraft in service, he will provide unlimited business at 12 hours/day utilization. We cannot," wrote Lassiter, "get a signed contract until we have become a qualified supplemental air carrier; however, Bill Redell is a close friend of mine for the last 20 years and I can depend on his word" [9]. The supplementals were small operators with slender financial resources. To them, Executive Jet appeared to combine the best possible entrée into the military with the financial backing and power of one of America's largest corporations. It is not surprising that these carriers treated Executive Jet's application as a matter of life and death [10].

Pan American's position was different. Ironically, it had encouraged the railroad to invest in Executive Jet when EJA was to be solely a taxi service. Pan American had decided not to establish its own taxi fleet; yet it held the franchise to sell the small Falcon aircraft and wanted EJA as a customer. But when the air taxi service tried to become a nonscheduled airline, Pan American opposed it and began to monitor all its activities. This was unfortunate because, as Patman's staff noted, "Pan Am has an intelligence system that makes the CIA look like a bunch of little boys reading graffiti on the bathroom wall" [11].

Examiner Shapiro's decision of April 11, 1967, did not please the supplemental airlines and they immediately appealed it [12], stressing the illegality of a railroad's controlling an airline. This was a straw issue, because the nonscheduled companies really feared a well-financed Executive Jet and opposed its backing by any large corporation whether or not it was in the transportation business. The opposition made it unlikely that the Pennsylvania could submit a plan that would win CAB approval, and the hearings dragged on. The railroad's first try, which had been prepared on the advice of Bruce Sundlun and Howard Westwood and had been approved by Stuart Saunders, was rejected. Sundlun told EJA's Executive Committee at its meeting on December 15, 1967, that the supplementals had bypassed Examiner Shapiro and had gone directly to the highest level in the Civil Aeronautics Board. As a result, the CAB general counsel took a strong position against Executive Jet's financial plan, insisting "it did not amount to divestment of PRR control." Sundlun said this was in direct contrast to what he had been told to expect by Examiner Shapiro and a Mr. Kenyon of the CAB's Bureau of Operating Rights [13].

The opposition made the acquisition of Johnson Flying Service, which had seemed certain at the beginning of 1967, an open question in December 1967. On January 24, 1968, all participants in the dispute met in the Civil Aeronautics Board's chambers before Examiner Shapiro, who said he would try and settle the issues through "informal" procedures [14]. In February, Bevan told Stuart Saunders that "the position taken by the examiner and the Bureau of Enforcement for the CAB was not favorable" [15]. Although Bevan and the railroad's lawyers felt that the Pennsylvania could apply for reargument, they agreed the better course was to sell. Consequently, in March the newly organized Penn Central began to work out a formula for the sale of its stock in Executive Jet and the transfer of the airline's indebtedness from American Contract Company to a third party [16].

THE PENN CENTRAL TRIES TO SELL

The railroad then began a systematic search for a buyer. Bevan was concerned that no legal technicality should prevent the railroad from making the best deal it could. By the end of 1967, Lassiter and EJA's counsel, Bruce

Sundlun, were at loggerheads, and it had also become evident that the airline needed more specialized advice on CAB matters. Bevan, after conferring with Howard Westwood of Covington & Burling, recommended to Lassiter the engagement of William C. Burt of the Washington law office of Koteen & Burt. As the latter firm was recognized as expert in the field of aviation law, Lassiter readily accepted Bevan's advice, and Burt entered the case in February 1968. Simultaneously, Bevan requested Hodge and Lassiter to review with Burt all past conversations with foreign aviation interests to make certain that no CAB violations had occurred. In the future, Bevan stressed, a representative of Koteen & Burt should be present at any meeting with foreign airline officials.

In April, after talking with several large corporations, the railroad came to a tentative agreement to sell its interest in EJA jointly to the United States Steel Corporation and Burlington Industries (a large textile firm). In June, a formal memorandum of understanding was executed, by the terms of which Penn Central would sell its interest in EJA to U.S. Steel and Burlington subject only to two conditions: the CAB's approval of Executive Jet's control of Johnson Flying Service, and the CAB's approval of the transfer of the Penn Central's interest in EJA to the two new corporations. Finding a buyer proved the easiest step. The hard problem was to get CAB approval for the deal.

Meanwhile, Executive Jet was still losing money and would continue to do so until it could obtain a supplemental air certificate and fly its four new Boeing aircraft. Therefore the railroad had to keep the airline alive financially until Burlington and U.S. Steel could take over. Much has been made of the continued flow of railroad money into Executive Jet after the CAB's unfavorable rulings of late 1967 and early 1968. The Patman Committee, relying principally upon accusations made in the Cole Report, asserted that this had been willfully and secretly done at Bevan's insistence. While it is true that the Penn Central's chief financial officer fully supported keeping Executive Jet alive, he did so with the full knowledge and enthusiastic backing of Board Chairman Stuart Saunders. Howard Westwood, the railroad's counsel, also reported to the CAB all railroad advances to EJA.

The evidence for this is overwhelming. On May 21, 1968, C. F. Myers of Burlington Industries interviewed Saunders about Executive Jet. Immediately afterward, Myers summarized the conversation for his fellow Burlington officers. Myers's memorandum indicated that Saunders knew much about EJA and approved of Bevan's actions. Reported Myers: "Saunders first said that they [the Penn Central] were distressed that the CAB made them divest as they felt strongly that this was an excellent growth investment." Myers then observed that Saunders considered "Lassiter and his operating team as being very top grade, very knowledgeable, and operators with the very highest standards. He thinks that both from a sales and operating standpoint this is a very strong team. In summary, he gave the very highest enthusiasm

[sic] to the management and to the company's potential and indicated that he sincerely hoped that they [the Penn Central] could come back in an equity participation at some future date." In the meantime, Saunders said, "the Penn Central will continue to give every support possible to expediting the growth and success of EJA" [17].

Saunders's statement of continuing support for Executive Jet was far stronger than any made by Bevan. In fact, it later embarrassed Saunders because, in the fall of 1968, Myers's memorandum came to the attention of the CAB. In October, Bevan's assistant, Gerstnecker, wrote Saunders that Covington & Burling "feel it is necessary to get any detail from you regarding writing this memo and your conversation, particularly with respect to the last sentence where it is alleged that you said we would continue to give every support possible to EJA." Gerstnecker tried to put the best possible face on the situation by suggesting to Saunders that "even if that was the language you used, that all you meant was we were still optimistic about the future of the company and that we intended to continue to use its services and do whatever we were permitted to do to continue its growth and development pending a decision in this case" [18]. Saunders replied, "Your letter of October 23 placed the correct interpretation upon the language attributed to me in the Burlington Industries memorandum" [19].

As 1968 wore on, the supplemental certificate holders, led particularly by Theodore I. Seamon, the attorney for Capitol International Airways, asserted that the Penn Central, U.S. Steel, and Burlington were linked together in a plan to achieve economic domination of the nonscheduled airline business. As 1968 drew to a close, Seamon and his fellow attorneys were able to capitalize on a series of blunders made by Executive Jet's management and destroy any chance of its control of Johnson Flying Service.

EJA'S EUROPEAN MISADVENTURES

April 1967 marked the start of what became in 1968 a series of disastrous decisions by Executive Jet's president, General O. F. Lassiter, who was encouraged at every step by Glore Forgan's Charles Hodge. David Bevan, in common with the rest of Pennsylvania's management and the railroad's lawyer, Howard Westwood, knew nothing of Hodge's and Lassiter's actions. Ironically, it was the prospect that the railroad would be forced to divest itself of the airline that emboldened Lassiter and Hodge. Many of the details were revealed by private memoranda in EJA's files, not available to anyone at the railroad until after the CAB had subpoenaed the files of all parties to the application to purchase the Johnson Flying Service in the fall of 1968. On February 22, 1968, Lassiter and Bevan discussed the railroad's future relationship with EJA. Bevan told EJA's president "that the Pennsylvania Railroad would accept a liquidation trust in the CAB case, if necessary." The next day, Sundlun noted that Hodge, in recognition that the railroad was terminating its interest in EJA, was actively planning to attract new money into the airline. Some would come from United States sources such as the Keystone Fund, but other potential money would be from foreign sources, including the Suez American Trust and the German industrialist from Ravensburg, Fidel Goetz [20]. Both Hodge and Lassiter had expectations that extended beyond any idea of Bevan's about Executive Jet. This was especially so since, after February 1968, Bevan's main concern was selling the Pennsylvania's interest in it to another party in order to satisfy the CAB. The Patman investigators assumed that the interests of Lassiter, Hodge, and Bevan ran together. Nothing could be further from the truth. Lassiter was primarily ambitious to become the chief operating officer of a worldwide airline. Hodge was primarily a stockbroker who specialized in finding investment capital for new corporations. His involvement in EJA seemed special. He apparently saw it as an opportunity to create a worldwide air empire which would bring him profit, power, and prestige. Bevan's main concern was the Penn Central.

At the beginning of 1968, Hodge accepted the fact that the railroad's influence in Executive Jet was waning. An additional factor also influenced him: At the end of 1967, Executive Jet still had four large Boeing jets that it could not fly. Hodge agreed with Lassiter that foreign airlines were a logical place to lease the surplus equipment.

Both Hodge and Lassiter underestimated the problems Executive Jet faced with the Civil Aeronautics Board. What they failed to understand was that Executive Jet's original concept, which had won CAB approval, had been new and did not compete with established airlines. EJA's taxi service proposed to replace aircraft owned and operated by individual corporations for the benefit of their personnel. Most airlines favored this concept since the companies subscribing to EJA's services would probably eliminate their private fleets. Thus, business could actually be put on the commercial carriers. Executive Jet's proposal to buy the Johnson Flying Service was different because it put the company directly into competition with the supplemental carriers and also some of the scheduled airlines. Expansion by purchasing foreign systems also would have intruded EJA into an existing business and would have guaranteed opposition. Like Executive Jet's attempt to purchase the Johnson Flying Service, any agreement to purchase an interest in a foreign airline would have to be approved in advance by the Civil Aeronautics Board. Both Lassiter and Hodge knew this, but they failed to take it seriously.

Aided by EJA's private files, it is now possible to trace much of what happened through Executive Jet Aviation's directors' minutes. At the time, Bevan was not privy even to this source of knowledge since he was not a member of the company's board of directors nor did he attend the directors' meetings. This was one of the penalties under the terms of the railroad's investment in the airline. Bevan never even saw the minutes until 1972 when he received the right to copy them in the preparation of his defense in the criminal action brought against him, Hodge, and Lassiter by Philadelphia's district attorney, Arlen Specter.

Lassiter's European adventures began innocently enough with the extension of the air-taxi service to Europe soon after the company became operational. This was perfectly legal, and to provide maintenance and staffing Lassiter created a European subsidiary, Executive Jet, S.A. It was eventually located in the Swiss city of Basel, using facilities leased from Carl Hirschmann, a wealthy Swiss banker and industrialist. After EJA decided to acquire the Johnson Flying Service, Lassiter thought of securing European landing rights through the purchase of foreign carriers. Early in 1967 Charles Hodge found that a German airline, Sudflug, was for sale. He suggested the purchase of Sudflug to EJA's board, but Bruce Sundlun, the airline's counsel, said no action should be taken until after the CAB ruled on the purchase of the Johnson Flying Service [21]. Sudflug was not acquired and Lufthansa later bought it.

Hodge and Lassiter then found another German airline for sale, Sudwestflug (which later became Germanair). The pair moved quickly and brought a purchase agreement to EJA's directors at their July 20, 1967, meeting, and they voted unanimously to buy Sudwestflug [22]. Very soon thereafter, EJA's board reversed its decision on the airline counsel's advice that no such agreement should be made while the Johnson Flying Service matter was pending before the CAB. But Hodge and Lassiter were determined not to let the Sudwestflug matter die. In all the European deals, they worked closely with two Washington attorneys, Joseph and Francis Rosenbaum, whose law firm also represented the German industrialist Fidel Goetz. In this case, the Rosenbaums arranged for Goetz to purchase and hold Sudwestflug until EJA could acquire it [23]. The deal was private and the Rosenbaum law firm and Glore Forgan entered into a guarantee that protected Goetz from any loss on the transaction. The Sudwestflug agreements were made without the knowledge of Executive Jet's board of directors, who were told on April 1, 1968, that no foreign agreements had been made, and that none would be presented to the board until the Johnson Flying Service case had been concluded by the CAB [24].

In February 1968, Hodge and Lassiter went to Europe, where they made still further deals. These were to purchase control of two airlines owned by Carl Hirschmann, Transavia, a Dutch carrier, and Hispanair, a Spanish corporation. These agreements, too, were kept from EJA's board although Lassiter reported them in detail to Bruce Sundlun at a February 23, 1968, meeting in Washington [25]. In addition, an open and legal arrangement was made to lease a surplus Boeing 707 to Transavia, starting in May 1968. This was approved by EJA's board and reported to the CAB [26].

Another of Lassiter's and Hodge's dreams was for Executive Jet to develop a cut-rate transatlantic air service via the so-called southern gateway from Florida. Lassiter apparently got this idea from a friend, Julian Lifsey, who, with Mrs. Irene Bowen, was part owner of a Tampa, Florida, travel agency. Lassiter unveiled his plans before an EJA directors' Executive Committee in December 1967. He had discovered that Major Norman Ricketts, a British subject, held a license to operate aircraft in regular service between the Bahamas and Luxembourg. Ricketts's certificate had a major advantage. Neither the Bahamas nor Luxembourg subscribed to the rules of the International Air Transport Association (IATA). This association is an international cartel that set uniform, noncompetitive international air fares. Most nations required their air services to abide by the IATA rules. An important exception was Iceland, and for years Icelandic Airlines has operated a cut-rate air service from the United States to Europe. It did so through a technicality. The United States, because of Iceland's strategic importance, is forced to give American landing rights to Icelandic Airlines. Tiny Luxembourg, with no airlines of its own, feels no allegiance to IATA and gives landing rights freely to all. The United States, a member of IATA, did not allow any cut-rate airline to fly directly from New York to Luxembourg. Icelandic evaded this regulation by going from New York to Reykjavik and then on to Luxembourg. General Lassiter saw an opportunity to create a similar operation in the south Atlantic by flying from the Bahamas direct to Luxembourg. It would be a simple and cheap matter for passengers to take local flights between Florida and the Bahamas to connect with Lassiter's line.

In 1967 Major Ricketts's airline, International Air Bahamas (IAB), had only a paper charter. Lassiter informed EJA's Executive Committee that the opportunity existed to purchase a controlling interest in IAB. He suggested that even if this were not done, it might be possible to lease one of Executive Jet's large aircraft to IAB. Lassiter arranged for Mrs. Bowen to attend the December 15 meeting to discuss traffic potential through the southern gateway [27].

At the airline's regular January 1968 board meeting, the directors recognized that the Pennsylvania relationship was ending. Charles Hodge, who, though no longer a director, attended meetings as the firm's investment banker, led a discussion about replacing the Pennsylvania's financial support by other investors [28]. Mrs. Bowen also came to this meeting and reported on the opportunities associated with International Air Bahamas and the southern gateway to Europe. This marked the beginning of a close association between Executive Jet and IAB. The record is confused, but it appears that Lassiter and Hodge were influential in activating the IAB's charter. Carl Hirshmann, the prominent Swiss industrialist who had been involved in other of Hodge's and Lassiter's overseas schemes, financed IAB, and in July, Executive Jet leased one of its Boeing 707s to the new venture. IAB promptly inaugurated service between Nassau and Luxembourg with the lowest trans-atlantic round-trip fare, undercutting even Icelandic. This fare earned maxi-mum visibility in the air world. *American Aviation* reported that in the sum-mer of 1968, "Icelandic noticed a drop in patronage and discovered that the substantial trade it was drawing from the southern part of the U.S. and Mexico and Central America was going to Nassau and taking IAB" [29]. This so upset Icelandic's president, the magazine said, that he immediately, in the company of a member of his government's diplomatic corps, appeared before the CAB and demanded all available information about the new competitor. In September 1968, Pan American, which was also losing business to IAB, complained to the Civil Aeronautics Board that Executive Jet controlled the Bahama airline and that it carried through traffic from the United States to Luxembourg via Nassau. Pan American insisted that the Civil Aeronau-tics Board review the leasing arrangement between Executive Jet and IAB [30].

Hodge and Lassiter succeeded temporarily in keeping their under-the-table European deals secret from EJA's board and the railroad's officials. They may have even thought their arrangements were entirely confidential. Unfortunately, the deals were reported in the European press and news of them filtered back to America. Later, Bevan remembered how he gradually learned of EJA's European entanglement. He knew that Hodge, LeMay, and Lassiter wanted to expand EJA's activities to Europe, but in view of the CAB's increasingly hard line toward the application to take over the Johnson Flying Service (JFS), the Penn Central's chief financial officer urged caution. He thought that any action ought to be carefully monitored by expert law-yers. That was why he insisted that William Burt be retained. Bevan expected that a representative of Koteen & Burt would be present at all meetings.

Koteen & Burt started working with EJA in early February 1968. Almost immediately thereafter, Lassiter and Hodge went to Europe where they worked out the preliminary agreements aimed toward control of Transavia and Hispanair. Neither Howard Westwood nor William Burt was aware of the purpose of the trip or of the secret agreements made. On April 1, after Lassiter and Hodge returned from Europe, Lassiter presided at Executive Jet's annual board of directors' meeting. Bruce Sundlun and Charles Hodge were also present. The minutes of the executive session record that Lassiter "outlined various proposals which had been advanced to the company for involvement with other air carriers, foreign and domestic, but emphasized that no agreement had been or could be made without CAB approval, and reiterated as a matter of policy that no such proposals would be submitted to the board for consideration until after the pending EJA/JFS case was concluded" [31]. Lassiter's statement was contrary to the facts, since he and

Hodge had made oral and written agreements for Executive Jet to take control of Transavia and Hispanair.

Actually, Hodge and Lassiter had left a broad trail. The Capitol Airways' attorney, Theodore Seamon, soon learned of it. Ironically, Howard Westwood found out more about EJA in Europe from Seamon than from his own clients. As early as March, he alerted David Wilson, the Penn Central's attorney, that Seamon knew "what we had assumed; i.e., obviously he has substantial information concerning what he believes to be various dickers between EJA representatives and various foreign aviation interests. Among other things, there has been considerable reporting thereof in the foreign press of which Seamon is aware. He probably has additional sources of information as well." Westwood warned that "sooner or later—we must assume—Seamon is likely to get some access to EJA's records, notably minutes of their board of directors' meetings. From various things he has said I have the impression that he at least thinks that some rather indiscreet things have been said at EJA directors' meetings. Whether, if this is so, they relate to the railroad I do not know" [32].

Lassiter and Hodge had indeed been indiscreet. At Burt's urging, on April 30, 1968, Bruce Sundlun summarized all of Executive Jet's relations with foreign airlines. As Bevan remembered, on May 8 a meeting in Washington was attended by himself, Howard Westwood and Brice Clagett of Covington & Burling, William Burt of Koteen & Burt, General Lassiter, Hodge, and William Gerstnecker. The topic was EJA's foreign involvements [33]. "Burt was furious that Hodge had not previously disclosed his and Lassiter's activities in Europe. He was particularly angered to find that some of the agreements had occurred immediately after he had been retained." To make matters worse, Hodge and Lassiter, in talks to representatives of United States Steel and Burlington, emphasized, not EJA's unique air-taxi service, but the profit potentialities of becoming a major international freight and passenger carrier. Here again, however, they reiterated to U.S. Steel's management that there were no oral or written commitments with foreign interests. The notes the Burlington and U.S. Steel executives made of Lassiter's and Hodge's ideas eventually came to the attention of the CAB.

HOLIDAY INTERNATIONAL TOURS

Before long, another embarrassing incident occurred. One day in August, Brice Clagett of Covington & Burling called Bevan and asked if he had ever heard of HIT. Facetiously, Bevan said, "No, what is it—a government agency?" Clagett answered, "No, it stands for Holiday International Tours." Bevan replied that he had never heard of it. Clagett responded that it was a small travel agency and then asked if Bevan knew about Penphil. The Penn

Central's chief financial officer said, "Yes, that is a small investment club to which I belong." The lawyer had heard a rumor that Penphil owned half of HIT. Bevan told Clagett that as far as he knew, "It is the Bowen Travel Agency, unless the name has been changed." He then asked why it mattered. In Clagett's opinion, it might be important in the coming CAB hearings examining the transfer of Penn Central's interest in Executive Jet to U.S. Steel and Burlington and the acquisition of the Johnson Flying Service. Clagett explained that he understood that some of Penphil's members worked for the Penn Central and that EJA was leasing a plane to International Air Bahamas. The involvement came because apparently HIT was to become the exclusive sales agent for IAB. Clagett feared that the Civil Aeronautics Board might assert that the railroad had used Penphil to found a travel agency for the express purpose of controlling International Air Bahamas. Bevan told him he would investigate and call back.

Bevan remembered the Bowen Travel Agency of Tampa, Florida, very clearly. In late 1967 the agency came to the attention of Penphil member Olbert Lassiter. An old friend of his, Julian Lifsey, a Tampa attorney, told Executive Jet's president about Irene Bowen's business. Lifsey explained that there seemed to be no future in the retail travel business and that Mrs. Bowen wanted to move from Tampa to Miami and convert her enterprise into a wholesale agency. Lifsey and Bowen were partners, but, he explained, the venture needed a substantial infusion of new capital. Lassiter took the idea to his friend Hodge, who arranged a meeting in Boca Raton attended by Bevan, Mrs. Bowen, Lassiter, Hodge, Gerstnecker, Sawin, and Lifsey. The group thought Mrs. Bowen was "quite articulate." She stated that she proposed to develop travel through the southern gateway between Florida and Europe and that her venture might require approximately $200,000. The Penphil members suggested that Mrs. Bowen draw up a set of cash-flow figures to support her estimates and give them to General Hodge. If Hodge were satisfied, Penphil would buy 50 percent of the stock in the new company for $25,000 and would lend up to $200,000 over a 2-year period. Mrs. Bowen would provide all of the management since none of the Penphil members had either the time or the necessary experience to do so.

As far as Bevan knew, Lassiter was the only one at the Boca Raton meeting who had met either Lifsey or Mrs. Bowen. Both were brought in and introduced to each one of the Penphil members in turn, including Charles Hodge. What Bevan did not know was that both Lifsey and Bowen had attended a December 15, 1967, meeting of EJA's Executive Committee. This was one of the meetings at which the possible EJA investment in the dormant International Air Bahamas charter held by Major Ricketts was discussed [34].

In January 1968, Julian Lifsey sent Hodge and other Penphil members copies of an analysis of the Bowen Travel Agency's potential [35]. This prospectus gave no indication that the Bowen Travel Agency would have any relationship to International Air Bahamas. After analyzing the data, Hodge approved, and for $25,000 Penphil bought 50 percent of the stock in the Bowen Travel Agency and shortly thereafter made a loan of $40,000 against the $200,000 credit line which Penphil pledged itself to extend.

Bevan first heard of International Air Bahamas (IAB) in the spring of 1968, when Lassiter told him that Executive Jet would lease a large Boeing aircraft to that airline, which was to begin a new service between Nassau and Luxembourg.

But Bevan never connected IAB with the Bowen Travel Service until he received Clagett's call. Then he telephoned Hodge and asked whether the Bowen Travel Agency and Holiday International Tours were the same. Hodge said yes, "that the name had been changed." Bevan asked whether or not it was true that HIT was to be the exclusive sales representative for IAB. Hodge replied "Yes," adding that he did not like the arrangement and had told Lassiter that he opposed it. When Bevan asked why he had not been informed, Hodge said that, whether Bevan realized it or not, his "preoccupation with the problems of the Penn Central" had made it virtually impossible for him to reach Bevan. Hodge also added that he did not think the matter was very important.

Bevan told Hodge about his conversation with Clagett and said that he did not want "the affairs of Penphil to become involved with those of the railroad." He stated that Penphil must immediately dispose of its interest in HIT, "if necessary, selling it back to Mrs. Bowen, and taking her IOU in return." Hodge agreed. After talking with several other Penphil members, Bevan called Lassiter and told him that Penphil would have to terminate its association with HIT. Lassiter agreed that, under the circumstances, this was the proper course. Bevan then asked him, since he knew her "better than anyone else, to advise Mrs. Bowen of the situation, and at the same time to explain that it was not a lack of confidence in her, but a situation which had arisen unfortunately which we could not have foreseen." Bevan then asked his brother, then Penphil's president, to arrange to sell Penphil's interest in the agency back to Mrs. Bowen. Bevan observed that within 48 hours from the time he learned of the involvement of HIT with IAB, Penphil's interest in the travel company had been sold. This was one of Penphil's bad investments. To get rid of the stock, the investment club took Mrs. Bowen's IOU for $25,000 and never received a cent of interest or principal on the $40,000 loan. In the end, Penphil wrote off the entire $65,000 as a loss.

This was not the last of HIT. In the hearings before the CAB in the fall of 1968, attorneys for the nonscheduled airlines brought out that Mrs. Bowen and Lifsey had attended EJA's Executive Committee meeting of December 15 and had discussed establishing an air service through the southern gateway to Europe. There was an ironic twist to these disclosures. The interveners before the CAB argued and the regulatory agency agreed that the railroad had used Penphil in order to establish a travel agency to control International Air Bahamas. But the Patman Committee maintained that Bevan planned to use Penphil and IAB to milk profits from Executive Jet and the railroad. In either case, the question was moot because HIT did not actually sign an exclusive contract with International Air Bahamas until the fall of 1968, and by that time Penphil had terminated its relationship with the travel agency.

When Howard Westwood and William Burt discovered the full impact of EJA's foreign involvement, they recommended that all the agreements made by Hodge and Lassiter be voided. Two figures dominated most of the arrangements: Carl Hirschmann and Fidel Goetz. The latter was the more important of the two. Bevan recalled that he discussed EJA with Joseph Rosenbaum, an attorney who represented Goetz's American interests. Rosenbaum felt he could have Goetz reverse the transactions involving Hispania and Transavia. Hirschmann also had become interested in IAB and it seemed possible that this involvement could be undone too. This would mean that all understandings between Executive Jet and the foreign interests would be eliminated, and if, after EJA had acquired the Johnson Flying Service, it still wanted to buy into foreign airlines, it would have to renegotiate. Bevan stressed to Rosenbaum, "There would have to be absolutely no understandings of any kind, or options outstanding."

THE COLLAPSE OF EJA'S CASE
BEFORE THE CAB

Nothing could be done to save the situation. Theodore Seamon, several other attorneys for the supplemental airlines, and Pan American representatives brought Lassiter's and Hodge's European deals to the attention of the CAB. This move resulted in a full-scale CAB investigation of the files of Executive Jet, Penn Central, United States Steel, and Burlington. One by one, embarrassing details emerged and were used with telling effect by EJA's opponents, who argued that Penn Central, U.S. Steel, and Burlington Industries wanted to dominate the supplemental air carrier business. Moreover, Seamon said, the foreign agreements were a flagrant violation of CAB rules. The airline made its plans, acted, and finally came to the CAB for approval. This, said the supplementals, was exactly the way Executive Jet had entered the air-taxi service business and was the pattern of the airline's behavior from the very first.

Howard Westwood summarized the problems caused by the CAB's investigations of the files of the petitioners. So "we have now substantial further information, but there is still a large amount of documents in hand that we have not finished examining." He found that the CAB believed "that the railroad knew of Lassiter's foreign involvements, that Steel knew of them, and that Steel entered into an understanding (despite being told of the decision of May 8 to undo what had been done) with the assurance that in some way . . . the foreign program would be adhered to." Westwood concluded [36]:

> The case, at this point, is lost. This is due to three things: (1) Lassiter and Hodge have no credibility and in some respects the mistakes in their testimony may not be explicable in terms of forgetfulness. (2) With Goetz still so prominently in the picture, the foreign entanglements have not been undone—and all signs point to him still being in the picture; there is not a syllable of legal proof that he is not; the so-called affidavits are not proof and, indeed, do not affirmatively deny that he is still in the picture. [Although Rosenbaum had told Bevan that the agreements would be undone, the evidence is confused and unconvincing.] (3) The fitness of EJA in terms of prudence of expenditures and in terms of responsible regard for legal requirements has been discredited.

In another letter, Westwood commented [37]:

> One of the more ironical aspects of the problem is that the charade of secrecy in which Lassiter and Hodge were indulging created secrecy only from the lawyers. It now turns out that European newspapers were carrying items telling virtually the complete story. If we and Burt had been told what was up, effective guidance could have been provided that would have prevented the present shambles and at the same time could have preserved the essence of Lassiter's dream. As it is, the whole picture is one of amateurish intrigue, vividly colored with the devious, that suggests a consciousness of guilt deeper even than is justified by the bare facts.

Westwood found some things "incomprehensible." For example:

> It looks as though, after the initial meeting in Philadelphia with Burt and Simpson, Lassiter and Hodge immediately went to Europe and produced the February "consortium." Unless I misunderstand, I can view this as nothing short of a double-cross of the railroad. And in my effort to understand the facts, I am constantly frustrated because I have lost confidence that anyone involved in EJA's foreign entanglements can tell the truth.

On January 3, 1969, Burlington Industries withdrew from its agreement with United States Steel to buy Penn Central's interest in Executive Jet. Ten days later, Westwood and Burt concluded that the CAB would not approve Executive Jet's acquisition of the Johnson Flying Service and EJA withdrew its application. U.S. Steel then terminated its agreement with the railroad. This left Penn Central with the problem of what to do. There was no simple answer. Although Executive Jet had withdrawn its request, the Civil

Aeronautics Board still planned to continue its investigation and would eventually rule upon the relationship between the air-taxi service and the railroad. No one could foretell what the CAB's ruling would be, but the railroad's lawyers believed that the chances for a favorable outcome were slight. It was equally evident that the nonscheduled airlines, together with Pan American and Icelandic, wanted to kill Executive Jet as a competitor once and for all. They continued their pressure on the CAB to rule against Penn Central.

Through 1969 the railroad's problem was how to liquidate its interests in Executive Jet and minimize its losses. By September of the previous year, Penn Central had invested approximately $18.5 million in the air-taxi service. In addition, EJA had borrowed from banks to finance the purchase of its large Boeing aircraft. For these the airline had no use, since it would never control the Johnson Flying Service. The railroad had two choices. It could immediately attempt to liquidate its entire interest in Executive Jet. This would mean a sale at panic prices and the sacrifice of the railroad's investment, an unacceptable solution. The other path was to try and put the airline's affairs in order to make it attractive to a new investor. The most important part of this strategy was the sale of Executive Jet's large aircraft. Unfortunately, there was little demand in 1969 for such planes and it was almost impossible to find a buyer who would pay a reasonable price. William Gerstnecker summarized the railroad's thinking in a note to Bevan, saying "that the withdrawal of our application does not remove the finding by the CAB that we are in economic control and the necessity for us to put our stock in a voting and liquidation trust." He emphasized that the Penn Central was currently "proceeding on the basis that under the present conditions we can bring about an orderly disposition of our so-called 'economic control' based upon continuing improvements in Executive Jet Aviation's business-jet operations which are being streamlined to fit that type of operation" [38]. There was a temporary short-term danger: the airline's taxi revenues could not sustain the interest charges on the large jets. These either had to be paid or the creditors, the most important of which was New York's First National City Bank, could force the company into bankruptcy and distress liquidation. The railroad would be the biggest loser. The only sensible course seemed to be to continue financial support of Executive Jet until the Boeings had been sold.

The railroad had a vehicle for handling the orderly disposal of its interests in Executive Jet. On August 28, 1968, Penn Central entered into an irrevocable voting and liquidating trust agreement with the Detroit Bank & Trust Company of Michigan. This agreement placed Penn Central's stock and notes in the hands of the trustee who was authorized to vote the stock independently of Penn Central's interests. On October 21, 1968, an amendment empowered the trustee to "make loans of money to EJA, up to the total of

$3 million in principal outstanding at any time, either secured or unsecured, upon such terms and conditions as the trustee may deem fair and reasonable, for the purpose of protecting the corpus of the voting and liquidating trust by sustaining EJA until the Civil Aeronautics Board issues its final decision in Docket No. 17657" [39]. Since the railroad had already invested $18.5 million, this amendment increased the maximum possible railroad commitment to approximately $21.5 million.

The 1968 voting trust and amendments were to endure for 5 years, since at that time the railroad was uncertain as to the outcome of Executive Jet's application to take over the Johnson Flying Service and as to whether the CAB would approve the transfer of the railroad's interest to Burlington and United States Steel. The trust's sole purpose was to keep Executive Jet alive until the outcome of the CAB hearings was known. After the January debacle, the railroad modified its agreement with the Detroit bank into a liquidating trust. Westwood and Burt worked to achieve the best possible settlement with the CAB. Finally, in October 1969 the railroad and Executive Jet entered into a "settlement agreement and consent to the issuance of an order to cease and desist." Penn Central signed this order, as did Executive Jet and General Lassiter. They did not make any admission with regard to any issue of fact or any conclusion of law. The CAB, however, found the railroad in violation of its regulations and agreed to accept Penn Central's offer of $65,000 in "compromise of civil penalties" and Executive Jet's offer of $5,000. Bevan felt that his critics did not put these penalties in proper perspective. He noted that in 1969, the U.S. Post Office fined the railroad over $100,000 in violation of its regulations, and in May 1970, the Interstate Commerce Commission claimed $471,500 as penalties against the Penn Central for violation of service regulations from May 1969 to February 1970. He found it ironic that the Patman Report, which blamed him for the Executive Jet penalties, said nothing about the railroad's operating penalties, which were Perlman's responsibility. Later, Bevan said he did not think that Perlman deserved criticism, but asserted that such penalties were an inherent part of doing business under government regulations.

The cease-and-desist order, signed by the railroad and accepted by the CAB, cleared the way for EJA's final act. Under the agreement, the railroad placed all its interests in EJA in an irrevocable liquidating trust similar to that already established, to be operated, as before, by the Detroit Bank & Trust Company. In this case, the trustees were directed to dispose of the interest by March 1, 1971, on terms determined by the trustees. Ironically, the railroad's own bankruptcy came before its interest in Executive Jet could be sold. The Penn Central's trustees took office with problems far more serious than Executive Jet. It is not surprising that they welcomed the first opportunity to dispose of their holdings in the airline even though it meant selling them at a total loss of the railroad's $21 million investment.

INVESTIGATIONS—AND PROSECUTIONS

Executive Jet Aviation turned sour not only for the railroad, which lost its money, but for its founder, General Lassiter, whom the bank trustee removed on July 1, 1970, in favor of Bruce Sundlun. Starting in 1969, Bevan's association with Executive Jet received the most detailed scrutiny. The first investigation began with the Kunkel suit, an action filed by a small shareholder who was also an Executive Jet employee who had been fired. Kunkel used the information collected by CAB to charge the Penn Central, Bevan, Hodge, and Lassiter with mismanagement that included the acquisition of foreign airlines in violation of the CAB rules. Out of Kunkel's charges grew several probes by Penn Central's directors and top management. They culminated in an exhaustive review headed by the new Penn Central president, Paul A. Gorman, who had come to the railroad after the investment in Executive Jet had failed. Gorman's committee consisted of five members. Four represented the railroad's legal, financial, and executive departments and the fifth came from the corporation's outside counsel, the firm of Dechert, Price and Rhoads. Gorman, after reviewing their massive collection of documentation, concluded [40]:

> The investments in EJA may well result in sizable losses, but no indication was found that the decision or actions of any company personnel were motivated by any purpose other than to enhance the value of the company's investments or that any such person had any interest that interfered or conflicted with the proper discharge of his duties to the company in this matter. [Gorman added that] during the course of the investigation, there was concern, of course, over the recitals in the CAB's consent order of possible knowing violations of aviation law by company officers. These related to EJA dealings with foreign interests. Nothing brought out by this investigation persuades me our people knew that EJA was doing more than having preliminary negotiations subject to CAB approval. [He concluded that] the important thing now is to devote the company's efforts to salvaging as much of the investment as possible in the present circumstances.

It is interesting to note that Gorman's conclusion was carefully couched in such terms that it was unnecessary to state that his sponsor for the presidency of the railroad, Charles Hodge, was involved in "knowing violations of aviation" and so recognized by the CAB.

Gorman's report might have settled the matter had the Penn Central not collapsed and had not Patman launched his investigation. It is significant that despite Patman's urging, no department of the federal government launched criminal proceedings against David Bevan or any other Penn Central or Executive Jet officer as a result of the congressman's Executive Jet allegations.

The one person who took up the challenge was Philadelphia County's district attorney, Arlen Specter. On January 4, 1972, Specter obtained warrants charging Bevan, Hodge, and Lassiter "with illegally diverting more than $21 million from the railroad" into Executive Jet [41]. The district attorney's charges made headlines in all the Philadelphia newspapers for several weeks in early 1972—especially because Lassiter, residing in California, refused to go to Pennsylvania and resisted extradition. Lassiter retained the noted criminal lawyer, F. Lee Bailey. After the initial publicity, Specter allowed the case to slide. Finally the inactivity became embarrassing. On August 10, 1973, Frank Brookhouser of the *Evening Bulletin* headlined his "Talk Around Town" gossip column, "Bevan, Hodge Held for Grand Jury 15 Months Ago, Still Not Indicted." Brookhouser reported that Specter blamed the delay "in part on stalling by defense lawyers for the two top-ranking officers of the railroad" [42]. But it soon became evident that Specter had not prepared his case very well. The *Philadelphia Daily News* wrote on October 8 that "the 2-year statute of limitations on fraudulent conversion charges had already expired when the attorney's office arrested two Penn Central executives in 1972. . . ." The article said that "sources in the D.A.'s office say that unless Bevan and Hodge can be indicted on new charges, the entire case may have to be dismissed." A few days later, Specter announced that he would now prosecute Bevan and Hodge for "embezzlement by a corporate officer," a charge on which the statute of limitations had not run out [43]. Still the district attorney did not press his case vigorously. Actually, in the fall of 1973 Specter was running hard for reelection for another term as district attorney. For some reason, he must have concluded that the case against Bevan and Hodge had become an embarrassment rather than an asset.

Philadelphia's voters defeated Arlen Specter in November 1973, and he was replaced by a Democrat, Emmett Fitzpatrick, who inherited the action against Bevan and Hodge. In the meantime, on December 10, 1973, death removed Olbert Lassiter from the case. In early 1974, Fitzpatrick arranged a meeting in his office with Bevan's attorney, Edward German. Fitzpatrick announced he had nearly finished a review of the case against Bevan and had been able to find no evidence to support it. Although he had a few additional things to investigate, at that moment he thought he had little alternative but to withdraw the charges against Bevan. German suggested that the district attorney consult the judge who had jurisdiction over the case. Fitzpatrick answered that he had already done so and that the judge appeared to believe the case should be dropped. He then asked German if he had any idea about the position of Edward Rome, the counsel for the Penn Central's trustees. Bevan's lawyer said that Rome had talked to Specter before he filed charges against Bevan and told the former district attorney that as far as the complaint against Bevan was concerned, "If Specter went ahead with the proceedings, he either knew nothing about the case, or was doing it solely for publicity purposes. Rome then added that he knew far more about the case than Specter possibly could and that Bevan, like all the directors of the Penn Central, and many others were involved in civil suits but there was absolutely no evidence to support criminal charges" [44].

Fitzpatrick asked German if he thought Rome would say the same thing to him. German, pointing to the telephone, said, "Call him." Rome confirmed German's account. Fitzpatrick then asked Rome if he would put his remarks in writing. Rome said he would, and on February 7, 1974, wrote Fitzpatrick [45]:

> I have received your letter of February 5, 1974, in which you enquired about my views concerning the criminal charges brought against Mr. David Bevan growing out of his role as an official of Penn Central Transportation Company, and his involvement with Executive Jet Aviation. In my capacity as special counsel to the trustees of the Penn Central Transportation Company, I have had the duty of making an extensive investigation of a variety of matters which have been the subject of public enquiry by the Congress, the press, and the trustees. I have, on behalf of the trustees, charge of the litigation instituted against former officers, directors and others, connected with the PCTC [Penn Central Transportation Company], including Mr. Bevan, charging the defendants with a variety of civil wrongs. That litigation is pending in the United States District Court for the Eastern District of Pennsylvania under the charge of Chief Justice Joseph S. Lord III.

> During the investigation conducted by the office of the District Attorney of Philadelphia County under your predecessor, I was on several occasions interviewed and asked to confer concerning my knowledge of the events revolving around EJA, the deposit of moneys in Liechtenstein, and other matters that were then under scrutiny. I, of course, cooperated fully and supplied all the information that was requested of me. In those discussions and meetings, I stated my view that Mr. Bevan's conduct did not violate any criminal law of which I was aware. Our intensive investigation has never revealed any embezzlement of PCTC's funds, and as a matter of fact the entire Executive Jet Aviation project was something that was known and supported by the board of trustees [sic] of PCTC and was the subject of public comment as a desirable plan of diversification by the railroad.

> In short, whatever civil responsibilities may rest upon Mr. Bevan, along with other persons and entities connected with PCTC, is being vigorously pursued in the Federal Court, and I am obliged to say that in my view the criminal charges brought against Mr. Bevan are unfounded.

Rome expanded upon this theme in an interview with the author. He criticized Bevan for failing to exercise enough supervision to curb the irresponsible acts committed by Hodge and Lassiter. But he felt that the concepts behind Executive Jet Aviation were sound and that Bevan had always tried to act in a way that benefited the railroad and not himself. When asked about the Cole Report, which had such an important impact on Patman's staff, Rome replied that he thought its major purpose was to shift the blame for the failure of Executive Jet from Saunders's to Bevan's shoulders. Rome concluded that he placed little credence in the report, which he regarded as both hastily prepared and biased [46].

Fitzpatrick acted quickly. On March 22, 1974, one of his assistants went before Judge Leo Weinrott in the Philadelphia Municipal Court, and he quashed all charges against Bevan. The case against Hodge was also dismissed for the same reasons. In retrospect, the Penn Central's involvement with Executive Jet Aviation had nothing to do with the company's collapse. Of the $21 million lost, $16 million had been expended prior to the merger. The approximately $4.5 million spent after February 1968 was minuscule compared with the railroad's operating losses. Furthermore, Bevan had not acted alone. He had had the support and cooperation of the railroad's highest officers, who had acted with the full knowledge of the corporation's board of directors. The assertion that Bevan ploughed money into Executive Jet in order to protect himself from embarrassing disclosures lacks any foundation in fact. Well over $15.5 million had been invested prior to Lassiter's employment of Ricciardi, whose allegations triggered the charge. The money invested after 1967 was spent in a vain attempt to keep Executive Jet alive until its future could be determined. This was done with the knowledge of Stuart Saunders. As late as November 1968, Saunders defended the EJA investment to Paul J. Tierney, the chairman of the Interstate Commerce Commission. He stated that the railroad's investment had "been made over recent years and the Civil Aeronautics Board has ordered Penn Central Company to divest itself of that interest. We feel," Saunders argued, "this action of CAB is unfortunate and a clear example of the unwarranted insistence in some areas upon a compartmentalized transportation industry and the resulting protection of competitors which is not in the public interest" [47]. The more than $4 million which the railroad lent Executive Jet in late 1968 and during 1969 was done openly through the railroad's trustee for its interests in EJA, the Detroit Bank & Trust, on its own initiative and judgment, and the Civil Aeronautics Board monitored all advances.

CONCLUSION

The Patman Committee's attempt to focus on the sensational and false Ricciardi charges did the American public a disservice. Executive Jet's real significance is its experience with the inner workings of the American aviation regulatory system. While it is true that the railroad's management erred in its decision to invest in an airline, its mistake lay not in corruption or mismanagement, but in its failure to understand the nature of the regulatory system with which it had to deal. The railroad's leaders, including Saunders and Bevan, were particularly ill-equipped to assess the risks they were taking. In the latter half of the twentieth century, no person or corporation can easily enter the railroad business without enormous investment in physical plant. Once that investment is made, it cannot be transferred to another business.

Exactly the reverse is true in airlines. The single most important asset an airline has is not its aircraft, and certainly not the airways system. The latter, including the air navigational network, airports, maps, weather reporting, and traffic control, is provided at public expense. An airline's single most essential asset is a certificate granted by the government that allows it to use public facilities to transport freight and passengers between certain points. Certificates are not granted openly to all, but are restricted in number, a fact that limits or prevents competition. Furthermore, until recently the regulating agencies set the tariffs, limiting what competition existed to service rather than prices. The airline's most costly assets are its airplanes, which are easily purchased and readily transferable from one route to another or from one owner to another.

Recently, some political leaders, including Massachusetts Senator Edward Kennedy and former President Carter, have come to recognize that federal airline regulation has operated to the detriment of the public by restricting competition. The major air operators, such as Eastern, TWA, and Western, have—to a corporation—mouthed platitudes about private enterprise but defended the CAB policies that restricted the number of airlines on any particular route and set prices for services.

Until recently, CAB regulation has ensured that what competition existed in the airline industry centered on the grant of federal certificates—not on other airlines once they were authorized to fly. It was almost inevitable that the granting of airline certificates was political. This fact has been demonstrated most nakedly on the international routes where the United States has bargained spiritedly with other nations to obtain landing rights for its carriers. Domestic certificates were no less political, but their being so was not always bad. Sometimes regional interests have benefited by political regulation. Such a case was the Civil Aeronautics Board decision to save Northeast Airlines, a marginal local New England line, by granting it the right to operate services on the highly profitable Boston–New York–Miami route.

The point here is that the CAB should be regarded as a political, rather than a legal, body. It is in this context that the whole Executive Jet struggle makes sense. General Lassiter came to aviation with a new concept: a jet-taxi service that would be sold to large businesses. This idea stepped on no toes in the airline industry because it proposed to replace privately run aircraft with commercial planes. In fact, as already noted, airlines did not get much business from those executives who maintained their own planes, but stood to profit by the reduction in company aircraft that EJA would bring about. Therefore, a major airline, Pan American, had only encouragement for the Pennsylvania at the start of its EJA investment. The Civil Aeronautics Board, too, was unconcerned about the railroad's investment in Executive Jet so long as the firm was solely an air-taxi service. The CAB thoroughly examined the Pennsy's investment in Executive Jet in 1965, and in November of that year it closed the case without taking action [48].

It was only when Executive Jet, with the full knowledge of both Stuart Saunders and David Bevan, changed its direction by purchasing the Johnson Flying Service to obtain a supplemental air certificate that the CAB became concerned. Even then, the initial contact between Executive Jet's officers and the CAB proved encouraging. Executive Jet argued that its air experience and capital would improve competition in supplemental air transport and benefit the American public, including the government. Examiner Shapiro's initial decision applauded this argument. However, the things that made Executive Jet's purchase of the Johnson Flying Service appealing to Examiner Shapiro menaced important vested interests in the airline industry. Lassiter's flying experience, together with his military influence, threatened the life-blood of firms such as Capitol International Airways, Saturn Airways, and World Airways. At the very least, Executive Jet would have forced a severe price competition for the right to carry troops and military supplies to South-east Asia. The line would also have menaced Pan American's war profits.

The record of the Atlantic route is much more confusing because of the clandestine activities of Hodge, Lassiter, and Goetz. Still, the outline is plain enough. Lassiter and Hodge saw the possibility of making money out of cut-rate transportation in the manner pioneered by Icelandic Airlines. They took an active interest in several carriers, including International Air Bahamas, Transavia, and Hispanair, all of which were aimed at the cut-rate travel market. They apparently convinced the German industrialist Fidel Goetz that Executive Jet would profit from opening a rival to Icelandic Airlines via the southern gateway, and they won his support. The record is fuzzy because they kept their activities secret. This was especially a problem in the case of Goetz, a German citizen. He chose not to come under United States jurisdiction and did not have to tell the CAB anything. His actions were so secretive that even the railroad's lawyers could not follow them.

It has already been noted that when, in the summer of 1968, International Air Bahamas set a transatlantic fare that was lower than Icelandic's, the officials of this foreign airline, together with a representative of the Icelandic government, appeared before the CAB. It seems ironic that a company that for years had profited by portraying itself as an antimonopolistic, low-cost airline competing against the cartel established by IATA should immediately run to an American regulatory agency when its own monopoly of low-cost transatlantic air traffic was threatened. The opposition of Pan American, which had to operate under IATA rules, should have been expected as a matter of course. David Bevan, the railroad attorneys (particularly Howard Westwood and William Burt), and Edwin Rome all tended to lay the blame for Executive Jet's failure to achieve its goals directly upon General Lassiter and Charles Hodge. The attorneys argued that the two men had rushed into illegal deals without taking into consideration the impact that such actions might have on the CAB and that forced the adverse ruling. Lassiter's and Hodge's actions allowed Penn Central's opponents to portray Executive Jet as a corporation that cut corners with the CAB.

Westwood summarized the problem by saying that Executive Jet "appears to be telling the CAB one thing and planning another." He observed [49] that the airline had

> a considerable history of running afoul of CAB rules and regulations. First, of course, it operated in common carriage without a certificate. This violation was not willful, but the CAB ruling should hardly have been a surprise. Then followed the abortive attempts to acquire foreign supplemental air carriers. While it was always intended that EJA would seek CAB approval, the point is that Lassiter acted first and asked questions later, a pattern of conduct which appears to be characteristic of him and which might lessen his value as a witness. Finally, there is the program to make EJA a major international freight and passenger supplemental carrier. This concept was so central to the sales pitch made to [U.S. Steel] and Burlington as to raise a doubt concerning EJA's current projections, which disclaim any intention of operating on that scale.

That Lassiter's and Hodge's activities were damaging, there can be no doubt. They acted in contradiction to statements they made to Executive Jet Aviation's board of directors, who proclaimed that they had made no agreements with foreign airlines and that none would be made until after the CAB ruled on the Johnson Flying Service application [50]. Later, Bruce Sundlun informed EJA's board that a CAB search of the files of EJA, Penn Central, and Glore Forgan had revealed that the airline "had, without prior CAB approval become involved with certain foreign air carriers" [51]. As a result, the board acted on January 20, 1969, to repudiate the actions of any of the airline's "officers or directors or employees" in making agreements to acquire Sudwestflug, IAB, Transavia, and other foreign interests. This resolution came too late.

No one will ever know the entire story of EJA's ill-fated European relationships. General Lassiter is dead. Fidel Goetz, who played such a key role in most of the arrangements, always kept himself and his records in Europe beyond the reach of American investigators. Finally, Goetz's death in 1976 removed any possibility that he one day might tell his story. On the Penn Central side, the evidence is abundant. No railroad official declined to testify in the many government investigations of EJA. David Bevan spent weeks answering questions before the Securities and Exchange Commission in Washington. He appeared before many other government bodies as well. Bevan never declined to answer a single question. His total cooperation was one of the things that made such a favorable impression on Edward Rome, special counsel for the Penn Central's trustees after the railroad's bankruptcy. So secure was Bevan in his knowledge that he had done nothing wrong and that he had nothing to hide that he spent hours alone, without even his counsel present, answering Rome's questions. Gorman's investigations of the Penn Central concluded that no railroad official had prior knowledge of EJA's European deals. The CAB, however, specifically charged that General Hodge "actively aided and assisted EJA in implementing its 'World Operating Rights Program,' " but made no similar charge against Bevan [52].

The key participant in EJA's activities who has never told his story was Charles Hodge, former chairman of the Executive Committee of the Wall Street firm of Glore Forgan. The facts about Hodge tell much about the quality and fairness of the government investigations that followed the Penn Central's collapse. As an investment banker, Hodge came directly under the regulatory power of the Securities and Exchange Commission. In view of his position as EJA's financial adviser and the CAB's charge that he had been a leading force in EJA's illegal World Operating Rights Program, it would be reasonable to expect that the SEC investigation of EJA would have concentrated on the New York stockbroker. This is especially logical because of the very large coverage EJA received in the Patman Staff Report, and because of Hodge's connection with Penphil. Hodge himself apparently feared what an investigation might reveal. When asked to appear before the SEC, he sent an affidavit, dated May 4, 1972, that stated: "Upon the advice of my counsel, I will exercise my rights under the Fifth Amendment to the United States Constitution and decline to answer any and all questions put to me concerning the above [the Matter of *Penn Central Company,* et al.]" [53]. As far as can be determined, Hodge took the Fifth Amendment in all the investigations that followed the railroad's collapse [54].

What is surprising is not Hodge's action, but the SEC's reaction. That body brought no charges in the official complaint filed by it after its Penn Central investigation. Even more surprising is the preferred treatment Hodge received in the SEC Report, *The Financial Collapse of the Penn Central Company.* Hodge is often mentioned in the Report, but it would be difficult for a reader to determine that Hodge had flatly refused to testify on all matters concerning the Penn Central. His lack of testimony is mentioned only in three obscure footnotes. On page 139 he is described as "not available for consultation during this period," and on page 310 his views are recorded as "presently unknown." Only on page 164 does a footnote reveal the reason why Hodge's views were "unknown." The Report states that in the inquiry into Gengras's election to the Penn Central's board, Hodge "refused to testify on Fifth Amendment grounds." Although the SEC reviewed the EJA affair, there is no mention of Hodge's refusal to testify on that subject. Contrast this with the treatment given to another important witness in the EJA case, Joseph Rosenbaum. In a paragraph on page 74 entitled "EJA Addendum: The $10 million Liechtenstein account," the SEC Report states, "we encountered great difficulties in exploring the facts in this area. The key witness, Joseph Rosenbaum, a Washington attorney, declined to testify, asserting his rights under the Fifth Amendment." The question that emerges is, why did Hodge receive such preferred treatment? This is a question that cries for further investigation.

As fascinating as the scandal surrounding the World Operating Rights Program is, it is doubtful that this was a real, or even a primary, reason, why EJA lost its application to acquire the Johnson Flying Service. Pan American, Icelandic, and the nonscheduled airlines that intervened before the CAB feared the creation of a strong new competitor, and it is unlikely that their opposition would have subsided even had Hodge and Lassiter acted correctly in every respect. Theodore Seamon, the attorney for Capitol International Airways, devoted a great deal of his energy to the portrayal of United States Steel and Burlington Industries as acting in concert with the railroad to create a dominant position in the nonscheduled airline business. The thrust of his argument was that an Executive Jet enterprise owned by a steel company and a textile firm was as unacceptable as an airline backed by a railroad [55]. What is even more revealing is that after United States Steel withdrew its effort to buy into Executive Jet, it attempted on its own to purchase Johnson Flying Service. In this, U.S. Steel acted independently of either Burlington or the Penn Central. Nevertheless, the same people raised the same objections that they had previously leveled against Executive Jet's takeover of Johnson. It is not surprising that U.S. Steel failed in the effort even though it clearly had not been guilty of any previous fast and sharp dealings with the Civil Aeronautics Board.

It is ironic to analyze what happened to Executive Jet's interests. None other than Icelandic Airlines purchased International Air Bahamas. Thus a foreign airline used an American regulatory agency, the Civil Aeronautics Board, to eliminate a potential competitor. Equally bizarre is that Executive Jet, which had no use for its large Boeing planes, was forced to lease them at distress rates to the Icelandic-operated International Air Bahamas and to an American supplemental carrier, World Airways. The CAB was fully informed of these actions and no one raised an objection [56].

In Executive Jet the railroad tried to play a game for which it was woefully unprepared. In this, Bevan's business judgment was no better than Saunders's. It was a mistake, but no worse than many other decisions made by business executives who underrate the forces arraigned against them. Neither Bevan's nor Saunders's EJA decisions were criminal, nor did they contribute to the Penn Central's collapse. Rather, they illustrated the foibles of the American air regulatory system that at that time tended to stifle competition and favor entrenched interests. Had Patman and his staff been interested in these issues, his committee might have made an important contribution to a long-term debate over the future of government regulatory commissions.

REFERENCES

1. Minutes of EJA's board of directors' special meeting, September 23, 1966.

2. Minutes of EJA's board of directors' regular meeting, January 12, 1967.

3. *The Financial Collapse of the Penn Central Company*, a Staff Report of the Securities and Exchange Commission to the [House of Representatives] Special Sub-Committee on Investigations, Hon. Harley O. Staggers, Chairman, Government Printing Office, Washington, D.C., August 1972, pp. 158–159. Hereafter referred to as the SEC Staff Report. Kunkel never carried through with his suit, and Bevan was not served notice of it.

4. Cole to Saunders, March 8, 1970. This letter came into Bevan's possession as a result of investigations following the railroad's collapse.

5. Saunders to Bevan, March 9, 1970.

6. Graham to Bevan, March 8, 1970.

7. The Cole Report, March 20, 1970.

8. *The Penn Central Failure and the Role of Financial Institutions*, Staff Report of the Committee on Banking and Currency, 92d Congress, First Session, House of Representatives, January 3, 1972, pp. 55 ff. Hereafter referred to as the Patman Report. The Report asserts that Cole prepared the document at the request of the Conflict of Interest Committee of the Penn Central board of directors to help in its investigation of Bevan, Penphil, and EJA. This is not true. There is no mention of any investigation by Cole in the Report by the Information, Disclosure and Conflict of Interest Committee of its investigation into matters raised by Marion E. Sibley. This was the board's investigation of the charges against Bevan regarding Penphil and Executive Jet Aviation.

9. Lassiter to Bevan, January 23, 1967.

10. The carriers opposing Executive Jet's application were American Flyers Airline Corporation, Capitol International Airways, World Airways, Saturn Airways, Trans International Airlines, and Trans-Texas Airways.

11. Patman Report, p. 72, quoted by Patman's staff from *Business Week,* August 16, 1969.

12. See Order as Adopted by the Civil Aeronautics Board, June 30, 1967, Order No. E-25371, Docket No. 17657, et al.

13. Minutes of EJA's board of directors' Executive Committee meeting, December 15, 1967.

14. Shapiro, Notice to All Parties, May 23, 1968.

15. Bevan to Saunders, February 15, 1968.

16. E. K. Taylor (Penn Central legal staff), Memorandum for File, March 13, 1968.

17. C. F. Myers, Memorandum, May 21, 1968, Subject EJA. This memorandum, made for the internal reading of Burlington executives, came into CAB's possession when that agency examined the Burlington Files. Later, it became part of the record and came into the Penn Central's Files.

18. Gerstnecker to Saunders, October 23, 1968.

19. Saunders to Gerstnecker, October 28, 1968.

20. Sundlun, Memorandum for EJA Files, February 23, 1968, of Sundlun's and Lassiter's meeting of February 22 in Washington.

21. Minutes of EJA's board of directors' annual meeting, April 13, 1967.

22. Minutes of EJA's board of directors' regular meeting, July 20, 1967.

23. Sundlun, Memorandum, for EJA's Files, February 23, 1968.

24. Minutes of EJA's board of directors' annual meeting, April 1, 1968.

25. Sundlun, Memorandum for EJA's Files, February 23, 1968.

26. Minutes of EJA's board of directors' annual meeting, April 1, 1968.

27. Minutes of EJA's board of directors' Executive Committee meeting, December 15, 1967.

28. Minutes of EJA's directors' meeting, January 10, 1968.

29. Wayne W. Parrish, "IAB: Aviation's Big Whodunit," *American Aviation,* December 23, 1968, p. 13.

30. Minutes of EJA's directors' special meeting, September 9, 1968.

31. Minutes of EJA's directors' annual meeting, April 1, 1968.

32. Westwood to Wilson, March 7, 1968.

33. Sundlun, Memorandum for EJA File, April 30, 1968. Memo of meeting on April 26 of Sundlun and Carl Hirschmann in New York City.

34. Minutes of EJA's board of directors' Executive Committee, December 15, 1967.

35. Lifsey, Jr., to Lassiter, January 18, 1968.

36. Westwood, Supplement No. 1 to the Attorney's Summary, December 17,1968.

37. Westwood to Gerstnecker, December 17, 1968.

38. Gerstnecker, Memorandum to Bevan, January 21, 1969.

39. Voting and Liquidating Trust Agreement between American Contract Company and the Detroit Bank & Trust Company, August 28, 1968, Exhibit ACC-102 in CAB Docket No. 17657; Amendment No. 1 to Voting and Liquidating Trust Agreement entered into as of August 28, 1968, between American Contract Co. and Detroit Bank & Trust Co., October 21, 1968, ibid.

40. Gorman to Hanley, May 28, 1970.

41.   *Philadelphia Evening Bulletin,* January 4, 1972.

42.   *Philadelphia Evening Bulletin,* August 10, 1973.

43.   *Philadelphia Evening Bulletin,* October 10, 1973.

44.   Author's interview with German, May 23, 1977.

45.   Rome to Fitzpatrick, February 7, 1974.

46.   Author's interview with Rome, May 23, 1977.

47.   Saunders to Tierney, November 29, 1968.

48.   Wilson to Gerstnecker, November 10, 1965.

49.   Memorandum from Westwood's office to Bevan's office, September 26, 1968. See Westwood to Bevan, September 27, 1968.

50.   Minutes of EJA's board of directors' annual meeting, April 1, 1968.

51.   Minutes of EJA's board of directors' regular meeting, January 20, 1969.

52.   Order to Cease and Desist adopted by the CAB on the matter of Docket 17657 et al., October 14, 1969, pp. 13–14. The CAB looked very hard for evidence that Bevan knew of the European deals beforehand. It could find none, so it had to link the railroad by implication, saying "PRR, through its officers David Bevan and William R. Gerstnecker and through General Hodge, has had general knowledge of the activities of EJA set forth above. PRR, through one or more of the aforementioned individuals, has aided and assisted EJA in a number of these activities." That "one" was obviously Hodge, whom the CAB cited in the previous paragraph as having actively aided the World Operating Rights Program.

53.   Benjamin Greenspoon, Chief Trial Attorney, Securities and Exchange Commission, in a letter to Edward German, March 1, 1978.

54.   For example, while Hodge did give a deposition in the Penn Central Securities Litigation (M.D.L. Docket No. 56, All Cases in the United States District Court for the Eastern District of Pennsylvania) on November 28, 1972, he did take the Fifth Amendment time after time and on all important questions. In fact, Hodge tried to avoid giving a deposition in this case, but was prevented from doing so by an order of Judge Joseph S. Lord III, on August 24, 1972. See Memorandum and order sur Motion of Defendant Charles J. Hodge for a protective order in re Penn Central Securities Litigation, filed August 25, 1972.

55.   Theodore Seamon, Memorandum of Capitol Airways Inc., on the failure of compliance by applicants with orders E-25371 and E-26170 before the CAB, Attachment 1, June 24, 1968.

56.   John W. Simpson (EJA's attorney from Koteen & Burt) to Alphonse M. Andrews, director, Bureau of Operating Rights of the Civil Aeronautics Board, July 11, 1969.

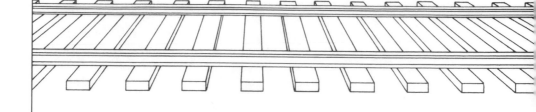

Chapter 18
THE MYSTERY OF
THE MISSING $4 MILLION

THE BERLINER BANK LOAN

Extensive investigation proved that the criminal charges that grew out of Patman's investigation of David Bevan's role in Executive Jet were without foundation. This caused Arlen Specter's successor as Philadelphia district attorney, Emmett Fitzpatrick, to drop all charges against the Penn Central's former chief financial officer. There was, however, one criminal act uncovered, the theft of $4 million from a Penn Central account that was alleged to implicate Bevan. Furthermore, circumstances linked this theft with Executive Jet, since the Penn Central entity from which the funds had been stolen was the American Contract Company, which had advanced funds to the air-taxi service. In addition, the recipient of this stolen money was Fidel Goetz, the European financier who had been involved with EJA's president, Olbert Lassiter, and Hodge in their ill-fated attempt to control several European airlines and International Air Bahamas.

The story began in September 1969 when the Penn Central, through its subsidiary American Contract Company, borrowed 40 million deutschmarks (DM) ($10 million) from a consortium of German banks headed by West Berlin's Berliner Bank. Almost simultaneously with the creation of the Penn Central in early 1968, money conditions changed. Inflation, fueled by the Vietnam war, caused the Federal Reserve to contract the United States money supply. John H. Shaffer, the Penn Central's treasurer, testified that in 1968 and 1969, "Everyone was out trying to borrow money and there wasn't any available" [1]. At the same time, the railroad's credit position slipped as the Penn Central borrowed ever-increasing amounts to meet its growing operating deficits. These two factors forced Bevan to look outside the United States for financing.

In 1967 Bevan and William Gerstnecker met a man who was later to play an important part in Penn Central's attempt to tap overseas financing. That man was Joseph Rosenbaum, and the Penn Central officers met him casually on a visit to the New York offices of Glore Forgan. Joseph Rosenbaum and his brother Francis had a Washington law office. One of Francis's clients was a wealthy German industrialist, Fidel Goetz, who employed the Rosenbaum law firm on a retainer of $5000 a month from 1960 through early 1970 [2].

In the first part of 1969, Joseph Rosenbaum approached Gerstnecker with an offer to borrow funds in Europe through a consortium headed by West Germany's Berliner Bank for the purpose of leasing rehabilitated freight cars to the railroad. The deal was completed in the spring of 1969 and was handled through R. W. Pressprich, a New York investment banking house that specialized in railroad equipment financing [3].

In the summer of 1969 Gerstnecker approached Pressprich to find an additional $10 million of financing for rehabilitated equipment under a conditional sales contract. Pressprich arranged financing through the Berliner Bank. It later transpired that Francis Rosenbaum had helped the New York investment firm find the money. For the Penn Central, equipment financing was routine. Every year the railroad rebuilt many millions of dollars worth of old freight cars into what amounted to new equipment. In this process the railroad took worn-out hulks to the company's Altoona, Pennsylvania shops where they were completely rebuilt. The Penn Central borrowed money for this on a short-term basis at the prime rate from New York or other banks. Each year the railroad accumulated millions of dollars worth of rebuilt equipment. When equipment was again usable, the railroad replaced the temporary financing with long-term borrowing with the equipment as security.

Gerstnecker worked out the basic details of the $10-million loan in August 1969. The major problem was a difference in custom between American and German financial institutions. Whereas, in the United States, banks routinely lent money to finance railroad equipment trusts, German banks were unfamiliar with this procedure. As security the Germans preferred a direct promissory note from the Penn Central, not a lien on railroad equipment. The Germans felt the corporation's pledge had a greater value than a lien on the equipment. But the Penn Central found it awkward to give a direct pledge of its own credit because such action had to be explicitly approved by the Interstate Commerce Commission, a long and complex procedure.

So-called conditional sales agreements, unlike equipment trusts, did not require ICC authorization. Consequently, in order to avoid dealing with the ICC and at the same time yield to German demands for a promissory note, Gerstnecker decided to work through the wholly owned Penn Central subsidiary, American Contract Company, which could give its note without ICC approval. Furthermore, the refurbished equipment served as additional security. These negotiations took considerable time and it was not until September that the loan could be accomplished. Meanwhile, Bevan's office faced a drain of key personnel because of dissatisfaction with Saunders's and Perlman's policies. One of the most serious losses was William Gerstnecker, who resigned on September 1 to become vice-chairman of Philadelphia's Provident National Bank. Gerstnecker did agree to follow through on the Berliner Bank loan until its completion, even though he no longer worked for the Penn Central. After September 1, he no longer had an office at the railroad. Bevan, as a matter of convenience, allowed Gerstnecker to use a conference table in the chief financial officer's very large office to conclude the loan agreement. This accommodation later provided problems for both Bevan and Gerstnecker.

As the loan date came closer, Penn Central officials faced an additional difficulty. The Berliner Bank was lending the American Contract Company DM40 million, which at current exchange rates was approximately $10 million. In September, the railroad had only $6 million of refurbished equipment. It would take some time before an additional $4 million in freight cars became available. The problem was what to do with the surplus $4 million while the railroad waited for the rest of the rolling stock. One solution was to convert the remaining deutschmarks into dollars and transfer the funds to one of Penn Central's American accounts. Had the loan been made several years earlier, this probably would have been done. However, in 1969 the value of the American dollar began to depreciate relative to that of the deutschmark. The threat of rapid and continued dollar depreciation made it inadvisable to convert deutschmarks to dollars until they were actually needed. Therefore Bevan elected to keep the funds in Europe in a deutschmark account until the railroad required them. At this time Joseph Rosenbaum recommended to Gerstnecker that the funds be kept at interest in the care of an institution controlled by Fidel Goetz.

Gerstnecker worked out the final arrangements in Bevan's Philadelphia office on September 11, 1969. The former Penn Central employee had previously told Bevan of Rosenbaum's recommendation and the chief financial officer replied that this arrangement seemed proper provided that the money was put in trust for the railroad. On September 12, the American Contract Company sent the First Financial Trust of Vaduz, Liechtenstein, which Gerstnecker thought was a Goetz bank, the following letter [4]:

Gentlemen:

We have directed the Berliner Bank from whom we are borrowing DM40,000,000 to credit the proceeds of this loan to your account. By your signature below you are evidencing your agreement that such funds are to be held in trust and invested and reinvested for our account to the extent not advanced to us for the rehabilitation of equipment to be leased to Penn Central Transportation Company or for the payment of principal or interest on the aforesaid loan.

It is understood between us that, while the responsibility for investment decision is yours, the investments are intended not merely to provide a return on the funds but also to protect us in so far as possible against the possibility of revaluation of the deutschmark. We will, moreover, keep you fully informed in advance of the progress of our equipment rehabilitation program, so that you may plan your investment program accordingly.

For your services and expenses you are to receive 25 percent of the amount by which the income of the funds so invested exceeds the interest rate on the aforesaid loan, applicable to that portion of the funds.

Very truly yours,

American Contract Company
Signed J. E. Dermond, President

The decision to put the proceeds of the Berliner Bank loan into the hands of the First Financial Trust was unwise. Nevertheless, it should be seen from the perspective of Bevan and Gerstnecker in 1969. For both officers, borrowing $10 million from the Berliner Bank did not loom as a relatively important act. After all, Bevan had borrowed for the Penn Central during the years 1968 and 1969 more than $950 million. Moreover, in the months ahead the Penn Central faced financial problems that caused Bevan to continue to deal in loans expressed in hundreds of millions of dollars. The magnitude of the railroad's financial troubles pushed any detailed consideration of the handling of the Berliner Bank loan into the background. Besides, both Gerstnecker and Bevan had a favorable image of Joseph Rosenbaum and Fidel Goetz. Bevan had run a check on Goetz with several New York banks and found that the German industrialist was estimated to have assets valued between $150 million and $300 million. His character was considered good. Bevan also checked Joseph Rosenbaum with two members of the Penn Central's board of directors who knew and dealt with him, John M. Seabrook and Howard Butcher III. He also asked the Washington law firm of Covington & Burling and Charles Hodge about Joseph Rosenbaum. All reports were positive.

Unfortunately, unknown to Bevan and Gerstnecker, Fidel Goetz, Francis Rosenbaum, and Joseph Rosenbaum had a sinister side. One of Goetz's many ventures was a dirty-money laundry. Francis Rosenbaum used this dirty-money laundry to send dishonest money to Europe where Goetz ran it through several of his corporations, some of which were based in Liechtenstein, and it came back "clean." For this service the German industrialist charged 2½ percent on receipt of the funds and an additional 2½ percent upon returning them [5].

Francis Rosenbaum had been a director in the Alsco Chromcraft Corporation, a prime contractor for rocket launchers ordered by the United States Navy. He became involved in a scheme that set up phony subcontracting firms that provided fraudulent invoices from European corporations for material that was never delivered. Rosenbaum used Goetz's laundry in this scheme.

FRANCIS ROSENBAUM AND THE FIRST FINANCIAL TRUST

What Bevan and Gerstnecker did not know was that on the date when the American Contract Company wrote to convey DM40 million to the First Financial Trust in Liechtenstein, it did not even exist. The story of the First Financial Trust is a complex one and reveals much about the dangers to the uninitiated in dealing with Swiss and Liechtenstein entities. Gerstnecker completed the final arrangements of the Berliner Bank note on September 11, 1969. Francis Rosenbaum attended this meeting and then left Philadelphia for Europe. On September 15, he arrived in Vaduz, Liechtenstein, the capital of the obscure European principality wedged between Austria, Switzerland, and Germany.

Once in Vaduz, Rosenbaum went to the office of Dr. Peter Marxer, a prominent local attorney. In public life, Marxer led one of Liechtenstein's parliamentary political parties and was the personal lawyer for the Prince of Liechtenstein [6]. Peter Marxer knew Fidel Goetz well. His law firm kept a stock of empty corporate shells that could be sold to individuals wishing to use them. A purchaser of such an entity could assign it any name he or she desired. There was one big advantage: secrecy. The owner of the firm would not be known except to the Marxer law office, and all correspondence and other communications would be funneled through that office, where various lawyers associated with Dr. Marxer would act as officers. In this manner, the real owner of the entity need never surface.

Francis Rosenbaum arrived at the Marxer law firm in the company of two Goetz employees, Mr. Hohl and Mr. Hillsinger. Franz Pucher, one of Marxer's associates, met Rosenbaum. Pucher had been expecting the American lawyer who, he had been told, apparently by someone associated with Fidel Goetz, was an attorney representing the Penn Central. Pucher later testified that Rosenbaum purchased one of Marxer's empty corporate shells called Finimobeil, formerly owned by a Mrs. Daisy Stehli. Francis Rosenbaum purchased for 20,000 Swiss francs what were known as founder's rights in the firm, the name of which he changed to the First Financial Trust.

After Francis Rosenbaum purchased this entity, he told Dr. Pucher that the Marxer firm would receive a check for approximately $10 million. He instructed the German lawyer to open a 2-day call deposit with a Liechtenstein bank for the money which he knew the Penn Central would need immediately for its refurbished freight cars. Then Rosenbaum signed a document authorizing the transfer of the remainder of the money, some DM16.8 million, worth approximately $4 million, to the Vileda Anstalt, a Goetz corporation. Pucher later testified that, while he thought Rosenbaum to be an American lawyer representing the Penn Central, he did not ask for a power of attorney nor did he have any written evidence to so indicate [7]. This failure to verify Rosenbaum's status would later cause Marxer acute embarrassment. Rosenbaum made arrangements for the Penn Central to be paid its $6 million on demand, knowing that it would be a while before the railroad would call for the rest of the money.

Events initially worked in favor of the Rosenbaums. Gerstnecker had left the Penn Central and was no longer concerned about its affairs. The increasing financial crisis of the railroad occupied most of Bevan's attention. However, several times before June, 1970, members of Bevan's staff reminded him of the $4 million sitting in Europe and asked if it should be brought to the United States. Each time Bevan directed that the funds stay in Liechtenstein. He had solid reasons for his actions. The dollar was rapidly depreciating against the German mark. Keeping the money in Europe meant the railroad would receive more dollars when the exchange was finally made. Since the railroad would repay the loan in marks, not dollars, it was important to receive maximum value on the exchange. On June 8, 1970, the date Bevan left the railroad, the DM16,800,000, worth approximately $4,230,000 when the railroad borrowed it, had an exchange value of $4,587,000 [8]. In the 9 months since the railroad had made the loan, the West German mark had appreciated approximately 8 percent against the U.S. dollar. Had Bevan stayed with the Penn Central, he might have kept the funds in Europe even longer. But Bevan's sudden dismissal from the railroad changed this plan. Almost immediately after he was fired, Bevan believed the funds ought to be withdrawn. He talked to Joseph Rosenbaum about the matter and learned for the first time that there was some question about the deposit. He promptly notified Paul Gorman, the Penn Central's new chief executive officer, who had replaced Stuart Saunders. Gorman asked one of the railroad's own attorneys, George Miller, to investigate. This assignment was cut short by the Penn Central's collapse on June 21, which brought the corporation under the control of the United States District Court for the Eastern District of Pennsylvania. The court assigned Judge Fullam to handle the matter, who in turn appointed trustees. Later in 1970 Judge Fullam appointed Edwin Rome as special outside counsel for the trustees. As such, Rome was an officer of the court and had widespread powers of investigation and recommendation into all aspects of the Penn Central's collapse. In the fall, Rome began a detailed investigation into the question of why the Penn Central was having difficulty in recovering its $4 million.

ROME STARTS AN INVESTIGATION

It was Rome's detective work, done almost in the style of Erle Stanley Gardner's Perry Mason, that eventually uncovered the facts behind the theft of Penn Central's $4 million. But, in the beginning, Rome thought the inability of the railroad to withdraw funds from First Financial Trust was a matter of misunderstanding. He believed the money could be recovered by contacting the proper people and explaining to them his role as special counsel for the trustees of the bankrupt Penn Central. One of Rome's first acts was to talk with the major participants in the original loan: William Gerstnecker, the Rosenbaum law firm, and David Bevan. On September 18, 1970, Rome met with Bevan and his attorney, Edward German. Rome later testified before a federal grand jury about Bevan's role in the recovery of the money. Said Rome, "There was never anything that I asked Mr. Bevan by way of question that he was unwilling to answer; and he did answer. . . . He stated from the outset that nobody had any right to the money other than the railroad and that it should be returned. And that, since it had not been returned, he was concerned even before the bankruptcy. He had taken this up with Mr. Paul Gorman, who was then president of the transportation company" [9].

Rome could not easily communicate with Francis Rosenbaum. The Washington attorney had pleaded guilty in the Chromcraft case and in 1970 was serving time in a federal penitentiary in New York State. As a substitute, Rome had a number of conversations with Francis's brother Joseph. From the beginning, Joseph appeared cooperative, and he intimated to the special counsel for the trustees that he, too, believed the Penn Central's money was still in the First Financial Trust.

At the beginning, Rome, in common with all the Penn Central officials, thought the money was safely on deposit in a Liechtenstein bank. Accordingly, in October 1970, he made a formal demand upon First Financial Trust for return of the funds.

Matters came to a head on October 18. On that date Dr. Muller, an attorney on Peter Marxer's Liechtenstein staff who was vacationing in North America, came to Rome's Philadelphia office. A meeting took place which included Rome, Muller, Bevan, German, and Joseph Rosenbaum. Muller told Rome that Marxer's law firm represented the First Financial Trust and that the money was still on deposit in that organization in Liechtenstein. Rome said, "Well, fine, let's get on the phone right now, we will place a call to Liechtenstein to Dr. Marxer, and I want to tell him directly that I want the money immediately cabled back to Philadelphia, and that if he [does] not do so, I [will] pursue every legal remedy available." When Rome reached Marxer by telephone, he received the impression that the $4 million was still in the First Financial Trust. He demanded the return of the money. At that point, Rome testified, "there was a hesitation on the other end of the wire, and they said they would have to talk about this and reply to me, and I demanded that they reply to me by the next morning, or else I would feel myself free to take any possible action" [10].

After the phone conversation, Rome became agitated. He "was considerably upset by the fact that Dr. Marxer, who was said to be a reputable lawyer in Liechtenstein, was giving [him] what seemed to be a run around with regard to the return of the monies, which his own colleague, Dr. Muller, had said was there and was being held for American Contract Company and Penn Central." Bevan, Rosenbaum, German, and Rome began to discuss ways of forcing the return of the money to the railroad. Some of the proposed methods included making a formal demand, "reporting it to the government, getting in touch with the ambassador for Liechtenstein," and discussing the matter with the attorneys for the Berliner Bank. During the entire conversation both Bevan and Rosenbaum affirmed "that they knew of nobody who had any authority whatever to divert those funds or to do other than to cause their return to the Penn Central." Joseph Rosenbaum did not admit knowing anything about the owners of First Financial Trust but intimated that the money was still there and that "it was only a matter of persuading Fidel Goetz, who was taken to be the owner, to release it" [11].

The next morning, October 19, Rome received [the] following cable from First Financial Trust [12]:

> Our American lawyers confirm now [the] view that there has been no breach of contract of the 15th of September, 1969, between American Contract Company and First Financial Trust. All actions taken by us done on instructions, page 2 of authorized attorney of Penn Central, and known by Penn Central management. Happy to discuss situation with you in Vaduz, but insist we are in no duty to send money to you.

Marxer's reply mystified Rome because he had had no knowledge of any attorney in Europe who represented the Penn Central in its dealing with First Financial Trust. Rome inquired within the railroad and could find no one who knew of any attorney for the Penn Central who had the authority to disburse $4 million. He came to the inescapable conclusion that "nobody within the railroad and no lawyer on behalf of the railroad had given such authority" [13]. Consequently, Rome cabled Marxer on October 20 [14]:

> Your cable from Paris received Philadelphia, 9:30 A.M. October 19. Dr. Muller, your representative, stated to us in Philadelphia that First Financial Trust held remaining proceeds of loan from Berliner Bank amounting to not less than sixteen million eight hundred thousand DM in trust for account of American Contract Company and trustees of Penn Central Transportation Company. Neither Dr. Muller nor you in our telephone conversation of October 14 claimed you were holding these funds for anyone else. At that time, Dr. Muller, David Bevan, and Colonel Joseph Rosenbaum confirmed in my presence that no authorization existed permitting diversion of trust funds other than in accordance with the original loan from Berliner Bank in favor of American Contract and Penn Central. Demand is made upon you for disclosure of person or entity for whom you hold funds contrary to our direction for immediate remittance. In particular, disclosure is demanded of you as trustee of circumstances attending deposit of funds with Vileda Anstalt and of any transactions or affiliations you have had with interest connected with Fidel Goetz. I am only attorney authorized to act for Penn Central in respect of this trust and there is no evidence to support your reference to page 2 of any instructions.
>
> Your failure to honor demand for transmittal of funds constitutes breach of trust for which you will be held to strict account including notice to appropriate government authorities. We have made full disclosure of our demand and your breach to attorneys for Berliner Bank for their appropriate action as creditor against all involved parties. Demand for immediate remittance reiterated.
>
> Edwin P. Rome

ROME GOES TO LIECHTENSTEIN

Rome conferred with Joseph Rosenbaum, David Bevan, and Edward German about the next step. Rosenbaum offered to pay Rome's way to Liechtenstein so that he could discuss the matter directly with Dr. Peter Marxer. Rome demurred, saying that he would go to Liechtenstein only when there was genuine prospect that something could be accomplished. Finally, he added, he would go only when authorized by Penn Central's trustees and at their expense. Rosenbaum said he would go over to Liechtenstein to talk with Marxer. German told Rome that he too was going to Vaduz at Bevan's expense to investigate. On hearing these statements, Rome replied, "You go ahead and go. It's all right with me, if you are willing to go. It's agreeable with the trustees that you go at your own expense, and phone me from over there. Depending upon what you learn when you are over there and the kind of story you tell me, I will then take up with the trustees whether or not they will authorize me to go over to have a meeting" [15]. Bevan's attorney, Edward German, immediately left for Vaduz, as did Joseph Rosenbaum, in company with his own attorney, William McInerney.

The various parties reported to Edwin Rome. McInerney, representing Rosenbaum, was the first to telephone. He stated that he had met with Dr. Marxer and two of his associates, Franz Pucher and Adulf Peter Goop. Rosenbaum's attorney said that in view of the threat implied in Rome's telegram, Peter Marxer had retained an American lawyer, Lawrence Brodie, a resident member of the London law firm of Coudert Brothers. McInerney had also seen Fidel Goetz, who insisted that Rosenbaum represented the Penn Central. When Rome learned that, he thought it was "healthful news, because if I could persuade Goetz that Rosenbaum did not represent the Penn Central, which he did not—and I have been assured from everyone within the Penn Central, including Mr. Bevan and Mr. Gerstnecker, that Rosenbaum did not represent the Penn Central—that Mr. Goetz, being an honorable man, I assumed, would return the money" [16].

Edward German's call was not so optimistic. He told Rome that Penn Central faced a difficult situation but nevertheless recommended that Rome come to Vaduz. The next day, Rome flew to Zurich, where he was met by McInerney. Together, they drove to Liechtenstein, arriving just before lunchtime on October 27.

That afternoon Rome and McInerney went to a conference room in Peter Marxer's law suite. Also present were Bevan's lawyer, Edward German, Marxer's American attorney, Lawrence Brodie, Franz Pucher, Adulf Goop, Fidel Goetz, his lawyer, Dr. Auftermatt, and two of the German financier's employees, Mr. Hilsinger and Mr. Hohl. Joseph Rosenbaum was in the building, but Goetz made a big show of refusing to be in the same room as the Washington attorney. At the beginning of the meeting, Rome still believed that the First Financial Trust was a bank owned by Fidel Goetz. The next few hours stripped away a veil of duplicity behind which the Rosenbaum brothers and Goetz were hiding. Rome introduced himself and said that he was in Vaduz in his official capacity as the lawyer for the Penn Central trustees. He stated that he wanted to be as cooperative as he could and that he "was given to understand that Mr. Goetz was an honorable man, and if he was an honorable man, I assumed upon our conclusion he would return the money." Rome stressed that if Goetz had a claim against Penn Central, he should present it whether it was for $4 million or some larger sum. Rome insisted that Goetz should make his claim in the proper way, "rather than just grabbing money that belonged to Penn Central." Rome said he would be glad to assist Goetz in the presentation of a claim because he "was in the fortunate position of being court-appointed lawyer for court-appointed trustees and, therefore, we were court officers, not just adversaries." Rome added he "had a separate kind of responsibility to the court beyond merely being a lawyer for a client" [17].

Rome's firm stand, particularly his threat of action through the United States Government and Liechtenstein diplomatic authorities, had frightened Peter Marxer, who decided that he could no longer protect the Rosenbaums. Marxer's American attorney, Lawrence Brodie, explained the Liechtenstein attorney's relationship to the Washington attorneys. He produced the file containing all Marxer's correspondence relating to the First Financial Trust and gave photocopies of the documents to Rome. Brodie then explained the nature of the First Financial Trust. "I learned," testified Rome, "then, for the first time, that it was not a bank; it was just a name, really. It was a piece of paper that was created, the way one here would go in and register a fictitious name in City Hall. It was not a bank: it was not even a corporation. It was a different kind of entity, under Liechtenstein law." Rome then discovered that the First Financial's founder was Francis Rosenbaum and that Joseph Rosenbaum was the alternate owner. In fact, after Francis went to prison, Joseph became the sole owner. Moreover, Marxer's files exposed Joseph's duplicity. For example, in Philadelphia Joseph Rosenbaum attended several meetings in Rome's office and pretended not to know who owned First Financial Trust. All the cables that had been sent from Europe had been signed by Marxer's office. The file produced by Brodie contained copies of Rome's cables to Marxer demanding a return of the money along with communications from "Dr. Marxer to Joseph Rosenbaum, asking him how Marxer should answer, [Rome's] own cable demanding return of the money, and a letter from Rosenbaum suggesting how that should be answered" [18].

The files also contained the documents by which Francis Rosenbaum had transferred Penn Central's money to Goetz's own entity, the Vileda Anstalt. By this time, Rome was not surprised to learn that this was another entity like First Financial.

Rome's questions to Marxer, Goop, and Pucher disclosed exactly how the Rosenbaums became involved with First Financial. Marxer told Rome that in the fall of 1969, immediately preceding the Berliner Bank's loan to the Penn Central, Fidel Goetz, for whom he had done some legal work, phoned and asked Marxer "whether within his law office, he had any entity available, an *Anstalt* [entity] that could be utilized. . . . Dr. Marxer said yes." Goetz gave Marxer instructions on what he wanted done, with an indication that more were to follow. Marxer then said that on September 15, 1969, at a time when he had gone to Switzerland to visit his mother, Goetz, accompanied by Hillsinger and Hohl, came to his office. Rome testified [19]:

Now I was still rather doubtful and suspicious, and I pursued a variety of questions to try and pin down whether Dr. Marxer was, in fact, there. And he got out his desk book, and he talked with his own secretary, who had her own calendar where Dr. Marxer had been on given days, and it reflected, in fact, that he had gone to a place in Switzerland to visit his mother, and similarly Dr. Goop and Dr. Pucher had acknowledged that they had been present when Goetz, Hillsinger, and Hohl, and a person a stranger to them, had appeared at Dr. Marxer's law office.

This person was Francis Rosenbaum, whom Goetz introduced to them as the Penn Central's representative and the man who was going to have this entity, First Financial Trust. He would make the deposit of money into it, and then and there he signed an accounting, which caused the release of the balance of the money to Vileda Anstalt, Mr. Goetz's entity.

Rome then asked Goop and Pucher "what reason they had to believe this man was the lawyer for Penn Central. They said . . . he was introduced in that way by Mr. Goetz, who was a very prominent German citizen, a man of immense wealth, a man who they had no reason to doubt or feel was being dishonest in any way and they accepted that." Rome then queried Marxer's associates as to why they did not attempt to verify Rosenbaum's position, or at least ask for some written evidence that he was indeed a Penn Central lawyer. Rome however testified that they "then said to me, 'Well, how do we know you, Mr. Rome, are the authorized representative of the trustees? You have come over here and told us you are the lawyer for the trustees, but you don't have anything to show for that.' And I had to acknowledge that I didn't have anything" [20].

Rome observed that Dr. Marxer and his colleagues had apparently acted legally under Liechtenstein law. Actually, they had sold the Rosenbaums a legal entity and they acted as lawyers for the Rosenbaums throughout the affair. The mistake that Marxer's office made was in not checking Rosenbaum's position. While this was negligent, Rome knew that his major quarrel was not with Marxer but with Goetz.

GOETZ TAKES HIS STAND

The episode obviously embarrassed Peter Marxer. The same cannot be said for Fidel Goetz, whose actions were brazen and deceitful. After Brodie's disclosures, Dr. Auftermatt stated Goetz's position. The German lawyer claimed that the Penn Central owed Goetz more than DM19 million, or an amount greater than the DM16 million that Goetz had received from Francis Rosenbaum. Auftermatt then told an elaborate story about how Goetz had been asked to put money into the Penn Central's acquisition of certain airlines involved with Executive Jet. He referred specifically to International Air Bahamas, Transavia, Hispanair, and German Air. Auftermatt then as-

serted that Goetz had still further claims against the railroad, to which Rome
retorted "he was going to have a tough time collecting that."

Auftermatt claimed that Goetz had lost money in an alleged deal with
Penn Central and that because of this he had "a legal and moral claim to the
$4 million." Rome tried to find out whether Goetz had any evidence to
substantiate this claim. He repeatedly asked Goetz to show him "or to
establish the fact that he had done whatever he had done at the direction or
request of anyone in Penn Central, and why he thought . . . he had a claim
against the Penn Central." Rome stressed that "the money that was there in
the First Financial Trust was money that belonged, not to Executive Jet
Aviation, and not to a variety of entities within the Penn Central family, but
explicitly to American Contract Company and Penn Central Transportation
Company." Rome further explained "that there were several hundred different corporate entities within the Penn Central family," and that Goetz should
name the entity for which he had put up DM19 million, "and he would have
a claim against that company." Rome testified that Goetz "never showed me
anything to support his claim that it was Penn Central Transportation Company or American Contract Company with which he was involved. He
showed me a variety of papers, copies of which he gave me and which have
been turned over to you in the past, Mr. Burt [C. Oliver Burt, an assistant
U.S. attorney who later prosecuted Bevan in this case], but not one of them
even contained the words "Penn Central," except one. And when I had
focused on that, Dr. Auftermatt himself said, 'Oh, well, that has nothing to
do with this situation. You can put that to one side.' " Rome observed that
every one of Goetz's documents which allegedly established the authenticity
of his claim against the railroad was "from either Joseph or Francis Rosenbaum, and they did reflect certain requests or instructions or directions,
recommendations being made by the Rosenbaums to Mr. Goetz to come up
with certain monies, to advance certain monies, to do certain things. But
many of them contained language—this on behalf of a client of this [the
Rosenbaums'] office without the client ever being named, no reference ever
to the fact that the client was Penn Central Transportation Company or
American Contract Company. And in frequent copies of these letters the
language was that this obligation was an obligation of this office, meaning Mr.
Rosenbaum's law firm." Rome then told Goetz, "You may have a claim
against the Rosenbaums, but you certainly haven't shown me anything to
support your contention that you have a claim against Penn Central Transportation Company or against American Contract Company."

Rome testified that Goetz always came back "with the fact that they dealt
with the Rosenbaums, who were the lawyers for Penn Central." Rome
retorted, "Well, how can you tell me that they are lawyers for Penn Central?
There is no documentation anywhere within the company files that reflects
anything wherein they are the Penn Central's lawyers, and moreover, I am

given to believe they are your lawyers." At this point Auftermatt said, "No, that the Rosenbaums were never Mr. Goetz's lawyers; that they functioned as business brokers, as finders of businesses for Mr. Goetz, but they were not his lawyers." Rome later discovered that this statement was an outright lie. Investigation produced correspondence between the Rosenbaums and Goetz in which the Rosenbaums had sent Goetz's requests for fees in "payment for legal service rendered." Letters came back from Liechtenstein "enclosing our check for payment for legal services." Finally, it developed that Goetz had been paying the Rosenbaum firm a regular retainer of $5000 a month since 1961 [21].

On the following day Rome had a further conversation with Auftermatt and Goetz during which the two Germans still tried to convince him that they held Penn Central's money legitimately. Rome took careful notes of this conversation, which he read into his testimony before the federal grand jury in 1974. Auftermatt argued:

> We understand your point that internally, within the Penn Central group of companies, that company should pay Mr. Goetz which actually got the funds from Mr. Goetz. We cannot determine which company that was. Yesterday we spoke about the company [Executive Jet Aviation] which handled the airline business, . . . but we made it clear that we didn't mean Executive Jet Aviation is our debtor. We meant the mother company of Executive Jet Aviation. But we pointed out that the guarantee to hold us [meaning Goetz] harmless came from the chairman of the finance committee of Penn Central Transportation Company [David Bevan].

Auftermatt then argued that "the problem has to be straightened out within the group of companies within the Penn Central family." He asserted "the wrong firm has paid us. The right one should pay over to the company from which the funds came. And that frequently happens with a group of companies." Rome pointed out to the Germans that their demands could not be met and that, in addition, the letter upon which Goetz relied did not even warrant "the accuracy of the claim for 19 million deutschmarks."

Rome asked them if Bevan had ever personally promised them to return the losses that Goetz claimed he sustained in the service of Executive Jet. Rome testified that they did not claim that Bevan "ever did it directly." Goetz and Auftermatt said that they had relied upon a statement "which they said had been made by Mr. German [Bevan's attorney] in Liechtenstein" the day before Rome had arrived from Philadelphia! It did not seem to bother them that Bevan and German had not been associated in any way until after the Penn Central's collapse, or more than 9 months after Goetz had used Francis Rosenbaum to grab the railroad's funds [22].

THE ROSENBAUMS' STORY

Nothing that Rome said could convince Fidel Goetz that he should release the railroad's $4 million. On the contrary, he defied Rome to do anything about it, suggesting that if the Penn Central had a claim against him, it should come to Liechtenstein or Germany and institute a suit. The revelations of Dr. Marxer and the conversations with Goetz raised almost as many questions as they answered. Goetz did not try to hide his possession of the entire missing $4 million. The most perplexing question was, what did the Rosenbaums have to gain in cooperating with Goetz in such a venture? Certainly, in September 1969, the two Washington lawyers could not have foreseen Penn Central's collapse, nor could they have hoped that the defalcation would not be discovered.

The first session of conferences with Goetz and Marxer lasted all afternoon and well into the night. It did not conclude until 1 A.M., and after the Germans left, Rome went immediately to Joseph Rosenbaum to see whether he could unravel some of the mystery. That interview lasted until 4 A.M. Rome seethed with anger against Rosenbaum and "really upbraided him" because he "had been leading us down the garden path all this time, and I couldn't understand how he had told us one story about how he was going to help us get the money back, and at the same time he was giving instructions to fob us off." Despite Rome's rage, Joseph Rosenbaum "never got angry no matter what was said. He was calm. 'Well now, let me tell you. ...'—he then proceeded to tell me a very elaborately detailed story." This story had nothing to do with the Penn Central's alleged debt to Goetz. Instead, it involved Joseph Rosenbaum's brother Francis, who had illegally siphoned money from the Chromcraft Company in that firm's contract to build rocket launchers for the United States Navy. Joseph said that his brother had taken the money and sent it to Europe where Goetz had "laundered" it. Unfortunately for Francis, his activities were discovered and he faced criminal indictment by the federal government. Francis felt that he could destroy the government's case if Goetz cooperated. The Washington attorney proposed that Goetz supply certain affidavits certifying that the money handled through the laundry had no connection with Chromcraft. Francis's September 14, 1969, trip to Europe was primarily aimed at gaining Goetz's support in this scheme. Joseph asserted that immediately after Francis arrived, Goetz grabbed him and took him to Vaduz, where he forced him to sign over the Penn Central's money to the Vileda Anstalt [23].

When Rome returned to the United States, he made arrangements to confer with Francis Rosenbaum in the New York prison. Edward German, Bevan's lawyer, was also at the meeting, as was Joseph Rosenbaum. Rome later testified extensively about the interview. It was then that

Francis admitted that he had never been a representative of the Penn Central in any way. He told of his long association with Fidel Goetz and confirmed that the German industrialist had paid him a monthly retainer of $5000 since 1961. He was in serious trouble, he said, when he arrived in Liechtenstein on September 15, 1969. He had used Goetz's money laundry to hide the theft of money from the United States government in the Chromcraft case. Francis was under indictment, and he had gone to Europe for the purpose of asking Goetz to provide data to foil the government's case. When he arrived in Vaduz, "before he even had a chance to take off his hat," Goetz grabbed his arm and took him to Peter Marxer's law office. There Goetz told him to sign over the Penn Central's money to the Vileda Anstalt. Goetz said if Francis did that, he would "be prepared to speak . . . about the other matter" [24].

Although Francis Rosenbaum did Goetz's bidding, the German financier did not cooperate. After Rosenbaum transferred the Penn Central's funds to Vileda Anstalt, Goetz refused to discuss a plan to falsify records in the Chromcraft case. The German financier merely told Rosenbaum to call him the next day. When Rosenbaum did so, Goetz said he could be of no help. He did not act for frivolous reasons. Rome testified that "Goetz apparently had been advised by his lawyers that it might be possible for the United States authorities to open Finanz's [the corporation Goetz used as a money laundry] books and they couldn't take a position in the affidavit that could not be sustained if the books were indeed opened" [25]. The risks for Goetz in supporting Rosenbaum were great. If United States authorities received permission to examine the books of Goetz's money laundry, there was no telling what might be disclosed.

ROME ATTACHES GOETZ'S DELAWARE SECURITIES

Francis Rosenbaum went to jail for his actions in Chromcraft. Even worse from his point of view, in a futile effort to save himself he committed a serious crime by participating in the theft of the $4 million from the Penn Central. This episode destroyed the Rosenbaums' loyalty to Goetz and explains why the two Washington attorneys decided to cooperate with Rome. Their theory apparently was that, since Francis had paid the full price in the Chromcraft case, they would try to ease their position in the Penn Central affair. The Rosenbaums did indeed have information that could damage Fidel Goetz. Because they had acted as his attorneys for years, they had detailed knowledge of the German's American investments. Therefore the Rosenbaums were able to furnish Edwin Rome with a list of more than $6 million of Goetz's investments in United States corporations chartered in the State of Delaware.

The Rosenbaums' information provided Rome with a weapon. The Philadelphian had smarted at the challenge hurled by Goetz's lawyer, Dr. Auftermatt, in Vaduz: "Well, if you think there is some claim, why don't you come over and sue Mr. Goetz in Germany, in Liechtenstein?" Knowing that a European suit would be "a long, difficult problem," Rome "tried to think of a way to sue in the United States." He knew that there was an obscure statute under Delaware law that allowed somebody "who claims against an individual who owns stock in a Delaware corporation" to attach that stock. The information supplied by the Rosenbaums allowed Rome to file an action on behalf of the Penn Central trustees in the United States District Court of Delaware, which attached more than $6 million of Goetz's assets. He explained to the grand jury the nature of the procedure. He said that all "that Mr. Goetz would have to do, if he wanted to dispute our right to that money, this $6 million, would be to come into court and enter an appearance, as a result of which an attachment on his funds would be dissolved in the court. But he would then be subject to the jurisdiction of the court in the United States, and I would be able to cross-examine him under oath and he would then also be available for the process of the United States government" [26].

It is significant that none of Goetz's statements in Liechtenstein was made under oath. Unlike Bevan, Gerstnecker, and the two Rosenbaums, as long as Goetz stayed outside the United States he remained beyond the reach of American courts. He could not be subpoenaed by the grand jury, nor did he have to testify. Goetz apparently did not dare enter the United States even at the cost of freeing his $6 million in Delaware corporations.

Goetz's fear of what Rome might discover was so strong that he allowed this attachment to run from 1971 until his death in 1976. The heirs of the Goetz estate then settled with the Penn Central trustees for $1,125,000. These negotiations were carried out by the Securities and Exchange Commission and the outstanding question remains why the settlement was so small. The securities, together with the income they generated, had been impounded. Punitive damages were also involved and the claim against Goetz had skyrocketed, since it was in deutchmarks that had almost doubled against the 1969 value of the dollar.

REFERENCES

1.   *United States of America vs. Joseph H. Rosenbaum et al.:* Criminal Action No. 74-514 in the United States Court for the Eastern District of Pennsylvania (Hereafter cited as *United States vs. Rosenbaum*), Philadelphia, Pennsylvania, Seventh Day, March 3, 1977, pp. 67–68.

2.   Testimony of Joseph Rosenbaum read into *United States vs. Rosenbaum,* Eleventh Day, p. 4.

3.   Testimony of J. H. Shaffer, *United States vs. Rosenbaum,* Seventh Day, pp. 66–67, tells how the Rosenbaums actively sought to arrange various loans.

4.   Quoted from *United States vs. Rosenbaum,* First Day, pp. 25–26.

5.   Testimony of Edwin P. Rome before the United States Grand Jury, May 12, 1974 in the United States District Court for the Eastern District of Pennsylvania, p. 65. Hereafter cited as Rome Grand Jury Testimony.

6.   Rome Grand Jury Testimony, p. 32.

7.   The information on Francis Rosenbaum's negotiations with Dr. Pucher is taken from *United States vs. Rosenbaum,* Tenth Day, pp. 9, 26–27, 63–64, 83.

8.   Exchange quotations were 1DM = 25 U.S. cents September 11, 1969, and 1 DM = 27.3224 U.S. cents June 8, 1970. Source: *New York Times,* September 12, 1969, and June 9, 1970.

9.   Rome Grand Jury Testimony, pp. 12–13.

10.   Ibid., p. 14.

11.   Ibid., pp. 19–21, passim.

12.   Ibid., pp. 14–15.

13.   Ibid., p. 16.

14.   There was a difference in the date between the conversation over the telephone testified to before the grand jury and this telegram. The difference is undoubtedly due to Rome's distance from the event at the time he testified. The error does not affect the weight of the evidence. Telegram citation from *The Penn Central Failure and the Role of Financial Institutions,* Staff Report of the Committee on Banking and Currency, 92d Congress, First Session, House of Representatives, January 3, 1972, pp. 266–267.

15.   Rome Grand Jury Testimony, p. 23.

16.   Ibid., p. 25.

17.   Ibid., pp. 29–30.

18.   Ibid., p. 31.

19.   Ibid., p. 36.

20.   Ibid., pp. 36–37.

21.   The entire account of this meeting, ibid., pp. 38–42.

22.   Ibid., pp. 45–47.

23.   Ibid., pp. 54–55.

24.   Testimony of Rome in *United States vs. Rosenbaum,* Eighth Day, pp. 27–31. (Note the difference here between this and Rome's earlier testimony that Goetz's money-laundry charge was $2\frac{1}{2}$ percent each time, rather than 2 percent.)

25.   Ibid., Ninth Day, p. 55.

26.   Rome Grand Jury Testimony, pp. 55–56.

Chapter 19
THE TRIAL AND ACQUITTAL

THE INDICTMENT: THE
GOVERNMENT'S CONTENTION

By January of 1971 Edwin Rome had completed his extensive investigation of the theft of the Penn Central's $4 million. He had concluded that the sole beneficiary of the money had been Fidel Goetz. And because Rome was unable to bring the German industrialist within the reach of the United States court system, he had taken steps to try and force Goetz to make restitution through the attachment of his interests in Delaware corporations. Rome's major interest lay in the recovery of the Penn Central's money. A second issue remained: the criminal prosecution of wrongdoers. This was a question for the federal courts.

Before any action could be taken, Wright Patman released his committee's Staff Report. Although alleging a complete probe, the Patman staff relied almost entirely upon Rome's investigation. All the documents printed in Patman's report on the Goetz affair came directly from the file that Rome had forced from Marxer in Liechtenstein in the fall of 1970 [1]. Given Patman's bias, it is not surprising that he used Rome's material to crucify Bevan. He released his Report in March 1971 together with a letter saying "The episode illustrates 'how tangled the personal, financial, and corporate affairs of Penn Central and its management became, thus contributing ultimately to the collapse of the Penn Central." The *Philadelphia Evening Bulletin* reported that Patman's Committee staff with abundant detail "told a story which, in the report's words, 'has all the elements of a film script of international intrigue.' It said Bevan placed $10 million in a Liechtenstein trust under the control of Fidel Goetz, who had been involved with the Penn Central's ill-fated attempt to turn Executive Jet Corporation into a worldwide transportation system.'' The newspaper quoted Patman as saying, "by permitting Penn Central to become so intimately involved in Executive Jet Aviation's illegal ventures, the disclosure of which would have proven extremely embarrassing to both Penn Central and himself, David Bevan placed himself in a position where men far more expert in the art of international manipulation were able to misappropriate $4 million in Penn Central funds'' [2]. Patman sent a copy of his staff report to every appropriate official, including George M. Stafford, chairman of the Interstate Commerce Commission, John M. Mitchell, Attorney-General of the United States, and Governor Milton J. Shapp of Pennsylvania. In his letter of transmittal, Patman "requested that appropriate investigations or inquiries be instituted regarding the facts contained in the report to determine any criminal or other violations that might have occurred'' [3]. He asked that his committee be kept appraised of the results.

The Justice Department placed Assistant United States Attorney C. Oliver Burt in charge of investigating and prosecuting the theft of funds from the Penn Central in Liechtenstein. The case moved very slowly. The grand jury did not finish its deliberations until the middle of 1974, by which time much of the publicity attending the Penn Central's collapse had abated. Despite this, Burt followed the thrust of Patman's contentions. Burt called for and received an indictment of five men: David Bevan, William Gerstnecker, the two Rosenbaums, and Goetz. The German industrialist remained in Europe, where he was beyond the reach of American law. The Justice Department elected to try all four men simultaneously before the same judge and jury. This partially explains the long delay between the indictment in 1974 and the beginning of the trial in February 1977. All four men and their attorneys had to be present, and this proved difficult. Several of the defendants had health problems, and Joseph Rosenbaum's lawyer, William Hundley, also represented a codefendant of Maryland's Governor Marvin Mandel in his prolonged graft trials. The Mandel case continued throughout much of 1976 and made it impossible for Hundley to be in Philadelphia. It was not until after New Year's Day, 1977, that a date could be fixed when all could attend. Even after the trial began, illness struck. Government prosecutor Oliver Burt contracted mumps and the proceedings were further delayed.

The reason for the indictment of the two Rosenbaum brothers is clear enough. Rome's investigation produced more than enough solid evidence to justify it. The question remained as to why David Bevan and William Gerstnecker should also be charged. Edward German asked this question of Oliver Burt, who replied casually, "You cast your net as wide as possible and see how many fish it will bring in'' [4]. Burt's charges were three in number. The first and most important one asserted that Bevan and Gerstnecker had conspired with the Rosenbaums to place money where it could be stolen by Fidel Goetz. The second charge, a variation of the first, alleged that Bevan and Gerstnecker had embezzled, stolen, extracted, or willfully misapplied funds belonging to a common carrier. The third charge was mail fraud, specifically that they had used the United States mails in their illegal acts.

From the beginning, the government faced serious problems in its case against Bevan and Gerstnecker. The first was that neither Bevan nor Gerstnecker received a penny of the stolen funds. Even Patman's staff had never claimed that the former Penn Central officials received any of the money [5]. Oliver Burt was forced to concede this point at the very beginning of his opening remarks in the trial itself. Edward German, Bevan's lawyer, made a big point of this, stating, "On page 1 Mr. Burt started right out by saying, 'I want to make it very clear to you right at the outset that none of these defendants is charged with personally stealing and putting in his own pocket the $4 million that the railroad lost in this case. That is not what the indictment charge is and that is not what we are here to prove' " [6]. If financial gain was not the reason, then what was? Wright Patman had evolved a theory that "David Bevan was anxious to placate Fidel Goetz in view of the damaging story he could tell about Bevan's EJA ventures," and that Bevan had diverted corporate funds "from normal banking channels to attempt to compensate Mr. Goetz for keeping quiet about his financial efforts with an illegal venture" [7]. The very full records available in the files of the Pennsylvania and the Penn Central do not support Patman's assertions. Bevan had no role in Hodge's and Lassiter's overseas involvements, except, when learning of them, to try to have them reversed. The government attorneys apparently concluded that Patman's charges could not stand up to scrutiny in court and abandoned them. What, then, did the government argue was Bevan's motive? A careful reading of Oliver Burt's 38-page opening statement at the trial reveals that he attributed no motive whatever for Bevan's actions. In fact, his statement implies that Bevan expected the $4-million deposit to be returned [8]. The government's failure to find a motive for Bevan's supposed conspiracy was to be one of the weak points in the prosecution's case.

BEVAN'S RELATIONSHIP WITH GOETZ

Actually, in September 1969 Bevan faced problems unrelated to those discussed at the trial. This was the time when Saunders finally decided to face up to Perlman's failure to operate the railroad and to bring in a new president, Paul Gorman. Bevan had already tried to resign his position with the railroad and had agreed to stay on only until his normal retirement date in late 1971. In the fall of 1969, he confronted a railroad that was both accumulating enormous operating deficits and running perilously close "to exhausting its capacity to borrow." Bevan had faith that the Penn Central could surmount its crisis if a good professional business manager could be found, and he thought the company had discovered such a person in Gorman. The problem for Bevan was to buy time so that Gorman could bring the railroad's operating losses under control.

When William Gerstnecker worked out the Berliner Bank loan, Bevan could only be pleased. He felt that this contact might smooth a way for further European borrowings. His investigations in the New York banking community gave him no reason to distrust Fidel Goetz. Joseph Rosenbaum suggested to Gerstnecker that the $4 million be placed in a deutschmark account at a Goetz institution as a token gesture in recognition of Goetz's alleged cooperation in reversing the European transactions of Hodge and Lassiter. Bevan saw no basic objection, but he did insist that the funds be placed in trust for the railroad. His main concern was to protect the railroad against the devaluation of the United States dollar against the mark, an event that did occur. The charge to the First Financial Trust was that "by your signature below, you are evidencing your agreement that such funds are to be held in trust and invested and reinvested for our account, to the extent not advanced to us for the rehabilitation of equipment to be leased to Penn Central Transportation Company or for the payment of principal or interest on the aforesaid loan." The instructions also specified that First Financial Trust was to protect the railroad against a dollar devaluation.

Everything would have been fine had the First Financial Trust been a reputable bank. The real culpability on the part of Gerstnecker, to whom Bevan had delegated full authority to consummate the loan, was his failure to investigate the nature of First Financial Trust. There were several reasons for this omission. Most important, both Bevan and Gerstnecker mistakenly trusted Fidel Goetz. And there were still other factors. In September 1969, the Penn Central was in turmoil. Perlman, the president, was being removed in favor of a new man, Gorman. Bevan's own immediate subordinate, Gerstnecker, had resigned and a new replacement had to be trained. Bevan's attention was occupied in trying to produce a reliable income budget for Gorman and at the same time to raise the necessary money to sustain the railroad through its most severe crisis. For Bevan, the Berliner Bank loan and the arrangement for the investment of $4 million in Europe did not hold a high priority.

The crux of the government's case was whether or not, when Bevan and Gerstnecker authorized the placement of money in First Financial Trust, they knew that it was not a bank but merely a device to siphon money into Goetz's pocket. This was a vital question also for Edwin Rome. The outside counsel for the Penn Central's trustees had many conversations with Bevan, probing every aspect of the former chief financial officer's relation with Goetz. Rome particularly asked whether Bevan had promised to replace the money Goetz lost in reversing the transactions involving Executive Jet. Rome testified before the grand jury [9]:

> I could summarize that which represents Mr. Bevan's consistent story in all the discussions that I have had with him. He has said that Goetz was of help in connection with the reversal of the Executive Jet situation; that as a result he felt that Goetz was going to be able to make a profit on the deal in the sense that, if Goetz acquired these foreign aviation rights, they would be profitable things, because they would have been profitable had Executive Jet Aviation been able to hold on to them. But since the law wasn't able to permit it, somebody else was going to pursue a good business deal, and, therefore Goetz would have a good business opportunity.
>
> But if Goetz did not, he, Bevan, felt another opportunity would in due course present itself, where a business deal could be made available in which Goetz could participate to seek profit. By way of illustration: Goetz had a textile empire in Germany. Penn Central Transportation Company at the time, as one of his diversification efforts, was talking about acquiring Kayser-Roth, a clothing company here in the United States. Goetz was aware of that because it was publicized internationally. Goetz got in touch with Penn Central to find out if Penn Central was interested in acquiring one of Goetz's textile factories. But that never came about. But that was the kind of thing that was involved. But Penn Central was involved with Great Southwest Corporation. It was going to be very profitable. Goetz was interested in buying stock in that company and therefore, Bevan thought that if he suffered a loss on the reversal of the aviation deal, if he were to buy stock in Great Southwest which was going up, in due course he would make it back. But Bevan and Gertsnecker had always said they never gave any authorization to Goetz or to Rosenbaum or to anybody else to turn this money over to Goetz.

Rome had tried to check Bevan's testimony in every possible way. He asked Francis Rosenbaum about it. Rome said that Francis confirmed that neither Bevan nor Gerstnecker knew the truth about First Financial Trust [10]. Rome also testified that all the railroad officials with whom he dealt thought initially that First Financial Trust was a bank. He told the grand jury "when the $10 million became available, it had been deposited in an entity in Liechtenstein called First Financial Trust, which, as I then learned, people within the railroad felt was a bank, as one would hear the name over here of X Bank and Trust Company." Earlier, Burt, the government attorney, had asked, "Did Mr. Bevan indicate that it was his belief that it was a bank?" Rome had responded, "Yes" [11].

FRANCIS ROSENBAUM'S POSITION

It is significant that Francis Rosenbaum consistently maintained that he and Goetz only knew of the nature of the First Financial Trust. His story was that he did not realize until he got to Liechtenstein that he would be forced to turn over the money to Goetz. There are a number of questions about Francis's testimony. He gave his account in a way that absolved his brother from any criminal responsibility, claiming that Joseph had learned what had happened only after the fact. Joseph Rosenbaum's story was that he acted to try to protect his brother as much as possible. He asserted that he did not tell Rome the truth about the First Financial Trust initially because he hoped to convince Goetz to make restitution of the money and therefore stop the investigation. The Rosenbaums' testimony on these two points may be self-serving. It is difficult to see, however, how Francis Rosenbaum benefited from his denial that Bevan and Gerstnecker were in on the plot. Quite the contrary. He had almost everything to gain by implicating Bevan. The government attorneys obviously wanted to convict Bevan, and they might very well have let Francis off with a light sentence if he helped convict the Penn Central's former chief financial officer. The government's problem was that Francis Rosenbaum did not change his story and that Edwin Rome believed what Bevan and Gerstnecker told him.

THE TRIAL

The trial of Bevan, Gerstnecker, and the Rosenbaums began in mid-February 1977, in Philadelphia before Judge J. William Ditter, Jr. The prosecution went through 11 days of testimony and argument, finally concluding on March 11. From the beginning, prosecutor Burt recognized the problems that beset his side of the case. He lacked any evidence of conspiracy. Everything was circumstantial. Burt emphasized that Francis Rosenbaum had been present when Gerstnecker made the final arrangement for the Berliner Bank loan and that the conference took place in Bevan's office. Even this point lost its punch when witnesses testified that Bevan did not take part in the proceedings.

Most of the early part of the trial never mentioned any conspiracy at all. For the first 4 days, witnesses discussed a possible technical violation of an Interstate Commerce Commission (ICC) regulation that a railroad needed approval to give its note. It was to overcome this problem that Gerstnecker handled the transaction through Penn Central's wholly owned subsidiary, the American Contract Company, which was not a railroad. The witnesses discussed whether this procedure involved a violation of ICC regulations, and they disagreed. The whole issue was irrelevant to the trial, anyway. In fact, the Interstate Commerce Commission had received a copy of the Patman Report, had thoroughly investigated the Penn Central in 1970 and 1971, and had made no charge of a violation of these rules, which would be a misdemeanor. It did not take Edward German, Bevan's attorney, long to unmask Burt's strategy. He complained to Judge Ditter, quoting an article in the *Philadelphia Bulletin* saying that "this case is being tried, not on the charges against these defendants, but on the collateral issue, and this jury is being misled into believing there is a lot of strange things that went on that didn't go on" [12]. At one point during the proceedings, German taunted Burt by saying that the prosecutor was following the old strategy of "If you don't have a case, try another case."

The prosecution, however, had one surprise. This was the testimony of Dr. Wolfgang Muller, an attorney in Dr. Peter Marxer's Liechtenstein law office. Muller came to Philadelphia on October 18, 1970, to tell Edwin Rome the status of the First Financial Trust. It was in response to his statements that Rome placed a transatlantic call to Dr. Marxer. Rome testified that Marxer himself gave the impression that the missing $4 million was still in the First Financial Trust [13]. Muller never appeared before the grand jury that indicted Bevan, Gerstnecker, the Rosenbaums, and Goetz. However, unbeknownst to the defense, the government had sent Richard Pointer, a postal inspector, to Europe to interview Muller. Pointer talked to Muller at Feldkirch, Austria, on August 15, 1974. At that time Muller told a story which, if true, would have been highly damaging to Bevan. He said that during his October 1970 visit to the United States, he informed Edwin Rome that Dr. Marxer's law firm was innocent of any wrongdoing in the case of First Financial Trust. Muller said that when he arrived in Washington, he was met by Colonel Joe Rosenbaum and driven to his house, where he met Bevan and German. He recalled a conversation in Rosenbaum's living room during which Rosenbaum asked him "to tell Ed Rome that he [Joe Rosenbaum] was not involved in the First Financial Trust matter." Muller alleged that Joe Rosenbaum wanted him to tell "Ed Rome 'the $4 million was available but subject to lien,' although all present were aware the money was not available." Muller added that "both Bevan and German were present when Rosenbaum said this and they did not contradict what Rosenbaum said." He further claimed that he "was under the impression that Rosenbaum was in a 'difficult situation.' " He then said that he "took a 'fast train' to Philadelphia, Pa., where he met with Ed Rome." At the meeting with Rome, Muller said that "the money was available but subject to a lien." Neither Joseph Rosenbaum, David Bevan, nor German, who were present, "disputed this." Muller stated that he then left Philadelphia for Miami, where Rosenbaum had arranged hotel accommodations. In Miami, he said, he had pangs of conscience about the lies he had told Rome. He claimed that "on several occasions he wanted to call Ed Rome and tell him the truth as to what happened to the $4 million but he was concerned about his safety. . . . He thought Rosenbaum, Bevan, and German were connected with the Mafia." Muller further stated that he was "unfamiliar with the telephone system in the United States of America" [14].

Dr. Muller did not testify before the 1974 grand jury that indicted Bevan. However, Postal Inspector Pointer read the results of his interview into the record. His account was certainly one of the factors that helped persuade the grand jury to indict Bevan. Because the entire grand jury proceedings were secret, German and Bevan remained ignorant of Pointer's interview with Muller.

The government planned to produce Wolfgang Muller as a surprise witness at Bevan's trial, but it was forced to telegraph its punch because of the Jencks Act. In *Jencks v. United States*, the Supreme Court ruled that defendants had the right to receive, for impeachment purposes, declarations made to government agents by government witnesses during investigations that occured prior to the trial. The defense was to receive such evidence at the time of cross-examination. The Jencks ruling had been further strengthened by being enacted into law by Congress [15]. In the case against Bevan, the court ruled that the government had to supply German with "voluminous" material at least 2 weeks in advance. However, the government had to produce short material only the evening before calling a witness.

Edward German clearly recalled the government strategy. One day during the trial, the government handed him the two-and-a-half-page typed transcript of Richard Pointer's interview with Dr. Muller. This was to be preparatory to Muller's testimony on the following day. German read the statement and could hardly believe his eyes. He remembered meeting with Rosenbaum, Muller, and Bevan in Joe Rosenbaum's Washington house on October 18, 1970, with Rome's full knowledge. He also recalled the meeting the following day in Rome's Philadelphia office. German viewed Muller as "a young handsome lawyer who had a language difficulty since he spoke English with a decided accent." His memory of the meeting was that Dr. Muller insisted that the Penn Central's agreement with First Financial Trust "was intact and that the funds were still available." German remembered that most of the evening at Rosenbaum's home was spent "having a couple of cocktails"; there was "little or no discussion concerning the case." As a matter of fact, "Dr. Muller was interested in making the meeting the following day as short as possible, as he had a young lady lined up in Florida with whom he was going to spend the following week." German was also familiar with the meeting in Rome's office where Muller told the same story he had told the night before. "As a matter of fact, in the presence of all of us, Ed Rome placed a call to Dr. Peter Marxer and he confirmed that the trust was inviolate and that Goetz was asserting a lien against the funds." It was Rome's call to Dr. Marxer that brought into question Muller's entire statement. Rome testified that Marxer backed Muller's assertion that the Penn Central's money was still in the First Financial Trust subject to a lien by Goetz. Marxer's quick support of Muller indicates that a story must have been worked out by Marxer and Muller before the latter left Vaduz. If this were true, neither Bevan nor German could have possibly been involved because neither had met Marxer or Muller at the time. Joseph Rosenbaum's position was different. He was actively trying to deceive Rome about the First Financial Trust. However, his statements to Rome after the trustee's special counsel discovered the truth on his visit to Liechtenstein indicate that Rosenbaum was also trying to fool Bevan and German as well. This would make it most unlikely that he would try to arrange Muller's statements to Rome in front of Bevan and his lawyer.

The Jencks material particularly disturbed German because Muller had supposedly told Pointer that "in the presence of Bevan and German, Rosenbaum told Muller what to say." If this were true, German and Bevan were guilty of subornation of perjury. Muller claimed he acted because he thought Rosenbaum, Bevan, and German were part of the Mafia and he feared for his life.

When German first read this material, he "found it rather hilarious." On second thought, his blood pressure "went up about 50 points." He was particularly outraged because the government provided no explanation of why it had withheld for 2½ years Richard Pointer's statement casting doubt on German's reputation as a lawyer. German regarded Muller's testimony as a pack of lies contradicted by the statements of one of the government's most important witnesses, Edwin Rome. German felt the government's attempt to include Muller's statement was a "dirty trick," and found it shocking. "As a lifelong conservative Republican," German "had never believed the accusations directed toward the law enforcement agencies until he had seen at first hand how far they would go in their attempts to get a conviction" [16].

Furthermore, German had good reasons to suspect the accuracy of Postal Inspector Pointer's account of the Muller interview. Earlier in the trial, also as part of the Jencks material, the government had given German a transcript of a May 1, 1974, interview Pointer had with Heinz Gottwald, a senior vice-president of the Chemical Bank's International Division. Gottwald was a key government witness because after the Penn Central consummated the loan with the Berliner Bank, the railroad deposited the DM40 million in the Chemical Bank in Frankfurt, Germany, which in turn transferred the funds to First Financial Trust in Liechtenstein. According to Pointer, Gottwald clearly recalled the transfer of funds from the Chemical Bank to First Financial Trust as though it had happened yesterday. Gottwald said "that Peter

Schumann [a bank official] had received a telephone call from Loder of Penn Central who advised him to transfer the loan proceeds of $10 million to First Financial Trust in Liechtenstein. Gottwald was surprised to learn that the money was to be disbursed in Liechtenstein since he knew that there was no such bank in Liechtenstein as First Financial Trust; [and] he told Schumann that the Chemical Bank wanted to do the conversion [change the money from marks to dollars]." At that point, Gottwald, miffed because he feared the Chemical Bank would lose out on the conversion, telephoned David Bevan. Gottwald allegedly recalled "that he told Bevan that First Financial Trust was not a bank." He remembered that "Bevan gave him the brush-off by saying that this had been decided 2 months ago and that Gottwald should talk to Gerstnecker about it" [17]. Gottwald then supposedly said that Bevan "had his call transferred to Gerstnecker." Gottwald allegedly told Gerstnecker "that First Financial Trust was not a bank and that the Chemical Bank would like to have the opportunity to bid on the conversion." If true, this testimony would have devastated Bevan because he consistently maintained that he believed First Financial Trust was a legitimate financial institution. This also had been Gerstnecker's position.

When German read Pointer's summary of Gottwald's testimony, he was worried. However, also included in the Jencks material was a copy of Gottwald's testimony before the United States grand jury on Friday, May 17, 1974. Pointer claimed that Gottwald was very certain that he had told Bevan First Financial Trust was not a bank. He concluded, "I asked Mr. Gottwald to tell me again what he recalled about his telephone conversation with Bevan and Gerstnecker on September 18 (1969), and he repeated just what he told me earlier."

Gottwald's testimony under oath before the grand jury was quite different, however. The government's attorney, Oliver Burt, asked Gottwald about it [18].

Q. Now do you recall that on the day you talked to David Bevan after Peter Schumann came into your office, did you not, in fact, tell Mr. Bevan, among other things, that First Financial Trust was not a bank, that there were only two banks in Liechtenstein, the Bank in Liechtenstein and the Bank of Liechtenstein?

A. Well, I know that Mr. Pointer put it down that way, but I tell you, I cannot swear that I put it to him that way, that First Financial Trust—all I did was —First Financial Trust was mentioned to me by Mr. Peter Schumann. Whether I mentioned it—my main concern was with Bevan to get the conversion and ask him why marks were being transferred to Vaduz.

Later on, Oliver Burt again attempted to have Gottwald say that he had told Bevan that First Financial Trust was not a bank.

Q. And it may well then have been something that you mentioned to him; is that not correct?

A. Could be. Could be.

Q. You are not willing to say positively that you did not mention it to him, are you?

A. No. I tell you—

Q. Can you answer that yes or no?

A. I am not positive.

Q. Are you willing to say positively that you did not tell Bevan during that telephone conversation that First Financial was not a bank?

A. No.

Q. You cannot say?

A. Either way, either way. If you say it was on my mind, obviously it was on my mind, because it was in the morning, but I would not say positively that I mentioned it nor can I positively say that I didn't mention it, you know.

Government attorney Oliver Burt was obviously concerned that Gottwald's grand jury testimony did not support Pointer's account and he questioned him still further. But Gottwald steadfastly refused to support Pointer's statement [19]. Finally, when Gottwald testified at the trial, he did not claim to have told either Bevan or Gerstnecker that First Financial Trust was not a bank [20].

In view of the record and his own knowledge of events, Edward German regarded the government's use of Pointer's statements as another "dirty trick." Consequently, Bevan's attorney asked for an immediate meeting with Judge Ditter. German told the judge that he "would have to move for a mistrial, since it would be necessary for me to be a witness in the case." Furthermore, he demanded that the court call Muller as a witness "so that his testimony would be under oath, then call Joe Rosenbaum, Dave Bevan, Ed Rome," and himself so that the truth could be determined. German told the judge that he intended to move that the court lift Dr. Muller's passport and charge him with perjury. Judge Ditter responded that he did not know whether he had the authority to take Muller's passport, and German did not know either. However, German responded that the court had a problem because he was making the motion verbally and would put it in writing the following day.

Immediately, the government attorneys went into a huddle and then asked German what would satisfy him "so far as Dr. Muller was concerned." He told them that if they called Muller as a witness, they were not to ask

questions concerning either Bevan or himself. The government agreed to the
condition, but Joe Rosenbaum's counsel would not approve since it would
allow the prosecution to ask questions about his client. The government
refused to grant Joe Rosenbaum any concession, and since it was getting late,
Judge Ditter proposed that the court adjourn and the matter be settled on
the following day. At this point, German told the court it was his intention
to obtain his own counsel to represent him if the matter was not disposed
immediately. The government attorneys went into another conference and
agreed not to call Dr. Muller as a witness for any purpose. In discussing this
incident with the author, German warned that any conclusion he might draw
would be prejudiced, and the lawyer suggested that I (the author) "might
draw my own conclusions with respect to the government's actions" [21].

ACQUITTAL

Prosecutor Burt's decision not to use Muller as a witness ended any hope of
proving that Bevan knew of the plot to divert funds from the railroad. The
prosecution knew that Edwin Rome believed Bevan and Gerstnecker were
innocent of any criminal wrongdoing, but it had to put Rome on the stand
in order to have a chance to convict the Rosenbaums. In his direct examination, Burt avoided asking Rome questions that might exonerate Bevan or
Gerstnecker. It was Rome's answers on cross-examination that destroyed the
prosecution's case. German began his examination thus [22].

Q. It has been mentioned that you met with Bevan and me from time to time.

A. Yes, sir.

Q. And isn't it a fact—well, is it a fact that Mr. Bevan was cooperative with
    you at all times?

A. From the very beginning.

Q. And was he at all evasive? Did he give you answers that seemed to be
    candid? Did he avoid answering questions?

A. Mr. Bevan never avoided answering any questions about any matter which
    I ever took up with him at any time from the beginning of our assignment
    right straight through.

Q. And you knew that I was meeting with others than you, as was Mr. Bevan
    from time to time in connection with the Berliner Bank and other mat-
    ters?

A. Yes, sir.

Q. And was there anything sinister or suspicious about my being at these
    meetings with you or Mr. Bevan?

A. On the contrary. Far from being anything sinister about it, it was something that I welcomed and, moreover, it was, in my judgment and in the view of persons with whom I worked, a further manifestation of the cooperation that was being proffered by Mr. Bevan and yourself.

Q. Mr. Rome, you have talked about the meeting that we had in Liechtenstein which, if my memory serves me right, was October 29 and 28 or thereabouts.

A. Yes, sir.

Q. The latter part of October?

A. 1970.

Q. And you mentioned, I guess, on the morning of the twenty-eighth—you got there on the twenty-seventh—that we had a meeting with Mr. Rosenbaum which lasted from 1 A.M. until 4 A.M.

A. Yes, sir.

The Court: This was Mr. Joseph Rosenbaum?

A. Mr. Joseph Rosenbaum, Yes, I'm sorry.

Q. And during that meeting did Mr. Rosenbaum say that this was the first time that he was telling the full story of what happened to the money?

A. Indeed he did say so.

Q. And did he not make it clear that Mr. Bevan did not know until that point what had happened to the money?

A. Yes, sir.

Q. And did he not make it clear that at the time that the money went over there, Mr. Bevan did not know that the money would not be coming back?

A. He did make it clear.

The Court: He did?

A. He did.

Q. And did he not make it clear that this was the first time that Mr. Bevan would have any knowledge that First Financial Trust was owned by him?

A. Yes, sir.

Q. Joseph Rosenbaum and Frank Rosenbaum?

A. Yes, sir.

Q. And did he not make it clear for the first time that the railroad or Mr. Bevan could have no knowledge of the fact that First Financial Trust was not a bank?

A. Yes, sir.

The government rested its case on March 11. At this point Edward German joined with Gerstnecker's lawyer, Robert W. Sayre, to ask that all charges be dropped against the former Penn Central officials. The Rosenbaums made similar motions. If the judge granted these motions, the defendants would not even have to put on a case nor would the issue go to the jury. German summarized the problem of the prosecution in the case of his client, David Bevan [23]:

> The trial . . . has been one where the government has failed to prove a conspiracy and they have tried their best to do so, strictly on the basis of guilt by association, by getting into a purported ICC violation which even John Young [a prosecution witness] would not support, a perhaps-CAB violation, and, of course, we have heard more about Chromcraft than we have [heard about] any criminal conduct in this case on the part of even Mr. Frank Rosenbaum, who has been, I think, very candid.

German continued that it was an unusual conspiracy case.

> Normally in such violations, one coconspirator comes forward to admit, "Yes, I did something wrong." He has made a deal with the government for which he has gotten a great benefit in order to indict other people.

> In this case Frank Rosenbaum has been completely candid. He has gotten absolutely no benefit out of it. He has stuck his neck way out . . . and as a result he has left the jury and the court, I think, with the clear picture of no conspiracy because he has said, "Yes, I did it," and he has said that without getting any benefit, without making any deal. He said, "I did it and I had a reason for doing it and these other guys had nothing to do with it," and he has no reason to protect any of them.

The prosecution and the defense finished their arguments after dinner. Judge Ditter announced that he would retire, examine the arguments, and then announce his decision. It was not until after 10 P.M. that the court reconvened. Then the court announced, "So far as Mr. Bevan is concerned, I will grant the motion for judgment of acquittal. So far as Mr. Gerstnecker is concerned, I will grant the motion for judgment of acquittal. So far as Mr. Joseph Rosenbaum is concerned, I will refuse it" [24].

Thus, in a few seconds, Bevan's long ordeal came to an end. He and Edward German walked out of the courtroom and over to the nearby Hotel Benjamin Franklin and had a drink. The newspapers took scant note of Bevan's day in court. On March 13, 1977, the *Philadelphia Sunday Bulletin,* which for days had headlined Patman's charges augmented with numerous pictures, ran a modest 600-word article in the Sunday edition entitled "2 Ex-Pennsy Aides Acquitted in Conspiracy." Monday's *New York Times* put the story on page 43 and headed it "2 Ex-Penn Central Aides Are Free of All Charges." It did run pictures of both Bevan and Gerstnecker, but the article contained little more information than appeared in the *Philadelphia Sunday Bulletin.*

Bevan went home free of the burdens of his career for the first time since the collapse of the Penn Central in June 1970. He could watch with interest the results of the trial in Judge Ditter's courtroom of the remaining two defendants, Francis and Joseph Rosenbaum. Finally, the case went to the jury, which convicted Francis Rosenbaum but acquitted his brother Joseph. So ended the saga of the Penn Central's missing $4 million.

REFERENCES

1. *The Penn Central Failure and the Role of Financial Institutions,* Staff Report of the Committee on Banking and Currency, 92d Congress, First Session, House of Representatives, January 3, 1972, especially pp. 259–269. Hereafter cited as the Patman Report.

2. *Philadelphia Evening Bulletin,* March 11, 1971.

3. Patman Report, p. 269.

4. Edward German, statement to author.

5. See Patman Report, Bevan's role, pp. 268–269.

6. *United States of America vs. Joseph H. Rosenbaum,* et al.: Criminal Action No. 74-514 in the United States District Court for the Eastern District of Pennsylvania, Second Day, Philadelphia, February 24, 1977, pp. 60–61. Hereafter cited as *United States vs. Rosenbaum.*

7. Patman Report, pp. 263, 268.

8. *United States vs. Rosenbaum,* C. Oliver Burt's opening statement, February 22, 1977, pp. 33–34.

9. Edwin P. Rome, testimony before the United States Grand Jury in the United States District Court for the Eastern District of Pennsylvania, May 29, 1974, pp. 67–68. Hereafter cited as Rome Grand Jury Testimony.

10. Ibid., pp. 69–70.

11. Ibid., p. 9.

12. *United States vs. Rosenbaum,* Fifth Day, pp. 6–7.

13. Rome Grand Jury Testimony, p. 14.

14. Quotations from Richard Pointer's interview with Dr. Muller at Feldkirch, Austria, August 15, 1975. This statement was part of the Jencks material handed to German during the trial.

15. United States Code 3500.

16.   Quotations from Edward German's statement to author.

17.   R. Pointer, Memorandum of interview with Heinz Gottwald at his residence on May 1, 1974, included in the Jencks material given to Edward German during the trial.

18.   Heinz Gottwald, Testimony, May 17, 1974, in the United States District Court for the Eastern District of Pennsylvania United States Grand Jury, pp. 17, 18–19.

19.   Ibid., pp. 23–24.

20.   *United States vs. Rosenbaum,* Seventh Day, pp. 15–18.

21.   Quotation from German's statement to author.

22.   *United States v. Rosenbaum,* Ninth Day, pp. 27–30.

23.   Ibid., Eleventh Day, pp. 51–52.

24.   Ibid., p. 143.

Appendix A
THE PENSION FUND

The pension fund of the Penn Central had nothing to do with the railroad's collapse. It remained solvent and was able to meet all its obligations. The only reason to include material on it is that the allegations made by the Patman Committee have undoubtedly misled some observers to connect the management of the pension fund with the railroad's problems. The Patman Report is unfortunate in another way. It totally obscures the real issues involved in the management of private pension plans.

SOME BASIC QUESTIONS

No reader of the Patman Committee's Staff Report could possibly have a favorable view of David Bevan's stewardship of the railroad's pension fund. The Staff Report confined itself mostly to questions of a broad policy nature that can be classified into three major areas. First, should a company manage its own pension fund or turn it over to a bank or some other outside managers? Second, should pension contributions be invested in the securities of the company itself? Third, is it ethical for pension monies to be invested in securities in which the nominal head of the fund or any company officer or director has an interest?

These policy questions are important; but there is an even more significant aspect to a pension fund, and that is, its results. It is quite possible to make all the right policy decisions and still have an unsuccessful fund. The Penn Central's employees who were covered by the pension fund were most interested in the following questions. First, could the pension fund pay its benefits? Second, were the fund's assets equal to its liabilities, or, phrased differently, was it fully funded? Third, did the collapse of the railroad have an adverse effect on pension rights? It is significant that Patman's staff did not even ask these questions, let alone attempt to answer them. It is possible only to speculate why the questions were not asked. However, it is clear that the answers were favorable to David Bevan and Robert Haslett. Bevan was proud that when the Penn Central collapsed, the pension fund was not affected and was able to meet every obligation. This result was impressive because, when Bevan took responsibility for pensions in 1951, he inherited a system that had large unfunded liabilities. When he left the railroad, the fund was fully financed. Moreover, its sound condition had been achieved while pension benefits had been substantially increased at no cost to the railroad. In summary, Bevan took an unsound plan and made it solvent, increased benefits, and at the same time reduced the financial burden carried by the railroad.

BEVAN'S REFORM OF THE
SUPPLEMENTAL PENSION FUND

When David Bevan joined the Pennsylvania Railroad in 1951, he became chairman of the managers of pensions. His main responsibility in this area was for the Supplemental Pension Plan. The purpose of this plan was to give augmented pension benefits to union and nonunion (nonagreement) railroad employees beyond those already provided under the Railroad Retirement Act. In the beginning, participants in the plan made contributions from their salaries. As of December 31, 1969, the program covered 21,700 active employees and paid benefits to 15,200 retirees [1].

When Bevan assumed responsibility for the fund, he found approximately 97 percent of its assets were in fixed-income securities (see Figure A-1). He believed that fixed-income securities did not appreciate in an inflationary economy and were unsuited for a retirement fund. Moreover, the fund contained 32 percent of its assets in the debt of the Pennsylvania Railroad and its subsidiaries. While in 1951 Bevan had no idea that the railroad would ever become insolvent, he thought it was bad practice to risk so much of the fund's assets in a single venture. Worst of all, the pension plan had unfunded liabilities of $51,722,000, or almost twice the fund's assets of $26,211,000. The only way an unfunded liability could be met was through direct contributions from the railroad itself. (See Table A-1.) If the plan had not moved toward full funding, it would depend largely on the economic health of the railroad to meet its obligations. In other words, had the Penn Central's plan not been fully funded at the time of the corporation's collapse, the members of the pension fund would have been seriously affected.

Bevan immediately gave the following goals high priority. First, he desired to reduce the plan's unfunded liability. Second, he wanted to eliminate the fund's heavy dependence upon the success of the Pennsylvania Railroad. Third, he wanted to reduce the cost of the fund to the railroad, and finally, he aimed to make the fund better able to cope with inflation. He proposed to accomplish these goals by changing the fund's investment philosophy. This meant a major shift out of fixed-income securities into common stocks. However, Bevan did not propose to rely on common stocks alone. He thought the ratio should merely be changed so that common stocks would represent between one-half and two-thirds of the investment portfolio. At the same time, he also desired wide diversification in the investment portfolio to minimize risk.

Bevan moved carefully. He gradually replaced fixed-income holdings, and by 1968 the fund had 65.9 percent of its investments in common shares and 34.1 percent in fixed-income securities, largely bonds. Unfunded liability climbed initially, reaching a peak of more than $96 million in 1956 (see

Figure A-2 and Table A-1). However, in 1957 unfunded liability began to drop, and by 1964 the fund showed its first surplus, which amounted to $7,346,000. The unfunded liability rose in 1965 and 1966, but this rise was due mainly to a substantial increase in benefits. As of February 1, 1965, the plan became noncontributory for all nonunion members. By 1967, the fund was doing so well that, upon Bevan's recommendation, the pensions of all members who retired on or before November 1, 1967, were increased by 10 percent. This change was designed to help retired employees cope with inflation. The increase was accomplished without increasing railroad contributions and was possible solely on the basis of the investment records. Even with these increased benefits, the plan had a surplus of assets over liabilities at the end of 1968.

THE PENSION FUND'S INVESTMENTS IN PENN CENTRAL–RELATED SECURITIES

Simultaneously, Bevan reduced the pension fund's investments in the securities of the Pennsylvania Railroad and its affiliated companies. These had amounted to about one-third of the portfolio on December 31, 1950, but accounted for approximately 10 percent in 1969. It is ironic that the Patman staff members severely criticized Bevan for maintaining any investments in railroad securities at all. They wrote, "There is another aspect to the pension fund's investments that raises a serious ethical question. The pension plan had investments in the railroad itself and certain of the railroad's subsidiaries." The Patman Report then commented that the investments "illustrate, once again, the excesses that can occur when the employees' pension fund is controlled by the company. Bevan, as chief financial officer of the railroad, was responsible for marketing the railroad's debt paper. Through his control of the pension plan, he could use the employees' pension fund to purchase stock and debt paper of the railroad and its subsidiaries." The Report observed that this was "a very convenient situation for the railroad," but asked, "How fair is it to the pension plan's beneficiaries? Was it right to invest the employees' pension fund in the mismanaged, financially failing railroad?" [2]

The Patman Report gave the impression that the pension fund had been severely damaged by Bevan's investment policy, especially the monies invested in the railroad and its affiliated companies. In reality, this was not true. The summary provided by Patman lists Penn Central–related securities amounting to $35,781,124, or approximately 10 percent of the fund's assets. But Patman's Staff Report neglects to say that most of these securities survived the railroad's collapse and maintained their value. The fund held no Penn Central stock. Patman's staff listed

$4,460,000 of preferred stock in the Wabash Railroad, which in 1969 had been absorbed by the financially strong Norfolk & Western Railroad and had no affiliation with the Pennsylvania whatsoever. Approximately $15 million of the Penn Central debt paper held by the fund was of the Pennsylvania Car Leasing Company. In this case, the pension fund held liens against railroad equipment that could have been foreclosed and sold had not the trustees of the Penn Central continued to make payments. Another $7,287,000 was in the debt of the Great Southwest Corporation which, although it experienced financial problems after the railroad collapsed, did not default on its debt. The fund held minor amounts of lease obligations (less than $500,000) of the securities of the United New Jersey Railroad & Canal Company and the Philadelphia, Baltimore & Washington Railroad. These obligations had been acquired before Bevan became the manager of the pension fund and had not yet been liquidated. The pension fund held comparatively little of the debt paper of the parent Penn Central and Pennsylvania Railroad companies. This holding amounted to approximately $4.3 million. Despite the railroad's collapse, even this paper was never worthless. Immediately after the Penn Central's bankruptcy, all its debt depreciated rapidly on the market. However, if the Penn Central's fund held onto these securities, they would regain much of their value; as of 1978, it appeared that they might regain all of it [3]. Even the $3,182,000 invested in the preferred and common stock of the Great Southwest Corporation was not a total loss. In summary, of the $35,787,000 pension fund monies invested in the Penn Central or its subsidiary companies, well over $27 million survived the crash of the corporation. Also, it is quite possible at this writing that if these securities are held they will shortly be worth at least their value prior to the railroad's collapse. Thus, the portion of employees' retirement funds invested in the Penn Central were placed in securities that were relatively free of risk even when the system collapsed financially.

In April 1969, Bevan summarized his management of the Penn Central pension fund for the company's board of directors. His memorandum, with supporting tables and graphs, is reproduced here. The Patman Committee never challenged its facts—and the fund's continued solvency is the best testimony to the memorandum's accuracy.

MEMORANDUM   April 21, 1969

This memorandum contains the highlights of the administration of our Pension Fund since I became Chairman of the Managers of Pensions 18 years ago. Attached is certain backup information which gives additional details in connection with the operation of the Fund. [See Figures A1 and A2 and Tables A1, A2, and A-3.]

At the end of 1950, the Fund at cost totaled $22,359,000 and the market totaled $22,001,000, slightly less. Approximately 97 percent was invested in fixed-income securities, preferred stocks and bonds, and 3 percent in common stocks. At the end of 1968, on a cost basis, the Fund aggregated $268 million and on a market basis, $375 million. On a cost basis, approximately one-half was invested in bonds and preferred stocks and one-half in common stocks. On a market basis, 34 percent was invested in bonds and preferred stocks and 66 percent in common stocks.

During this period, the unfunded liability of the Pension Fund reached a peak of $96,462,000 in 1956, as contrasted to total assets in the Fund of $68,-173,000 at that time. Since then, increased benefits built into the plan to make it competitive with other pension funds have added estimated actuarial liabilities of $53.4 million. Despite this, at the end of 1968, on an estimated basis, there was an overfunding of the plan on a market basis of $8.2 million, or a net overall improvement in the unfunded liability of $158 million covering a period of 12 years.

Charges to operating expenses for current and past service on an actuarial basis reached a peak in 1958 of $9,700,000 and have been reduced to an all-time low of $1,147,000 in 1968. It should be noted that the last figure is for the combined Penn Central Railroad as contrasted to $9,700,000 in 1958, charges solely for the Pennsylvania Railroad.

Finally, as of December 31, 1950, on a cost basis, 32 percent of the Fund was invested in Pennsylvania Railroad or affiliated company securities and, as of February 28, 1969, on the same basis, ownership in company and affiliated securities had been reduced to 7 percent.

David C. Bevan

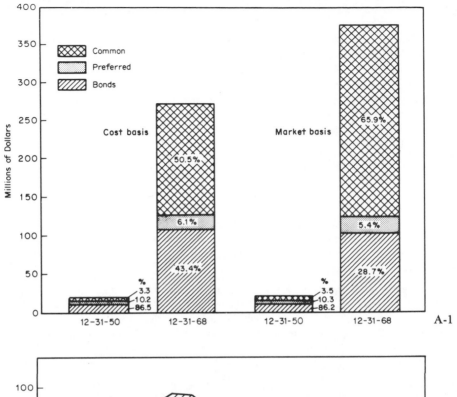

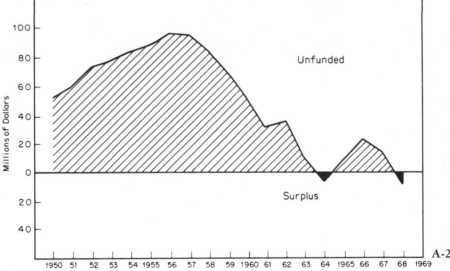

Figure A-1.　The Penn Central system plan for supplemental pensions, showing the composition of securities in the pension fund on December 31 of 1950 and 1968. (Data for the Pennsylvania Railroad through 1967. The 1968 figures include the former New York Central Plan.) **Figure A-2.**　The Penn Central system plan for supplemental pensions—unfunded liability for 1950 to 1968, inclusive. (Data for the Pennsylvania Railroad through 1967. The 1968 figures include the former New York Central Plan.)

TABLE A-1. Penn Central System Plan for Supplemental Pensions: Unfunded Liability* (*in thousands of dollars*)

December 31	All companies	December 31	All companies
1950	$ 51,722	1960	52,505
1951	60,020	1961	30,752
1952	74,578	1962	35,561
1953	77,541	1963	9,052
1954	81,617	1964	(7,346)†
1955	85,738	1965	7,316
1956	96,462	1966	22,234
1957	95,189	1967	14,746
1958	82,969	1968	(8,181)†
1959	68,169		

SOURCE: Secretary, Managers of Pensions, April 1, 1969.

*Pennsylvania Railroad only, through 1967. In 1968, figures include former New York Central Funded Plan.

†Surplus.

TABLE A-2. Comparison of Penn Central Supplemental Pension Fund with One Educational Institution and Common Trust Funds in Philadelphia and New York Banks

Date	Pennsylvania Railroad–Penn Central* Supplemental Pension Plan	Indexes					
		A (6/30)	B (7/31)	C (10/31)	D (11/30)	E (10/31)	F†
8/31/56	100	100	100	100	100	100	100
8/31/57	97	94	95	93	96	93	97
8/31/58	105	98	99	108	113	108	100
8/31/59	117	99	114	114	116	113	114
8/31/60	121	99	111	113	115	114	113
8/31/61	139	104	128	133	137	138	125
6/30/62	129	103	118	121	130	116	112
6/30/63	153	115	132	138	139	139	132
6/30/64	170	118	145	150	150	155	142
6/30/65	181	120	145	154	152	167	145
6/30/66	189	110	135	137	137	146	138
6/30/67	208	110	144	139	138	175	143
6/30/68	231	106	148	152	165	182	150

SOURCE: David Bevan, Memorandum, April 21, 1964, incorporated in the minutes of the Penn Central board of directors.
*Pennsylvania Railroad, only through 1967. In 1968, figures include former New York Central plan.
†Date missing from original document.

TABLE A-3. Penn Central System Plan for Supplemental Pensions: Charges to Operating Expense* (*in thousands of dollars*)

December 31	Current service	Past service	Total
1952	$ 2,037	$ 2,850	$ 4,887
1953	2,011	6,517	8,528
1954	1,556	966	2,522
1955	1,459	4,498	5,957
1956	1,938	5,199	7,137
1957	2,249	4,399	7,648
1958	2,300	7,399	9,699
1959	2,087	6,499	8,586
1960	1,814	7,099	8,913
1961	1,829	6,199	8,028
1962	1,964	5,749	7,713
1963	1,874	5,638	7,512
1964	1,693	3	1,696
1965	1,989	—	1,989
1966	1,237	—	1,237
1967	1,343	—	1,343
1968	1,147	—	1,147

SOURCE: Secretary, Managers of Pensions, April 1, 1969.

*Pennsylvania Railroad only, through 1967. In 1968, figures include former New York Central Plan.

References

1. *The Penn Central Failure and the Role of Financial Institutions,* Staff Report of the Committee on Banking and Currency, 92d Congress, First Session, House of Representatives, January 3, 1972, p. 287. Hereafter referred to as the Patman Report.

2. Patman Report, pp. 293–294.

3. See Paul Strauss, "The Penn Central: Born Again," *Financial World,* May 15, 1977, pp. 29–33.

Appendix B
PENNSYLVANIA RAILROAD–NEW YORK CENTRAL CAPITAL EXPENDITURES: A COMPARISON

TABLE B-1. Pennsylvania Railroad Company and Leased Lines: Capital Expenditures (*in thousands of dollars*)

Year	Road	Equipment			Grand total (road plus equipment)
		Owned*	Acquired under lease	Total equipment	
1946	$17,702	$ 16,018	$ —	$ 16,018	$ 33,720
1947	19,090	33,585	—	33,585	52,675
1948	23,248	83,089	—	83,089	106,337
1949	23,874	81,896	—	81,896	105,770
1950	24,008	63,790	—	63,790	87,798
1951	27,979	133,875	53,739	187,614	215,593
1952	33,928	89,393	—	89,393	123,321
1953	42,106	38,403	—	38,403	80,509
1954	28,979	12,016	—	12,016	40,995
1955	31,101	37,869	—	37,869	68,970
1956	36,316	56,095	—	56,095	92,411
1957	22,578	42,668	32,445	75,113	97,691
1958	12,394	38,404	13,050	51,454	63,848
1959	14,968	31,157	79,113	110,270	125,238
1960	8,665	39,955	107,234	147,189	155,854
1961	9,946	38,289	12,634	50,923	60,869
1962	13,381	35,773	13,797	49,570	62,951
1963	13,605	59,836†	8,950	68,786	82,391
1964	28,962	67,081†	4,800	71,881	100,843
1965	50,189	160,177	33,870	194,047	244,236
1966	52,578	144,860	—	144,860	197,438

TABLE B-1. Pennsylvania Railroad Company and Leased Lines: Capital Expenditures (*in thousands of dollars*) (*Continued*)

Year	Road	Equipment			Grand total (road plus equipment)
		Owned*	Acquired under lease	Total equipment	
Averages, 1946 through 1966					
Postwar (1946–1966)	$ 25,505	$ 62,106	$ 17,125	$ 79,231	$ 104,736
10 years (1957–1966)	22,727	65,820	30,589	96,409	119,136
5 years (1962–1966)	31,743	93,545	12,284	105,829	137,572
3 years (1964–1966)	43,910	124,039	12,890	136,929	180,839

SOURCE: Pennsylvania Railroad, Accounting Department, David Bevan to A. J. Greenough, May 2, 1967.

*Including the following equipment acquired by Pennsylvania Company and leased to Pennsylvania Railroad. and excluding purchase of equipment from Pennsylvania Company.

1953	$ 7,712
1955	3,186
1956	6,321
1957	5,988
1958	3,607
1959	669
1960	19,000

†Including equipment acquired by Associates of the Jersey Company and leased to the Pennsylvania Railroad.

1963	$21,896
1964	2,640

TABLE B-2. New York Central Railroad Company and Leased Lines: Capital Expenditures (*in thousands of dollars*)

| Year | Road | Equipment | | | Grand total (road plus equipment) |
		Owned	Acquired under lease	Total equipment	
1946	$ 12,625	$ 28,575	—	$ 28,575	$ 41,200
1947	14,294	34,074	—	34,074	48,368
1948	21,923	68,247	—	68,247	90,170
1949	18,801	81,748	—	81,748	100,549
1950	15,662	47,338	$ 7,560	54,898	70,560
1951	26,140	87,931	11,588	99,519	125,659
1952	32,969	107,522	7,907	115,420	148,398
1953	20,838	62,141	5,005	67,146	87,984
1954	23,391	15,744	—	15,744	39,135
1955	12,502	27,099	—	27,099	39,601
1956	24,232	55,112	—	55,112	79,344
1957	37,579	76,620	—	76,620	114,199
1958	12,585	5,631	—	5,631	18,216
1959	13,922	14,806	—	14,806	28,728
1960	19,835	19,753	—	19,753	39,588
1961	13,189	18,826	—	18,826	32,015
1962	15,126	20,855	4,221	25,076	40,202
1963	14,201	14,343	10,995	25,348	39,549
1964	16,461	56,135	8,682	64,817	81,278
1965	18,334	54,169	35,421	89,590	107,924
1966	24,356	39,383	32,111	71,494	95,850
Averages: 1946 through 1966					
Postwar (1946–1966)	$ 19,475	$ 44,574	$ 5,880	$ 50,454	$ 69,929
10 years (1957–1966)	18,559	32,053	9,143	41,196	59,755
5 years (1962–1966)	17,696	36,979	18,286	55,265	72,961
3 years (1964–1966)	19,717	49,896	25,404	75,300	95,017

SOURCE: IBS statement.

341

TABLE B-3. Annual Average Capital Expenditures: of the Pennsylvania Railroad and the New York Central* (*in thousands of dollars*)

Period	Road		Equipment†		Total	
	Pennsylvania	New York Central	Pennsylvania	New York Central	Pennsylvania	New York Central
Postwar (1946–1966)	$ 25,505	$ 19,475	$ 79,231	$ 50,454	$ 104,736	$ 69,929
10 years (1957–1966)	22,727	18,559	96,409	41,196	119,136	59,755
5 years (1962–1966)	31,743	17,696	105,829	55,265	137,572	72,961
3 years (1964–1966)	43,910	19,717	136,929	75,300	180,839	95,017

SOURCE: Pennsylvania Railroad, Accounting Department, David Bevan to A. J. Greenough, May 2, 1967.
†Includes leased equipment.
*SOURCE: IBS statement.

Appendix C
PENPHIL GROUP STOCKHOLDING IN KANEB

TABLE C-1. Penphil Group Stockholdings in Kaneb Pipe Line Company

Total Kaneb common shares outstanding	Holdings of Penphil, its members, and Penn Central	Percent in holdings of Penphil, its members, and Penn Central	Breakdown of Penphil, its members, and Penn Central holdings				
			Penn Central	Penphil	Herbert Fisher	David Bevan	Total
1,259,053	271,528*†‡§	21.56	122,500†	30,488‡	115,496§	3044	271,528

SOURCE: Patman Report, p. 212.
*Does not include any stockholdings of Glore Forgan or its members. Glore Forgan and its members held almost 107,000 shares at March 10, 1965. Comparable information not available for 1969.
†Does not include warrants held by the Penn Central for an additional 41,021 shares of Kaneb common stock.
‡Does not include warrants held by Penphil for an additional 7,653 shares of Kaneb common stock.
§In addition, Mr. Fisher is the cotrustee of two trusts for his daughter's benefit. The trusts collectively own 24,835 shares of Kaneb common stock.

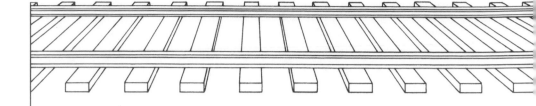

INDEX

Accidents, 19th-century, 6
Accounting:
  collapse of Penn Central and confusion
    in, 194–195
  conflict over, 108–114
  confusion in, 149–152
  in Conrail system, 138
  defects in, 51–52
  in disarray, 172–173
  establishing new, 52–55
  head of, 100–101
  management failure in, 189, 190,
    195–197, 209–210
  in merged railroads, 117–125, 192
  in new administrative structure,
    128–132
  railroads as pioneers in cost, 7, 8, 13
  recommendations on (1969), 163–164
  reforming (1951), 188–189
  removed from Bevan's control,
    123–131, 193, 194
  resignation of staff from, 148
  responsibility, as tool, 52, 53
  SEC investigation of policies on,
    206
  standards of, criticized, 104–105
  (See also Data processing; Interstate
    Commerce Commission
    accounting system)
Acheson, Dean, 246
Acuff, John, 216
Adams, Charles Francis, Jr., 9
Adams, Henry, 9
Adamson Act, 18

Administrative system:
  attempt to provide reformed, 45
  centralized, 118, 191–193
  and consolidation of personnel,
    139–140
  control in, 52–55
  decentralized, 118, 191–193
  differences in, of merged railroads,
    191–192
  modernization of, 50–52
  new, 123–126
  undermining Bevan's staff in, 147–149
  (See also Management)
Airlines, 19, 244, 283
  (See also specific airlines)
Allegheny Ludlum Steel Corporation, 78,
    124, 225
Alsco Chromocraft Corporation, 295, 305,
    306, 322
American Aviation (publication), 238, 271
American Contract Company, 69, 244,
    246, 248, 260, 265, 292–295, 298,
    299, 303, 314
American Telephone and Telegraph, 29
Amtrak, 138
Annual report(s):
  1951, 31
  1952, 48
  1969, 177–179
Arvida Company, 64, 69, 180, 197, 219,
    221, 229
Atchison, Topeka, & Santa Fe (railroad),
    14, 31, 32, 34
Atkinson, Arthur, 90

Auditing and accounting (*see* Accounting)
Auftermatt, Dr., 300, 302–304, 307

Bailey, F. Lee, 280
Baltimore & Ohio Railroad, 8, 16, 29, 76–77, 83, 84, 140, 142, 194
Banking and Currency Committee (House of Representatives):
  diversification criticized by, 64, 70–72
  (*See also* Patman, Wright)
Bankruptcy Act, 81
Barrett, William A., 211, 212
Barriger, John, 179
Barron's (newspaper), 77, 81–82, 92
Barter, Arnold, 141
Baylor, Werner, 206
Berliner Bank loan, 291–295, 298, 299, 301, 312, 314, 317, 320
Bevan, David Crumley, 26
  accounting and (*see* Accounting)
  acquittal of, 320–323
  in administrative system (*see* Administrative system)
  assumes new post (1951), 33–35, 37, 39, 44
  attempts by, to prevent collapse, 189–192
  background of, 40–44
  bright spots in career of, 197–198
  capital budget crisis and resignation threatened by, 155
  and capital needs (*see entries beginning with term:* Capital)
  challenges facing, 188–190
  characteristics of, 42
  and Clement, 34–35
  criticized for his reporting manner (1970), 176–177
  data processing problem and, 120, 121
  debt restructuring program of, 47–50
  decision to resubmit resignation, 165–166
  diversification under (*see* Diversification)
  dividend payments and, 171, 172
  duties of (1951), 39–40
  and eastern railway mergers, 85
  EJA and (*see* Executive Jet Aviation)
  in fiscal crisis, 179–182
  German as attorney for (*see* German, Edward C.)
  and Greenough presidency, 89, 90
  Hartke and, 203–204
  Hodge and (*see* Hodge, Charles J.)

Bevan, David Crumley (*Cont.*):
  indicted, 309–313
  intention of, to resign (1967), 125–128
  investigations of, 198–199
  Kunkel and, 260, 279
  as leader, 22–25
  merger as viewed by, 117
  missing $4 million (*see* $4 million, missing)
  and operations breakdown, 144
  opposes Lehigh Valley acquisition, 84
  ousted, 182–194
  and Penphil (*see* Penphil Corporation)
  Perlman and (*see* Perlman, Alfred Edward)
  reforms by, resented, 119–120
  renewed power of, 171–173
  resigns, 157–161, 163
  retirement benefits of, 208
  in Ricciardi affair, 239–240
  Saunders and (*see* Saunders, Stuart)
  as scapegoat (*see* Patman, Wright)
  sidetracking of, 128–132
  Specter charges against, 198, 207, 240–241, 280–282, 291
  stock holdings of, and losses, 152–153
  strategy of, to save Penn Central, 172–174
  threatens to resign, 113
  trial of, 314–320
  trustees' suit against, 207–208
  withdraws resignation, 164
  in World War II, 41–42
Bevan, Howard Sloan (father), 34, 40
Bevan, John (ancestor), 40
Bevan, Mary (Mary Gilbert Heist; wife), 42
Bevan, Thomas (brother), 217, 220, 229, 274
Bezilla, Michael, 20
Billing and collection, breakdown of, 143–144
Billups, Fred H., 218, 224
Binzen, Peter, 117, 140, 208, 240, 255
Blank, Rome, Kaus & Comisky, 231
Bodman, Warren, 216, 217
Bookkeeping (*see* Accounting)
Borrowing (*see* Credit)
Boston Globe, The (newspaper), 177
Boston & Maine (railroad), 209
Boston & Worcester (railroad), 6
Bowen, Irene, 270, 273, 274
Bowen Travel Agency, 273–274
Broad Street Station (Philadelphia terminal), 49, 58
Brodie, Lawrence, 300–302

Brookhouser, Frank, 280
Brookings Institution, 79
Brown, Manning, 43
Brown, Nick, 142
Buckeye Pipeline Company, 64, 68–69, 71, 163, 197, 219
Budgetary control:
    as management tool, 52–54
    (See also Accounting)
Budgets:
    absence of, 51
    (See also Accounting; Capital budgets; Income budgets; entries beginning with term: Cash)
Bureaucracy (see Management)
Burlington Industries, 266, 267, 272, 275, 276, 278, 285, 287
Burlington Northern (railroad), 16
Burstein, Robert, 248
Burt, C. Oliver, 199, 207, 303, 310–323
Burt, William C., 266, 271, 272, 275, 276, 278, 285
Business institutions, railroads' role in rise of modern, 4–9
Butcher, Howard, III, 66, 294

CAB (see Civil Aeronautics Board)
Campbell Soup Company, 225
Canadian National (railroad), 15
Canadian Pacific Railroad, 14, 15, 244
Cannon, Francis, 216–217
Capital:
    driven out of railroads (early 20th century), 17
    providing working, 46–47
Capital budgets, 101–108
    conflict with operating department over, 189
    developing, 102
    impossible, 154–155
    lacking, 51
    1956–1965, 103
    1964–1966, 103
    1966–1967, 105–106
    1968 and 1969, 195
    1970, 171, 173
    Perlman favoring, 108, 153
Capital expenditures:
    accounting statistics for planning, 13
    forecast of, 101–108
    1952, 47

Capital expenditures (Cont.):
    1968 and 1969, 156
    1970, 174
    of Pennsy and New York Central, compared, tables, 339–342
    under Perlman, 152–156, 191, 196
    raising funds for, 155–157
    restricting, as goal, 25
Capital gains on sale of Norfolk & Western, 67, 68
Capital improvements, 144
    diversification and, 136–137
    increase in funds for, 190
    of proposed merged railroads, 120
    using Norfolk & Western funds for, 66, 67
Capital needs:
    postwar, 22
    (See also Commercial paper; Credit; Debt)
Capitol International Airways, 264, 267, 272, 284, 287
Carpi, Fred, 38–39, 85
Carter, Jimmy, 283
Cash:
    accusation of drain of, through Pennsylvania Company, 208
    diversification blamed for drain on, 204
    drain on: 1964–1967, 191
        1968, 138, 191
        Penn Central collapse and, 70
    on hand at merger, 189, 195
    inadequate, 187–188
    working, on merger date, 153
Cash flow, 189
    absence of projections on (1951), 188
    absence of statements on, 51
    decline in, from operations, 190
    estimate of, and merged railroads, 192, 194
    as main problem prior to merger, 108–109
    management confusion over, 195
    management failure and, 190–191
    and merged railroads, 125, 193–194
    1968–1970 problem with, 136–138
    1970 statement of, 171–174
    preparing estimates on, 101–102
Cash loss in life of Penn Central, 237
Cash shortage, 1968, severe, 194–195
Cassatt, Alexander Johnston, 30, 59
Cassidy, Leslie, 218
CBK Industries, 206, 216
Central Intelligence Agency (CIA), 265
Central of New Jersey (railroad), 209

Central Soya (firm), 142
Centralization, administrative, 118, 191–193
Certain-Teed Products (firm), 43
Chandler, Alfred D., Jr. 3–5, 7, 10, 12, 50
Chapters of Erie (Adams and Adams), 9
Charter, 5
    of Pennsy, 29
Chase Manhattan Bank, 72, 225
Chemical Bank, 72, 175, 181, 317
Chesapeake & Ohio (railroad), 16, 64, 77–79,
    82–84, 140, 194
Chicago, Burlington & Quincy (railroad), 11,
    15, 80
Chrysler Corporation, 20
CIA (Central Intelligence Agency), 265
Civil Aeronautics Board (CAB), 19, 265, 322
    collapse of EJA case with, 275–278
    consent order and EJA activities, 261, 263
    EJA and, 238, 282–288
    EJA-Pennsy relationship and, 248
    and EJA as taxi service, 246–247
    IAB and, 271
    Johnson Flying Service and (*see* Johnson
        Flying Service)
    leasing to Transavia reported to, 270
    major air operators as defenders of, 283
    Patman charges on EJA-Pennsy connection
        and, 244
    Patman investigation and, 242
    as political body, 283, 284
Clagett, Brice, 272–274
Clarke, Philip, 90, 91, 110
Classification yards, 153–154
Clement, Martin W., 34–39, 49
Cline, C. C., 143
CMI (Continental Mortgage Investors), 221,
    222, 227–228, 233, 234
Coff, Gail, 142
Cole, Basil, 111–113, 124, 130
    accounting and budgeting confusion and,
        150–151
    and Bevan as scapegoat, 211–212
    criticized, 107–108
    and failure of EJA, 261, 262
    and Meehan's resignation, 149
    Patman investigation and, 242
    report by, on EJA, 262–264, 266, 282
Cole Report, 262–264, 266, 282
Collective bargaining, 18, 188
Commerce, Committee on (Senate), 26, 136,
    137
    (*See also* Hartke, Vance)

Commercial and Financial Chronicle
    (magazine), 178
Commercial paper:
    crisis in (1970), 174–176
    fear of run on (1970), 177
    government investigation of, 206–207
    issue of, 155–156
    run on (1970), 180–181
Commuter services, 138
    (*See also* Passenger service)
Competition, new methods of (19th century),
    8
Compulsory arbitration, 18
Computers, 54–55, 119, 121, 123, 153, 192,
    209–210
    (*See also* Data processing)
Conrail (Consolidated Rail), 138, 196, 197
Continental Mortgage Investors (CMI), 221,
    222, 227–228, 223, 234
Contingent Compensation Fund, 148, 208,
    218–219
Cook, William S., 118, 121, 122, 149, 151, 210
    and accounting practices prior to merger,
        109
    background of, 100
    new administration and, 127, 128, 132
    as part of Bevan's team, 111–114, 188–189
    resigns, 148
Corning, Erastus, 12
Corporate form, use of, 3–5
Coudert Brothers (firm), 300
Covington & Burlington, 166, 246–248, 250,
    254–255, 266, 267, 272, 294
Cox, Hugh B., 246, 247, 250
Credit:
    1954 revolving, 47
    1969 revolving, 156, 161
    1970 available, 174
    1970 revolving, 175
    requirements in, of Penn Central, 72
    revision in rating for, 105
    situation leading to massive borrowing,
        190
    (*See also* Commercial paper; Loans)
Cuneo Press, 143
Curtin, John, 42
"Cybernetics," 123

Dalzell, Stewart, 212, 231–232
Data processing, 100–101, 163
    Bevan loss of control on, 193, 194

Data processing (*Cont.*):
  Bevan problem with, 120, 121
  confusion in, and collapse of Penn Central, 194–195
  in disarray, 172–173
  installing program of, 154–155
  management failure in, 196, 209–210
  of merged railroads, 124, 125, 192
  New York Central, 121–122
  in reform of financial system, 189
  (*See also* Accounting; Computers)
Daughen, Joseph, R., 117, 140, 208, 240, 255
Day, William, 65, 67, 184, 225
Debentures, 175–176, 191
Debt:
  bonded, 47–48
  increase in (1964–1965), 103
  management of, 187–188
  1951 Pennsy, 187
  1952–1964 total, 102
  for 1970–1974 period, 178
  by 1982, 117
  reduction of (1951–1963), 47–50, 66
  yearly interest on (1952–1964), 47, 50
  (*See also* Credit)
Dechert, Price and Rhoads, 279
Decker, Robert, 142
Defense, U.S. Department of, 184
Deficit:
  1958, 75
  1967, 111
Delaware, Lackawanna & Western (railroad), 77
Denton, Frank, 43, 44
Denver & Rio Grande Western (railroad), 24, 80, 81, 154
Denworth, Raymond, 212, 231–232
Derailments, 1970, 144
Dermond, J. E., 294
Detroit, Toledo & Ironton (railroad), 46, 139
Detroit Bank & Trust Company, 239, 277–278, 282
Dickey, Charles, 44
Dieselization, 93, 194
Ditter, J. William, Jr., 314, 315, 319, 320, 322, 323
Diversification, 57–74, 197
  blamed for cash drain, 204
  and capital improvements, 136–137
  and collapse of Penn Central, 135
  critics of program of, 69–73
  Daughen and Binzen on, 208

Diversification (*Cont.*):
  EJA and (*see* Executive Jet Aviation)
  goal of, 57
  Great Southwest as part of, 230
  Hodge role in, 219
  income from, to offset losses, 179
  major, 64–69
  and new administrative structure, 124, 125
  as no reason for failure, 196
  Penphil and, 216
  total investment in, 70
  (*See also* Land; Pennsylvania Company)
Dividends:
  cash loss through, 137
  1848–1968, 30
  Long Island Railroad, 59
  1955 New York Central, 81
  1956–1963 Norfolk & Western, 92
  1958, 75
  1969, stop, 138, 171
  1970s Buckeye, 69
  Penn Central, 171–172
  Pennsylvania Company, 65
Dorrance, John T., Jr., 225
Doty, Ethan Allen, 241
Dowling, Robert, 63
Dresser Industries, 229
Drew, Daniel, 9
Drexel and Company, 218
Drinker, Biddle and Reath, 212, 231
Duane, Morris, & Heckscher, 217
Du Pont, E. I., Co., 13, 17, 35, 232
Du Pont–Glore Forgan, Inc. (*see* Glore Forgan and Company)

Earnings:
  accounting manipulation and, 104–105
  continuing low, 187–188
  management failure and, 190–191
  of merged railroads, 118
  1931–1939, 22
  1951, 46
  1955 and 1957 New York Central, 81
  1956–1963 Norfolk & Western, 92
  1967 statement of, 111–112
  1969 consolidated, 174
  1969 statement of, 178
  1970 consolidated, 177
  poor record of, 108–114
  retained (*see* Profit)
  (*See also* Dividends; Pension funds)

Eastern Airlines, 283
Eaton, Cyrus, 79, 84–85
8-hour day, 18
Eisenhower, Dwight D., 179
EJA (*see* Executive Jet Aviation)
Electrification, 20–22, 49
    cost of, 22
    Long Island Railroad, 59, 60
Elkins Act (1903), 16
Enterprise Denied (Martin), 17
Equipment:
    classification yards for, 153–154
    dieselization of, 93, 194
    electrification of (*see* Electrification)
    leasing rehabilitated, 292
    locomotives, 21
    1955–1964, 102–103
    1959 program for, 66, 67
    1966 and 1967 maturities and depreciation
        of, 103, 105
    1966–1970 plan for, 104
    1970 funds for, 173
    trust certificates for, 48–50
    (*See also* Capital expenditures)
Equitable Life Assurance Society, 35
Erie Canal, 4–5
Erie-Lackawanna (railroad), 209
Erie Railroad, 8–10, 12, 76, 77
Estes, A. B., 253
Executive Jet Aviation (EJA), 64, 215, 218,
        219, 237–291, 310
    Bevan's view of major mistake on, 248
    CAB and (*see* Civil Aeronautics Board)
    charges resulting from investigation of,
        207
    committee investigating, 164–166
    conclusion on situation involving, 282–
        288
    as disaster for Bevan, 164–165, 238
    European misadventures of, 267–272
    Goetz and, 311, 313
    and Hartke Committee, 204
    and Holiday International Tours, 272–275
    investigation and prosecution of, 279–282
    investments in, 69–70
    new opposition to, 264–265
    Patman concept of, 205, 241–242
    Patman misjudgment of, 237–238
    Penn Central seeks to sell, 265–267
    Pennsy involvement in, 242–248
    purchase of Johnson Flying Service by (*see*
        Johnson Flying Service)

Executive Jet Aviation (EJA) (*Cont.*):
    Ricciardi affair and, 238–241
    and Rome investigation, 302–304

FAA (Federal Aviation Agency), 246, 248, 250,
    251
FBI (Federal Bureau of Investigation), 207
Federal Aviation Act (1958), 246–248, 251
Federal Aviation Agency (FAA), 246, 248, 250,
    251
Federal Bankruptcy Act, 59
Federal Bureau of Investigation (FBI), 207
Federal Reserve Board, 204
Federation for Railway Progress, 81
Fenninger, Carl W., 41
*Financial Collapse of the Penn Central
    Company, The* (SEC report), 286
Financial planning, merger and, 120–121
Finanz (firm), 306
Finn, George, 141
First Bancshares, 218
First Bank and Trust Company, 221, 222,
    229
First Boston Corporation, 86, 93, 175,
    216–217
First Financial Trust, 293–303, 312–318,
    321
First National City Bank, 43, 47, 72, 175, 181,
    182, 265, 277
First Pennsylvania Banking and Trust
    Company, 65
Fisher, Herbert E., 218, 222–223
Fisk, Jim, 9
Fitzpatrick, Emmett, 280–282, 291
Flannery, Robert G. (Mike), 124, 210
Fleming, Thomas F., 218
Flying Tiger Airlines, 19, 244
Forbes (magazine), 105, 233
Fortune (magazine), 29, 75, 93
$4 million, missing, 199, 291–308
    acquittals in trial over, 320–323
    and Berliner Bank loan, 291–295, 298, 299,
        301, 312, 314, 317, 320
    and First Financial Trust, 293–303,
        312–318, 321
    Goetz and (*see* Goetz, Fidel)
    indictment over, 309–311
    investigation of, 207
    Patman view of, 205
    Rome investigation of (*see* Rome,
        Edwin P.)

$4 million, missing (*Cont.*):
  Rosenbaum involvement in (*see*
    Rosenbaum, Francis N.; Rosenbaum,
    Joseph H.)
  trial over, 314–320
Fox, Paul D., 127, 217
Franklin, Walter S., 33, 44, 57
  Bevan supported by, 189
  and debt reduction, 49
  managerial structure and, 37, 52
  as president, 37–39
Freight:
  competition with trucks over, 32
  EJA in handling of (*see* Johnson Flying
    Service)
  and ICC power over rates for, 16, 17, 19
  in income budget, 101
  lost business in, 142–144
  1955 source of revenue from, 79
  1956 and 1957 volume of, compared, 75
  piggy-back, 39
  traditional setting of rates for, 31–32
Fullam, John P., 208, 297
Funkhouser, A. Paul, 106–111

Gateway Center (Chicago, Illinois), 57, 59
General Electric Company, 100, 128
General Motors Corporation, 13, 17, 29, 35,
    159, 232
Gengras, E. Clayton, 163, 183, 255–256,
    286–287
German, Edward C., 211, 241, 310, 315, 316
  and Cole Report, 263
  and indictment of his client, 310
  Muller testimony and, 316, 317
  in Rome investigation, 297
  Specter charges and, 280, 281
Germanair (Sudwestflug), 269, 285, 302
Gerstnecker, Willlam R., 63, 113, 127, 162,
    242
  acquitted, 320–323
  and Berliner Bank loan, 292–295, 312
  and EJA, 243, 244, 246, 247, 255, 267
  and EJA foreign involvements, 272
  and Holiday International Tours, 273
  indicted, 310, 315
  investments of, 207
  and liquidation of interests in EJA, 277
  as Penphil member, 217
  replaced, 171
  resigns, 161–162

Gerstnecker, William R. (*Cont.*):
  in Rome investigation, 297, 300, 307
  Francis Rosenbaum and, 314
  Rosenbaums' scheme and, 296
  suits agains, 207–208
  trial of, 314–320
Glatfelter Paper Company, 217
Glore Forgan and Company (E. I. du
    Pont–Glore Fogan, Inc.), 86, 159,
    162–164, 175, 205, 217–219, 224, 227,
    228, 243, 253–255, 260, 269, 285, 286
Godfrey, Arthur, 238
Goetz, Fidel, 205, 275, 284, 285
  and Berliner Bank loan, 293, 294
  Bevan and, 311–313
  death of, 285
  Delaware securities of, attacked, 306–307
  expected investment of, 268
  and First Financial Trust, 293–303,
    312–318, 321
  indicted, 310, 311, 315
  investigated, 207
  laundered money operation of, 294–295
  in Patman report, 309, 310
  as recipient of stolen money, 291
  Rome investigation of, 298–306, 309
  Rosenbaums and, 292
  as sole beneficiary of stolen money, 309
  Sudwestflug and, 269
  undoing relationships with, 275, 276
Goldman, Sachs, 155, 156, 174–175, 178, 180
Goop, Adulf Peter, 300–302
Gorman, Paul A., 164, 171, 279, 286, 311, 312
  Bevan on, 174
  collapse and, 182, 183
  cost-cutting program of, 180
  and missing $4 million, 296–300, 304, 305
  as president, 158–160, 164, 172, 173, 176
Gottwald, Heinz, 317–319
Gould, Jay, 8, 9
Government aid, 180–182, 184, 197–198, 203,
    212
Government and collapse of Penn Central,
    25–26
Grady, Sandy, 240
Graham, Walter, 262
Grand Central Terminal (New York City),
    79–80
Grand juries, 199
Grant, Walter R., 121, 124, 127, 149, 151, 154,
    193
Great Northern Railway, 14, 15

Great Southwest Corporation, 64, 69, 70, 125, 152, 175, 176, 180, 197, 219, 230, 232, 313
  and Hartke committee, 204
  investments in, 221, 222, 225–227
Greenfield, Albert M., 58
Greenough, Allen Jackson, 89, 90, 95, 106–108, 113, 124, 139, 248
Guthrie, Robert, 182

Hage, R. E., 250
Hanley, Edward J., 124, 131, 132, 164, 183, 225
  and Bevan's resignation, 126–127
  and EJA investigation, 164, 165
Hanna Mining Company, 225
Harlem Railroad, 8
Harriman, Edward H., 14–15, 17
Hartke, Vance, 172, 238
  Bevan and, 203–204
  investigation under, 205
  report by, 211
Hartwell, Samuel, Jr., 253, 254
Harvard College, 224
Haslett, Robert, 127, 148, 217, 218, 224, 229, 230
Hemphill Noyes & Company, 216
Hepburn Act (1906), 16, 17
Highways, 32–34, 76, 188
Hill, Charles S., 148–151
Hill, James J., 14–15, 17
Hilsinger, Mr., 295, 300–302
Hirschmann, Carl, 269–271, 275
Hispanair, 269, 271–272, 275, 284, 302
HIT (Holiday International Tours), 221, 222, 229, 230, 272–275
Hodge, Charles J., 279
  Bevan to, on Penphil, 219–220
  Bevan breaks with, 162, 219
  and Bevan's resignation, 163, 164
  charges against, 207
  EJA creation and, 243, 244
  EJA as disaster for, 238
  and EJA failure, 285
  EJA–Johnson Flying Service connection and, 254
  EJA–Pennsy connection and, 246, 247
  European misadventures of, 267–272, 275, 276, 284, 286, 291, 311, 312
  fails to understand opposition to EJA, 264

Hodge, Charles J. (*Cont.*):
  foreign aviation interests of EJA and, 266
  as founder of Penphil, 217
  Gengras and, 255, 286–287
  in government investigation, 205
  Holiday International Tours and, 273–274
  IAB and, 270
  and investment in National Homes, 228–229
  investments by Penphil and, 215–216, 218
  Johnson Flying Service and, 253
  Kunkel sues, 260, 279
  relationship between Bevan and, 219
  and replacement of Perlman, 159–160, 163
  in Ricciardi affair, 239
  role of, in diversification program, 219
  Joseph Rosenbaum and, 294
  Specter charges against, 240–241, 269, 280, 281
  takeover plans of, 162–163
  and Tropical Gas, 224
  trustees' suit against, 207–208
Hohl, Mr., 295, 300–302
Hoisington, Gen. Perry, 244
Holiday International Tours (HIT), 221, 222, 229, 230, 272–275
Holmes, Frederick, 217
Hoogenboom, Ari, 16
Hoogenboom, Olive, 16
Hudson River Railroad, 8
Hundley, William, 310
Huntington, Collis P., 14, 17
Hurst Performance, Inc., 240

IAB (International Air Bahamas), 270–271, 273–275, 284, 285, 287, 291, 302
IATA (International Air Transport Association), 270, 284–285
IBM (International Business Machines), 100, 101, 122, 189
ICC (*see* Interstate Commerce Commission)
Icelandic Airlines, 270, 271, 277, 284, 287
Ickes, Harold L., 22, 49
Income (*see* Dividends; Earnings)
Income budgets, 189
  absence of, 51, 188
  management failure over, 195–196
  and merged railroads, 124, 125, 192–194
  1970, 171–175
  preparing, 101–102
Indianapolis Grain Corporation, 142

Inflation, 20
  1968, 155
  1970, 176
Innovations, economic, of railroads, 3–4
Inselbuch, Elihu, 239
Interest, yearly (1952–1964), 47, 50
Interest rate:
  omission of dividends and, 172
  prime, 1968 and 1969, 155
Interlocking directorships (*see* Penphil
  Corporation)
International Air Bahamas (IAB), 270–271,
  273–275, 284, 285, 287, 291, 302
International Air Transport Association
  (IATA), 270, 284–285
International Business Machines (IBM), 100,
  101, 122, 189
Interstate Commerce Commission (ICC), 91,
  322
  authorization on sales and credit by,
    292–293
  Berlin Bank loan and violation of
    regulations of, 314–315
  Bevan's testimony before (1962), 117, 132,
    209
  and collapse of Penn Central as political
    issue, 198
  Conrail losses according to standards of,
    138
  and control of Lehigh Valley, 84
  diversification attacked by, 64, 72
  "early warning report" on Conrail by,
    197
  hearings of, on merger, 119
  and loss of business, 142
  merged railroads and, 121
  and merger of Baltimore & Ohio and
    Chesapeake & Ohio, 85
  and merger of Virginian and Norfolk &
    Western, 93
  1967 earnings statement and, 112
  penalties claimed by (1970), 278
  permission from, to issue commercial
    paper, 156
  post-World War II regulation by, 19
  power of, over rates, 16, 17, 19
  and price for New Haven line, 137
  problems associated with ratemaking by,
    196–197
  and relationship between employees of
    merged railroads, 139–140
  retarding change, 16

Interstate Commerce Commission
  (ICC) (*Cont.*):
  rules against merger of New York Central
    and Chesapeake & Ohio, 78
  Saunders' view of investments in EJA and,
    282
  unresponsiveness of, 188
Interstate Commerce Commission (ICC)
    accounting system, 16–17, 19, 192
  abandoning, 54, 101, 188, 210
  and accounting systems of merged
    railroads, 118–119, 193
  Perlman and, 122, 123, 125
  policy on, 51, 52
  and responsibility reporting, 53
Interstate Commerce Commission (ICC)
    investigation, 26, 199, 205–206, 310
  accounting and budget confusion and,
    150–151
  and criticism of ICC, 210–211
  into lack of planning, 141, 144
  into lost business, 142, 143
  into volume of traffic, 141–142

Jencks Act, 316
Jencks v. United States, 316
Jensen, Julius, III, 228
JFS (*see* Johnson Flying Service)
Johns-Manville (firm), 218
Johnson, Lyndon Baines, 95, 106, 155
Johnson, Robert R., 249
Johnson Flying Service (JFS):
  CAB and chance for control of, destroyed,
    267–274, 284, 285, 287,
  decision to purchase, 249–250
  expected CAB approval of purchase of,
    and acquisition of aircraft, 259–260
  fatal error of EJA over, 259–264
  first CAB ruling on, 250–256
  purchase of, and CAB approval in
    question, 265, 266
Jones, Rufus, 40
Jordan, Stanley G., 137

Kaneb (firm), 218, 221–223, 228, 231, 232
  Penphil holdings in, table, 345
Kattau, Fred, 124, 130
Kennedy, David, 180, 181
Kennedy, Edward, 283
Kenyon, Mr., 265
Keystone Fund, 268

Kling, Vincent C., 63, 218, 229
Knox, Seymour H., 225
Knuby, Max, 143
Kogan, Max B., 239
Koteen & Burt (firm), 266, 271, 272
Kroger Company, 143
Kunkel, John, 164, 165, 260, 262, 263, 279
Kusik, John, 85

Labor, 196
  as cash drain, 137–138
  as conservative force, 11
  1965 cut in, 120
Labor unions (see Trade unions)
Lackawanna (railroad), 77
Laird, Melvin, 184
Large, Henry, 105–108, 111, 249
Land, 69, 79, 209
  development projects and, 58, 59
  sales of, 49–50
  (See also specific sites)
Lassiter, Gen. Olbert F., 164, 278
  aircraft purchased by, 260
  charges against, 207
  death of, 280
  EJA as creation of, 243–245
  EJA as disaster for, 238
  EJA failure and, 285, 287
  and EJA–Pennsy connection, 247
  European misadventures of, 267–272, 275,
    276, 284, 291, 311, 312
  funds diverted by, 261
  Holiday International Tours and, 273
  IAB and, 270, 274
  Johnson Flying Service and, 250
  Kunkel suit against, 260, 279
  as member of Penphil, 218
  new concept of, 283–284
  and opposition to EJA, 264
  Patman's view of, 242
  and Pennsy involvement, 244
  removed, 279
  in Ricciardi affair, 238–240
  Specter charges against, 240–241, 269,
    280–281
  Sundlun and, 265–266
Lehigh Valley Railroad, 77, 83–84, 209
LeMay, Gen. Curtis, 238, 243, 249, 260, 264,
  271
Levy, Gustave, 155, 174
Lifsey, Julian, 270, 273–274

Loans:
  Berliner Bank, 291–295, 298, 299, 301, 312,
    314, 317, 320
  government, 180–182, 184, 197–198, 203,
    212
  1970, 173, 175
Lockheed Aircraft Corporation, 20
Locomotives, 21
Loder, Robert W., 318
Long Island Railroad, 30–33, 37–62, 70, 136
Long Island Transit Authority, 60
Lord, Joseph S., III, 281
Lufthansa, 269
Lunding, Frank, 184

Macco Corporation, 64, 70
Macco Realty Company, 69
McCron, Raymond, 147, 148
McDonnell Aircraft Corporation, 250
Macey, David, 177–178
McInerney, William, 300
McKinsey & Company, 124, 129
McMartin, Phil, 240
McTernan, J. J., Jr., 127, 128, 148, 149
Madison Square Garden (New York City), 57,
  59, 64, 66, 103, 180
Madison Square Garden Corporation, 58, 59
Maintenance costs in income budget,
  101–102
Management, 3–26
  conditions allowing innovation in (19th
    century), 9–10
  forces retarding innovation in (19th
    century), 10–11
  innovation and stagnation in (19th century
    and early 20th century), 9–18
  institutions and managers, 22–26
  modernizing, 37–44
  19th century, 3–9
  in period of stagnation, 18–21
  problems of, 33–35
  reform of, 188
  response of, to institutional rigidity, 21–22
  techniques of railroad, 3–4
  two philosophies of, 118–119
  (See also Administrative system)
Mandel, Marvin, 310
Mann-Elkins Act (1910), 16, 17
Mapco Corporation, 225
Marietta & Cincinnati (railroad), 8
Martin, Albro, 17

Marting, Walter A., 225
Marxer, Peter, 295–302, 305, 306, 315–317
Meads, Donald, 43
Meanor, Edward D., 217
Meehan, Thomas, 128, 148–149
Mellon, Richard King, 44, 49, 62–63,
    126–127, 157, 243–245
Mellon National Bank and Trust Company
    (Mellon Bank), 43–44, 62, 152
Mellon–United States Steel Building, 43–44
Menk, Louis, 159
Merger, 23, 24, 75–78, 117–133
    advantages of, 77–78
    and Bevan's intention to resign, 125–128
    capital budgets and, 101–108
    and conflict over accounting, 108–114
    cost accounting concepts and, 16
    difficulty of (post-World War II), 18
    and diversification, 64, 72
    eastern railway, 82–86
    first studies on, 119
    government scrutiny of, 20
    as method of solving problems (1960s),
        15–16
    new administrative structure and, 123–126
    and 1967 earnings statement, 111–113
    after Northern Securities decision, 15
    operating failure following (see Operations
        breakdown)
    proposed, 82–86
    reasons for failure and, 187–199
    as Saunder's goal, 99
    as solution, appraised, 189–190
    Symes and, 52
    and two managerial philosophies, 118–119
    Virginian and Norfolk & Western, 16, 84,
        93
Metropolitan Commuter Transportation
    Authority (New York State), 60
Michael, John R., 139–141, 144
Midland Marine and Trust Company, 225
Miller, George, 296
Miller, Paul, 281
Milwaukee Road (Chicago, Milwaukee, St.
    Paul, & Pacific Railroad), 47
Missouri Pacific (railroad), 47
Mitchell, John M., 310
Monopoly on inland transportation, 32
Morgan, J. P., 15
Morgan Guaranty, 225
Morgan Stanley (investment house), 86, 175
Muller, Wolfgang, 297–299, 315, 319–320

Myers, C. F., 266–267
National Homes Corporation, 221, 222,
    227–229
National Starch, 142
Nelson, James C., 79
New York, Chicago & St. Louis (the Nickel
    Plate; railroad), 16, 77, 84, 91, 93, 94
New York, New Haven & Hartford Railroad,
    32–33, 76, 80, 135, 137, 180, 209
New York, Ontario & Western (railroad), 209
New York Central Railroad, 3, 29, 52, 64, 72,
    77
    administration of (19th century), 11
    airlines and, 19, 244
    alliances formed by, 8
    assets of (1950s), 29
    extent of, 5
    illustrating institutional development and
        change, 12–14
    merger of (see Merger)
    passenger traffic on, 32, 79
    real estate holdings of, 209
    revitalizing, 78–82
    seeking to purchase a rival, 9
    situation of (late 1950s), 76–77
    system building by, 8–9
    track reduction and efficiency of, 22
    Western railroad under, 6
New York & Erie (Erie Railroad), 29
New York Life Insurance Company, 43, 44,
    155
New York Times (newspaper), 322–323
Newell, James P., 38–39, 90
Newsweek (magazine), 240
Nicholson, S. Francis, 41
Nickel Plate, the (New York, Chicago & St.
    Louis; railroad), 16, 77, 84, 91, 93, 94
Nixon, Richard M., 155, 176, 180, 184, 203
Norfolk & Western (railroad), 109, 209, 230
    as coal road, 77
    liquidation of interests in, 64–68, 70–72,
        85–86
    passenger traffic of, 32, 33
    and Penn Central loss of business, 142,
        143
    Pennsy dividends and interests in, 46
    Saunders as head of, 91–95
    shares of, backing debentures, 175–176
    and Virginian merger, 16, 84, 93
North American Review (magazine), 9
Northeast Airlines, 283
Northern Pacific Corner, 15

Northern Pacific Railroad, 14, 15, 80, 159
Northern Securities Company, 15, 16, 23
Noyes, Hemphill, 227, 228, 233

O'Herron, Jonathan, 150, 163, 171, 174, 180,
    261–262
Operating expenses, Long Island Railroad
    (1951), 30–31
Operating losses, 70
    of merged railroads, 195
    1954–1967, of Pennsy and New York
        Central, 151
    1968, 138, 156
    1968 and 1969, 137
    1969, 174, 177–179
    1970, 173, 175, 179–180
    1971 and 1973, 138
    1976, 138
    postwar, 187
Operating ratio:
    defined, 30
    1953, 46
    1956–1963, Norfolk & Western, 92
    1959, of coal-carrying railroads, 77
    Pennsy, 31
Operating revenues:
    increasing accuracy in predicting, 190
    (*See also entries beginning with term:*
        Capital)
Operations breakdown, 135–146
    at core of bankruptcy, 140–142, 196
    lack of planning as element in, 140–141,
        193, 194
Operations forecast in income budget,
    101–102
Oregon Short Line (railroad), 14
Overcapacity of railroads, 77

Pabst, George, 35
Pan American World Airways (Pan Am),
    244–245, 264–265, 271, 275, 277,
    284–285, 287
Parallel investments, 230–232
    (*See also* Penphil Corporation)
Parkinson, Thomas, 35
Parrish, Wayne W., 238
Passenger service, 188
    Amtrak absorbs long-haul, 138
    high-speed trains in, 106
    New York Central, 32, 79

Passenger service (*Cont.*):
    1951, 34
    1955, Pennsy and, 79
    and 1957 recession, 76
    Norfolk & Western, 32, 33
    write-off of, 174, 177
Patchell Study, 119
Patman, Wright, 184, 203–212, 286, 291, 322
    air regulatory system and, 288
    allegations of, 204–205
    background of, 204
    changes made by, 207
    Cole Report and EJA investigation under,
        263–264, 282
    collapse as political issue for, 198, 199
    concept of EJA, 205, 241–242
    conflicts of interest reported by, 232
    control of Penphil in view of, 217
    EJA and, 205, 207
    EJA investigation under, 237–238, 268, 279
    EJA penalties and, 278
    focus of investigation under, as public
        disservice, 282–283
    ICC and report of, 315
    implications of investigation under, 233
    on intelligence system of Pan Am, 265
    and investment activities of Penphil,
        220–230
    manner of handling investigation by, 26,
        210–212
    and missing $4 million, 309–311
    and Pennsy investment in EJA, 244, 248,
        266
    and Penphil as conglomerate, 219–220
    Penphil-IAB connection as viewed by, 275
    Penphil investigated by, 215–216
    premerger computer system and, 209–210
    Ricciardi affair and, 239–240
    in rivalry for Penn Central story, 206
    staff report of, 309, 310
    suits following disclosures by, 231
Peat, Marwick, Mitchell & Company, 51–55,
    101, 120, 122, 178, 179, 188–190, 192
Penn, William, 40
Penn Center (Philadelphia), 57, 58, 63, 69,
    187
Penn Central Transportation Company:
    Bevan's strategy to save, 172–174
    failure of, 135
    files bankruptcy petition, 184
    formed, 117–118
    leaders of, 22–25

Penn Central Transportation
    Company (*Cont.*):
outside investments and collapse of, 69–70
payment of dividends by, 171–172
Penphil and (*see* Penphil Corporation)
public view of collapse of, 25–26
as solution, 16
source of operational confusion of, 13
    (*See also* Merger)
Penn Plaza (New York City), 59
Pennsy (*see* Pennsylvania Railroad)
Pennsylvania Banking and Trust Company,
    225
Pennsylvania Company, 5–6
abandonment of bond issue by, 181
accusation of cash drain through, 208
building up investments of, 103
debentures and, 175–176, 191
dependence on, 109
floating loan backed by, 173
Great Southwest stock held by, 226, 227,
    230
importance of, 65
and 1970 operating loss, 174, 179
and Norfolk & Western liquidation, 64–67
soundness of, after collapse, 177
success of, 221
as vehicle for investments, 68–72, 136
    (*See also* Diversification)
Pennsylvania Railroad (Pennsy), 23, 29–36,
    77
administration of (19th century), 11
and airlines, 19
apparent prosperity of (1950s), 75
assets and track miles of (1950s), 29
decline of, 30–33
diversification program of (*see*
    Diversification; Pennsylvania
    Company)
electrification of (*see* Electrification)
extent of, 5
fails to adopt new managerial concepts, 45
illustrating institutional development and
    change, 12–14
as investment (1873), 5
management of (*see* Management; *specific
    areas of management, for example:*
    Accounting)
merger of (*see* Merger)
operations of (*see entries beginning with
    terms:* Capital; Cash; Operating;
    Operations)

Pennsylvania Railroad (Pennsy) (*Cont.*):
Penphil and (*see* Penphil Corporation)
postwar debt of (*see* Debt)
in railroad network (19th century), 8
record of dividends of (*see* Dividends)
situation of (1950s), 76–77
system building by, 8–9
track reduction and efficiency of, 22
and trade unions (*see* Trade unions)
Pennsylvania Reading Seashore Lines
    (railroad), 209
Pennsylvania Station (New York City), 30, 58,
    103
Penphil Corporation, 69–70, 205, 215–216,
    263, 286
charges involving, 207–208, 215–216
as conglomerate, 219–220
founding and founders of, 216–221
Holiday International Tours and, 273–275
implications and lessons of, 230–235
investigation of (*see* Patman, Wright)
investments of, 220–230
Kaneb and (*see* Kaneb)
Pension funds, 197, 327–335
alleged misuse of, 206, 216
investments by, 206, 218–219, 221–223
Penphil and (*see* Penphil Corporation)
supplemental, 216, 218–219, 328–329,
    332–335
Perkins, Charles E., 17
Perlman, Alfred Edward, 173, 192, 232, 278
accounting and budgeting under control
    of, 119, 123, 149–151
background of, 80
and Bevan, 83, 139
and Bevan's intention to resign, 126
and Bevan's staff, 148
and capital budgets, 108, 153
capital expenditures under, 152–156, 191,
    196
and data processing problem, 121, 122
dividend payments and, 171–172
before Hartke committee, 203–204
and Hodge's takeover plans, 162
and lack of merger operating plan,
    140–141
as leader, 22–25
management failures of, 188–190, 192–197,
    210, 212
management style of, 80–81, 135–136
merger opposed by, 119, 120
and mergers of eastern railways, 84–86

Perlman, Alfred Edward (*Cont.*):
  and new administrative structure, 123–129,
    132
  and New Haven line, 137
  ousted, 158, 172, 182–184, 311
  as president, 139–140
  retirement benefits of, 208
  and revitalization of New York Central,
    78–82
  Symes and, 82–83
Perlman Yard, 153
Pevler, Herman, 90, 91, 94, 95, 159
Philadelphia Daily News (newspaper), 241,
  280
Philadelphia Electric Company, 225
Philadelphia Evening Bulletin (newspaper),
  205, 210, 239–241, 280, 309
Philadelphia Inquirer (newspaper), 205, 206,
  240
Philadelphia Savings Fund Society, 165
Philadelphia Sunday Bulletin (newspaper),
  240, 322, 323
Physical plant:
  1970 funds for, 173
  (*See also* Equipment)
Pittsburgh, Fort Wayne & Chicago (railroad),
  8
Pittsburgh fiasco, 57, 62–64
Pittsburgh & Lake Erie Railroad, 179, 180
Pointer, Richard, 315–319
Post Office, U.S. 278
Pressprich, R. W., 292
Productivity, 20, 21
Profit:
  lack of railroad (since 1930s), 209
  1951, 46
  1951 and 1952, 47
  1960, 65
  1970 target for, 173
Provident National Bank (formerly Provident
  Trust Company), 40–44, 52, 161, 217,
  229, 293
Public Works Administration (PWA), 22, 49
Pucher, Franz, 295–296, 300, 301
PWA (Public Works Administration), 22, 49

Quesada, E. R., 250

Railroad Labor Board, 18
Railroads:
  in business history, 3–4

Railroads (*Cont.*):
  in rise of modern business institutions,
    4–9
  as unprofitable (since 1930s), 209
  (*See also specific railroads*)
Railway Progress (magazine), 81
Ramsey, H. C., 218
Rathbone, M. J., 238
Rauch, Stewart, 165, 166, 173
Reading (railroad), 209
Recession, 1957, 75–76, 92
Reconstruction Finance Corporation, 22, 80
Redell, Gen. Bill, 264
Redway, James, 250
Regulation:
  post-Civil War, 11
  as retarding change, 16
  spread of, 20
  (*See also specific regulatory agencies*)
Relyea, Bruce, 128, 148, 149
Ricciardi, Joseph H., 238–241, 282
Ricciardi affair, 238–241, 282
Richmond, Dean, 12
Ricketts, Maj. Norman, 270, 273
Rincliffe, R. George, 225
Rockefeller, David, 225
Rockefeller, Nelson, 60, 61
Rockefeller family, 226
Rome, Edwin P., 128–131, 193, 281–282, 285
  and acquittal of accused, 320–322
  and Bevan's activities in Penphil, 231, 232,
    286
  confused thinking of Saunders revealed by,
    195
  indictments following investigation by,
    309–311
  investigation by, 297–307, 309, 312–315
  Muller testimony and, 315–317
  Specter charges and, 280–281
  and trial of accused, 319
Ronan, William, 60, 61
Roosevelt, Franklin Delano, 22, 41
Roosevelt, Theodore, 15, 16, 23
Rosenbaum, Francis N., 207
  Berliner Bank loan and, 292
  convicted, 320–323
  and First Financial Trust, 295–297
  and Goetz-Bevan connection, 313
  indicted, 310, 311, 315
  laundered money and, 294–295
  nature of First Financial Trust known to,
    314

Rosenbaum, Francis N. (*Cont.*):
  Rome investigation of, 297, 306–307
  Sudwestflug and, 269
  trial of, 314–320
Rosenbaum, Joseph H., 207, 287
  acquitted, 320–323
  Berliner Bank loan and, 292–294
  European connection of, 275, 276
  and $4 million, missing, 296
  indicted, 310, 311, 315
  and nature of First Financial Trust, 314
  Rome investigation of, 297–307
  Sudwestflug and, 269
  trial of, 314–320

Samuelson, Robert J., 209
Sass, Fred, 111
Saturn Airways, 264, 284
Saunders, Stuart, 86, 93, 226, 232, 296
  and accounting practices, 104–105,
    150–151
  and accusations against Bevan, 212
  becomes board chairman, 90–91
  becomes president (1963), 39
  beginning of rift between Bevan and,
    108
  Bevan-Grant relations and, 154
  Bevan sidetracked by, 128–132
  Bevan as subordinate to, 95–96
  Bevan's cordial relations with, 91–92
  and Bevan's intention to resign, 125–128
  and Bevan's resignation, 157–158,
    160–166
  and Bevan's staff, 147–149
  and Bevan's view of capital expenditures,
    103–108
  capital expenditures and, 103–104,
    154–156
  and Cole Report, 242, 262–263, 282
  on collision course with Bevan, 99
  conflicting forces presided over by,
    119–122
  continued support for EJA by (1968),
    266–267
  debt management and, 188
  diversification under, 57, 71
  dividend payments and, 171–172
  EJA and, 243–244
  EJA failure and, 261–262, 287–288
  and EJA investigation, 164–165
  EJA investment defended by, 282

Saunders, Stuart (*Cont.*):
  and EJA–Johnson Flying Service
    connection, 249, 250
  EJA-Pennsy connection and, 243–246, 248
  fails to understand opposition to EJA, 264,
    265
  and first CAB ruling on EJA, 255
  in fiscal crisis, 179–182
  as head of Norfolk & Western, 91–95
  and Hodge's takeover plans, 162–163
  labor agreement under, 138
  as leader, 22–25, 283
  management style of, 135–136
  managerial failures of, 189–197, 209–210
  and merger, 117, 119
  as negotiator, 94–95
  new administrative structure and, 123–128
  1970 capital budget and, 173
  as obsessed with poor earnings record,
    108–114
  ousted, 182–184
  and Pennsylvania Company, 68
  Perlman fired by, 311
  Perlman replacement sought by, 158–160
  and Pittsburgh fiasco, 62–64
  retirement benefits of, 208
  and sale of Long Island Railroad, 60–62
  and SEC investigation, 206–207
  Smucker resignation and, 139
  stock holdings of, 152
  Symes and, 38
  turning point in relations between Bevan
    and, 113–114
  and use of railroad money to maintain EJA,
    266
Sawin, Benjamin F., 217, 221, 229, 273
Sayre, Robert W., 322
Schaekel, Tom, 110
Schiff, Jacob, 15
Schmidt, C. H., 142, 143
Schumann, Peter, 317–318
Scott, Thomas, 5, 17
Seabrook, John, 165–166, 183, 294
Seamon, Theodore I., 267, 272, 275,
    287
Sears, Roebuck & Company, 17
Securities and Exchange Commission (SEC),
    19, 20, 307
  and American Contract Company, 248
  and collapse as political issue, 198
  1969 annual report and lawsuit by, 177,
    178

Securities and Exchange Commission (SEC)
    investigation, 26, 67, 110, 193, 199,
    205–207, 228, 285–286
    of CMI, 228
    of Great Southwest shares, 227
    Hodge and, 286, 287
    implications of, 233
    of Kaneb shares, 222, 223
    lack of operating directives in, 119
    of National Homes, 228
    and new administrative structure, 124
    of 1965 loan, 152
    of Penphil Corporation, 215
    staff report on, 210–211
Securities regulation, 17
Security Insurance Company, 163
Seidler, Lee J., 178–179
Sempier, Carl G., 192
    background of, 100–101
    data processing and, 119, 121–125
    as part of Bevan's team, 188–189
Seward, Carroll, 216
Shaffer, John H., 148, 291–292
Shapiro, Milton H., 250–254, 259, 265, 284
Shapp, Milton J., 310
Shell Oil Company, 46
Sheridan, Bogan & Company, 216
Sherman Antitrust Act (1890), 15
Simpson, Howard, 84, 276
Sinclair, John F., 43
Smith, James Hopkins, 238
Smith, Robert, 91–93
Smucker, David E., 105–108, 111, 139, 154,
    159
Sotor, Nicholas G., 140, 141
Southern (railroad), 31
Southern Pacific (railroad), 14, 33, 34, 244
Specter, Arlen, 198, 207, 240–241, 280–282,
    291
Spokane, Portland & Seattle (railroad), 15
Stafford, George M., 310
Standard Oil of New Jersey, 29
State Street Investment Corporation, 223–224
Statistical data, 16, 35, 50, 52
    (See also Accounting; Data processing)
Stehli, Daisy, 296
Steubenville & Indiana (railroad), 8
Stevens, Lawrence M., 216, 217, 227, 228,
    233–234
Stewart, James, 238
Stocks, 19, 20, 176
    (See also Dividends)

Stokely–Van Camp (firm), 142–143
Strick Holding Company, 64
Subsidiary corporations, reduced number of,
    48–49
Sudflug (airline), 269
Sudwestflug (Germanair), 269, 285, 302
Suez American Trust, 268
Sundlun, Bruce G., 239
    EJA and, 243, 244, 246, 247, 254–255, 268
    EJA aircraft purchase and, 259, 260
    European misadventure and, 269, 272, 285
    Johnson Flying Service and, 250
    Lassiter and, 265–266
    and opposition to EJA, 264, 265
    replaces Lassiter, 279
Supplemental Pension Fund, 216, 218–219,
    328–329, 332–335
Symes, James M., 22, 64, 91–95, 99
    becomes board chairman, 89
    and Bevan, 89–90
    Bevan supported by, 189
    budgeting system under, 190
    capital expenditures under, 103
    on classification yards, 153–154
    on Clement, 35
    and debt reduction, 49, 50
    diversification under, 57
    and effects of 1957 recession, 76
    equipment program under, 66, 67
    land sales under, 58
    managerial system under, 52, 117–118
    merger backed by, 117, 119, 120
    and middle Atlantic railroad picture
        (1950s), 76–78
    and new administrative practices, 37
    as president, 38–39
    on recession (1957), 75
    Saunders and, 23
    supported, 55
Symington, Wayne, 221, 222, 227, 229

Tankersley, Ray, 144
Tariff agreements, 8
Taylor, James B., 245
Technology:
    innovation through, 21
    problem solving through, 21–22
    and railroads, 11–12
    rate of change in (late 19th century), 10
Terrell, Richard, 159
Thompson, Mr., 264

Thompson, J. Edgar, 12
Tierney, Paul J., 282
Tracey, Burke A., 140, 141
Trackage:
  1890s, 14
  of merged railroads, 118, 192
  obsolete (1951), 33–34
  reduction of, 22
Trade unions, 188
  electrification and, 20
  and merger, 137–138
  opposition to (19th century), 11
  railroads and first effective, 9
  restricting management options, 18
  work rules frozen by, 19–20
Traffic:
  regulating 19th-century, 8
  (See also Freight; Passenger service)
Trailer Train Company, 90, 197
Trans World Airlines (TWA), 19, 244, 264, 283
Transavia, 269–272, 275, 284, 285, 302
Transcontinental Air Transport, 19
Transportation Act (1920), 16–18
Trippe, Juan, 245
Tropical Gas, 218, 221–225, 231–233
Trucks, competition from, 32–34, 76, 188
Truman, Harry S, 246
Trust certificates for equipment, 48–50
Tuohy, Walter, 64, 82–86
TWA (Trans World Airlines), 19, 244, 264, 283

Union Pacific (railroad), 14, 31, 32, 34
United Airlines, 264
United States Freight, 81, 223, 225
United States Railroad Administration, 18
United States Steel Corporation, 29, 53, 266, 267, 272, 275, 276, 278, 285, 287
University National Bank, 221, 222, 229

Van, Harold, 239
Vance, William, 206
Vanderbilt, Cornelius, 8, 9
Vaughan, George C., 139
Vaughn, Linda (Miss Hurst Golden Shifter), 240
Vietnam War, 155, 176, 249, 264
Vileda Anstalt (firm), 296, 299, 301, 302, 305, 306

Virginian (railroad), 16, 77, 84, 93
Visible Hand, The (Chandler), 3,
Vogel, Jack A., 180

Wabash Railroad, 16, 46, 64, 65, 72, 84–86, 90, 91, 93, 94, 209, 261
Wall Street Journal, The (newspaper), 54–55, 138, 197, 203–204
Warner, Theodore, K., 127, 217
Washington Post (newspaper), 209
Weinrott, Leo, 282
Westec (firm), 112
Western Airlines, 283
Western Electric, 160
Western Railroad (Massachussetts), 3, 6–8, 12
Westwood, Howard, 250, 254–255
  and CAB investigation, 275–276, 278, 285
  EJA and, 266, 267
  European connection of, 271, 272, 275
  and opposition to EJA, 264, 265
White, William, 79
William R. Staats (firm), 175
Wilson, David L., 246, 248–249
  EJA and, 247, 272
  first CAB ruling and, 253–254
  and Johnson Flying Service, 249–250, 253
Wilson, Robert G., 174–175, 180
Woods, George, 93
Worcester, E. D., 12
Work measurement as management tool, 53–54
World Airways, 264, 284, 287
Worthington Corporation, 218
Wreck of the Penn Central (Daughen and Binzen), 117, 208, 240, 255
Wriston, Walter, 182, 183
Written reports in new administrative structure (19th century), 7
Wyatt, Henry, 92
Wynne, Angus, 69
Wynne, Toddy, Sr., 226
Wynne family, 226

Yale Express, 112
Yale University, 224
Yards, classification, 153–154
Yarnell, Biddle & Company, 216, 229
Young, John, 322
Young, Robert R., 23, 78–83

About the Author

Stephen Salsbury was formerly Chairman of the History Department at the University of Delaware. Since 1977, he has been Professor of Economic History and Dean of the Faculty of Economics at the University of Sydney in Australia. Born in Oakland, California and raised in San Diego, he received his Ph.D. from Harvard University in 1961. He is author of *The State, the Investor, and the Railroad: The Boston and Albany 1825–67* and coauthor with Alfred D. Chandler of *Pierre S. du Pont and the Making of the Modern Corporation.*